Print and Pleasure

Print and Pleasure

Popular Literature and Entertaining Fictions in Colonial North India

FRANCESCA ORSINI

permanent black

Published by
PERMANENT BLACK
'Himalayana', Mall Road, Ranikhet Cantt,
Ranikhet 263645
perblack@gmail.com

Distributed by
ORIENT BLACKSWAN PRIVATE LIMITED
Bangalore Bhopal Bhubaneshwar Chandigarh
Chennai Ernakulam Guwahati Hyderabad Jaipur
Kolkata Lucknow Mumbai New Delhi Patna
www.orientblackswan.com

ISBN 81-7824-512-6
ISBN 978-81-7824-512-6

Typeset in Agaramond
by Guru Typograph Technology, Dwarka, New Delhi 110075
Printed and bound by Manipal Technologies Limited, Manipal

MIX
Paper | Supporting responsible forestry
FSC™ C043100

For Peter

Contents

Illustrations

Acknowledgements

A book is shaped to a large extent by the sources one finds and the sources one does not find. This book is shaped very considerably by the material found in two libraries, and it is these libraries and their staff that I would first like to thank. In the British Library, the sections comprising Hindi and Urdu Books, Vernacular Tracts, *Reports on Native Presses*, and *Quarterly Lists of Books Registered* (SV 412) have provided the bulk of my material. The staff of the British Library have been invariably helpful and patient over all the time I spent there. Graham Shaw, head of the Asia, Pacific, and Africa Collections in the British Library, was generous in his encouragement and kind enough to go through a draft of the Introduction.

Equally important has been the Bharati Bhavan Library in Chowk, Allahabad, where I could feel somewhat like a late-nineteenth and early-twentieth-century Hindi reader, borrowing books, taking them off the shelves and seeing them in the form Hindi readers would have seen them. Even if I did not in the end use the musty borrowing catalogues that the librarian kindly took down for me from a *kali kothri*, to read those names and see those titles, and to step out into the market, was always evocative—and I am very grateful to Arvind Krishna Mehrotra for saying it so much better in his poem (reproduced before the Introduction). Finally, the Indian Institute Library in Oxford allowed me a generous glimpse of the Naval Kishore Press's Urdu publications, and I am particularly grateful to my former student Emma Bowes Mathieson for directing me towards the wonderful *Kissa Aurat Mard.*

I had two aims in this project: one was to see what had come before the Hindi boom of the 1920s, what exactly all those "perennials"—songs and tales—were which still constituted the bulk of publications in the 1920s and were called "old titles". The second aim was to move beyond the Hindi archive and consider Hindi and Urdu together. This has been a long process, and several people have helped along the way: Dr Tanvir Ahmad Alavi took out time to read through and comment on the Urdu *barahmasas* he had collected, and in Allahabad I also always profited from the vast knowledge of Shamsur Rahman Faruqi. The "Urdu reading" group that collected daily at tea time was by far the best way of acquiring speed and pleasure in reading Urdu, and my heartfelt thanks go to my dear friends Sara Rai and Alok Rai, and to Rajul and Aslam (and Peter, when he was there), for their patience and humour. I am not sure that hearing three adults read aloud at the same time was as enjoyable as they said!

Vasudha Dalmia has been part of all I have done and thought in the nine years it took to complete this project, and the gratitude I feel towards her goes beyond words. She also generously provided a rich community of colleagues and friends when she and Stuart Blackburn organized a very successful conference on "New Literary Histories for Nineteenth-Century India" in Berkeley in September 1999—Hans Harder, Dilip Menon, Christina Oesterheld, Ulrike Stark (whose wonderfully rich book on the Naval Kishore Press luckily came out early enough for me to read it) have been interlocutors and fellow panellists over these years, and I thank them all. At that conference I also first met Anuradha Kapur and Kumkum Sangari, whose friendship I greatly treasure, and whose conversations have helped shape and focus every wisp of an idea.

The bulk of this book was written during a blissful sabbatical in Venice in autumn 2005, leaving turbulent waters back in Cambridge. I would like to thank my Italian friends there for the good times we spent together: Lorenzo, Caterina e Paolo, Licinia e le due Elene.

The impressive conference organized at Jadavpur University in January 2006 by Rimi Chatterjee and Abhijit Gupta provided the perfect forum to try out the general ideas of the book, and so did invitations by V. Narayana Rao and Vasudha Dalmia to present them in Madison and in Berkeley afterwards. I wish also to thank my friends and hosts in Calcutta, Supriya and Sukanta Chaudhuri, for many stimulating conversations, and in particular one of the speakers at the Jadavpur conference, William St Clair, whose lectures on book history in the Romantic period at the English Faculty in the University of

Cambridge, years ago, first gave me a glimpse of what book history entailed and what it could achieve. I could blame the lack of sources to justify why this book does not remotely approximate his *The Reading Nation*, but that would be churlish.

Other useful forums were the History Seminar at SOAS, the Centre for South Asian Studies seminar in Cambridge, SARAI in Delhi, and, most recently, the University of Pennsylvania. I would like to take this opportunity to thank Daud Ali, Rachel Dwyer, Ravikant, and Sanjay Sharma for being such perfect interlocutors, as well as Sarah Beth and David Lunn for listening patiently all these years and finding it all so interesting.

Ideas on the early novel were shaped in conversation with Lise Smith, and in friendly disagreement with Franco Moretti. In Cambridge, Chris Bayly was always most generous with time and suggestions; discussions with Aishwarj Kumar always reminded me of the other dimensions of nineteenth-century Hindi; while Badri Narayan made very useful suggestions about the labour migration aspect of book reading and the book trade.

Book history in India is growing into a field, and I have treasured the pioneering work of Stuart Blackburn, Anindita Ghosh, Rochelle Pinto, Ulrike Stark, Farina Mir, and R. Venkatachalapathy, as well as Subhadra Sanyal's probing questions. And it has been great to have in Rukun Advani such a responsive publisher.

Finally, it could not have been more ideal to have a book historian with a book history library right at home. While Peter Kornicki's *The Book in Japan* remains magisterial in ways in which we, working on Indian book history, can only dream of yet, Peter in person has been much less daunting, always ready with advice, suggestions, encouragement, and love. So this book is dedicated to him.

As this book is intended for anyone interested in Indian literary, cultural, and social history, I have kept diacritical marks to a minimum. And all translations from Hindi/Urdu into English are mine, unless otherwise specified.

Bharati Bhavan Library, Chowk, Allahabad

Arvind Krishna Mehrotra

A day in 1923.
The reading room is full.
In pin drop silence,
Accountants, homoeopaths,
Petty shopkeepers, students, clerks,
Turn the pages
Of the morning papers.
At the issuing desk,
Some are borrowing books:
A detective novel in Urdu
In two volumes;
A free translation
Of a poem by Goldsmith-
Printed in Etawah,
Titled *Jogi Arthur*.

The books are still on the shelves,
Their pages brittle
And spines missing.
New readers occupy the chairs,
Turning the pages
Of the morning papers.
Turning the pages too,
But of dusty records
In a back room,
Is a researcher from Cambridge, England.
It's her second visit,
And everyone here knows her.
She's looking at Indian reading habits
In the colonial period.

Outside,
On the pavement,
Is a thriving vegetable market.
Amidst the stalls,
A knife-grinder sets up
His portable establishment
And opens for business.

1

Introduction

"Who am I, a stain on the family of poets, Narayan Prasad? The good for nothing son of Dullaray. I stuck the word 'Betab' (Eager) to my name like a tail so that this pen-name should encourage people to think that I am a poet." Thus begins the autobiography of one of the most successful commercial playwrights of the Parsi theatre, Narayan Prasad "Betab" (1872–1945), "born in a lineage of Brahmabhatt Brahmins in the *qasba* of Aurangabad, district Bulandshahar."[1] Hiding behind this humble and conventional opening are two of the most remarkable cultural phenomena of nineteenth-century North India—the emergence of a world of commercial publishing and entertainment, and the creation of a reading public. These have only recently started drawing the historian's attention and their consequences for the making of modern India remain to be explored in depth.

Born of an illiterate *halwai* (sweet-maker) who seems to have been deeply involved in the oral world of poetry and song, Betab made a set of intellectual journeys—from sweet-making in Bulandshahar district to working as a press compositor in Delhi, from illiteracy to professional knowledge of Urdu and Hindi grammar and spelling, from extempore oral versification to formal instruction in metrics, from the local world of poetry and song contests to the cosmopolitan and itinerant world of commercial theatre, from amateur poet to published and professional author. These journeys mark the emergence of new horizons of possibility, of new avenues into print for oral genres and neo-literate

[1] Narayan Prasad Betab, *Betab Charit* (1937; rpnt. New Delhi: National School of Drama, 2002), p. 15. Kathryn Hansen is translating this autobiography.

audiences. Stories like this, of Betab's career, help us understand what seems otherwise a puzzle in the history of print in nineteenth-century North India: how could a diverse, diffuse, and vibrant print culture emerge in the context of such low and sluggish increases in literacy and formal schooling?[2] And while colonial officers and Indian intellectuals often despaired at the lack of readership for their "good books", figures like Betab help us understand who commercial publishers were catering to when they churned out songbooks, tales, and theatre chapbooks, as well as how the habit of reading and buying books spread.

If print figures at all in histories of nineteenth-century India, the focus is usually on the printing efforts of missionaries, of the various colonial education departments, and of Indian intellectuals. This history of print starts conveniently in 1800, with the publication at Fort William College in Calcutta of separate texts in Hindi and Urdu, in different scripts and with different vocabularies by, respectively, Bhakha and Hindustani *munshis* (scribes) under the guidance of a Scottish professor, J.B. Gilchrist. It continues with the publication of textbooks and translations of scriptures by missionaries and school book societies, first in Calcutta again, and then in upcountry colonial centres from the 1840s with the educational efforts of Indian intellectuals in the colonial administration (Sir Syed Ahmad Khan, Deputy Nazir Ahmad, Raja Shiva Prasad), and the "Hindi movement" from the second half of the nineteenth century. Print—either in the form of the works written at Fort William College, or of school textbooks, journals, and the new, imported genres of "modern literature" such as the essay—has rightly been seen as crucial to this story, and virtually *all*

[2] Our best sources for book publishing in nineteenth-century North India are the annual colonial *Reports* and *Notes on the Native Presses* (from 1848 onwards), the provincial *Quarterly Catalogues of Publications* from 1867 onwards [OIOLC: SV412/38] for the North Western Provinces], the library catalogues by J.F. Blumhardt, and bibliographic studies—such as Krishnacharya, *Hindi ke Adimudrit Granth [1801–1870]*, Delhi: Bhartiya Jnanpith, 1966, and Nazir Ahmad, 'A Bibliography of Urdu Printed Books', in idem, 'Development of Printing in Urdu, 1743–1857', unpublished M.Phil. thesis, University of London, 1976. For statistics on literacy, see Table 1.3 at the end of this Introduction.

Indian reformist intellectuals of this period were linked to the world of print.[3]

Commercial publishing, by contrast, was shaped to a much greater extent by the cheap technology of lithography—that is, by what Indian printers and publishers felt could make it into print from among pre-print oral or written traditions, and by their sense of potential audiences.[4] It was also shaped by the momentum of publishing itself. Printed books themselves created tastes and attracted new audiences by easily crossing the Hindi–Urdu script divide, thanks to lithography and the availability of bilingual copyists. Strictly speaking, commercial publishing in North India includes the production and marketing of textbooks, religious books, and books for entertainment, since the same commercial publishers printed them all. Religious publishing spanned a wide range, from canonical texts, booklets of prayers and religious songs, polemical tracts, religious periodicals, and the texts of local or sectarian traditions. It forms at least another history of print in North India, just as substantial in terms of bulk and variety of output, and as crucial in creating a reading public. But it raises issues of content, audience, and religious transformation that the present

[3] For J.B. Gilchrist and the books published at Fort William College, see Sisir Kumar Das, *Sahibs and Munshis: An Account of the College of Fort William*, Calcutta: Orion Publications, 1978; Shardadevi Vedalankar, *The Development of Hindi Prose Literature in the Early Nineteenth Century*, Allahabad: Lokbharati Publications, 1969; and Samiullah, *Fort William Kalij: Ek Muta'lla*, Sultanpur, 1989. The classic account of the Hindi–Urdu divide is C.R. King, *One Language, Two Scripts: The Hindi Movement in Nineteenth Century North India*, Delhi: Oxford University Press, 1994. See also Alok Rai, *Hindi Nationalism*, Delhi: Orient Longman, 2001. For missionary efforts, Vedalankar, *Development*, pp. 105–14; Ulrike Stark, *An Empire of Books: The Naval Kishore Press and the Diffusion of the Printed Word in Colonial India*, New Delhi: Permanent Black, 2007, pp. 37–9. For Bharatendu, print, and the new genres, see Vasudha Dalmia, *The Nationalization of Hindu Traditions. Bharatendu Harishchandra and Nineteenth Century Banaras*, Delhi: Oxford University Press, 1997.

[4] As Ulrike Stark puts it, "The successful publisher's choices not only *responded* to readership tastes and reflected processes of canonization as well as current trends in literary activity, they also *shaped* these processes." Stark, *An Empire of Books*, p. 11.

book could not begin to address. So, for the purposes of this book, commercial publishing will indicate only books aimed at entertainment and leisure: this is the story that I chart.[5]

That entertainment publishing should be more flexible and fluid and mixed than literary or educational publishing will of course come as no surprise to historians of the book. So, while the relationship between the two dominant Indian languages in North India (or Hindustan, as it was called in Mughal times), Hindi and Urdu, was largely antagonistic and competitive in the reformist field, it was symbiotic in the field of commercial publishing and theatre. The relationship between these two fields was often complementary. For, while the genres of commercial publishing seem to reflect exclusively local traditions as compared to "serious" publishing—the latter shows a more obvious engagement with reformist patriotism and the intensified circulation of ideas accompanying nineteenth-century empire and globalization—in fact the commercialization of leisure which books and the theatre introduced incorporated discourses, tropes, and images that could acquire political overtones. Certain genres of commercial theatre and publishing were in fact crucial to the creation and diffusion of a popular nationalist idiom.[6] Thus, while Hindi and Urdu *qissas*,

[5] For Islam and printing in South Asia, see Francis Robinson, 'Technology and Religious Change: Islam and the Impact of Print', *Modern Asian Studies* 17, 1 (1993): 229–51, reprinted in *Islam and Muslim History in South Asia*, New Delhi: Oxford University Press, 2000. For reformist literature in print, see Barbara D. Metcalf, *Islamic Revival in British India: Deoband, 1860–1900*, Princeton: Princeton University Press, 1982; Marc Gaborieau, 'Late Persian, Early Urdu: The Case of "Wahhabi" Literature (1818–1857)', in F.N. Delvoye (ed.), *Confluence of Cultures: French Contributions to Indo-Persian Studies*, New Delhi: Manohar, 1994, pp. 170–96; Kenneth Jones, *Arya Dharm: Hindu Consciousness in Nineteenth Century Punjab*, Berkeley: University of California Press, 1976, and *Religious Controversy in British India: Dialogues in South Asian Languages*, Albany: State University of New York Press, 1992; and Dalmia, *Nationalization*, ch. 6.

[6] Pinney argues this for allegorical printed images, and Kapur for mythological plays. See Christopher Pinney, *Photos of the Gods: The Printed Image and Political Struggle in India*, Delhi: Oxford University Press, 2004; Anuradha Kapur, 'The Representation of Gods and Heroes: Parsi Mythological Drama

songs, and theatre chapbooks from this period appear oblivious of the colonial state and even of the British presence in India—in this they are unlike comparable Bengali texts from the colonial capital, Calcutta[7]—the diffusion of the habit of reading connected up with oral and visual forms of entertainment to find a political use with the cow protection movement of the 1880s. This then paved the way for a deluge of nationalist ("*rashtriy*") *lavanis*, *kajlis*, *khyals*, *svangs* and *bhajans* in the 1920s.[8]

To anticipate the general arguments of this book and outline the broader picture here, I see commercial publishing in Hindi and Urdu in the nineteenth century as a unified field created by three different but interrelated forces. First, there was the insertion of neo- or non-literate audiences and their oral traditions into the print market. The publication of songs and short qissas shows this process. These songs and qissas were part of both rural and urban oral traditions. Evidence from Lucknow and Banaras testifies that urban popular culture had incorporated songs and poetic (as well as dramatic) forms from the countryside (e.g. seasonal songs, *barahmasas*), as well as making possible new oral forms—such as public recitation of *dastans* and *masnavis* in the bazaar (see chapters 2–4).

The second force was represented by educated writers such as Ratannath Sarshar and Devkinandan Khatri, who responded to the new possibilities of print and the print market as represented

of the Early Twentieth Century', in V. Dalmia and H. von Stietencron (eds), *Representing Hinduism*, Delhi: Sage, 1995, pp. 401–41.

[7] Cf. Anindita Ghosh, *Power in Print: Popular Publishing and the Politics of Language and Culture in a Colonial Society, 1778–1905*, New Delhi: Oxford University Press, 2006.

[8] For a nationalist *nautanki* on the Jallianwalla Bagh massacre, for example, see Kathryn Hansen, *Grounds for Play: The Nautanki Theatre of North India*, Berkeley: University of California Press, 1992, p. 109. The cover of the chapbook shows an allegorical image of Gandhi sitting pensively while a woman, held by her sari by a whip-holding English soldier—representing "oppressed Punjab"—begs Vishnu in the sky. This is evidence of what Pinney has called the "interocular field" between theatre, commercial printed images, and commercial books.

by newspapers and commercial fiction publishing. They created hybrid forms that harnessed resources—characters, aesthetic, narrative models—from old genres for new textual dynamics and new discourses (chapters 5 and 6).

And third, there was the world of commercial theatre and professional performers, such as courtesans, various types of singers, storytellers, and *naqqals*, which put a premium on eclecticism. Theatre and its assortment of pleasures, in particular, acted as a catalyst for various poetic and musical forms, for flexible and talented writers (such as Agha Hashr Kashmiri, Narayan Prasad "Betab", and Radheshyam Kathavachak), and for multiple and overlapping audiences in terms of class and gender.[9] The interaction between these three forces created a varied and vibrant print culture that crossed script boundaries and caused a mixing of narrative and poetic traditions.[10]

Who were the readers of these books? Given the absence of prefaces addressing prospective readers, and of traces left by the readers themselves, only through indirect reference, stray observation, and the rare autobiographical notation by neo-literate writers such as "Betab", can

[9] As work on ticketing, theatre spaces, and audiences has shown: see e.g. Kathryn Hansen, 'Parsi Theatre and the City: Locations, Patrons, Audiences', *Sarai Reader 02. The Cities of Everyday Life*, Delhi/Amsterdam 2002, pp. 40–9.

[10] Christopher Pinney and Jyotindra Jain have demonstrated that in the nineteenth century commercial prints and photographs were produced and consumed in close relation with the domain of the theatre. The same could be said of the texts, illustrations, and songs of printed books. Whether it was a dramatic dialogue, a character's costume, the representation of a garden or a palace in a book or in a painting, or a model's artistic pose in a photographic studio, the aesthetics of contemporary theatre and painting were never far off. As Anuradha Kapur has argued, Parsi theatre and its poorer cousin, the nautanki, offered "a new assortment of pleasures" which, by all accounts, bowled spectators over, made stars of actors, and turned the scripts and tunes of plays into independent saleable commodities. See Anuradha Kapur, 'Impersonation, Narration, Desire, and the Parsi Theatre', in S. Blackburn and V. Dalmia (eds), *India's Literary History: Essays on the Nineteenth Century*, Delhi: Permanent Black, 2004, p. 87; and 'Love in the Time of Parsi Theatre', in F. Orsini (ed.), *Love in South Asia: A Cultural History*, Cambridge: Cambridge University Press, 2006, pp. 211–27.

we start drawing a picture of reading habits. What the evidence points to is a twofold process. First of all, literacy and book-reading habits were in this period often acquired "on the side" by upwardly mobile individuals and groups who sought to avail themselves of the occupational possibilities opened up by the colonial administration and the new market for jobs. The irony in a circulating proverb, "*parhe Farsi, beche tel*" (study Persian to sell oil) attests to a perceived mismatch between the traditional high status of the Persian-educated elite on the one hand, and on the other to either the hard times on which they had fallen, or to the fact that lowly groups like oil-makers were looking to a bit of education as a way of improving their status. In Muhammad Hadi Rusva's novel *Sharifzada* (1900), set in post-1857 Lucknow, the protagonist, a "*sharif* by birth" but of slender means, begins his transformation into a "modern sharif" by teaching the son of a Hindu coal seller—"*parhe Farsi beche koyla*" in this case. The sooty and noisy compound where he teaches contrasts starkly with the innate refinement of the destitute sharifzada, but it is also his only source of income and the beginning of his social resurgence. In Pandit Gauridatt's *Devrani Jethani ki Kahani* (1870) a family of Agrawal grain traders debates the advantage of educating one son in order to gain through him a steady income from his *naukri* (salary) and a foothold in the administration.[11] We can also think of Betab, who learnt proper spelling from a fellow worker while training to be a compositor at the Qaiser Hindi Press in Delhi.[12]

By reading the complaints of the educated elite against the grain, we can see that this was a period of great social mobility which was linked to literacy, but not necessarily acquired through education. "Every commoner [*'āmī*] believes himself to be a scholar [*'ālim*] and every ignoramus regards himself as a learned man merely on the basis of having *read a few chapbooks* on religious issues and a translation of

[11] Mirza Muhammad Hadi Rusva, *Sharifzada*, 1900; rpnt. New Delhi: Maktaba Jamia, 1992; Gauridatt, *Devrani Jethani ki Kahani*, rpnt. Patna: Grantha Niketan, 1966.

[12] Betab received no pay while learning the job, and after a month he was given Rs 5 per month. He learnt spelling from his fellow compositor Pandit Shambhunath, who had himself become a compositor after failing to secure a teaching job; Betab, *Betab Charit*, pp. 27–37.

the Qur'an, and that too in Urdu, with some ordinary teacher [*ustād*] or just *through his own effort*", complained Syed Ahmad Khan in the 1840s.[13] As David Lelyveld has emphasized, this sort of reaffirmation of *sharafat*—which we might roughly translate as good breeding and gentlemanliness—should not be read as a sign of continuity, but rather of contestation. Old elites and emerging groups were disputing whether sharafat was based on lineage or on education; whether it was a *habitus* acquired through generations or a comportment that could be learnt; or whether it was simply a reputation that could be flaunted through the shrewd use of conspicuous consumption. This last is evident in *Qissa Qazi-e Jaunpur*, in which a donkey-cart driver becomes sharif by giving sumptuous parties (see chapter 4).[14] The autobiographies of Parsi theatre playwrights Betab and Radheshyam Kathavachak (1890–1963) suggest that would-be clerks were not the only ones to acquire an education in this period. The fathers of both had eagerly taken part in the oral poetic world of svangs and lavani competitions. On their part, Betab and Kathavachak gained literacy without any formal education, composed and read poetry and theatre chapbooks, and migrated to the city, where they became professionals in the world of print and theatre (see chapter 3). In fact, while much attention has been devoted in recent years to recasting women as *sharif bibis* and *bhadramahilas* through education and "useful reading", the scores of books teaching *adab* and polite letter-writing through the medium of Urdu point towards aspirations to sharif status of non-elite males. Once literacy was acquired, though, it could be put to use for pleasanter purposes as well.

At the same time, elite males eagerly availed themselves of the new pleasures offered by print. Whether a wealthy merchant like Bharatendu bought songbooks or not, he certainly wrote them and had them

[13] Syed Ahmad Khan, *Āsār-al-Sanādīd*, ed. Khaliq Anjum, rpnt. New Delhi, 1990, vol. II, p. 65, quoted and translated by C.M. Naim, 'Ghalib's Delhi', *Urdu Texts and Contexts*, New Delhi: Permanent Black, 2004, p. 265, emphases added.

[14] David Lelyveld, personal communication, July 2005. See also, for example, Munshi Debi Parshad and Munshi Nathhan Lal, *Guldasta-e Adab*, Lucknow: Naval Kishore, 1875.

published.[15] And the poet Ghalib wrote in a letter to a friend of his delight at having received a massive volume of the dastan of Amir Hamza: "And there are seventeen bottles of good wine in the pantry. So I read all day and drink all night. 'The man who wins such bliss can only wonder/ What more had Jamshed? What more Alexander?'"[16]

Low literacy was not the only challenge commercial publishers in nineteenth-century North India had to face, for forms of entertainment used to be *embodied* in storytellers, singers, mimes, dancers, actors, and so on. Whatever the venue—whether the aristocratic circle, the *kotha* (courtesan's house), the private house, the temple, the fair, or the street—pleasure was a visual and oral experience provided by specialist individuals and communities. Other forms of communal singing also relied on oral transmission. Under such conditions, how did commercial publishers manage to win over to the printed page a society habituated to oral and visual entertainment? I will argue that commercial publishers managed to succeed by offering a range of "texts of pleasure" which tagged along with, reproduced, or multiplied the pleasures offered by oral performers. Books infiltrated existing sites and patterns of leisure—whether neighbourly women's sessions during hours of rest, or joint trips to market fairs, or after-work community singing by migrant workers living together in the city. Chapbook sellers doubled as storytellers, and storytellers kept some books for sale as they stood at crossroads in bazaars and fairs, blaring out their wares and their tales.[17]

[15] E.g. Bharatendu Harishchandra, *Gulzar-e Purbahar* (The Garden of Spring), an anthology of songs, Banaras: Gopinath Pathak, 1879 (500 copies), 12mo, 96 pp., printed with moveable type, 5 annas; and *Phulon ka Guccha* (A Bouquet of Flowers), an anthology of lavanis, Banaras: Chandraprabha Press, 1882, 2nd edn (1000 copies), 18 pp., 1 anna and 6 paise.

[16] R. Russell and K. Islam, *Ghalib: Life and Letters*, Delhi: Oxford University Press, 1994, p. 255, quoted in F. Pritchett, *The Romance Tradition in Urdu. Adventures from the Dastan of Amir Hamzah*, New York: Columbia University Press, 1991, p. 28.

[17] In 1864 the missionary John Murdoch warned of a rapid increase in the number of native presses, bookshops, and book-hawkers in his pamphlet *Mission Book-Shops in Connection with Bazar Preaching* [OIOLC: 11903.f.33(1)].

But before we explore the commercialization of leisure and the creation of a reading public, let us first consider the technology that made such processes possible.

Lithography and Multilingual Publishing

Though the beginnings of Hindi and Urdu publishing were under the aegis of moveable type, commercial publishing owed its success to another technology, that of lithography. Lithography was crucial in transforming a technological innovation—printing—into a commercial enterprise and a cultural phenomenon. The arrival of lithography can be counted as one of the most successful technology transfers to India, one to which, scholars have pointed out, local amateurs contributed with their search for local materials.[18]

The first books published in Hindi and Urdu in India were typeset and printed in Calcutta. Though technical innovation and the first large-scale printing of books in Indian characters is attributed to the Baptist Mission Press at Serampore,[19] the early publication of Hindi and Urdu books is largely connected to Fort William College and the

---

Several decades later the Punjabi Hindi novelist Upendranath Ashk described "two hawkers of qissas, dressed in *tahmads* [unstitched dhoti-like undergarment] and open-necked shirts of coarse longcloth with turbans awry on their heads and lips red with betel, singing [in the bazaar] the qissa of the quarrel between the illiterate mother-in-law and educated daughter-in-law, and the crowd was lapping it up . . ." U. Ashk, *Girti Divaren* (Falling Walls), Allahabad: Neelabh Prakashan, 1947, p. 26.

[18] As Graham Shaw puts it: "It can be argued quite forcefully that the introduction of lithography in India in the 1820s had a far more significant impact on the history of printing in South Asia than the arrival of typography in the 1550s." His article 'Calcutta: Birthplace of the Indian Lithographed Book' is the most detailed discussion of the introduction and early spread and improvements on the technology in India: *Journal of Printing Historical Society* 27 (1998): 89–111. For lithography's role in making the printed book acceptable among Muslims, see Francis Robinson, 'Islam and the Impact of Print'; for further technological advances, see Stark, *An Empire of Books*, pp. 45ff.

[19] The first Devanagari types are attributed to the East India Company employee Charles Wilkins and to the ironsmith Panchanan Karmakar (and

Hindustani Press (1802) in particular, which owned Naskh and Nastaliq Urdu types from the start.[20] Purchasing and running a printing press required significant capital investment. First of all, purchasing or making Urdu and Hindi typefaces was costly: at the beginning of the nineteenth century a set of Nagari types forged in Britain cost as much as £700, while at Serampore it cost around £100, or Rs 1500.[21] Missionary presses almost exclusively used Naskh fonts

---

later his nephew Manohar), who was employed by the Baptist missionary William Carey to develop a set of Nagari fonts. The mission at Serampore became the first Indian foundry for Devanagari, Bengali, and other Indian types. See Krishnacharya, *Hindi ke Adimudrit Granth*, Delhi: Bhartiya Jnanpith, 1966, pp. 12, 21, which discusses also the different typefaces developed at Calcutta. Though Serampore was the first foundry to create Nagari fonts, the fonts developed at the foundry in Bombay belonging to Javji Dadaji—who had learnt the art from the American Mission in Bombay that owned the important Nirnayasagar Press—were the ones that later gained currency in North India. Until the 1830s, presses had to purchase fonts either from Serampore or from foundries in Britain (p. 16). For early printing in Hindi and Urdu, see also Stark, *An Empire of Books*, pp. 35–44.

[20] For a list of the first Hindi books printed, see Krishnacharya, *Hindi ke Adimudrit Granth*, which also includes details on Devanagari types occasionally used in Europe since 1667, pp. 8–11. For Urdu books, see N. Ahmad, 'Development of Printing in Urdu, 1743–1857'. This contains a 'Bibliography of Urdu Printed Books from 1743 to 1857', pp. 273–376. For a history of European printing and presses in Calcutta, see Graham Shaw, *Printing in Calcutta to 1800: A Description and Checklist of Printing in Late 18th-Century Calcutta*, London: Bibliographical Society; New York: Oxford University Press, 1981. The first Urdu book printed in India was J.B. Gilchrist's *Dictionary English and Hindoostanee* (1786), and a few European-owned presses in Calcutta printed books with Urdu typeface; Ahmad, *Development*, p. 1. For information on Urdu books printed by the Hindustani Press, see Ahmad, *Development*, pp. 77–80; see also Stark, *An Empire of Books*, pp. 40–3.

[21] Compared to 26 Roman letters, there are just under 200 letters in the Naskh script, and over 600 character combinations in Nastaliq; the Devanagari fonts at Serampore amounted to 1000 characters, later reduced to 700. See M. Siddiq Khan, 'William Carey and the Serampore Books (1800–1834)', *Libri*, vol. 11, no. 3, 1961, pp. 247–8, quoted in Krishnacharya, *Hindi ke*, pp. 13–14. An 1807 advertisement by William Carey for the Serampore Nagari fonts sets the cost at Rs 1500; idem, p. 22.

and the Hindustani Press owned both Naskh and Nastaliq. Indian-owned presses stuck to the even more expensive Nastaliq, which looked far more familiar to Indian readers. The high cost of paper also contributed to making these printed books prohibitive: the price in 1811 of the complete Tulsidas *Ramcharitmanas* or of Lallujilal's *Prem Sagar* was Rs 20![22] The high cost of typefaces for Indian alphabets, and possibly of oil-based ink for printing with moveable type, has often been counted as one of the main reasons for the late spread of print in India. But another significant factor was the alien look of the typeset book, with its pagination, wide white margins, and fonts.[23] Another reason was the availability of copyists to make handwritten copies at request.[24] Thus, while Hindi and Urdu titles coming out of Fort William College proved to be popular with North Indian audiences in the nineteenth century—Frances Pritchett rightly called them "perennials"—in the form in which they were originally printed they catered to a rather different public: to students at Fort William, to an international audience of scholars, to current or former Company officers, and to amateurs dabbling in "Oriental languages".[25] The fact

[22] Krishnacharya, *Hindi ke*, pp. 8–9. Naval Kishore's pioneering efforts in establishing a paper mill in Lucknow in 1880 were integral to the success of his publishing business, and that paper mill, incidentally, became the largest Indian industrial concern in the North-Western Provinces at the time; Stark, *An Empire of Books*, pp. 187–92.

[23] Interestingly, especially when we think of printing in East Asia, block-printing never took off as a technology. Krishnacharya mentions only one book published by this method by Europeans (*Hortus indicus malabarius*, n.pl.), and one *Bhagavadgita* commissioned by the Maratha minister Nana Phadnavis in 1805 on copper; *Hindi ke*, p. 15. I owe the suggestion on the expensiveness of oil-based ink to Peter Kornicki.

[24] C.A. Bayly, *Empire and Information: Intelligence Gathering and Social Communication in India*, Cambridge: Cambridge University Press, 1996, p. 238.

[25] Witness the European editions of these texts and of grammars for Hindustani, as well as Trübstein's flourishing book trade: see Peter Friedlander, 'Hindustani Textbooks for the Raj', *Electronic Journal of Foreign Language Teaching*, vol. 3, suppl. 1 (2006): 39–56. Fort William College books were printed in editions of 500 copies, of which the college bought either 100 copies, or else the full printrun, and then gave the books to the students, kept them for the college library, and sent them to colleges in Agra and Banaras.

that Gilchrist was both the proprietor of the Hindustani Press and Professor of Hindustani at the college—he both commissioned the texts and ordered the books for the college—makes the enterprise seem rather corrupt. The title page of a multilingual glossary compiled by Lallujilal, *Angrezi Hindi Parsi Boli Likhyate* (Calcutta: Baburam Chapakhana, 201 pp., 1867 Samvat/1810) suggests that Lallujilal was at least envisaging the practical needs of an Indian audience not educated in Persian in the colonial capital as well: "with the help of Shri Taranicharan Mitra, I made a [glossary] of 3,600 spoken words [*boli*] of English and 3,600 of Hindi and 3,600 of Persian in *shastri* letters [i.e. in Nagari] and had it printed so that people here will learn to speak and understand English and Persian."[26]

As Graham Shaw has convincingly argued, lithography, a technology invented in 1798 by Alois Senefelder (a native of Prague) and which remained marginal to the history of printing in Europe, was *the* technology that allowed the spread of printing and publishing in North India, as well as in Egypt and other Muslim societies.[27] The technology allowed several options: while the lever press was quicker, the cylinder (or star) press demanded less labour. For Urdu books a third option, the relief stone printing method, was used, which allowed for greater speed and a greater number of impressions. As this method required brush and pen work, it was greatly appreciated by Urdu calligraphers; and it was well suited to the printing of illustrations, too.[28] J.N. Rind's detailed information about the Government Lithographic Press he ran in Calcutta in the 1820s gives us a sense of the

[26] Krishnacharya, *Hindi ke*, p. 8 of the bibliographic list.

[27] Shaw, 'Calcutta', which brings to light the French contribution to the introduction of lithography in Calcutta. Shaw also notes that whereas lithography in Europe was employed mainly for reproducing music and art, in India the technique met with immediate success, and almost three times more works were lithographed in India than in Europe in the early period. The technical and historical information in the following paragraph is taken from Shaw's article. The point was also briefly made by Krishnacharya, *Hindi ke*, p. 35. See also Ahmad, *Development of Printing*, p. 112.

[28] Ahmad, *Development of Printing*, p. 115. For the later technological developments of the iron press (1801), and the steam press (1811) which "raised the output of a press from approximately 300 to 1100 sheets per hour and lowered printing costs by twenty-five percent", see Stark, *An Empire of Books*, p. 65.

economics of the enterprise. A writer of English texts was paid a maximum of Rs 150 and a minimum of Rs 60 per month, while writers in Urdu and Nagari scripts received a salary of Rs 35 each, a little over that of printers, who were paid Rs 30 per month—Rind himself received Rs 500. The average cost of impressions was Rs 2 per hundred, "or less than the lowest charge made by private lithographers for the most trivial form they print."[29] The paper used was common China paper, which in the shops cost Rs 8–Rs 10 per ream. Five men were employed to work at each press, one to work the roller on the ink slab; the second to apply the ink to the drawing; the third to wet the stone; the fourth to work the handle of the press; and the fifth to stand behind the press and give assistance.[30]

The first upcountry litho press was established in Patna by an East India Company servant: this was the Behar Amateur Lithographic Press (1826); but one of the important effects of lithography was the shift to private Indian ownership of printing presses, a shift undoubtedly encouraged by the more liberal legal framework of the Metcalf Act of 1835.[31] By the 1840s litho presses had sprung up in Agra, Lucknow, Meerut, Banaras, Bareilly, and so on.[32] The success of lithography in North India can be attributed to three factors. First, it was a cheap technology requiring low initial investment and low running costs. Second, it was a flexible technology that accommodated itself to the local needs for printing in multiple languages and scripts. Multi-script printing was of course possible with moveable type as well, but it was infinitely easier and cheaper when done by hand and then transferred onto the lithographic stone.

Third, by reproducing the calligrapher's hand, lithography made printed books more familiar to Indian audiences. In part this was by making them look like manuscript books and maintaining the books'

29 Board's Collection, no. 51650, p. 79, quoted in Shaw, 'Calcutta', p. 102.

30 Rind, quoted in Shaw, 'Calcutta', p. 98.

31 See Stark, *An Empire of Books*, pp. 46 and 83ff. for a full discussion of official acts and the censorship of press and publications.

32 Ahmad, *Development of Printing*, pp. 115–40; and *Notes on Native Presses in the North Western Provinces for the Year 1848*, in *Selections from the Records of the Government, North Western Provinces*, Agra: Secundra Orphan Press, 1854, p. 237.

Fig. 1: An example of the flexibility of lithograpy: *Navarasatarang*, a collection of songs by Pandey Madan Gopal Varma, owner of the Kayastha Granthalay, Gorakhpur, 1950Vi. [1893]. Courtesy Bharati Bhavan Library, Allahabad.

aesthetic value—in the form of ornamental frames, woodblock illustrations and, in the case of Urdu and Persian books in particular, the peculiar arrangement of the text onto the page. Calligraphers (*katib*) thus found new employment as copyists, and every print workshop had a few on its payroll.[33] Lucknow, in particular, became famous for its beautifully calligraphed printed books, and introduced innovations such as a separate title page and pagination.[34]

While Persian and Urdu books were almost universally lithographed, in the case of Hindi books a hierarchy came into place, as the cases of Naval Kishore in Lucknow and of E.J. Lazarus's Benares Medical

[33] On calligraphers and copyists, see Stark, *An Empire of Books*, pp. 45ff.
[34] Ibid., pp. 55–6 (quoting Shlegova).

Hall Press show. Publications for government, or for wealthy patrons, and textbooks that guaranteed high sales were printed with moveable type, while books published on a smaller scale and those brought out by smaller or purely commercial printers were lithographed until the 1890s.[35] The visual impact, as we have already seen, was quite different depending on the technology used: printed books shared in the mystique of English publications, while lithographed books reproduced the visual experience of manuscripts, albeit often with a different format and pagination. In Hindi, while lithographed books maintained

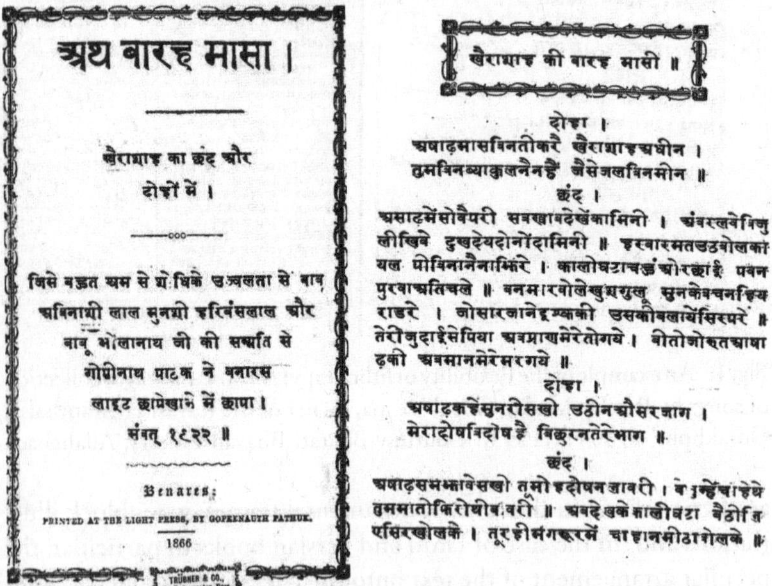
अथ बारह मासा ।

खैराशाह का छंद और

दोहों में ।

जिसे बहुत श्रम से औ धिके उज्वलता से बाबू

अविनाशी लाल मुनशी हरिबंसलाल और

बाबू भोलानाथ जी की सम्मति से

गोपीनाथ पाठक ने बनारस

लाइट छापेखाने में छापा ।

संवत् १९२२ ॥

Benares:

PRINTED AT THE LIGHT PRESS, BY GOPEENAUTH PATHUK.

1866

TRÜBNER & CO.,
60, Paternoster Row,
LONDON.

खैराशाह की बारह मासी ॥

दोहा ।

अषाढ़मासबिनतीकरै खैराशाहअधीन ।

तुमबिनब्याकुलनैनहैं जैसेजलबिनमीन ॥

छंद ।

असाढ़मेंसोवैपरी सबखावदेखेंकामिनी । अंबरलवेबिजु लीखिवे दुखदेयदोनोंदामिनी ॥ इसबारमतउठबोलका यल पीबिनानैनाभिरे । कालीघटाचहुंओरछाई पवन पुरवाअतिचले ॥ बनमारबोलेखुशगुलू सुनकेबचनहिय राडरे । जोसारजानेद्रम्मकी उसकोबलायेंसिरपरें ॥ तेरीजुदाईसेपिया अबप्राणमेरेतोगये । बीतोजोरुतआषा ढ़की अबमानमेरेसरगये ॥

दोहा ।

अषाढ़कहैंसुनरीसखी उठीनऔसरजाग ।

मेरादोषबिदोषहै बिछुरनतेरेभाग ॥

छंद ।

अषाढ़समझावेसखी तूमोहदोषनजावरी । बेजुल्हेंचाहेथे तुममातोफिरोथीबावरी ॥ अबदेखकेकालीघटा बैठीजि एसिरखोलके । तूरहीमगरूरमें चाहानमीठाबोलके ॥

Fig. 2: Cover and first page of Khairashah's *Barahmasa*, one of the most reprinted texts of the 1860s and 1870s, printed with moveable type by the Benares Light Press in 1866. Note the indentations used to signify new paragraphs. Compare this with the look of the lithographed edition (Fig. 5, p. 54), which does not have indentation or paragraphs, but whose hand approximates that of the typeface.

[35] The Naval Kishore Press may well have been the exception to this trend, since it could afford moveable type for other Hindi genres as well; cf. ibid., p. 48, fn. 33.

the arrangement in continuous lines of old manuscript books, the form of the letters changed to reproduce the shape of Hindi typefaces.

In fact, we can see the shift even in handwritten manuscript copies from this period, with the hand seeking to reproduce the typeface. As the industry grew, more and more North Indian litho printers acquired presses with moveable type, and new lithographic workshops sprang up: thus, the expansion took place at both the higher and lower ends of the industry.

A universal feature among nineteenth-century Indian printers was the fact that they invariably brought out books in more than one language. E.J. Lazarus's Benares Medical Hall Press and the Naval Kishore Press in Lucknow owned Arabic, Persian/Urdu, Devanagari, and Roman fonts.[36] In the case of litho presses—the overwhelming majority—the matter was simpler and more economic, for the book needed only to be copied in a fair hand in the other script—"with great effort", the colophon usually said. In fact, lithography also allowed books written in "substandard" dialects to be printed at no extra cost if the printer or the author envisaged a market for them. In Banaras some printers specialized in Sanskrit publications, but even they would print books in Hindi, and the great majority of printers in Banaras brought out books in Hindi, Sanskrit, and Urdu. Urdu printers would be more likely to publish Persian and Arabic books, but they did also bring out books in Hindi, an example being Muhammad Hanif of the Gulzar-e Banaras Press.[37] Before the development of Darjeeling, Banaras was also the centre of Nepalese publishing, and, among the several Bengali printers in the city, one at least specialized in Bengali books.[38]

[36] See Ulrike Stark, 'Hindi Publishing in the Heart of an Indo-Persian Cultural Metropolis', in Blackburn and Dalmia, *India's Literary History*, pp. 251–79; and idem, *An Empire of Books*.

[37] See *Quarterly List* for 1883. Though lower key compared to Sanskrit and Hindi publishing in the city, and to Urdu publishing in Lucknow and Delhi, about ten Urdu printers brought out a mixed fare of religious, medical, and poetic titles. E.J. Lazarus's Benares Medical Hall Press brought out Urdu editions of its Hindi and English textbooks.

[38] It was in Banaras that Bhanubhakta's Nepalese *Ramayana* was published in 1884 by Ramkrishna Varma, see *Quarterly List* for 1884. As for Bengali printers and publishers, see e.g. Bhutnath Mukherjee; *Quarterly List* for 1883.

A substantial number of publications were in two languages, and the volume of such bilingual printing did not diminish throughout the nineteenth century. This prominent and persistent tradition—whether of bilingual publications, translations, or educational books—requires some attention. It certainly had a lot to do with education, learning and knowledge, which were multilingual as a matter of fact, since valuable knowledge was preserved and transmitted in the classical languages: Sanskrit, Arabic, and Persian. In order to access this knowledge, there existed a large corpus of grammatical, lexicographic, and commentarial literature. Like most literate cultures, Indian literate culture too, in its various traditions, was highly hypertextual: texts referred back to other texts and presented themselves as translations, commentaries, compendia, or guides to other texts—even though they were in fact original works. Moreover, the new government schools required the use of a significant number of new books, which consisted mainly of translations from English into Hindi and Urdu. Multilingualism in this wider sense thus included:

(a) books *published* in different language editions (e.g. government textbooks, entertaining stories or barahmasas);
(b) books *written* in more than one language (e.g. text and commentary or translation);
(c) a few books where the text in the same language was printed in more than one *script*; and
(d) the existence of more than one print language in the same market.

In nearby Allahabad, another member of the Bengali diaspora, Chintamani Ghosh, set up the Indian Press in 1884, which became the largest publishing house in the region, publishing in English, Hindi, Sanskrit, Urdu, and Bengali. It was here that Ramanand Chatterjee's influential journal *Modern Review*, and indeed all of Rabindranath Tagore's early books, were printed. See Mushtaq Ali, 'Hindi Sahitya ke Itihas Men Ilahabad ka Yogdan, Indian Press ke Vishisht Sandarbh Mein', unpublished Ph.D. thesis, University of Allahabad, 1989; and Francesca Orsini, *Hindi Public Sphere. Language and Literature in the Age of Nationalism*, Delhi: Oxford University Press, 2002, pp. 52–72. For a recent account of the fortunes of the Indian Press, see the introduction in Arvind Krishna Mehrotra (ed.), *The Last Bungalow*, New Delhi: Penguin India, 2007.

The first reason for multilingual publishing was the plural nature of knowledge: several traditions of knowledge coexisted within the same society. The other, related, reason was the existence of plural audiences. In the case of books or journals printed in English and an Indian language, the English text addressed the government or the British/international community of scholars (and, increasingly, the pan-Indian one). Text and translation side by side suggested an equivalence between languages. In the case of Marathi–English newspapers, as Veena Naregal has argued, it was a purposeful statement: it showed that Marathi was as able as English to carry intellectual reflection.[39] Religious audiences also made multilingual publishing necessary: since Hindus made up a significant part of the Persian-educated service elite, Urdu versions of religious texts like the *Bhagavata* and *Shiva Purana*, of Tulsidas's *Ramcharitmanas* and of the *Mahabharata*, were made available to them.[40] Finally, as literacy spread more widely among upwardly mobile castes, migrants, and women, Hindi publications also grew in number and range. Thus, in the second half of the nineteenth century, after pilgrimage guides, prayer books, and other religious publications such as Tulsi's *Ramcharitmanas*, Lallujilal's *Prem Sagar* and religious songs, popular genres like qissas, barahmasas, and other kinds of songs were made available in the Devanagari script. Kempson, the Director of Public Instruction who compiled the annual report on printing presses for 1864, was clearly puzzled by the hybridity of tastes: "I am sorry to report that Hindi translations of Mahomedan poetry of the amatory kind are becoming popular. The increase in the number of persons able to read their own vernacular has created a demand for books which illiterate and unprincipled printers meet with trash of this description." The shared taste for qissas and poems puzzled the colonial officer and was clearly at variance with his neat historical-ethnographic categories: "It is almost incredible that a Hindu, capable of contrasting the principles of the English Government with the rule of his Mahomedan conquerors, should learn his own language with

[39] Veena Naregal, *Language Politics, Elites, and the Public Sphere: Western India under Colonialism*, New Delhi: Permanent Black, 2001.

[40] As Ulrike Stark has shown, Naval Kishore undertook a systematic programme of publishing Hindu scriptures in Urdu: *An Empire of Books*.

the aid and encouragement of the former and apply it to a revival of the literature of the latter."[41]

First, though, we need to reflect on the ways in which bookreading became a pleasurable habit.

Books, Pleasure, and Sites of Leisure

I have suggested above that commercial publishers met the challenge of "embodied pleasures" in the persons of performers by offering a range of texts of pleasure. These texts sought to reproduce and multiply the pleasures offered by oral performers, thus infiltrating existing forms and patterns of leisure.

The first evidence for this is the genres that fuelled the boom in commercial publishing, in both Devanagari and Urdu scripts, in the second half of the nineteenth century: tales/qissas (chapter 4), songs and popular poems like barahmasas (chapters 2 & 3), and theatre chapbooks.[42] All these were "oral-literate" genres that allowed multiple forms of consumption: oral recitation, reading aloud in a communal setting (e.g. *qissa sunana*), and silent or almost-silent reading—a pattern that seems to have continued into the early twentieth century. In fact, I see at least four different kinds of experiences:

(a) oral performance: either listening to a qissa recited by a *qissa-go* or a hawker or a song performed by a singer, sharing the singing of a song or bhajan, or watching a sketch performed by a mime actor;

(b) reading aloud: if we go by the internal evidence of qissas, this was mostly done at home, among family and neighbours. This kind of reading was a shared experience. It included the sound of the reader's voice and the comments of the audience; it involved mostly qissas, but also the new serialized novel, e.g.

[41] *Report on Native Presses for the Years 1862,1863, 1864 & 1865*, by M. Kempson, in *Selections from the Records of the North-Western Provinces of Agra and Oudh*, Allahabad: Government Press, 1866, p. 17. For an assessment of Kempson's position, see Stark, *An Empire of Books*, pp. 92–7.

[42] For a history of a genre, detailed list of the theatre chapbooks held in the British Library, and a masterly study of the theatre form, see Hansen, *Grounds for Play*, which made a systematic study of their printing history unnecessary.

Fasana-e Azad (see chapter 5), which collected around the reader an audience at home or even on train journeys, and produced an identification of its characters as real people.

(c) A third kind of reading was the almost silent one in which the reader moved his or her lips, mouthing but not uttering the words; this was the kind of reading used for religious books and prayers, and, though I have no written evidence from North India in this period, it is the typical mode of reading among neo-literates elsewhere.

(d) Finally, there is silent reading which, like oral recitation, has the most power to envelop the reader and spirit him or her away into a different world; both qissas and novels were read in this way.

Taken together, the genres of commercial publishing can be said to span all these reading experiences, though in different combinations. Moreover, if the printed book could not by itself reproduce the pleasure of the grain in the narrator's voice, or the shrewd use of pauses and glances to capture and hold attention—not to speak of music and song—it must have counterbalanced this lack by other pleasures. Such pleasures could be internal to the text (as in the humorous description of the school in the qissa of the qazi of Jaunpur in chapter 4), or external to it, as for example the ready availability and multiplication of titles, and easy access to the text; or the eclecticism of having texts from different poetic and narrative traditions side by side in both Devanagari and Urdu letters. While these various forms of using oral-literate texts continued, we can also argue that a gradual process of familiarization with the printed book took place. This finally allowed, in the 1890s, a genre like the detective novel—which did not have an oral antecedent and which was read only silently, as far as I know—to be very successful and fuel a kind of "novel-writing industry" (chapter 7).

I am well aware that pleasure is not confined to texts of "entertainment". One can derive pleasure from a beautifully sophisticated poem or from mastering a satisfyingly difficult manual. Here, Roland Barthes's distinction between *texts du plaisir* and *texts de jouissance* becomes useful. Pleasure as *plaisir* indicates the kind of intellectual as well as emotional pleasure that the discerning reader experiences when relishing the finesse of language, the intelligence of the writer, the play of intertextual allusions, the richness of a classic. In nineteenth-century North India, we can immediately think of the Urdu ghazal and sophisticated (*riti*) poems in Braj Bhasha. Pleasure as *jouissance*, bliss, is pleasure that cannot be explained through words, an all-absorbing and obsessive experience that totally overwhelms the reader. Barthes was thinking of Jules Verne when trying to find words to describe indescribable *texts de jouissance*, which can only be reached "*through another text of bliss*: you cannot speak 'on' such a text, you can only speak 'in' it, *in its fashion*."[43] We can think of dastans, and of novels like Devkinandan Khatri's *Chandrakanta* (1892), or Parsi theatre plays as *texts de jouissance* whose pleasure can only be reproduced in their own modes.

I would also like to follow the insight of an Italian writer on children's literature, Ermanno Detti, who has suggested the term "sensuous [or sensual] reading" for the particular way of reading which is exclusively focused on pleasure. Though often frowned upon by educationists, this kind of fundamental and deeply pleasurable experience is absolutely necessary, Detti argues, to develop a taste for reading. To acquire an enduring reading habit, "it is necessary to go through a phase in which the individual is able to relish reading so much as to long to relive that pleasure all through his life."[44] Stretching Detti's point, I would add

[43] Roland Barthes, *The Pleasure of the Text*, translated by Richard Miller, New York: Noonday Press, 1975, p. 22. Emphasis in the original.

[44] Ermanno Detti, 'La lettura sensuale', in *Il Piacere di Leggere*, Firenze: la Nuova Italia, 2002, pp. 19–20. My translation. Detti highlights two aspects of this reading experience: firstly, our marked annoyance towards anything that can interrupt or distract us from reading. "Even the most pleasurable things, if they interrupt and call us back to reality, become odious to us, and the reader desires nothing better than to remain in that state of laxity, in that flux which keeps him or her in its world outside the world." The second point relates to the deep impact of such an absorbing reading: 'even years later, the book, the pages—and not, it should be observed, the deep meaning or the content of that work—give us a tender memory of who we were." Detti calls this kind of reading "sensuous [or sensual] reading", because, despite detaching us from the outside world, it affects all our bodily senses (p. 12). Detti's study stems from a completely different, and more pragmatic, interest than Barthes': fifty years of

that Indian elites and colonial officers of the Department of Public Instruction, when deploring the fact that neo-literates in nineteenth-century North India chose texts of pleasure instead of useful and uplifting ones, failed to appreciate that sensuous reading was absolutely necessary in order to win people over to the printed page.

The slender evidence we have on book-buying and reading patterns shows that books insinuated themselves mostly along already established spatial and gendered patterns of leisure, both inside and outside the home. Accordingly, it may be useful to map these spaces to see how books penetrated them. In her against-the-grain reading of the attempt by nineteenth-century Hindu and Muslim reformist intellectuals to "sanitize" women's spaces inside the home, and to restrict their access to public spaces, Charu Gupta has pointed to women's largely segregated leisure practices inside and outside the home: "Amusements, performances and festivals were closely interwoven into the fabric of daily life, and these provided arenas of sociability across genders . . . marriages, festivals and religious practices [were] . . . part of neighbourhood life and social gatherings in villages, markets and towns."[45] Following her cue, we can try to extricate more precisely how and when practices of leisure were separate for men and women, and how and when they overlapped, for it was precisely this overlap that made male colonial intellectuals and fathers anxious. While poetic and singing traditions rooted in women's genres, or mimicking women's voices, were much enjoyed by male audiences and found ample space in the publishing market (see chapters 2 and 3), women partook of these in separate gatherings. But books signified a kind of open access, a breaking down of boundaries that most males in the nineteenth

---

national compulsory school have brought near-total literacy to Italy (where, in 1951, 11.9 per cent were illiterate and 89.8 per cent were educated only up to primary school) and also produced mass "post-literacy"—i.e. the literacy of those who never read a book or a newspaper. School gives literacy but not the pleasure to read.

[45] Charu Gupta, *Sexuality, Obscenity, Community: Women, Muslims, and the Hindu Public in Colonial India,* New Delhi: Permanent Black, 2001, p. 86. See also Sumanta Banerjee, *The Parlour and the Street: Elite and Popular Culture in Nineteenth-Century Calcutta*, Calcutta: Seagull, 1989.

century found hard to digest.[46] In fact, as we shall see, reading for pleasure may well have reinforced gender-segregated leisure.

In a society where female seclusion continued to be a marker of status, and where gender segregation became even more widespread among upwardly mobile castes, it has been easy to accept the ideal distinction that colonial intellectuals upheld between a female "inner domain" and a male "public domain" as representing reality—public space for men, and private or domestic space for women. But while historians have rightly argued against this simple binary by pointing to female employment and mobility outside the home,[47] it is also true that the public–private binary was powerfully internalized as a discursive pattern by nineteenth-century men and women, even if in practice it continued to be variously modulated so as to negotiate pragmatic needs and conflicting aspirations.[48] In fact, "private" and "public" spaces varied, depending upon gender and class. Rather than simply "private" and "public", we should think of two different polarities for men and women: for men, as Katherine Brown has suggested in her work on the Mughal *mehfil*, this was a polarity between intimacy and

[46] For one typical example, see V. Dalmia, 'Generic Questions: Bharatendu Harishchandra and Women's Issues', in S. Blackburn & V. Dalmia (eds), *India's Literary History*, pp. 402–34. See also Gail Minault, *Secluded Scholars: Women's Education and Muslim Social Reform in Colonial India*, New Delhi: Oxford University Press, 1998, ch. 2; and Meera Kosambi, *Feminist Vision or 'Treason Against Men'? Kashibai Kanitkar and the Engineering of Marathi Literature*, Ranikhet: Permanent Black, 2008, *passim*. This anxiety about what women read arose whenever the education of girls became an issue of debate; see e.g. P.F. Kornicki, 'Unsuitable Books for Women? Genji Monogatari and Ise Monogatari in Late Seventeenth-Century Japan', *Monumenta Nipponica* 60, 2 (Summer 2005): 147–93; and Kate Flint, *The Woman Reader, 1837–1914*, Oxford: Clarendon, 1993.

[47] The simple binary has been criticized as one that discounts the household as a place of production and reproduction of economic, kin, and political "goods", and establishes upper-caste patriarchal ideology as the norm: see Kumkum Sangari and Sudesh Vaid, 'Introduction' in *Recasting Women. Essays in India's Colonial History*, New Delhi: Kali for Women, 1989, pp. 1–29.

[48] For example, scholars have pointed out that while purdah as an ideology appears a general and fixed norm, in practice it is flexible according to age, location, activity, etc. H. Papanek and G. Minault (eds), *Separate Worlds: Studies of Purdah in South Asia*, Delhi: Chanakya, 1982.

distance; and for women the polarity was between related and unrelated others.[49] Moreover, rather than "public space" in the singular, it is more useful to think in terms of a typology of spaces, of a *topology* recognized by all participants, which translated into norms about comportment and dress that were administered by neighbours and the extended family.

Moving away from the equation male = public, female = domestic helps us, first of all, to appreciate the house as a place with *both* private and public dimensions, both amenable in different ways to the penetration of books.[50] Books could enter segregated public gatherings which featured music, dancing, feasting, and gift-giving at the time of religious or life-cycle rituals, when the family house was thrown open to all.[51] Sources mention *marsiya* recitations at the time of Muharram, or the reading of religious books by the ladies of the house to their female visitors.[52] A similar "segregated open space" was the *chhat* (roof), the *mohalla* equivalent of the courtyard, where urban

[49] Katherine Brown, 'If music be the Food of Love: Masculinity and Eroticism in the Mughal *mehfil* ', in F. Orsini (ed.), *Love and South Asia*, pp. 61–86.

[50] Anthropologists have suggested that, in gender-segregated societies, it is better to look at the house from "inside out" rather than "outside in"—to see the house at the centre of a network of spaces and relations that go well beyond it. See J.N. Gray and D.J. Mearns (eds), *Society from the Inside Out: Anthropological Perspectives on the South Asian Household*, New Delhi: Sage, 1989.

[51] As Amineh Ahmed writes of contemporary elite Pukhtun women in the North-Western Frontier Province of Pakistan: "Wedding and funeral ceremonies, however, represent less the interruption of an otherwise secluded space, than bespeak the duality of the [house] as the site for transactions between outside and in. Even during everyday non-*gham-khadi* occasions, Bibiane [i.e. elite Pukhtun women] understand the house as *presumptively public* and invest continuous efforts to prepare it for future events (storing up cloths, cutlery; getting together trousseaux). Furthermore, the acts of 'making kin' and negotiating brides' marital assimilations portray the *ongoing transactions between inside and out*": Amineh Ahmed, " 'The World is Established through the Work of Existence'": The Performance of Gham-Khadi among Pukhtun Bibiane in Northern Pakistan', unpublished Ph.D. thesis, University of Cambridge, 2004, p. 48, emphases added. She notes that these rituals and festive gatherings act as important occasions for kin and local cohesion, and even for political influence.

[52] C.M. Naim, 'How Bibi Ashraf Learnt to Read and Write', reprinted in idem, *Urdu Texts and Contexts*, p. 211.

women would assemble in the slack time of the afternoon or evening for conversation, company, and singing, and presumably where song-books purchased by women would be read out and sung.[53] If we follow an internal reference in *Kissa Aurat Mard* (1882), this was one space where tales would be told and which the *Qissa* itself tries to enter (see chapter 4). When Aloys Sprenger noted in the early 1850s that "of late, several tales and religious works written expressly for ladies have been printed and seem to meet with a rapid sale", we can imagine the ladies reading and sharing them in this space of sociability.[54] *Ustanis* (female teachers) and small girls' schools inside a neighbour's home are also mentioned in nineteenth-century accounts of education for Muslim women, suggesting the house as a place for the reading of another kind of book, i.e. educational books and "suitable books" for women. These included some of the earliest novels, written especially for this purpose. Nazir Ahmad's fine novels became truly popular, combining instruction with entertainment.[55] Writing in the 1920s, when the taste for reading sensational or romantic novels had spread among Hindi readers, the remarkable woman Ayurvedic doctor and writer Yashoda Devi lamented that "in the trunks of educated women are kept at least one or two of such novels."[56]

[53] Marwari "girls from the *mohalla* gather in the evening to practise singing", wrote Melaram Vaishya in the late 1920s, in *Gande Git Vahishkar* (Boycott of Dirty Songs), Bhivani, 1932, 2nd edn, p. 13. A perspective from inside out also allows us to see the *gali*/lane—and nowadays the local shop—as an intermediate space, between the inside and the outside, where women and girls can go.

[54] Aloys Sprenger, *A Catalogue of the Arabic, Persian and Hindustany Manuscripts of the Libraries of the King of Oudh*, Osnabrück: Biblio Verlag, 1854, rpnt. 1979, p. xiii.

[55] See C.M. Naim, 'Prize-Winning *Adab*: Five Urdu Books Written in Response to the Gazette Notification No. 791A (1868)', reprinted in idem, *Urdu Texts and Contexts*, pp. 120–50; Christina Oesterheld, 'Nazir Ahmad and the Urdu Novel: Some Observations', *Annual of Urdu Studies* 16 (2001): 27–42; Frances Pritchett, 'Afterword: The First Urdu Bestseller', in *The Bride's Mirror: A Tale of Life in Delhi a Hundred Years Ago* by Nazir Ahmad (trans. G.E. Ward), New Delhi: Permanent Black, 2001, pp. 204–23.

[56] Yashoda Devi, *Dampati Arogyata Jivanshastra* (Allahabad: 1931), p. 5, quoted in Gupta, *Sexuality*, p. 174.

Musical entertainment within the house, according to colonial travellers, was also gendered and took place in either the "female" or "male" (*zenana* or *mardana*) parts of the house. Performances for the male audience would take place in the hall of audience, or in the open space inside the compound, and sometimes the women of the house would be allowed to watch these from behind *chiq* blinds.[57] Mostly, however, such performances of musicians were segregated, and certain groups of female singers performed only for women. Outside the house, men enjoyed music and singing by visiting courtesans' quarters or performances in private houses by paying a small sum to the host.[58] Early songbooks strive to reproduce the mixed repertoire of courtesans and other singers. As one songbook advertisement put it, "The owner of the press Amir Singh has included the ghazals that people [*log*] have heard from singers [*ganevalon*] and that they want to learn by heart so that they learn them properly", adding that the book's final part, which included a more mixed fare of couplets and poems, "will come in use when you write a letter".[59] Other songbooks evoked the pleasures offered by street singers and even vendors selling their wares, while yet others evoked the bawdy songs sung by women at weddings.[60] Reformers in the early twentieth century objected to the continued singing by women of "obscene" songs at weddings and at Holi, and it seems fair to imagine that women would at this time have been among the buyers of these songbooks.[61] Writing in the 1920s about Marwari

[57] See Ketaki Kusari Dyson, *A Various Universe: A Study of the Journals and Memoirs of British Men and Women in the Indian Subcontinent, 1765–1856*, Delhi: Oxford University Press, 1978, pp. 336–56.

[58] Amlan Das Gupta, private communication, Calcutta, January 2006.

[59] Advertisement for *Chamanistan-e Bahar* at the back of Devkinandan Khatri's novel *Chandrakanta*, pt 1 (1892).

[60] E.g. *Churiharinlila*: "*Lavani* or songs by a bangle-seller and *lila* in *doha* and *chaupai*", ibid. See Gupta, *Sexuality*, for a comprehensive discussion of these songs in print and the campaigns against them.

[61] Already in the 1880s, Grierson suggested on linguistic grounds that the language of the women's folk songs collected by his assistant could have been influenced by printed songbooks: George Grierson, 'Some Bihārī Folk-Songs', *Journal of the Royal Asiatic Society of Great Britain and Ireland*, vol. XVI (1884): 201–4.

women in particular, Melaram Vaishya noted with horror that the fashion for "erotic songs" (*shringarik git*) had so far advanced that even wailing at funerals (*ghami ka rudan*) was set to *raginis*. "The songs that used to circulate secretly amongst men are now sung openly by women", he complained. Apparently Marwari women vigorously sang religious songs until midnight, but then, after their male relatives had gone to sleep, they started singing erotic songs. Vaishya inveighed particularly against lewd marriage songs (*sithnis*), but clearly he was referring also to the widespread habit of women singing together. While Marwari women would not dress up and sing when they went out alone—"Thank God the time has not come for a dressed-up woman alone to walk about singing"—when two or more went out they were sure to dress up and sing; and they would moreover sing also at home, alone or with friends, and so loud that the neighbours could hear.[62]

The most important public site for the circulation of books and the creation of a popular reading public was no doubt the *mela* (fair).[63] The mela was a festive space where women seem to have considered it part of their right to go to and display themselves, an arena which, in

[62] Vaishya, *Gande Git*, pp. 12, 14, 17.

[63] Dipesh Chakrabarty has argued that the street, mela, and bazaar are all part of one "spatial complex": 'Open Space/Public Place: Garbage, Modernity and India', *South Asia*, vol. XIV, 1 (1991): 15–31. Yet it seems useful to distinguish between the bazaar, the street, and the mela. While the bazaar carries implications of a "*haram*" space barred to respectable women (a "*bazaaru aurat*" is a prostitute, as Chakrabarty notes), the *chaupal* (village assembly) is a public space where men and women would be present together, yet still enforces segregation by having them sit apart in gendered groups. This arrangement is still prevalent in situations where men and women take part in public cultural, religious, or political activities together. This is undoubtedly true if we think of such spaces as non-segregated public arenas to which all have access, yet which in gendered terms carry different overtones. As Gloria Raheja and Ann Gold have pointed out, the style of women's participation "in the presence of men" differs greatly from when they are alone on the roof or in the courtyard, and this colours some male perceptions of female behaviour (quiet, submissive); G. Raheja and A. Gold, *Listen to the Heron's Words: Reimagining Gender and Kinship in North India*, Berkeley: University of California Press, 1994.

the words of a colonial administrator, "seem[s] to do away with . . . most of the distinctions of caste, and the separation of sexes."[64] Anand Yang has drawn attention to the volume and significant expansion of fairs and markets in nineteenth-century North India.[65] In the "widening constituency of melas", as he puts it, petty traders, peasants, and especially women seem to have swollen the files of pilgrims and visitors to such fairs. Women accounted in some cases for between half and two-thirds of the participants. As one cautionary tale, *Mela Ghumni* (Touring the Fair) puts it, "the men are few, women jostle and shove."[66] This versified tale has been read as exemplifying a moralizing critique of women at fairs.[67] But a closer reading suggests a somewhat different interpretation: it suggests the excitement of women preparing to go to the mela, dressed up in colourful clothes and jewels, their joyful singing together and snacking along the way. And, once at the fair, their enthusiastic meeting with relatives and friends, bathing, and enjoying a little flirtation with the priests, are all unmistakable in the text, whose refrain echoes such enthusiasm—"*mela ghumni, mela ghumni*". In this text the caution is directed rather against the threat of cheating shopkeepers, of ubiquitous thugs who could attack, rob, and dishonour a woman, and of the police who could gang-rape a woman in their custody.[68]

Melas, Yang notes, offered a cluster of religious, economic, and leisure activities. They not only provided a range of goods outside the "usual trade cycle", including cheap European imports, but also attracted, in the words of one witness, "parties of strolling actors, dressed fantastically . . . dancing and singing", nautch parties, performing

[64] Rankine, *Notes on Saran*, quoted in Anand Yang, *Bazaar India: Markets, Society and the Colonial State in Bihar*, Berkeley: University of California Press, 1998, p. 157.

[65] Ibid., ch. 3.

[66] Bhagavat Prasad, *Mela Ghumni*, published by the author, Muzaffarpur: 1925, p. 2. Although dating from a later period, it seems to be one of a string of such texts, published by several printers in Gorakhpur, Banaras, etc.

[67] Yang, *Bazaar India*; Gupta, *Sexuality*, p. 96.

[68] In fact, I wonder whether the *mela ghumni* booklets printed in the 1920s and 1930s could be reformist reworkings of an existing song genre, since their first half is all about pleasures, and the caution comes only at the end.

animals, jugglers, puppet shows, and theatrical troupes.[69] Melas also became a major site for the distribution and sale of books. Gayaprasad Bookseller of Nai Bazaar in Gorakhpur, who offered a mixed list of devotional and seasonal songs, a Hindi and Urdu primer, a *vratkatha*, and a collection of barahmasas, advertised in the 1890s that he set up shop at every fair.[70] A couple of decades later Yashoda Devi complained, "For two-three years I sent my books on women's education to the Magh mela on the banks of the Triveni. *The women who came to purchase books* went away after seeing my stall. *They named juicy novels* and used to demand them specifically, as well as the likes of *Albela Gavaiya* and *Ghazal sangrah* [two songbooks]. *Shops that sold such useless novels reported brisk sales.*"[71]

This provides a lovely vignette of Hindu women taking advantage of fairs to buy books, and conspicuously preferring genres of entertainment like songbooks and novels. Even if women could not go to theatrical performances, they could now read the chapbooks at home. An earlier mention of the woman's trunk also suggests that these books belonged to them personally, rather than being family possessions, and, by implication, that the consumption of such books was probably kept hidden from the men (and probably from female elders) at home. The authority figures may themselves have kept such books, without wanting younger women to have access to them. Consumption, therefore, could remain separate, even if the places from where the books were bought were common.

[69] Yang, *Bazaar*, pp. 150–1. Phanishwarnath Renu's story *Tisri Kasam* (The Third Vow), and the lovely film by Basu Bhattacharya based on it (1966), revolve around a cart-driver and an actress performing with a troupe from one fair to the next.

[70] Gayaprasad Bookseller sold bhajans and Krishna *pads* at four and a half annas: songbooks like *Chautal Basant Bahar* and *Holi Bahar* and *Anuthi Kajli* ranging between one and a half and three and a quarter annas, a collection of barahmasas at two annas, an Urdu–English primer at two and a quarter annas, and syllabaries in Devanagari and Urdu for half an anna or even less; customers or hawkers who bought four books received a fifth one free; see *Chautal Sangrah,* held in Bharati Bhavan Library, Allahabad.

[71] Yashoda Devi, *Dampati Arogyata*, p. 7, quoted in Gupta, *Sexuality*, pp. 174–5, emphasis added.

One last important space of leisure that encouraged book reading was the theatre, and later the cinema hall. Kathryn Hansen's study of Bombay theatre halls in the nineteenth century has shown that, while catering to a heterogeneous public, located as they were in two commercial areas in strategic proximity to Hindu middle-class localities, textile mills, and Muslim areas, the theatre "as an enclosed physical structure . . . was capable of restricting access" and enforcing internal compartmentalization through pricing and seating. In fact, she argues, the space of the theatre could be inscribed with different, even opposed, meanings: "Sometimes it tended to enclosure and separation, working in the interests of class differentiation. At others, it yielded openness and access, merging into the liminal space of its surroundings. The use made of the theatre space depended on the desires of its patrons, performers and audiences, who themselves were extremely diverse."[72] Whether women could access theatres or not, and whether they did so in a segregated or mixed fashion, theatrical performances were, as suggested, perhaps the greatest incentive to reading and buying books, and theatre companies made a brisk business of selling chapbooks of their productions.[73] This was true not just of larger cities. Remembering his childhood in the qasba of Bareilly at the turn of the century, Radheshyam Kathavachak recalled not just the intense activity of poetic competition that spilled over into songbooks, but also the frenzied expectation that surrounded the annual tours of Parsi theatre companies. Their songs were immediately learnt by heart and

[72] Hansen, 'Parsi Theatre', p. 44. Other modern public spaces—parks, colleges, restaurants ("hotels") and coffee houses—have also each acquired specific (and multiple) connotations and produced their own gendered behaviour, so much so that it seems difficult to generalize about "a" modern public space, or an attitude to public space. While the university campus can be perceived as the symbol of equal gender access to education and of a modern camaraderie between the sexes, this is a symbol that often clashes in North Indian universities—with a reality of aggression and anxious self-defence. Restaurants and some cafes are the quintessential spaces of modern romance/consumption, while other cafes (and bars) remain bastions of male leisure. Once again, we need the coordinates of gender and access to understand differences between spaces that otherwise all appear to be equally "public".

[73] Hansen, *Grounds for Play*, ch. 4.

sung throughout the city; and when he decided to shift from religious storytelling to writing plays and songs, he bought all the chapbooks he could find.[74]

The stray evidence available on leisure and reading matches the larger picture of socio-economic change in nineteenth-century North India. First of all—paraphrasing Gail Minault—with the British unequivocally in charge after 1857, the predominantly Muslim service gentry had to come to terms with the new institutional structures and competition from other groups for jobs. Moreover, for the generation born after 1857, "government service meant British government service, often at a very menial level, unless one served in a princely state."[75] Literacy and a smattering of *adab* (civility), still the dominant ethos, were now sought by other upwardly mobile groups, who also turned to books for entertainment. Second, the dispersal of court musicians, singers, and dancers and their regrouping around the new garrison towns and metropolitan centres allowed for a wider circulation of musical and song genres, and the crystallization of new theatrical forms such as Parsi theatre and nautanki.[76] Third, the greater circulation of people and goods even in rural areas—shown by the expansion of fairs and markets—allowed a faster exchange of performance and musical genres between urban and rural performers and audiences, this being something which booksellers capitalized on. Finally, migrant workers and women were among the beneficiaries of these enhanced pleasures which even a little literacy could now secure through books. The result is not a unified picture of book-reading practices, nor in fact of book buying. As is still largely the case within the Hindi-Urdu sphere, religious books, theatre chapbooks, songbooks and qissas, costing from a few paises to a few annas, were bought. Novels, marginally more expensive, were mostly borrowed from public libraries

[74] Radheshyam Kathavachak, *Mera Natak-kal*, rpnt. New Delhi: National School of Drama, 2001; see ch. 3.

[75] Gail Minault, *Secluded Scholars*, p. 59; see also David Lelyveld, *Aligarh's First Generation: Muslim Solidarity in British India*, 1978; rpnt. New Delhi: Oxford University Press, 1996.

[76] On the movement of *bais*, see the excellent article by Amlan Das Gupta, 'Women and Music: The Case of North India', in Bharati Ray (ed.), *Women of India: Colonial and Post-Colonial Periods*, New Delhi: Sage Publications, 2005, pp. 445–84.

or other individuals. By and large, novels are absent from the lists of popular booksellers, while they feature prominently in public libraries and the catalogues of publishers and book dealers of standing.[77]

Commercial Publishing and Literary History

How does a focus on book publishing affect our existing views of Hindi and Urdu literary history? Until the 1860s, the story is pretty much the available one in relation to the development of prose, of textbooks, and of the reproduction of old literary tastes. In fact, the first forty years of book publishing in Hindi and Urdu can be neatly encompassed by the books published by order of Fort William College in Calcutta; by the translations of Christian texts and tracts published at Serampore, and by other missionary presses in North India (Agra, Ludhiana, etc.) from the late 1830s; and by the primers and textbooks, almost exclusively translated from English or Bengali, published by school book societies in Calcutta and Agra. The total number of titles in the first forty years of Hindi publishing comes to a mere 126.[78] There were the voluminous grammars, readers, and dictionaries for foreign learners published by the presses connected to Fort William College—the Hindustani Press and the Sanskrit Press. Alongside these,

[77] Lise Smith has compared the library holdings of Bharati Bhavan, the public library in the market Chowk area of Allahabad, with borrowing patterns between 1900 and 1940. She concludes that while novels constituted the second largest category of holding after plays, they were the most borrowed (63 per cent of the titles borrowed, but 80 per cent of the total borrowings made), while qissas and songbooks were unrepresented and not very often borrowed: Lise Smith, 'Transmission and Reconstruction: The Role of Translated Texts in the Development of the Novel in Hindi, 1890–1920', unpublished Ph.D. thesis, University of Cambridge, 2005, ch. 2. Forty Hindi novels were available in 1908 at Ramkrishna Varma's Bharat Jivan Press in Banaras; see list at the back of Pandit Shankarprasad's *Balmitra*, Banaras: Bharat Jivan Press, available at Bharati Bhavan Library, Allahabad.

[78] See also Stark, *An Empire of Books*, ch. 1. For a list of all Hindi books available that were published in this period, see Krishnacharya, *Hindi ke*, pp. 1–29 of the bibliographic list. For a selection of texts and critical evaluation, see Vedalankar, *Development of Hindi Prose*. For a bibliography of Urdu books, which however excludes textbooks and religious books and tracts, see Ahmad, 'Development of Printing in Urdu', pp. 273–376.

the prose works commissioned by Gilchrist from Hindustani munshis and bhakha pandits are justly famous for having encouraged the shift from Persian and Braj Bhasha towards Urdu and Khari Boli Hindi, and for encouraging the writing of prose—mostly in the shape of translations and adaptations of earlier works. These longer narratives or story collections were to prove "perennial" favourites among Indian publishers and readers throughout the nineteenth century, in both scripts.[79] Collections of very short tales or sketches (*naql*), also compiled under Gilchrist's supervision at Fort William College, equally became part of the staple of publications in North India later in the century.[80] The few other books published in Calcutta drew upon the Urdu and Braj Bhasha poetic traditions: in Urdu, Mir Hasan's celebrated masnavi *Sihr ul-Bayan* (1805),[81] Miskin's marsiyas, and the longest book printed at the Hindustani Press, the complete works of the eighteenth-century poet Mir Taqi Mir, *Kulliyat Mir Taqi* (1811?), 1085pp. long![82] In Nagari we find a small number of editions of renowned works of Braj Bhasha poetry, such as Bihari Lal's 700 couplets and Matiram's *Rasraj*, as well as poetic anthologies.[83] There are also the first examples of what would

[79] Among them were Mir Amman's *Bagh-o Bahar* (1803), Nihal Chand Lahauri's *Mazhab-e 'Ishq,* his Urdu versions of the story of *Gul-e Bakawali* (1804), Haider Bakhsh Haideri's *Tota Kahani* in Urdu, the *Simhasan Battisi* (1802) by Qasim Ali Jawan and Lallujilal, the *Baital Pacchisi* (1802) by Mazhar Ali Khan Wila and Lallujilal, in both scripts, and Lallujilal's *Prem Sagar* in Nagari. For a bibliography of the texts produced at Fort William College, see http://www.columbia.edu/itc/mealac/pritchett/00urdu/baghobahar/BBFORTWM.pdf (viewed 3 September 2007).

[80] For a list, see Christina Oesterheld, 'Entertainment and Reform. Urdu Narrative Genres in the Nineteenth Century', in S. Blackburn and V. Dalmia, *India's Literary History*, p. 172.

[81] And also its prose version by Mir Bahadur Ali, *Nasri Benazir,* Calcutta: Hindustani Press, 1803, pp. 129.

[82] Ahmad, *A History*, p. 80.

[83] *Saptashatika (Satsai*), Calcutta: Pandit Baburam Chapakhana, 1809; another edn, Calcutta (Khidirpur): Sanskrit Press, 1810, 1813. Matiram, *Rasraj*, Calcutta (Khidirpur): Sanskrit Press, 1814, 86 pp. Lallujilal's anthology, *Sabhavilas,* first published in Calcutta: Sanskrit Press, 1815, 38 pp., contained poems by Rahim, Tulsi, Vrind, etc., and Brajvasidas's much longer collection, *Brajvilas* (1817, 739 pp.), which Lallujilal edited, were reprinted several times

Fig. 3: Cover and first page of *Divan Nazir Hindi* published by Matba Ilahi, Agra, no date [OIOLC: 14158.d.12].

---

in the 1820s and 1830s. The title page of the 1829 edition of the *Sabhavilas* says: "a collection of stanzas on various subjects, in Hindee, by different authors. Edited by Captain W. Price . . . professor . . . at Fort William." See Krishnacharya, *Hindi ke*, p. 21 of the bibliographic list. The Sanskrit Press also published a collection of Vrind's poems, a treatise on erotics (*Kok-sar*, 1818), and the prose story of *Sudama Caritra* (1819); see ibid., p. 25.

become a staple of the fledgling Hindi publishing industry—Tulsidas's *Ramcharitmanas* and other works attributed to him.[84] Clearly, apart from the important foray in Urdu and Hindi prose writing, publishing to this point was *reproducing* existing literary tastes and tapping a ready-made literary audience, both British and Indian. Perhaps the most striking fact is the publication in Devanagari in 1810 of the poems of Nazir Akbarabadi (1735–1830?), while the poet was still alive in Agra. His mostly humorous poems in a demotic idiom, breaking the elite–popular divide, were to be published in all formats and prices in both Urdu and Nagari throughout the nineteenth century.[85]

TABLE 1.1

Printed Editions of Nazir Akbarabadi

Wali Muhammad Nazir, *Ashar Miyai Nazar ke* Calcutta [Sanskrit Press?] (H) 1810[86]
Joginama, [in a miscellany: Lucknow: Matba Mustafai, 1848 (U)]
—Delhi: Mustafai Press (U), 1851; other ed. 1853
Banjaranama, Delhi: Mustafai Press (U), 1851; other ed. 1853
—Meerut, Ainah Sikandar Press (U), 1865, 1 anna
Layli Majnu, Kanpur: Mustafai Press (U), 1853 (1000), 3 annas
—Meerut: Ainah Sikandar Press (U), 6 pp., 6 paise
—Delhi: Muhammadi Press (U), 1868, 16 pp. (8000), L, 16mo, 4 paise
Divan-e Nazir, Meerut: Muhib Kishwar-e Hind, 1865 (H), 52 pp., 3 annas.

[84] E.g. *Gosvami Tulsidas Krit Krishnagitavali*, Calcutta (Khidirpur): Sanskrit Press, 1807, 25 pp., and *Ram Sagunavali*, printed the same year by the same press. The first *Ramayan*, edited by Sadal Mishra, one of the pandits employed at the college, was printed at the same press in 1811. Krishnacharya, *Hindi ke*, pp. 5, 9 of bibliographic list.

[85] See *Ashar Miyan Nazir*, Calcutta: Sanskrit Press, 1810, cited in Krishnacharya, *Hindi ke*, p. 26.

[86] According to Krishnacharya, this volume could have been edited by Lallujilal, who also hailed from Agra and owned the Sanskrit Press at the time: *Hindi ke*, p. 8 of the bibliography. I have not been able to see this volume, held in the National Museum, Calcutta, but it would mean that the first printed edition of poems by Nazir Akbarabadi was published during his lifetime, and came out first in Devanagari!

—Delhi: Brahm Press (U), 1874 reprint, 48 pp. (1000), L, 8vo, 1 anna and 6 paise

Burhapenama etc., Agra: Sheonarayan (U), 1868, 16 pp. (1400), L, 8vo, 1 anna

Majmu'a-e Nazir, Delhi: Brahm Press (U), 1875 rpnt, 16 pp. (2000), L, 8vo, 6] paise

Kulliyat-e Nazir Akbarabadi, Lucknow: Nawal Kishore (U), 1887, 5th ed., 194 pp. (3000), L, 6 annas and 6 paise

---

Source: Krishnacharya, *Hindi ke Adimudrit Granth*; N. Ahmad, 'Development of Printing in Urdu'; *Quarterly Lists of Publications.*

The local scholars and merchants who first set up commercial printing presses in North India towards the end of this period also initially reproduced existing literary or knowledge traditions, whether in Arabic, Persian, or Urdu, or in Sanskrit and Braj Bhasha.[87] This was particularly the case with printings sponsored by local rulers. Their patronage worked very much as an extension of traditional literary and scholarly patronage.[88] Most enterprises published books as well as periodicals, though only a handful of titles a year. The exception was the Matba-e Mustafai (est. 1839). Mustafa Khan, a glass merchant, was also a book dealer and had an extensive network of agents and colporteurs in all the main towns of the province: his press put out an impressive eighty titles in 1853 alone. The prices were considerably lower than those of other publishers and the quality of lithography was considered good. Mustafa Khan seems to have been the first to gauge the possibilities of the market and the dynamics of the business. He produced expensive, excellently lithographed, specialized books for

[87] For Sanskrit publishing in Banaras, see F. Orsini, 'Pandits and Printers in Banaras', in A. Gupta and S. Chakravorty (eds), *Print Areas: Book History in India,* New Delhi: Permanent Black, 2004, pp. 103–38; also Stark, *An Empire of Books*, section 5.5.

[88] At great expense, Nawab Ghaziuddin Haidar had founded a typographic unit in Lucknow with Arabic fonts which printed a few works in Persian; the earliest recorded was the dictionary *Haft Qulzum* (1821), which became something of a celebrity in Europe after the German scholar-poet Friedrich Rückert translated part of it as *Grammatik, Poetik und Rhetorik der Perser* (Leipzig: 1874); Sprenger, *Catalogue*, p. xi. For early printing and patronage in Lucknow and Banaras, see Stark, *An Empire of Books*, pp. 53–64.

the upper end of the market as well as more current genres at much cheaper prices. Thus textbooks for Persian education, Urdu qissas, masnavis, and the ubiquitous almanacs sold at 3 annas, with printruns as high as 1000 copies. Medical, religious, and law books were priced higher but also found a ready market.[89]

The map of printing in North India shows that, apart from Lucknow, British administrative towns and cantonments like Agra, Allahabad, Kanpur, Meerut, and Lahore were among the first to acquire printing presses.[90] Other important catalysts were missionaries and school book societies, and the Indian courts of Delhi, Lucknow, and Banaras. Mofussil towns like Moradabad, Aligarh, and Bareilly, and pilgrimage places like Mathura were other obvious centres since they had both the literate manpower and a ready-made market for publications.

In terms of texts for entertainment, we notice the publishing of some new tales by local writers, such as Rajjab Ali Beg Surur's *Fasana-e 'Ajaib* and Muhammad Bakhsh's *Nauratan,* alongside the long qissas and collections of short tales produced at Fort William College.[91] We also notice masnavis, which were apparently in great demand in Lucknow at the time.[92] Interestingly, while Urdu's own literary history centres predominantly around the ghazal and the sophisticated oral

[89] See Stark, *An Empire of Books*, p. 55. For a list of the books published by the Matba-e Mustafai in Delhi and Kanpur in 1853, see F. Orsini, 'Printers and Publishers', upon which this section is based.

[90] For a useful outline of the development of printing presses in Lucknow, Agra, and Banaras up to 1857, see Stark, *An Empire of Books*, pp. 49–62.

[91] Rajjab Ali Beg Surur, *Fasana-e 'Ajaib*, Lucknow: Matba-i Mustafai, 1845, pp. 198, and Muhammad Bakhsh, *Nauratan*, Lucknow, 1846 (reprinted in Banaras in 1849 and in Kanpur in 1850): see Blumhardt's Catalogues. For a critical evaluation of *Nauratan* and of the genre, see Oesterheld, 'Entertainment and Reform', in S. Blackburn and V. Dalmia (eds), *India's Literary History*, pp. 170–87.

[92] See Anna Suvorova, *Masnavi: A Study of Urdu Romance*, Karachi: Oxford University Press, 2000, chs 4 and 5. Some examples include: Muhammad Ali Shah, *Masnavi-e Habib*, Lucknow: 1843, 32 pp. *Masnavi Gul-o Sanobar*, Lucknow: Matba-e Mustafai (1845), 47 pp. Muhammad Sadiq Khan, *Masnavi Sarapa-e Soz*, Lucknow? (1845), 18 pp., as well as Mirza Shauq's *Bahar-e 'ishq*, Lucknow (1849), 42 pp., reprinted in 1851. Shauq's masnavis were reprinted several times in the 1860s, with prices as low as 1 anna: see *Quarterly List* for 1869.

world of poetic mehfils and *mushairas*, it was masnavis and qissas which more readily entered the world of commercial publishing.[93] Perhaps as a gesture towards the new potential popular audience acquiring literacy "on the side", from the 1850s we also see new, shorter, qissa titles in simple and colloquial language. These titles were reprinted any number of times in both scripts in the decades following (see chapter 4). We glimpse here the beginning of a real boom in commercial publishing. As we shall see, some tales, like that of the king of Byzantium (*Qissa Shah-e Rum*), were drawn from longer adventure cycles and repackaged in a simpler, shorter format. Others sketched out humorous situations about ordinary characters. Part of the same trend towards short, cheap lithographed books are the many reprints of pithy or funny poems by Nazir Akbarabadi, often published together with tales and barahmasas in the following decades. The 1860s also see the beginning of the great, systematic publishing projects of Naval Kishore, including his massive dastan cycles, these being real feats of publishing enterprise exuding confidence in the entertaining potential of print.[94]

As the Naval Kishore Press shows dramatically in the second half of the century, Urdu had become *the* language for written communication, employment, education, and learning, and, at least partly, entertainment.[95] In Hindi, by comparison, the number and range of publications in the middle decades of the century were much smaller and largely confined to textbooks and primers.[96] For the rest—apart

[93] Apart from masnavis, and the early, expensive, Calcutta edition of Mir's *Kulliyat*, there were two printed editions of *tazkiras*: Maulvi Abdul Bari's *Tazkira-i Khandan-i Gul*, Lucknow: Nigar Mission Press, 1824, pp. 480 [OIOLC: 14112.d.6], and Nawab Mustafa Khan, *Gulshan-e Bekhar*, Delhi: Urdu Akhbar Press, 1843.

[94] See Frances W. Pritchett, *The Romance Tradition in Urdu: Adventures from the Dastan of Amir Hamzah*, New York: Columbia University Press, 1991, pp. 21ff, and Stark, *An Empire of Books*, pp. 311–12.

[95] This is not to say that Naval Kishore published Urdu books alone. As Ulrike Stark has pointed out, he applied his systematic approach to Hindi publishing as well; Ulrike Stark, 'Hindi Publishing in the Heart of an Indo-Persian Cultural Metropolis', in Blackburn and Dalmia, *India's Literary History*, pp. 251–79, and idem, *An Empire of Books*, ch. 7.

[96] These were mostly printed by the Agra School Book Society, though undoubtedly many more must have come from Calcutta. Still, the presence of

from almanacs, editions, and commentaries on Tulsidas's works, reprints of Fort William College Hindi works like the *Prem Sagar* and *Simhasan Battisi*, and an occasional *Koksar* (Banaras, 1853)—we only find a few printed editions of renowned Braj Bhasha works, and the first, tentative versions in Nagari of popular Urdu qissa titles, anticipating what would be a major trend in the following decades.[97]

This discrepancy between Hindi and Urdu stands in sharp contrast with the publishing boom of the 1860s, in which the same genres were printed *both* in Urdu and Devanagari, as individual chapters in this book will show. After the traumatic events of 1857, which came as a severe blow to printing establishments in Delhi and Lucknow—as Ulrike Stark notes, the only publisher the British were happy to welcome in Lucknow was a non-Muslim outsider, Munshi Naval Kishore—printing presses mushroomed all over district towns in North India. Thanks to the *Quarterly Lists of Publications* compiled for each provincial government from 1867 onwards we have a much more detailed, though by no means complete, picture of the range and number of published books.[98] As Stark suggests, technological innovations

---

North Indian authors, first and foremost Shiva Prasad, signals a noteworthy change and the beginning of sustained local involvement in matters of public education. There is a substantial amount of work on Shiva Prasad: in Hindi, Vir Bharat Talwar, *Rassakashi: 19vim Sadi ka Navajagaran aur Pashchimottar Prant*, Delhi: Saramsha Prakashan, 2002; in English, see Dalmia, *Nationalization*, pp. 132, 184–5; Manu Goswami, *Producing India: From Colonial Economy to National Space*, Chicago: University of Chicago Press, 2004, and C.A. Bayly, *Empire and Information*.

[97] Among Braj Bhasha works, see Nanddas, *Anekarth* and *Nammala*, Calcutta: 1844, 29 pp. (Krishnacharya, *Hindi ke*, p. 29). Among qissa titles, see *Chahar Darvesh*, attributed to "Amir Khusrau", printed in Calcutta: Kashmiri Yantralay, 1847, 160 pp.; another edition was printed in Banaras at the Sudhakar Press in 1849 and priced a hefty Re 1, and a third one in Meerut by Matba-e Chasma-e Faiz, 1860, 232 pp.: Krishnacharya, *Hindi ke*, p. 42.

[98] See Stark, *An Empire of Books*, p. 58, fn. 47, for a list of the post-1857 Lucknow presses. While the statistics are to be taken with the usual pinch of salt, the *Report on Native Presses in NWP* for the year 1862 listed 442 books published in that year (interestingly, 139 in Urdu and 131 in Hindi, a much narrower gap than previously, and a still significant 93 in Persian and 51 in

such as the steam and iron presses and the growth of an indigenous paper industry can be considered preliminary factors in the publishing boom of the 1860s. As she notes, for the first time low-priced books (besides primers) emerged as a substantial share of the market (see Table 1.2).[99] Qissas, songbooks, barahmasas, and theatre chapbooks were central to this publishing boom and catapulted non-elite authors and performers like Maqsud, Khairashah, Khushdil, Yad 'Ali, Harnam, etc. into the world of print.

Let us look more closely at the constituent genres of this commercial boom and the pleasures they proffered in print. Qissas all went through multiple editions, and even the price of the longer ones dropped to a few annas.[100] Even the voluminous *Dastan Amir Hamza* could sell for as little as12 annas, though the price normally hovered over Re 1.[101] However, it was definitely the shorter, simpler qissas that

---

Sanskrit). The *Quarterly Lists of Publications* for 1868 included as many as 1239 books printed in the North Western Provinces, Oudh, and Punjab (including Delhi) for that year, an almost threefold increase. By 1888, there were 1239 books listed for the North Western Provinces alone (i.e. without Delhi and the Punjab). For details about the Registration Act of 1865, see Stark, *An Empire of Books*, pp. 83–90, which also comments on the reliability of the *Quarterly Lists*, still our best source for the period.

[99] Stark, *An Empire of Books,* pp. 65–6. "The introduction of mass-produced cheap formats, sewed and bound in paper covers, resulted in a situation where, for the first time, books became an affordable commodity for a large section of the urban literate classes"; ibid., p. 67. As suggested above, I believe we can assume a much wider penetration of books in the countryside through melas, and among neo-literate groups.

[100] For example, Haidari's lengthy *Araish-e Mehfil*, whose Nagari version cost a hefty Rs 2 and 8 annas in 1851, was sold by Naval Kishore in 1868 at 10 annas, and by the Hindu Press in Delhi a decade later at only 4 annas. In 1877 *Bagh-o Bahar* was in its fifteenth Naval Kishore edition, while Nihal Chand Lahauri's *Gul-e Bakawali* was in its eighteenth edition by 1888, with a printrun of 1500 copies, and selling at as little as 3 annas. Another fourteen editions by other presses in Calcutta, Lucknow, Kanpur, Delhi, Banaras, and Agra are listed in the British Library catalogues and the *Quarterly Lists*.

[101] Tota Ram, *Dastan Amir Hamza*, Lucknow: Naval Kishore, 1869, 324 pp. (1100 copies), Re 1, 8 annas; another edition by the Ijad-e Kishan Press in Agra in 1888 (1000), cost 12 annas and 8 paise.

flooded the market. The British Library alone holds twenty-one editions of Khushdil's *Qissa-e Sipahizada*, printed in the course of only ten years (1868–78), besides another eight editions collected with other short tales and poems (*majmu'as*) (see chapter 4). Of these thirty editions of *Qissa-e Sipahizada*, twenty-six were printed in Urdu and four in Nagari— signalling a growing overlap between texts in the two scripts.

Thanks to the information given in the *Quarterly Lists of Publications* we know that printruns oscillated between 1000 and 2000 copies, and prices between 9 paise and 1 anna in the case of this title, while shorter tales such as that of the qazi of Jaunpur, a mere four pages long, now cost as little as 3 paise. Even majmu'as oscillated between 1 anna and 5 paise.[102] Qissas, like dastans, were consumed in more than one way—they were recited by professional narrators, read aloud at home and silently by individuals.

Given the range of the most-published titles, we can suggest several different kinds of reading pleasure. Short, sketch-like tales were mostly farcical, inviting the reader to laugh at human folly and the weaknesses of the mighty. Adventure tales, whether recited or read silently, transported the reader away into another world, providing the kind of sensuous experience we noted above as *jouissance*—as indeed Ghalib suggested. While reading the printed dastans required considerable literate skills, adventure qissas like *Fasana-e 'Ajaib* flowed more easily after the initial virtuoso display by the author.[103] In chapter 4, I will focus on tales pitting men against women. It is easy to surmise that the pleasure these tales offered, while obviously gendered, would have included the spirited defence of one's sex against accusations made by the other; dismay at the cruelty of the other sex towards one's own; and the *frisson* resulting from witty repartee and sexual liminality. In the case of the woman author of *Kissa Aurat Mard* (1882), but probably also in the case of less-known male authors of qissas, we can also

[102] *Majmu'a-e Qissas*, Kanpur: 1877 (2000 copies), 32 pp., 5 paise; another collection published by Naval Kishore in 1878 with a high printrun of 4800 copies, 36 pp. cost 1 anna and 3 paise; see *Quarterly List* for 1878, p. 5. See ch. 4 for an analysis of these texts.

[103] For the pleasure of wonder (*'ajab*) in qissas, see Frances Pritchett, *Marvelous Encounters*, Delhi: Manohar, 1985.

include the pleasure of authorship, or the pleasure of utterance specially in order to counteract opinions which constituted the common sense of that time.

As Table 1.2 shows, the other genres fuelling the publishing boom were songbooks and small barahmasas (songs of the twelve seasons). As we shall see in chapter 2, this was a genre with a long history in North

TABLE 1.2

Price Range of Books[104]

1850s

Makhzan al-Tawarikh (History of India), Agra: Matba' Asad ul-Akhbar, 1853 (U), (300 copies), Rs 8

Jawahir al-Quran, Kanpur: Matba' Mustafai, 1853 (U), (1000), Re 1 and 12 annas

Akhlaq-i Jalali, Delhi: Matba' ul-Ulum, 1853 (400), Re 1

Mir Amman, *Bagh o Bahar*, Delhi: Matba' ul-Ulum, 1853 (U), (400), 12 annas

Sifdat ul-Masadir (Declension of Persian Verbs), Kanpur: Matba' Mustafai, 1853 (U), (1000), 4 annas

Almanac for 1854, Kanpur: Matba' Mustafai, 1853 (U) (H), (1200), 3 annas

Qissa Mansur Shah, Kanpur: Matba-e Mustafai, 1853 (U), (1000), 3 annas

Munajat Kalma (Prayers), Kanpur: Matba-e Mustafai, 1853 (U), (1000), 1 anna and 6 paise

1860s–1870s

Yatra Swamodah (tr. *Pilgrim's Progress* from Bengali), Banaras: Benares Medical Press, 1867 (H), P, 380 pp. (1500), Re 1 and 8 annas

Baital Pacchisi, Agra: Latafat Press 1867 (H), 104 pp. middle size (1500), L, 2 anna and 6 paise

— Lucknow: Naval Kishore, 1868 2nd edn (U), 8vo, 78 pp. (500) L, 8 annas

— Delhi: Fauq Kashi Press, 1878 reprint (H), 8vo, 104 pp. (1200), L, 2 annas

[104] Sources: *Note on Native Presses for the Year 1853*, pp. 396 ff., and *Quarterly Lists of Publications*, North-Western Provinces, 1868; and *Catalogue of Books Published in Oudh, 1868–1876* [OIOLC: SV 412/42]. P stands for printed and L for lithographed; U for Urdu and H for the Devanagari script.

Khushdil, *Qissa Sipahizada*, Delhi: Husaini Press, 1867 (U), pp. 16, 8vo, L (2000 copies), 9 paise.

Chhabili Bhatiyari, Agra: Muhammadi Press, 1868 (H), 48 pp. (1400), L, 1 anna, 6 paise

Nawab Mirza Shauq, *Zahr-e 'ishq, Bahar-e 'Ishq*, Lucknow: Central Press, 1868 (U), 22 × 29 (1000) L, 1 anna

Qissa Qazi-e Jaunpur, by Farjan, Delhi: Akbari Press, 1869, pp. 4, 3 paise

Majmu'a Barahmasa (Maqsud, Khairashah, Harnam, Shambhu Ray, Benimadho), Agra: Muhammadi Press, 1867 (U), (1200), pp. 16, 6 paise

Ambar Das, *Arsi Jhagra*, printed Pt. Keshab Das, Agra, 1868 3rd edn, small, 8 pp. (2000), L, 6 paise

Baramasi Gauri Sajan, Agra: Latafat Press, 1867 (H), 8 pp., small (1500), L, 2 paise

Bansuri Lila, Lucknow: Durgadass Press, 1868 (H), 4 pp, 26 × 0 (500) L, 2 paise

Indian oral and written literary culture in Avadhi, Braj Bhasha, and Urdu, but only two varieties appeared constantly in print in the 1860s and 1870s. These were either long narrative poems in Urdu modelled on masnavis or short stanzaic songs in a mixed language that first appeared in Devanagari. Two different forms of this genre—one developed in Urdu, and the other a Hindi/Urdu song—were now printed side by side in *both* scripts. Khairashah's *Barahmasa*, first printed in Devanagari in Agra in 1862, went through a staggering sixteen editions in sixteen years, mostly in Devanagari and in small format, but also in Urdu as part of majmu'as.

Evidence of the penetration of small books like barahmasas into the countryside is the presence of manuscript copies of printed editions dating from this period, at times imitating the hand of the litho copyist.[105] The large number of very short barahmasa songs attributed to Ram or Surdas also testifies to the significant convergence between

[105] See Blumhardt's *Catalogues*, and the table in ch. 3. For manuscript copies of the barahmasas by Khairashah (dated 1870), Maqsud, Wahhab (1849 and 1870), and Harnam (1860 and 1853), Jawaharlal Chaturvedi, *Braj Bhasha Riti Shastra Grantha Kosh*, Allahabad: Hindi Sahitya Sammelan, 1965, pp. 164–5. Interestingly, while poems, *sangit* chapbooks, songbooks, and qissas remained popular well into the twentieth century, barahmasas seem to have gone out of fashion by the 1880s.

entertainment, religion, and print that we also find in songbooks, theatre chapbooks, and printed images.[106] The covers, often depicting a group of women sitting by the side of a performer, suggest that these books were aimed at women's group singing sessions, while indicating that the author of the song was himself a performer (see Fig. 6 in chapter 2). In terms of the pleasures on offer, we find in the printed barahmasas both the pain and sensuality of the *virahini* (the woman longing for her absent husband) and of the pleasures of *suhagins* (happily married women). If one of the great novelties introduced by commercial publishing was to physically bring together male and female traditions of entertainment within the same book, we can conjecture that women reading and reciting these songs would have found a culturally valid and formalized expression for their emotions. Similarly, the men composing and singing them would have reproduced gendered structures of emotions, or identified with women's feelings.

Finally, chapbooks of plays, variously titled sangit, svang, or khyal, also made their appearance in the late 1860s.[107] Commercial theatre with its corollary, chapbooks and songbooks, were really what propelled so many song and poetic genres into print, as well as enthusiastic theatregoing audiences into the world of book-buying for leisure.[108] As Anuradha Kapur has argued, commercial theatre created new expectations of pleasure. Chapbooks and songbooks gave the reader the possibility of prolonging, augmenting and appropriating that pleasure for oneself, into one's own ordinary life. It was a possibility eagerly grasped by the following advertisement, which points to a

[106] For songbooks, see ch. 2. For mythological themes in theatre, see Hansen, *Grounds for Play*; and A. Kapur, 'The Representation of Gods and Heroes'. For printed images, see Pinney, *Photos of the Gods*.

[107] The earliest found by Kathryn Hansen were a *Prahlad Sangit* (1866) and *Gopichand Bharatari* (1867), both written by one Lakshman Singh or Lakshman Das and published from Delhi. A *Prahlad Sangit* published by Wazir Khan of the Mohammadi Press in Agra in 1869 (1400 copies), 48 pp., cost 1 anna and 6 paise; *Quarterly List*. For an extensive history of the genre in performance and in print, see Hansen, *Grounds for Play*.

[108] Although sangits seem to have had mostly smallish printruns of 1000 copies, an edition by Naval Kishore of the *kundaliyan* by the popular poet Giridhar Rai was reprinted in 3600 copies, with moveable type, for 3 annas. See *Quarterly List*.

habit of theatregoing and (reluctant) book-buying, even as it tries to undercut the profit theatre companies made by selling their own chapbooks:

> Take this, dear reader! This is the book without which you did not really enjoy yourself when you went to the theatre. Sitting in the theatre you had to stretch your neck until it hurt, and you were disappointed at not having the text. Today, we offer you the book for which you have already paid—and are still paying— the theatre companies a lot of money each time, and that too not of your own accord but because you were forced to. *Bahar Thiyatar* [The Springlike Pleasure of the Theatre] is a collection of songs from the famous plays you have been purchasing from theatre companies for three annas each. How expensive those books are—if you have ever thought about it, or do, you'll wring your hands in pain. And yet *you must buy* the songbooks from theatre companies, because *without the book with you, you cannot really enjoy the songs, your pleasure is reduced.* This is why we have decided to bring out a complete and illustrated collection of all the songs from the most renowned plays of the celebrated companies that are famous throughout Hindustan. No further praise is needed—does a golden bracelet need a thumb-mirror?[109]

Learning these songs by heart would transform the viewer into an active producer, thereby socializing the pleasure of the song and the play within circles of friends. If we are allowed to read back the pleasure of modern film songs into that of the theatre songs of the nineteenth century, we could also say that learning these songs meant appropriating for oneself, and playing with, the emotions and sensuality contained in texts and the tunes.

While it is clear that it was oral and performance traditions—storytelling, singing, and the theatre—that fuelled the publishing boom of the 1860s, three final points are worth making. First, the individual chapters of this book, each based on a particular genre, will try to show that in each case print did not simply reproduce an existing genre. Print provided new pleasures by multiplying the titles on offer. And it introduced subtle variations, often in terms of a hybridity of registers

[109] Ad for *Bahar Thiyatar*, pt 2, Upanyas Bahar Office, Banaras, date uncertain, emphases added; Bharati Bhavan Library, Allahabad.

and song forms, as if the variety of pleasures associated with different performance traditions were now being offered on a single plate. It is this same hybridity and assortment of pleasures that has been identified as the main attraction of Parsi theatre.[110]

Second, it is clear that the boom of the 1860s saw a parallel expansion of book publishing and reading at various levels. There was the creation of a popular reading public which cheap songbooks, barahmasas, and qissas shows. But there was also a substantial expansion of reading materials and reading habits within a serious/self-improving public. This is exemplified by the publication of didactic novels for girls, of journals and newspapers, and of a wide range of books on history and the contemporary world.[111] It is in this context that we must locate the first experiments at novel-writing in Hindi and Urdu—witness the success of Nazir Ahmad's *Mirat ul-'Urus* (1869) and of *Fasana-e Azad*, serialized in Naval Kishore's daily newspaper *Avadh Akhbar* (est. 1858, see chapter 5). However, it was with detective and *tilismi* novels in the 1890s that fiction first achieved mass appeal, and novel-reading became a widespread leisure activity—thanks to lending libraries and monthly novel publications (chapters 6 and 7). It is also at this time that most commercial genres in Devanagari began to be printed with moveable type, a sign either that the technology had become cheaper or that book publishing had become a business profitable enough to justify the initial investment.

Finally, it is the aim of this book to explore the sea of cheap reprints that surrounded the few "new titles" of poetry and fiction. The latter are the only titles that have made it into literary histories of this period.[112] It now seems clear to me that these much-despised "reprints"

[110] See e.g. A. Kapur, 'Love in the Time of Parsi Theatre', pp. 211–27.

[111] See the extraordinarily wide range of Urdu (and to a lesser extent Hindi) publications brought out by the Naval Kishore Press in this period; Stark, *An Empire of Books* provides an extensive list of titles.

[112] See e.g. R.S. McGregor, *Hindi Literature of the Nineteenth and Early Twentieth Centuries*, Wiesbaden: Harrassowitz, 1974; and A.J. Zaidi, *A History of Urdu Literature*, New Delhi: Sahitya Akademi, 1993. Literary histories of the nineteenth century often debate which was the "first" novel, journal, short story, play, literary history, and focus exclusively on new works, while conceding that "older tastes", such as that for Braj Bhasha poetry and the Urdu ghazal, remained popular and productive.

TABLE 1.3

Statistics on Literacy

Males	Population	Literate	Learning	Illiterate
1860			150,600	
1872	16,413,000		189,000 (1.2%)	
1881	22,912,000	1,033,000 (4.5%)	299,000 (1.3%)	21,579,000 (94%)
1891	24,303,000	1,257,000 (5.2%)	238,400 (1%)	22,808,000 (94%)
Females	**Population**	**Literate**	**Learning**	**Illiterate**
1860			465	
1872	14,367,000		10,500 (0.07%)	
1881	21,195,000	21,500 (0.1%)	9,700 (0.05%)	21,163,000 (99.8%)
1891	22,601,000	38,400 (0.2%)	8,400 (0.04%)	22,554,000 (99.8%)

These figures suggest between 1,363,000 and 1,542,000 potential readers. Note that many more people were literate than "learning", i.e. schoolgoing.[113]

in fact played a crucial role in expanding the Hindi and Urdu public much beyond the realm of the traditionally literate/educated, thus creating the basis for wide and relatively inclusive Hindi and Urdu public spheres. They also perpetuated, and possibly increased, the level of hybridity between literary as well as everyday registers of Hindi and Urdu at a time when reformist trends were clearly marking two separate paths.

[113] Sources: Education Reports and the Census for 1880 and 1890: Henry Stewart Reid, B.C.S. (Director of Public Instruction), *Report on the State of Popular Education in the North Western Provinces for 1856/57 and 1857/58*, Banaras: Medical Hall Press, 1859 [BL OP.1161.379.01]; Reginal Thornton, *Memoir on the Educational Statistics of the NWP*, 1850; *Report on the Progress of Education in the North-Western Provinces for 1869–70*, by M. Kempson, Director of Public Instruction, North-Western Provinces, Allahabad: Government Press, 1870; *Report on Public Instruction in the North-Western Provinces and Oudh* for the year ending 31st March 1880, by R.T.H. Griffith, Allahabad: Government Press, 1880. For recent considerations on literacy and potential readership, see Stark, *An Empire of Books*, pp. 12–21.

2

Hindi and Urdu Barahmasas in Print

Jis din se laga asarh rahi man mar, sabhi sansar chhavte mandir,
sakhiyon ne bichhai sej mahal ke andar.

From the day Asarh began, I've been dejected, everybody repairs
their homes,
inside my girl friends have spread their beds.

Mujhe yad piya tera ati, dharakti chhati, bijli darpati, garajte Indar,
sakhi umre nadi aur nale, bhare samandar.

Your memory haunts me, my love, my heart flutters, lightning
scares me, Indra thunders,
my friend, rivers and canals overflow, the sea is full.

Main dari dekh ke badar, kahin bole bairi dadar,
main piya bin beadar, roy roy bhije hamari chadar.
Charon or bolte mor, ghata ghanghor, sujhe ambar na.

The sight of clouds scares me, treacherous frogs croak,
without my love I'm disrespected, my wrap is soaked in tears,
All around peacocks cry, black clouds thunder, you cannot
see the sky.

Refrain:

Mere dil men aisi ave zahar khae marna.
Yun kahti sundar nar, suno bhartar, sej taiyar, dukh kuchh ghar na.
Piya hamka chhanr pardes gaman nahin karna.

I feel like eating poison and dying.
Thus says the lovely woman, listen husband, the bed is ready, no trouble at home.
My love, don't leave me to go away.

(*Allahbakhsh ka Barahmasa*, vv. 1–4)[1]

Fig. 4: The cover of a typical Urdu collection of barahmasas, Ghuncha Dil or *Majmu'a Dilpasand*, printed in Kangra at the Matba Fauq Kashi (1876) [OIOLC: 14119.d.6(9)]. Courtesy British Library.

This is the first stanza of one of the most frequently reprinted songs within perhaps the most commercially successful genre of the 1860s and 1870s, the *barahmasa* or song of the "twelve months". The barahmasa is a kind of poem in which an abandoned

[1] *Allahbakhsh ka Barahmasa*, Fatehgarh: Matba' Hasani Press, 1877, Devanagari, p. 2 [OIOLC: 14158.c.4(4)].

woman (*virahini*) pines for her absent lover or husband. It describes her pitiful state month by month against a backdrop of seasonal changes and ritual events. Today, barahmasas are perceived only as a kind of folk song, but a significant literary tradition attests to the attractiveness of its template for poets in all the literary languages of North India for centuries. The form was deployed for independent poems and for set pieces within longer narratives, these being overlaid with devotional or mystical overtones, inflected with Perso-Urdu poetic tropes, or used to illustrate courtly paintings. In fact the barahmasa is a genre remarkable for its flexibility and virtual ubiquity in literary traditions in North Indian vernaculars from the very beginning with poets adopting this popular, oral form for their first literary experiments.[2]

The female voice—her pining for and devotion to the absent lover—and the calendrical cycle are the core elements of this genre. It can be considered a particular sub-species of a general form of poetry centred on the female voice and typically expressing *viraha*, the pain of separation. Barahmasa songs had long been part of the literary repertoire, especially as a type of women's song. They had also circulated in written form as part of manuscript culture.[3] Since printed barahmasa songs, like that of Allahbakhsh or Khairashah, are all by male authors, we may surmise that, like *kajlis* and other types of folk songs, they circulated orally in a world of competitive popular singing (see chapter 3). Altogether, the British Library catalogues list forty-five barahmasa titles, some printed as many as twenty times in fifteen years. Allahbakhsh's poem went through a staggering nineteen printings in twelve years, thirteen in Delhi alone from at least five different printers, though the

[2] For an overview of the genre and examples from old Gujarati, Rajasthani, Avadhi, and Bengali, see Charlotte Vaudeville, *Barahmasa in Indian Literature*, Delhi: Motilal Banarsidass, 1986; and V.P. Dvivedi, *Bārahmāsā: The Song of Seasons in Literature and Art*, Delhi: Agam Kala Prakashan, 1980. For the tradition of Urdu barahmasas, see Tanvir Ahmad Alavi, *Urdu Mein Barahmase ki Rivayyat*, Delhi: Urdu Academy, 1988. For an overview of the genre in Hindi and Urdu, see F. Orsini, 'Hindi and Urdu Barahmasas', in *Hindi and Urdu Before the Divide*, Delhi: Orient Longman, forthcoming. This chapter builds upon that essay.

[3] See Jawaharlal Chaturvedi, *Braj Bhasha Riti Granth*, Allahabad: Hindi Sahitya Sammelan, 1965, pp. 162-9 for Hindi barahmasa manuscripts, all dating from the eighteenth and nineteenth centuries.

earliest edition dates from 1867 in Agra. The same text was printed nine times in Devanagari and ten in Urdu, with only minor changes in spelling.

Barahmasas are therefore interesting as a genre successfully reproduced in the world of print from the pre-print world of oral performance and manuscript transmission. To observe which varieties of barahmasas were taken up by print, and what effect print had on the genre in terms of focus and audience, is to discover more about the layered and heterogeneous world of Hindi/Urdu publishing from the 1860s. As we shall see, only two kinds of barahmasas found their way into print from the many existing traditions, while more were also produced in response to the genre's popularity in print.

The first kind was a song, like Allahbakhsh's, either secular or religious. The other was a long Urdu narrative poem which, like Maqsud's and the *Barahmasa Sundarkali*, stood halfway between the sophisticated world of Perso-Urdu poetry and that of popular songs. The initial publication of barahmasa songs in Devanagari in the early 1860s as cheap and flimsy chapbooks eight- or sixteen-pages long—along the lines of other religious and semi-religious poems like bhajans, *jhagras*, and *lilas*—seems to have targeted an audience of women and neo-literate readers. Their repackaging and publication in the standard Urdu 8vo format in the late 1860s and 1870s, often together in collections (*majmu'as*) and alongside the older *masnavi*-like barahmasa poems like Maqsud's and Wahhab's, suggests a publishers's strategy of reaching out to a different audience. Printer-publishers on the lookout for available popular genres to reproduce in print must have first thought of barahmasas as a genre suitable for women's singing and reading, as works with the same commercial potential as *Sone Lohe ka Jhagra* (The Dispute between Gold and Iron), and the collections of *phag* songs and the *dan-lila* and *nag-lila*, songs about Krishna's exploits—which all appeared in print around this time in the same format.[4] All these titles were successful, as the many printings of the

[4] See e.g. *Sone Lohe ka Jhagra*, Agra: Sheonarayan, 1868 2nd (2000), demy 16mo, 8 pp., Litho, 3 paise. For an exploration of the genre in nearby Punjab, see Anshu Malhotra, 'The Emergence of Bazaar Literature: Jhagrras, Kissas and Reform in Early Twentieth Century Punjab', *Studies in History*, vol. 18, no. 2, 2002. Oddly, she views this extensively printed genre as "new".

same works printed over the next decade in Agra, Mathura, Banaras, Kanpur, Delhi, Fatehgarh, Meerut, Lucknow, etc., attest. But though the Hindi reading public was growing—and it was not of course confined to women—the bulk of the *available* reading public was mainly an Urdu one of traditionally educated or neo-literate men. It seems reasonable to surmise that publishers simply repackaged barahmasas, originally aimed low at the popular Hindi audience, in the attractive format of standard Urdu books.[5] Not only that, the popularity in print of barahmasa songs by Khairashah, Allahbakhsh, and Harnam must have prompted publishers to also print the Urdu poems of Maqsud and others—those that were already circulating orally and in manuscript form.[6] New Urdu barahmasas, like those by Kanhayalal Talib (1870) and Abdullah Kanpuri (1874), came to be written after this publishing success. Barahmasas thus support the argument that the boom of commercial publishing rode on top of existing oral and performance traditions, brought together the more demotic strands of North Indian literary traditions (instead of those with greater literary authority), and that it favoured a language and a poetic idiom that was significantly hybrid (see also chapters 3 and 4).

Following the order in which the two sub-genres came into print, this chapter will first explore the shorter barahmasa songs before turning to the Urdu narrative poems.

[5] Thus the copyist of Jassu Singh's *Barahmasa Mard Birog* (1876) wrote at the end of the poem that it had been previously written in Hindi and had now been turned into Urdu "with great effort" (*nihayat koshish se*). The peculiarity of this poem was that it was written from the male point of view ("*Bin nari mard ki khvari bhari*"—grievous is a man's distress without a woman/wife—runs the refrain). Unfortunately the poet did not make much out of the difference: rather than being the barahmasa of the soldier or labourer away from home, this is also set in the village (his wife is possibly away at her *mayka*, but that is not mentioned), the others are as usual having fun playing Holi, the women prepare for Dussehra, etc. Jassu Singh, *Barahmasa Mard Birog*, Urdu, Delhi: Matba Burhan Press, 1876, 8 pp., 16mo [OIOLC: 14119.a.18(2)], p. 8. It was printed at least twice thereafter in Delhi, in 1875 and 1879, both times in Urdu.

[6] E.g. in the barahmasa by 'Ibadullah Ranj, composed in 1872 and published in 1876 in Lucknow, the author admits to having taken his cue from other texts: "this story is written in books" ("*kitabon men likhi hai ye hikayat*", v. 34), and his choice of language and details suggests familiarity with Maqsud's; Alavi, *Urdu Mein Barahmase*, p. 314.

Barahmasa Songs in Print

The very first printed barahmasa I have so far been able to discover is a *Barahmasa Khairashah* printed in Agra by the Matba Ilahi in 1862.[7] As already noted, the small format and the fact that the earliest barahmasa titles were printed first in Devanagari—in what was otherwise still an Urdu-dominated market—suggest that these barahmasa booklets were in the first instance aimed at what was perceived to be a segment of the reading market that could only be approached through Hindi, i.e. women.

The perception of barahmasas was in fact of a type of song sung at night, during the rainy season, especially by women.[8] As with other

Fig. 5: Cover and first page of the first available edition of the *Barahmasa* by Khairashah (Agra, 1862), here depicted holding a pen. Note that the lithographic edition does not have paragraphs [OIOLC: 14158.c.6].

[7] Printed barahmasa songs followed a strict stanzaic pattern of *doha* for the refrain and *chand* for the stanza, ranging from the very basic *Barahmasa Benimadho* (36 vv. altogether) to the longer song-poems like that by Allahbakhsh above (107 vv.), Khairashah, and Harnam (both 120 vv.).

[8] See e.g. Chaturvedi, *Braj Bhasha*, p. 168n.

women's song genres, several variations around divine and mythological characters (Yashoda, Shyam, Radha, Sita, Shiva) came to express feelings and dilemmas in women's lives: the fear of being abandoned by one's absent husband, jealousy against one's co-wife, sorrow at the departure of one's son.[9] "Devotional" barahmasas (Table 2.1) were often

Table 2.1
Devotional Barahamas on Divine or Mythological Characters (1867–1869)
DN=Devanagari

Baramasi Gauri Sajan, Agra: Latafat Press, 1867, DN, Litho, 8 pp., "small" (1500), 2 paise
Krishan Chandra ki Barahmasi, Agra: Mufid Khalaiq Press, 1868, 3rd edn, DN, Litho (2100), 3 paise
Ramchandra ki Barahmasi, by Bhawani, Agra: Mufid Khalaiq Press, 1868, 3rd edn, DN, Litho (2100), 3 paise
Ramchandraji ki Barahmasi by Ganesh, Fatehgarh: Ram Sarup, 1868, DN, Litho, demy 8vo, 14 pp. (800), 9 paise
Shri Ramchandra ki Barahmasi, Agra: Sheonarayan, 1868 2nd edn, DN, Litho, 16mo, 16 pp. (3000), 3 paise
Radhaji ki Barahmasi, Agra: Mufid Khalaiq, 1868, 2nd edn, DN, Litho (3000), 3 paise
Jugalkishori ki Barahmasi, id., Agra: Mufid Khalaiq, 1868, 2nd edn, DN, Litho, demy 16mo, 8 pp. (3000), 3 paise
Bhawani, *Ramchandra ki Barahmasi*, Delhi: Hasani Press, DN, Litho, 8 pp. (1000), 3 paise
Sudama ji ki Barahmasi, Agra: Mufid Khalaiq, 1869, DN, Litho, 16mo, 8 pp. (700), 3 paise
Shri Krishna Chandra ji ki Barahmasi, Agra: Mufid Khalaiq, 1869, 2nd edn, DN, Litho (2000), 3 paise
Benimadho ki Barahmasi, Agra: Mufid Khalaiq, 1869 2nd edn, DN, Litho (2000), 3 paise
Bharat ji ki barahmasi, Agra: Mufid Khalaiq, 1869, DN, Litho, 8 pp. 16mo (2000), 3 paise

Source: *Quarterly Lists . . . NWP*, 1867–1869: SV412/38, OIOLC.

[9] In this respect, the catalogue of printed barahmasas with mythological and divine characters (Table 2.1) matches the songs that Sivanandan Misra collected from the "ladies of Shahabad" for George Grierson in the early 1880s in

the shortest songs, with only a few, rather elementary, verses often attributed to Surdas or Tulsidas.

As the refrain in one of them indicated ("Krishna, Krishna repeat men and women"), devotional barahmasas were especially meant for group singing. The cover of one booklet shows a woodblock image depicting a *sant* (Surdas) sitting in front of a group of women, all singing a bhajan, with a temple in the background.[10] In this case the template of twelve months was used to evoke, within the two short lines of each stanza, incidents or lilas connected to the deity, while the refrain brought the mood back to devotional fervour or viraha. Thus, in the barahmasa attributed to Surdas, also known as *Barahmasa Benimadho*, each stanza contained a single detail from Krishna's exploits, while the name of the month at the beginning set the beat along the calendrical cycle. *Ramchandra ka Barahmasa* evoked moments in Ram's quest, and *Dropadiji*'s quickly retold the events related to the game of chess in the Mahabharata. Here is an example from the *Barahmasa Surdas* (or *Benimadho*)—the language is clearly Braj Bhasha, in this version perhaps slightly affected by the transition into Urdu script:

Katik kalol karen sab sakhiyan, Radha bichar kar man men ri
Madho piya ko an mila'o, nahin pran bache chhan men ri.

Refrain:
Hamkau chhanr chale Beni Madho, Radha sog kare man men ri

Agahan *gend banay Sanvare, ja'e khele tat Jamna ke ri*
Khelat gend giri Jamna men, kali nag Nathu chhan men ri.

---

the Bhojpur area. Grierson's article quotes a number of them which have the *gopis* and Udhav, Kaushalya, and Lakshman as protagonists; some of these songs collected from the ladies of Shahabad were, he noticed, in "nearly pure Bhojpuri"; others had probably been originally in Braj Bhasha and were transmitted orally by Bhojpuri-speaking women. George A. Grierson, 'Some Bihārī Folk-Songs', *Journal of the Royal Asiatic Society of Great Britain and Ireland*, 16 (1884): 204, 208. The pattern of reproduction and transmission seems thus to have been from the oral repertoire into print and back into the oral repertoire.

[10] *Barahmasa Surdas*, Agra date? OIOLC: 14109.a.10(1), U, Litho, 16mo, 8 pp. The same picture appears also in non-devotional ones, e.g. *Barahmasa Allahbakhsh*, Delhi, 1870, OIOLC: 14158.c.5, only this time with palms in the background instead of a temple.

Refrain.

Katik, the girlfriends all make merry, but Radha is deep in thought:
Come Madho, my love, my life will leave me any moment now.
Refrain: "'Beni Madho has left me and gone", Radha grieves in her heart.
Agahan, the Dark one made a ball, he went and played on the banks of the Jamuna.
The ball fell into the river, the Black Snake Nathu in a moment.
Refrain.[11]

The greatest circulation by far was achieved by the non-religious barahmasa songs of Khairashah, Harnam, Allahbakhsh, Shambhu Ray, etc. In their case, too, the numerous internal rhymes, the short and regular stanzas, and the presence of a refrain all suggest that they were meant to be sung, while the presence of the intercalary month of Laund, absent from more literary barahmasas, suggests that they were closer to folk songs.[12] Unlike folk songs, though, they were not in a local dialect but in the demotic mixture of Braj Bhasha and Khari Boli of other song genres (see chapter 3).[13] Thus in formal terms they are to be distinguished from folk and devotional songs as well as from poems in the local Hindi dialects, from courtly compositions in Braj Bhasha, and from the Urdu tradition of Afzal's *Bikat Kahani*.[14]

In terms of focus, they also seem to move away from a lyrical expression of the virahini's suffering (cf. Urdu barahmasas below) towards a representation of the pastoral within what could be called an aesthetic-ethic of worldly pleasures, with a greater emphasis on festivals, food, and festive clothes and activities. It is as if the women who were *not* abandoned by their husbands, or whose husbands returned regularly from their employment abroad (*pardes*), could now avail themselves of a great range of goods and entertainments which made ritual occasions all the more pleasurable. If we think back to Anand Yang's argument

[11] *Barahmasa Surdas*, p. 2.

[12] See Susan W. Wadley, 'The Rains of Estrangement: Understanding the Hindu Yearly Cycle', *Contributions to Indian Sociology* 17, 1 (1983): 51–85.

[13] The vocabulary, as we shall see, consisted almost exclusively of Hindi *tadbhava* words, mixed occasionally with simple Perso-Urdu vocabulary.

[14] Cf. F. Orsini, 'Hindi and Urdu Barahmasas', for a wider overview of various formal variations.

about the increase in local and regional fairs and the greater mobility of women, it is as if this shift finds reflection in the changed emphasis in the barahmasas. This shift is one from the lamentation of the wife, whose peasant husband must find employment elsewhere for the greater part of the year,[15] to a celebration of the pleasures available when he returns with the money to buy all the newly available goods. Compared to Afzal's lyrical poem and the women's songs, the emphasis in printed barahmasas was on the woman's sensual beauty—whether the raw and rugged beauty of the virahini, with her mixture of unfulfilled longing, taunting, and submission, or the resplendent and playful beauty of happily married women, the *suhagins*.

The authors, depicted on the frontispiece as either holding a pen or a tambourine (*daf*), sometimes a rosary,[16] and sometimes surrounded by accompanying musicians playing the sarangi and the tabla, seem to have been performers who "ordered" printers to publish their song-poems (Fig. 6). One of them, Kundan Misra, indicated in the colophon: "I have ordered Lala Hazarilal merchant and bookseller [*saudagar kutubfarosh*] to print this barahmasa. No one should print it without the order of the abovementioned Lala." Such stern declarations intended as deterents to pirated editions were common enough, though Kundan Misra uniquely added his signature (Fig. 6) in an attempt to strengthen his claim on the printed text.[17]

Three of the most oft-reprinted barahmasas were *Khairashah ka Barahmasa* (107 vv: 13 stanzas of 7 vv. + refrain), *Barahmasa Harnam* (110 vv.), and *Allahbakhsh ka Barahmasa*. Some of them, as we have seen, had already circulated in manuscript form.[18] They certainly

[15] See also Dirk Kolff, *Naukar, Rajput, Sepoy*, Cambridge: Cambridge University Press, 1990, ch. 3.

[16] E.g. *Khairashah ka Barahmasa*, Delhi: Matba' Brahm Press, 1874 [OIOLC: VT1127].

[17] *Barahmasa Kundan Misra*, Delhi: Matba' Hasani, 1870, DN, Litho, 8vo, p. 16.

[18] E.g. among Urdu poems Chaturvedi mentions a late-eighteenth-century ms of Wahhab's Urdu poem (Vikrami 1848/1791) and two mid-nineteenth century ones, while printed editions in Devanagari and Urdu date from the 1870s. He also mentions Maqsud's barahmasa, which, according to Alavi, dated from the 1790s (and was printed in the 1870s). His list also includes a

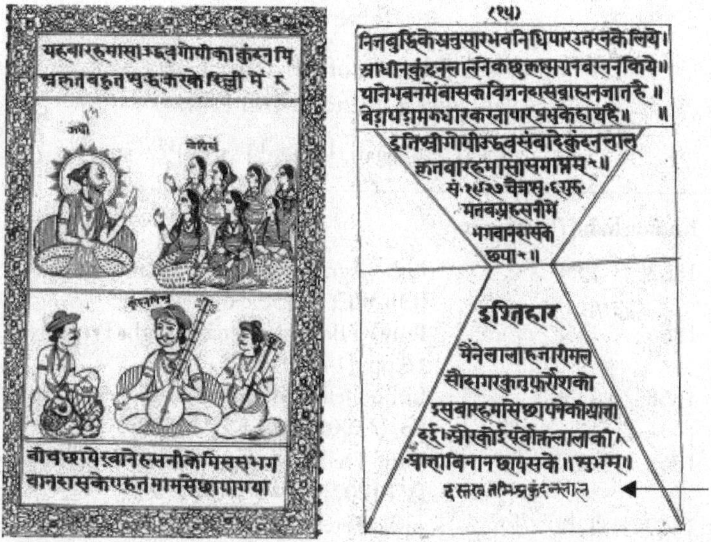

Fig. 6: Cover and last page (p. 16) of the *Barahmasa* by Kundan Misra, Delhi, Hasani Press (1870). The arrow points to the "signature" in a different hand from that of the copyists [OIOLC: VT 1088]. Courtesy British Library.

found great favour with the reading public both in Hindi and Urdu: Khairashah's barahmasa was printed twenty times in less then twenty years, Allahbakhsh's at least fifteen times in a decade, and Harnam's at least six times between 1869 and 1878 alone (Table 2.2).

---

manuscript copy of Harnam's barahmasa, dated Vikrami 1910 (1853), i.e. before it was first printed in 1869 in Devanagari in Delhi by the Matba' Ahmadi, copied by one Pyare Lal, 16mo, 16 pp. [OIOLC: VT 1202]. Chaturvedi's catalogue also includes other Muslim authors whose poems were not published, such as Sheikh Taqi, as well as specifically lower-caste names like Hiralal Halwai. Chaturvedi, *Braj Bhasha Riti Granth*, pp. 164–5. J.H. Garcin de Tassy, intriguingly, was interested enough in this genre to include one barahmasa (*Barahmasa Kanval Dah or Kanvaldai*) in his *Chrestomathie Hindie et hindouie* (1849, pp. 112 ff.), and to translate it into French as 'Analyse d'un monologue dramatique indien', *Journal Asiatique*, October 1850, pp. 310–28. According to Alavi, the author was a famous Sufi of Bihar, Hazrat Jauhri, and the poem is included as "a dastan" in his collected works, *Gauhar-e Jauhri*: Alavi, *Urdu Mein Barahmase*, p. 80.

Table 2.2

Printed Editions of Khairashah and Allahbakhsh in the British Library

(DN = Devanagari, U = Urdu script)[19]

Khairashah, *Barahmasa*		
1862	DN	Litho Agra: Matba' Ilahi, 12mo, 16 pp. [OIOLC: 14158.c.6]
1866	DN	Printed Banaras: Benares Light Press, 8vo, 16 pp. [14158.d.12]
1868	DN	Litho Delhi: Matba' Ahmadi, 16mo, 16 pp. (1500), 3 paise [VT1579(5)]
1869	DN	Litho Delhi: Matba' Ahmadi, 16mo, 16 pp. [VT1202]
1869	DN	Litho Fatehgarh: Matba' Hasani, 16mo, 16 pp. [VT 1579(6)]
1869	DN	Printed Calcutta: Gyanratna Press, demy 8vo, 13 pp. [VT1211]
1870	U	Litho Delhi: Matba' Hasani, 8vo, 8 pp. [VT693]
1872	DN	Litho Delhi: Matba' Narayani, 12mo, 16 pp. [14158.c.7 and VT 1136]
1874	DN	Litho Delhi: Matba' Brahm Press, 12mo, 16 pp. [14158.c.9 and VT1127]
1874	DN	Litho Lahore: printed by Chiragh Din *tajirkutub*, 16mo, 16 pp.
1874	DN	Litho Meerut: Matba' Muhibb Kishwar Hind, 16mo, 16 pp.
1875	DN	Litho Delhi: 16mo, 16 pp.
1875	DN	Litho Mathura: 16mo, 16 pp.
1876	DN	Litho Delhi, 16mo, 16 pp.
1876	DN	Litho Delhi: Matba' Gyan Press, printer Lala Srigopal (*Majmu'a* with *chha-rut*), 8vo, 8 pp.

[19] Chaturvedi mentions a printed edition of Khairashah's from the famous Venkateshwar Press of Bombay, dated Vi. 1907 (1850), but I have been unable to trace it. *Braj Bhasha Riti Granth*, p. 168.

1876	U	Litho Delhi: Matba' Brahm Press, (*Majmu'a Barahmasa*, with six other barahmasas), 8vo, 16 pp.
1877	DN	Litho Delhi: Matba' Brahm Press, 16mo, 16 pp.
1878	DN	Print Calcutta: Chaitanya Chandrodaya, Battala, 12mo, 12 pp.
1878	DN	Litho Delhi: Matba' Fauq Kashi, 16mo, 16 pp.
1878	U	Litho Delhi: (with barahmasa of Shambhu Ray), 8vo, 8 pp.
1878	DN	Litho Meerut: Matba' Jwalaprakash, 16mo, 16 pp.
1879	DN	Litho Meerut: Matba' Jwalaprakash, 16mo, 16 pp.

Allahbakhsh, *Barahmasa*

1867	DN	Litho Agra: Matba' Ijad Khan (with two thumris and one kabitt), 16mo, 16 pp.
1870	DN	Delhi: Matba' Hasani, printer Bhagvan Das, 16mo, 16 pp. (3000), 3 paise
1870	DN	Litho same edn?, 16mo, 16 pp.
1872 U	Litho	Lucknow (with *Qissa Gopichand Bhartrihari*), 8vo, 20 pp., pp. 18–20
1873	DN	Litho Delhi, 16mo, 16 pp.
1875	DN	Litho Delhi, DN, 16mo, 16 pp.
1875	U	Litho Delhi, 16mo, 8 pp.
1876	U	Litho Delhi, Matba' Brahma Press, 12mo, 8 pp.
1876	U	Litho Delhi: Matba' Faiz-e 'Am
1877	DN	Litho Delhi: Matba' Fauq Kashi, 12mo, 8 pp.
1877	DN	Litho Fatehgarh: Matba' Hasani, 16mo, 16 pp.
1877	DN	Litho Delhi: Gyan Press, printer Lala Srigopal, 16mo, 8 pp.
1878	DN	Litho Delhi: Matba' Narayani, 16mo, 16 pp.

1878	DN	Litho same edn? 16mo, 16 pp.
1879	U	Litho Delhi: Matba' Husseini, 16mo, 8 pp.
1879	DN	Litho Delhi, 16mo, 16 pp.

Let us look at the texts in some detail. Like folk songs, they all begin in the month of Asarh, without any introduction. They do not focus exclusively on the heroine's laments but include many details from the ritual calendar. Besides, to the folk song template they add some of the expressions of Urdu poetry (*javani*, *'ishq*) and place a greater emphasis on worldly pleasures. The texts are all very similar—they differ mainly in the arrangement of tropes and expressions—suggesting that the pleasure they offered was based on seriality, recognition, and variations in the selective mention of ritual and other details, rather than on novelty. The opening month of Asarh focuses on the virahini's suffering, following the typical barahmasa strategy of inverting the meaning of all the love-inducing elements of the "lovely" rainy season: with her husband absent, the clouds and rain, the thunder and lightning all frighten the virahini, and the frogs, peacocks, and *papiha* enhance her sense of loneliness. We have seen the stanza of Allahbakhsh's barahmasa (quoted at the start of this chapter). Here is how the other two popular barahmasas begin. First Harnam's:

Doha:

Laga asarh suhavna, ghan garajat chahun or.
Pi pi karat papihara, sakhi bolat dadur mor.

Lovely Asarh has started, thick thunder all around,
"Pi pi" calls the papiha, my friend, and peacocks and frogs

Verse:

Ab to sakhi asarh aya, meri sudh piya ne na lai.
Ghan garajat bairan badari,[20] *meri nind nainan se gai.*
Kis se kahun apna maram, sakhi rut agam,[21] *balam nahin.*
Kyonkar jiun bin pi, mujhe barkha ki rat bairan bhayin.

[20] *Badali* in the Urdu edition, *Majmu'a Dilpasand*, 1876 [OIOLC: 14119.d.6(9)], p. 6.

[21] *Alam* in the Urdu edition, ibid.

Now Asarh has come, my friend, but my love asked no news of me.
Thick thunder the clouds, my enemies, sleep has fled my eyes.
Who can I open my heart to, my friend? How to cross this season, my love is not here.
Why live without my love? The rainy night has become my foe.

Bedhna ne mere karam men piya ki judai likh dai.
Chakve ki jo gati pati bina sakhi, sou gati mere bhai.
Suna bhavan Harnam bin, pi pi papiha kar raha.
Gae bhul sab sukh, dekh dukh papi piya na ghar raha.

God wrote in my destiny that I would be parted from my love.
As the *chakva* pines without her spouse, my friend, so do I.
Without Harnam the house is empty, and the papiha calls "pi pi".
All joys forgotten; look sorrow, you sinner—my love did not stay at home. [Or: look at my sorrow, my sinful love did not stay at home.][22]

And Khairashah's, only slightly varying the elements and introducing a few words from the Urdu poetic vocabulary (*judai*, '*ishq*) and a generally more mixed vocabulary ("*ban mor bole khushgula*"):

Doha:

Asarh mas binati karai Khairashah adhin
Tum bin byakul nain hain, jaise jal bin min.

In the month of Asharh Khairashah the subject pleads,
Without you my eyes are restless, like a fish outside water.

Verse:

Asarh men sovai pari, sab khvab dekhen kamini,
Ambar lavai bijuli khive, dukh dey donon[23] *damini.*

During Asarh all the lovely women sleep sweet dreams.
The sky flashes lightning strikes, both flashes bring distress.

Har bar mat uth bol koyal, pi bina naina jhirai.
Kali ghata chahun or chhai, pavan purva ati calai.

[22] *Barahmasa Harnam*, Devanagari edn, Delhi: Matba' Ahmadi, 1869, '*baqalam* (copied) Pyarelal', 16 pp., 16mo [OIOLC: VT 1202], vv. 1–10.
[23] *Dūnī* in the Urdu edn, *Majmu'a Dilpasand*, 1876, p. 2.

Don't sing each time, cuckoo, without my love my eyes are worn out.
Black clouds spread everywhere, the easterly wind blows fiercely.

Ban mor bole khushgula, sunake bachan jiyara darai.
Jo sar na jane ishk ki, uski balayen sir parai.

The tuneful peacock sings in the forest, my heart sinks at hearing its call.
Who knows not the essence of love is hit by misfortune.

Teri judai se piya ab pran mere to gaye.
Biti jo rut asarh ki, ab man mere mar gaye.

Being apart from you, my love, makes me die.
Now that the season of Asarh has passed, I have lost all respect.[24]

Moving along the calendrical cycle, these barahmasa poets again and again juxtapose the suffering and longing of the virahini with the joyous "structure of feeling" connected with the seasons and the cycle of women's rituals. In fact, although occasional verses hark back to the suffering of the virahini, the attention in the poems soon moves to the festive calendar, presenting the "critical periods" (Susan Wadley) in the calendrical cycle as occasions for celebration and merrymaking (*manana* and *khelna* are the verbs most often used). Thus, Savan embodies the pleasure of the rainy season, with women on swings with their husbands singing *malhar* songs (Allahbakhsh); the women also wear clothes dyed with the saffron flower (*kusumbhi, kusumbi*) and plait their hair with *champa* flowers (Khairashah). Some barahmasas mention the festivals of Tij (Khairashah), Saluno (Maqsud), and Kanagat, "which women celebrate with their husbands" and at which they decorate their palms with henna. The heavy rains of Bhadon usually awaken the heroine's fear, while other women celebrate Nag Panchami (Khairashah) and go with mirasins to the fair playing the drum (*Sundarkali*). Kvar and Katik are the months of Dassehra and Divali, whose lights offers several possible metaphors to the poet. In Allahbakhsh's stanza on Kvar and Dassehra we see women longing for their husbands to come so that they can wear nice clothes and go to

[24] *Barahmasa Khairashah*, Agra: Matba' Ilahi, copied by Baldev Prasad, Samvat 1919 (1862) [OIOLC: 14158.c.6(1)], vv. 1–10, p. 1.

the fair. While having fun in the company of husbands is mentioned, one gets the feeling that the husband's presence is largely instrumental: without him, the wife would not feel entitled to go off and enjoy herself:

Sakhi chautha mahina kvar, a ja dildar, kahti yun nar dvar par khariyan.
Ham kis par paharen sakhi ri hari chunriyan.
Sab sakhi naurata khelati, dekhti mele piya sang, leke gunthti chhariyan.
Phulon ki barkha khari laga rahi jhariyan.
Main kis par dharun Dasahra, ghar nahin sajan mera.

My friend, the fourth month of Kvar, come to meet me, so say
the women standing on their doorways.
Who can I wear the green bangles for, my friend?
All my friends play *naurata*, they watch the mela with their loves,
with sticks decorated with flowers.
Torrents of flowers showering down.
Why should I keep Dassehra, when my beloved is not at home?[25]

While the pujas are mentioned, the women seem mainly interested in wearing nice clothes (Ilahi Bakhsh), playing cards (Harnam), making toy-houses (*gharaunda*, Ranj), and roaming around the fair buying toys (Allahbakhsh).[26] Religious activity in the barahmasas thus consists for women in celebrating festivals and turning out in nice clothes for their husbands. With Magh comes the festival of Basant (*panchami*). *Tesu* flowers are in bloom and women gardeners (*malin*) bring them to women's houses (Allahbakhsh). The women dye their *chunris* and saris yellow (*basanti*), they celebrate ("play") Basanti with their husbands (Ranj) and sing Basant songs in the shade (*Neh*). All the barahmasas mention Holi without fail, when the frolicking and flirting of women contrasts with the heroine's "empty youth"—in fact, the Urdu barahmasa *Sundarkali* dedicates the whole month to this.

The cold season offers no festivals but foregrounds other pleasures: as Harnam says, "these are the days of pleasure and bed" (*Ye din hain*

[25] *Allahbakhsh ka Barahmasa*, Devanagari, Delhi (1870), vv. 27–31.
[26] None of the barahmasas I have seen mentions Karva Chauth, Rakhi, Janmashtami, or any of the other festive-day rituals deemed important for women.

sukh aur sej ke, v. 64). And while the hot season is hardly pleasant for anyone, it becomes tolerable when the women sprinkle their courtyards with water (*chhirkav*), fan their husbands, and offer them cool sherbets (Neh): once again, the calender is reflected not through the prism of ritual obligations but of pleasure.

If the pleasures women can enjoy in every season are therefore a prominent attraction in this kind of barahmasa, the text also allows a voice to the anger, self-pity, and longing of the virahini. She reproaches her husband and bemoans fate (*taqdir*) and her *karam* (past lives) as solely responsible for her state. Some authors have the virahini regret her marriage and state that it must have been at an inauspicious moment (*bad ghari*—e.g. Najib, Ranj). Her laments over her lost youth and sexuality (*joban*), and her bad marriage, are in some texts developed into eloquent complaints against her parents' poor choice of a husband for her. This eloquence, together with her curses against the other woman, the *sautan*, oaths (*qasam*) and ritual gestures to avoid the evil eye (*balayen lena*) can all be viewed as part of a more general perception of "women's language" that seems to have played an important role, especially in the imagination of eighteenth- and nineteenth-century Urdu poets.[27] Khairashah adds to her viraha a dimension of repentant pride. This comes in the shape of a second stanza in which each month reproaches the virahini, saying that it was her past pride, or her lack of initiative when her husband was leaving, that put her in such a position.[28]

Even this short survey reveals the barahmasa as a fairly open genre. Male poets manipulated this genre to provide women the pleasures of

[27] E.g. Najib, vv. 115 and 128–9, and Ranj, v. 214, in Alavi, *Urdu Mein Barahmase*. For Urdu poets and women's voice, see the anthology and analysis by Carla Petievich, *When Men Speak as Women: Vocal Masquerade in Indo-Muslim Poetry*, New Delhi: Oxford University Press, 2007.

[28] E.g. "Asarha says: listen my friend, you did not rise when you had the chance./ I have no fault, parting was written in your fate./ My friend, do not blame me. He wanted you, it was your pride that turned your head and made you crazy./ Now you watch the black clouds and sit with your head in your hands./You were proud, you did not want to say sweet words./ Now you finally understand, when you have lost all respect." *Barahmasa Khairashah*, Agra, 1862, vv. 11–20, pp. 1–2.

identification, as well as the chance to express both longing and despair, while at the same time evoking the many enjoyments of festivals, rituals, and fairs. The strong erotic undertones, present both in the virahini's regret at her "passing youth"—joban being another term for sexuality—and in the flirtations of suhagins, could be enjoyed by both women and men.

Urdu Barahmasas in Print

The barahmasa by Muhammad Afzal 'Afzal' Jhanjhanvi (d. 1625), known as *Bikat Kahani*, has attracted critical attention as the first significant poem in Rekhta composed in North India, almost a century before Urdu poetic culture exploded in this region in the early eighteenth century.[29] Afzal's was the first within a considerable production of Urdu barahmasas—documented by Tanvir Ahmad Alavi—which continued well into the nineteenth century, and thence into the world of print. Alavi's work shows that although the barahmasa genre did not become part of the high Urdu literary tradition that centred around the ghazal, it was nevertheless practised by provincial poets, by men of service, by shaikhs and muftis all the way from Rajasthan to Bihar.[30] Generally speaking, in the hands of Urdu poets barahmasa developed either on the lines of romantic masnavis, sometimes with spiritual overtones; or else they were closer to the perceived realm of the popular/pastoral, which clearly drew upon viraha and Krishna-love material, especially for the theme of Holi. Only a few of the more sophisticated poets made use of the treasure trove of Perso-Urdu poetic themes and style, crafting metaphors that took the subject of romantic loss into

[29] S.R. Faruqi, *Early Urdu Literary Culture and History*, Delhi: Oxford University Press, 2001, p. 113.

[30] See Alavi, *Urdu Mein Barahmase*. Among the eighteenth- and nineteenth-century poets he includes in his collection, one can identify the following typology: (a) Sufis like Hazrat Jauhari, Maulvi Hafizullah Qadiri from Badaun, Shaikh Ibadullah Badal 'Ranj' and Shaikh Abdullah Ansari from Kanpur. With the exception of Jauhari's work—which, as we have seen, was picked up by Garcin de Tassy—their poems were preserved, but were usually not printed; (b) educated provincial officers and men of service like Mufti Ilahi Bakhsh, and possibly Najib; and (c) "bazaar" poets like Maqsud of Lucknow.

high levels of poetry. Most barahmasa writers, conversely, even when drawing upon a Perso-Urdu poetic vocabulary, used only first-level metaphors and simple tropes. So, even after Urdu poetry developed in North India along sophisticated Persian models in the wake of Vali's sensational ghazals, barahmasas continued to offer an appealing folksy idiom, a not-too-implicit sensuality linked to the feminine voice and the cycle of seasons. Consequently, the broad perception of barahmasas is that they constitute a "minor" form. This has had some predictable results: barahmasas were often not deemed important enough to be copied down and transmitted as part of a poet's corpus: hence manuscripts of this genre are rare or not extant. The case of Afzal's *Bikat Kahani* is typical: according to Alavi, the poem was transmitted mostly orally, and the oldest manuscript available dates from almost two hundred years after its composition. Also, while the relatively large number of manuscripts from all over North India and the Deccan testify to its enduring popularity, it is hardly ever mentioned in tazkiras of Urdu poets.[31] Yet Afzal's *Bikat Kahani* was still read in the nineteenth century, two hundred years after its composition. In fact it set the template for all subsequent Urdu barahmasas in several ways: in terms of metre; in the use of Rekhta (alternating verses in Persian and Hindavi/Braj Bhasha); in the presence of a preamble in praise of love and of famous lovers; in the relentless focus on the virahini's pain; and in some of the narrative elements, such as the husband's return at the end of the twelve months.[32] The presence of formulaic filler verses

[31] Alavi, *Urdu Mein Barahmase*, p. 22.

[32] Ilahi Bakhsh mentions first *hearing* Afzal's poem as a not-unusual occurrence ("you must have heard"), and then having had the opportunity to *see* it (i.e. read a manuscript copy); Alavi, *Urdu Mein Barahmase*, p. 272. According to the *Quarterly List* for Delhi in 1869, his *Bikat Kahani* was printed in Delhi in Urdu by the Hasani Press in 1868, 8vo, 16 pp. (1000 copies) for 1 anna and 6 paise, and again in 1869 for only 6 paise. I have been unable to trace these editions. *All* Urdu barahmasa writers after Afzal employed the *hazaj-i musaddas-mahzuf*, a metre common to Persian and Urdu masnavis, as was the prologue on love. Not all Urdu barahmasas actually employ Rekhta, but Ilahi Bakhsh does. For an analysis of these texts, see F. Orsini, 'Hindi and Urdu Barahmasas'. Perhaps also under the influence of the masnavi template, poets like Maqsud (1790s),

suggests that Afzal would have taken the cue for his barahmasa from folk songs—they are practically absent from the later, more polished Urdu barahmasas.[33] To the template of the calendrical cycle—with its web of climatic, ritual, emotional connections, and with its motifs of the pandit and the mullah, the bird-messenger, the dream, and leaving home as a *jogin*—Afzal added the symbolism and language of love of Perso-Urdu poetry. Either as a direct borrowing from women's folk songs, or because it was an intriguing voice to take up, Afzal also adopted for the virahini a strong woman's voice. She reproaches her "cruel" lover for "treason" (*dag͟habazi*) before swearing eternal servitude to him. This is the same pleasure in the colourful and down-to-earth "woman's language" that we find in other Urdu barahmasas, as well as in the mid-nineteenth-century masnavis of Mirza Shauq Lakhnavi.[34]

Three Urdu barahmasas entered the world of print in the nineteenth century—Wahhab's, Maqsud's, and the anonymous *Barahmasa Sundarkali*. While Wahhab's poem is remarkable for the absence in it of Perso-Urdu vocabulary, Maqsud's appears equally at ease with both the vocabulary of Perso-Urdu poetry and that of local, everyday speech. And *Sundarkali* incorporates several motifs from qissas of the time.

Nothing is known about Wahhab, while Maqsud was a *saqqa* (water-carrier) who lived in Lucknow. He must have been famous enough in his time because Mushafi disparagingly mentions him in his *Tazkira-yi Hindi*—a rare instance of the world of bazaar poetry intruding upon

---

the anonymous author of *Sundarkali*, Najib (1830s), and Ranj (1872) framed the barahmasa with a narrator who either hears the story from the virahini, or intervenes in the narration, especially towards the end, when the meeting (*vasl*) between her and her returning lover-husband takes place.

33 "*Sajan pardes, main nit dukh bharun ri*" (My love is away, I grieve constantly); "[*Agahan*] *dukh de gaya ab* [*Pus*] *aya*" ([One month] has gone, now [the next month] has come); "*Piya ke dard se bis kha marun ri*" (Pain for my love will make me swallow poison), etc.

34 See for example the heroine of Shauq's *Zahr-e 'ishq*, discussed by Anna Suvorova in *Masnavi: A Study in Urdu Romance*, Karachi: Oxford University Press, 2000, ch. 5; and F. Orsini, 'Love Letters', in *Love in South Asia*, pp. 235–8.

the elite world of the *mehfil*, but also a sign of the circulation of these poems in urban public space: "Maqsud—the water-carrier—is a bazaar poet, and apart from an agreeable and smooth [*ravan*] disposition he has no other quality. He does not take part in poets' assemblies. The sons of low-born [*kamzat*] people have become his pupils [*shagird*] and they read out his nonsensical poems in assemblies and fairs, especially at the time of Holi."[35]

Wahhab's poem, which had already circulated as a manuscript in Devanagari before it was printed in Kanpur in 1871, is really a ballad.[36] It refers to itself as being "sung" and "listened to":

Sakhi bichuran kahani main sunaun	*ke barah mas piv bin kyun ganvaun*
Sunat hai ans bharai nainan men	*jise bedan birah ki hoe tan men.*
My friend, I tell a tale of parting,	twelve months how can I spend without my love?
Whoever feels the pain of *viraha* in her	body will fill her eyes with tears upon hearing it.
Kahani pem ki Wahhab gave	*ke barah mas apna nam lave*
Wahhab sings a love story	which calls itself barah mas.[37]

Wahhab's poem seems closer to women's songs not only for the absence in it of Perso-Urdu vocabulary, but also for the wealth of local idiomatic words and expressions and its choice of images:

[35] Urdu translation by Alavi, *Urdu Mein Barahmase*, p. 71.

[36] According to the *Quarterly List* for Oudh and the Blumhardt *Catalogues*, it was first printed in Devanagari in Kanpur by the Matba' Nizami in 1871 [OIOLC: VT1107], and then again in 1877 [OIOLC: VT1088]; it was then printed in Urdu in Lucknow by the Khairkhwah-e Hindi Press in 'many editions', 20 pp. (1000 copies) and by the Gulshan-i Muhammadi Press, 16 pp., 1000 copies, no price mentioned.

[37] Ibid., p. 278, vv.1–2, p. 279, v. 32.

Sakhi main pit ka darsan bichhaun	*dosala pem ka upar urhaun.*
I'll spread my eyes for my love,	and wrap around me the shawl of love.[38]

There is even a pun on the word *puri*, meaning both "fulfilled" and "fried puri". All women enjoy cooking festive food, but "without my *bhagavan*" how can the virahini cook?

Jo ajhun na hamari as puri	*kaho kis bhanti bhave ham ko puri.*
If my hope is not fulfilled today,	how can I, tell me, enjoy puris?[39]

This also comes very close to the barahmasas by Khairashah, Allahbakhsh, and Harnam in its focus on women's pleasure in ritual occasions and pilgrimages to holy bathing places, when they go together, singing and joking, dressed in bright clothes. These happy suhagins go to the *tirath* (pilgrimage) all singing together (*sab git gaven*), they make offerings to Brahmins; then, all adorned for the special occasion (*singar*), they offer puja amidst jokes and laughter.

Maqsud's barahmasa is a strikingly confident poem of medium length and in the usual *hazaj* metre. In terms of both size and in language, his barahmasa in standard Khari Boli straddles the middle ground between folk songs and the more literary Urdu poems.[40] In linguistic

[38] Alavi, *Urdu Mein Barahmase,* p. 288. I am not giving the verse numbers because the order of pages and months is mixed up in Alavi's edition. For similar images in contemporary village women's songs, see Gold and Raheja, *Listen to the Heron's Words.*

[39] Alavi, *Urdu Mein Barahmase*, p. 285. It was printed in Urdu in Kanpur in 1877, pp. 12 [OIOLC: VT1087], and probably reprinted. Chaturvedi lists one (undated) manuscript copy in Devanagari, *Braj Bhasha Riti Granth,* p. 164.

[40] After a longish *hamd* in praise of God and the Prophet (vv. 1–27), it introduces the story of the virahini as one he heard direct from her—a trope common to several masnavis ("*suna hai hamne birahan ki zabani, kaha karti thi ro ro ye kahani*", v. 29), and then a customary reflection on the power of love (vv. 28–45). The language moves easily between Perso-Urdu and demotic registers: "God, let us be reunited soon, my days are so restless. Worse, the rainy season has come, and my beautiful dark one has gone away' (*Ilahi vasl hasil ho*

and literary terms, Maqsud's barahmasa provides an example of the successful blending of folk template, Khari Boli poetic diction, and a sprinkling of Perso-Urdu imagery that was replicated within printed barahmasa songs and collections. Interestingly, and uniquely within this barahmasa, the occupation that keeps the virahini's husband away is actually mentioned: he is a soldier at the service of an officer, a *hakim*. The virahini prays this employer will be transferred (*taghrir*) so that her husband returns home. Maqsud appears equally at ease with both vocabularies, of Perso-Urdu poetry and local everyday speech, and is able to mix them in an easy flow:

Birah ki fauj ne a mujhko ghhera,	*nahin mujhmen ab hosh mera.*
Nikal ankhon se lakht-e dil ki buti,	*zamin par ho gai bira bahuti.*
Piya jis roz ghar se sidhara	*qamar aqarab men aya sitara.*
Sitara nahus tha aur bad ghari thi	*shab-e furqat mere sir par khari thi.*[41]

The army of viraha surrounded me,	I am totally at a loss now.
My heart is bleeding out of my eyes,	falling on the ground like red ladybirds.
The day my love left our house,	the moon entered the house of Scorpio
Unlucky star it was, unhappy moment,	the night of separation was hanging over me.

(vv. 52–5)

At first Maqsud eagerly follows ritual events; but in the second part of the poem his attention wanders from the calendar to mundane details: thus, during Katik "people start making quilts and mattresses" (v. 102); other girls poke fun at the virahini by calling her crazy

---

shitabi, nihayat din kare hai istarabi. Tis upar mausam-e barsat aya. Salona-sanvra pardes chaya, vv. 44–5), ibid., p. 228.

[41] Ibid., p. 229. *Bira bahuti* are red cochineal insects that yield a scarlet dye.

and saying she is under the influence of an evil spirit ("shadow", *saya*, vv. 121–4); and she turns to various religious specialists, promising them generous reward for their services once her husband comes back:

Shagun tu khol pothi dekh pande	*piya avenge mukh se bol pande.*
Piya ka jis ghari darsan karungi	*tera ghi-khand se main mukh bharungi.*

Pande, open the book, look at the omen,	tell me my love will come.
The moment I see him back,	I'll fill your mouth with sweets and sugar.

(vv. 89–90)[42]

Incidentally, while Hindu festivals, fairs, bathing festivals and the Brahmin astrologer are mentioned in all barahmasas, only some of the poems authored by Muslim poets include the Sufi pir, the dargah, and the oracular mullah (Maqsud, Qadiri, Najib, Ranj)—in other words suggesting the kind of multiple devotion that characterized popular religion.[43] Thus, in Maqsud's poem the virahini calls the pandit again, a few months later, to avert the evil astral influence that keeps her husband away. She gives him offerings ("*dan-tika*"), but she also goes to the dargah to pray at the pir's tomb and promises offerings if her husband comes back (vv. 176–80, 203). Without belabouring this point,

[42] Ibid., p. 232.

[43] Ilahi Bakhsh's virahini has "many *ta'viz* [amulets] and *mantar* [mantras]" read (v. 169), while Najib's bewails the fact that "Neither this wretched book nor the Gita were of any use, they did nothing for me. Nor did any mullah or Sufi divine (*makhdum*, vv. 146–7)." Besides the pandit, the virahini goes to the mullah for his omen—he will open the Quran at random (*fal*) (Maqsud, *Neh*, Najib, and Ranj). Maqsud has his virahini also visit the dargah of the local pir and offer prayers upon his tomb. *Sundarkali* appeals to Khizr (vv. 31–4). After calling upon the Brahmin and the mullah, Ranj's heroine wishes to go and make an offering of water to "Shivji's as well, and sweep his temple with her hair" (vv. 154–5). See also Harjot Oberoi, *The Construction of Religious Boundaries: Culture, Identity and Diversity in the Sikh Tradition*, New Delhi: Oxford University Press, 1995, which explores the hybrid and diverse character of folk religion in North India.

it does seem worth noting that women's religiosity in the barahmasa songs includes only Hindu festivals and religious specialists, while the Urdu barahmasa poems include not only a mixed poetic vocabulary but also a mixed form of religious devotion.

The Urdu barahmasa most often reprinted, with at least six Urdu impressions from Lucknow in the 1870s and 1880s, is the anonymous *Barahmasa Sundarkali* (208 vv.). Its division into stanzas of eight to twelve verses, followed by a *dohra* couplet, suggests it was meant for oral recitation.[44] This is even more of a hybrid work: it takes greater liberties with the description of the months and includes narrative elements common to qissas (it is framed as the story of Prince Ratankuar and Princess Sundarkali).[45] Thus, the poem begins in Asarh but with no mention of the rain (which only comes in Savan), and the cold nights fall not in Pus but in Magh. Other seasonal and ritual events are absent, apart from Holi, which takes up the whole of the month of Phagun. Remarkable is the mention of other forms of entertainment within the text: after the pandit has promised Sundarkali that her husband will return, she asks her friends to call the mirasins in order to celebrate with singing and dancing. And when her husband does indeed come back, and they go to see a *tamasha* together (v. 199), Sundarkali dresses up in her finery like a true suhagin.[46]

As in the printed barahmasa songs, there is a strong undercurrent of eroticism. The "fire of viraha" that consumes the heroine from the

[44] The first was brought out by Naval Kishore in 1870, 12 pp. (550 copies), 1 anna; further printings were done by other publishers in Lucknow in 1871, 1873 (Karnama Press), 1874, 1876 (Matba' Benazir, Lucknow), and 1877: see *Quarterly Lists* and Blumhardt catalogues. The *Quarterly List* for NWP in 1888 mentions a "4th edition" by Naval Kishore, 8 pp. (2000 copies) for only 3 paise, in 1887.

[45] Not only does it include the greatest range of mixed cultural indicators (Hazrat Khizr, the pandit), it also has the greatest variety of narrative motifs: one night the virahini sees her distant husband in a dream; she sends a parrot (*ḥudḥud*) after him with enquiries. The parrot goes through a little subplot of his own. She then decides to become a jogin in order to go and look after Ratankuar (cf. qissas in chapter 4), but before this she consults a pandit-astrologer who promises her that Ratankuar will come back within ten days. She gives him *dan* (an offering) and her necklace as a gift.

[46] Soon after, she begins to feel ill and dies after a last embrace (v. 206).

very beginning is presented in decidedly physical terms. We are told that she and her husband were married as children and he immediately left "for the East", with her youth consuming her ever since:

Kite din so mujhe huyi javani	*javani ne kiya mujhko divani.*
Javani ne kiya mere upar josh	*kate bal apne men ab hua hosh*
Rangile sej par aram kije	*khushi o rang-ras ka kam kije.*
How long since I became a young woman,	youth has driven me crazy.
Youth has made me boil/burn,	my childhood has gone, I just realized.
Rest on your colourful bed,	enjoy your frolic.

(vv. 12–14)[47]

The cold season and warm clothing are described in loving detail, as a kind of introduction to the pleasures that colourful quilts and warm beds can offer. Desirable "things" feature prominently in the world these women inhabit:

Mahina magh ka parta hai pala	*sakhi sab ghar-baghar orhe dushala.*
Bichhauna toshak aur orhen nihali	*sabon ko ek taraf apni taiyari.*
Kisi ko chhint gujrati o romi	*kisi ko bandari patne ki momi*
Mujhe har vaqt ye jara satave	*nihali aur razai ko orhave.*
Bichaune ke upar phulon ki kaliyan	*piyari piyu ke sang karti rangreliyan.*[48]
In the month of Magh frost appears,	from house to house, my friend, all are wrapped in shawls.

[47] Alavi, *Urdu Mein Barahmase*, p. 214.

[48] So the Matba' Benazir edition (1876), p. 6. Alavi's text has "*piyare piu kahan vo rangreliyan*", p. 219.

Bedding, mattresses, quilts, — all are busy preparing themselves.

Some like *gujarati* or *romi* chintz, — others the *bandari* or waxed Patna kind.
This cold tortures me every moment, — though I wrap myself in quilts and covers.

The bedding is covered with blossoms, — the loved ones are enjoying themselves with their husbands.

(vv. 85–90)

Piya karan meri phatati hai ankhiyan — *jo ave piyu lagaun chhatiyan.*

Palang upar do tan liptae rahte — *khushi o rang-ras ka bhog karte.*
Ki jare men maza hota anutha — *jo gur-ghi se bhi lage hai mitha.*
Agar ana hai to jaldi se ao — *maza jare ka hai, akar chakhao.*

Because of him my eyes are swollen, — if he comes I'll take him in my arms.

We'd lie together on our bed — and take our pleasure to the full.

Unique is winter pleasure, — sweeter than *gur* and *ghee.*

If you are to come, come quickly, — and taste the pleasure of this season.

(vv. 94–7)[49]

Finally, for Chait the flowers in bloom, and the gardener taking his pick in the garden, offer the possibility of extending the metaphor to the heroine ingénue, with further erotic double meanings. These lines could come straight from a Parsi theatre song:

Hamare bagh men phule hai vo phul — *vo kis ke bagh men hua hai mashghul.*

Chameli si badan mahaki hamari[50] — *rasili ankh jyun nargis piyari.*

[49] Ibid., pp. 217–18, 219.

[50] In the Matba' Benazir edition (1876), p. 8. Alavi's texts has "*chameli si dehi sakhi hamari*", p. 221.

Nayan ke pas champe ki kali hai — *balak ye nak champe se bhali hai.*
Mera mukh hai ki jyun gulab ka phul — *na janun baghban kya ho gaya bhul.*
Vo joban hai ki jyun anar ka phal — *bhari mithas se misri ki jyun dal.*

That flower has bloomed in my garden, — but he has lost himself in another.
My body is like a jasmine, my friend, — my liquid eyes like narcissi.
Between the eyes is a champa bud, — no, my nose is even prettier than that!
My mouth is like a rose bud, — God knows what the gardener forgot!
My breasts, two pomegranates: — full of sweetness like sugar.
Bahar aya, dekhanhar na aya, — *anar aya, chakhanhar na aya.*
Spring has come, my saviour has not; — the pomegranate is ripe, but no one to taste it.

(vv. 128–32, 136)[51]

The continuous production of Urdu barahmasas shows that, parallel to the sophisticated Urdu literary culture centred on the ghazal and on Perso-Urdu models, there existed another poetic culture. This was not ignorant or oblivious of the former but provided, in a sense, an alternative aesthetic which employed elements from folk culture and from contiguous modes like the pastoral-devotional. In terms of language, while Afzal's barahmasa is written in a demotic Hindavi–Braj Bhasha interspersed with lines in Persian, subsequent Urdu barahmasas chose Khari Boli Hindi/Urdu, with only a few traces of Braj Bhasha, and with a wide-ranging vocabulary spanning the full

[51] Alavi, *Urdu Mein Barahmase*, p. 221.

range from Perso-Urdu to Braj Bhasha.[52] The result was thus a mixed/hybrid Hindi–Urdu poetic vocabulary, marked by a clear delight in everyday language, identifiable by the feminine voice of the virahini, and by descriptions of worldly pleasures such as swinging or playing Holi or spending a night of love in a warm bed. And while the twelve-month cycle remained in place, the suffering of the virahini came to be juxtaposed, as in the songs by Allahbakhsh, Khairashah, and Harnam, with women's worldly pleasure alongside quaint details about eclectic religious practices.

I have here documented and tried to explain the printing fortunes of a minor though significant and quite specific poetic and song genre—the barahmasa. This genre was peculiar to the Hindi–Urdu commercial publishing market of the 1860s and 1870s, and it petered out in the 1880s.

Why did barahmasas, more than other oral forms, make such a smooth transition into print, and why were they so successful, even if for a limited period? Long enough to be printed singly in small booklets, and short enough to be collected with others in standard Urdu collections, barahmasas I think fulfilled all the requirements of early commercial publishing in Hindi and Urdu. They were popular as a genre which circulated both orally and in manuscript form in urban and rural settings. The printed booklets tagged themselves along already existing forms of leisure, while print made available a greater range of titles in both Hindi and Urdu. The fact that the first barahmasas were printed in Devanagari, I have already suggested, indicates that the target audience was women—as independent sources also confirm.

Alongside the shorter songs by Khairashah, Allahbakhsh, and Harnam, and probably prompted by their success, longer narrative Urdu poems—which had circulated since the early seventeenth century and become part of the repertoire of "bazaar poets" by the late eighteenth—also found their way into print. What barahmasas show, therefore, is

[52] Typically, Persian or Persianizing verses described the virahini's pitiful state, while the vocabulary turned to Khari Boli–Braj Bhasha for rituals and festivals.

not only the convergence between rural and urban, Hindi and Urdu popular traditions, but also the preference (or, from another perspective, the success) of a hybrid language that could cross the barrier of differing scripts with only minimal adjustments.[53] Hybridity is in evidence in the poetic idiom—both devotional and erotic (*shringara* and 'ishq)—and it is this same idiom that we shall find in songbooks and qissas (see chapters 3 and 4). At the same time, the figure of viraha continued to resonate emotionally with the migrant's experience, both for those who had left and for those who were left behind.[54]

Also, whether as songs or as Urdu narrative poems, the barahmasas that found favour in the North Indian book market offered both the unfulfilled sexuality and sensuality of the virahini and the fulfilled sensuality of the happily married woman. This articulation by the male authors of nineteenth-century barahmasas of a worldly aesthetic centred on the figure of the woman and on the seasons (subsuming ritual activities and "things") marks the emergence of women as popular readers as well as the continued currency of the emotional structure of viraha.[55] To the Hindi–Urdu reading public, barahmasa songs and popular Urdu poems offered an attractive image of the woman "in her

[53] That this was a language clearly accessible to both Hindi and Urdu audiences is proved by the fact that barahmasas were printed in either script with minimal variation. Print did tend to fix the language one way or another, mostly in line with existing written models: thus editions in Urdu script (which of course do not differentiate between the verb ending "ai" "y", "e" and "ī", e.g. *karai, kare*) tended to bring the language closer to Khari Boli by spelling Braj Bhasha verb forms as Khari Boli ones ("pare" for "parai", "chor" for "chār") and occasionally using words more in line with Khari Boli ("divānī" for "dukhārī", "thālī" for "thārī", etc.). It is for this reason that the long Urdu barahmasa poem (397 vv.) by Munshi Kanhayalal Saxena "Talib" of Jalalabad, printed by Naval Kishore in 1871—with glosses for even common *tadbhava* words like *birah, sagar* (sea), *nayan* (eyes), and *samachar* (news)—appears so surprising. Were there really Urdu readers in the 1870s who could not understand these words, or did the glosses mark the difference between poetic forms and registers that were now considered non-standard from "chaste" and proper Urdu?

[54] For a brilliant discussion of viraha and the migrant's experience, see Kolff, *Naukar, Rajput and Sepoy.*

[55] And for a brilliant discussion of the rearticulation of viraha in nineteenth-century performance traditions, see Kumkum Sangari, 'Love's Repertoire: Qurratulain Hyder's *River of Fire*', in *Love in South Asia*, pp. 259–88.

own voice", and yet a woman flatteringly dependent on men for her fulfilment, most unlike the defiant beloved of the Perso-Urdu ghazal. Whether it was the virahini drawing attention to her wasted but youthful body, or beautiful suhagins enjoying sexual pleasure in harmony with the seasons, the message was a simple one: a happy woman is not just a married woman (for the virahini is also married, after all), but, as Hafizullah Qadiri's *Barahmasa Neh* puts it succinctly, "A woman who is wanted by her husband is a suhagin" (*Jise chahe sajan vo hai suhagan*).[56] After months of complaint and lamentation addressed to the husband who has deserted her and sent no news of himself nor asked any of her, the heroine is usually overjoyed to welcome him again at the end of the poem. Her position as a suhagin and her sensual appearance is immediately reinstated, with no admonitory lesson for the male reader.

[56] *Barahmasa Neh*, v. 269, in Alavi, *Urdu Mein Barahmase*, p. 252.

3

Songs in Print

The Hindi and Urdu barahmasas explored in the previous chapter showed the transition into print of certain sub-types within a genre that had enjoyed oral and manuscript transmission, and which had occupied more than one niche within multilingual literary traditions. Songbooks, another plentiful, cheap, and markedly heterogeneous genre that enjoyed great popularity from at least the 1860s, allow us to similarly observe the transition into print of performance traditions. In fact, because traditions and contexts of singing can be traced with greater precision, songbooks allow us to explore two other important aspects of the growth of commercial publishing—how the printed book inserted itself into spaces of oral and auditory leisure, and how it successfully captured pleasures earlier embodied in various sorts of singers and discrete singing experiences.

The period after 1857 has been recognized as one of great mobility and transformation in the world of performance, singing, and singers. Patterns and locations of patronage changed. Singers and musicians pulled increasingly away from courts, towards market and cantonment towns, and to the metropolitan centres of Calcutta and Bombay. New patrons emerged for the most famous singers; scholar-reformers sought to redefine the idea of "classical" for Indian music and separate it from courtesan-based practices; and the emerging commercial theatre drew abundantly from existing song traditions. Finally, at the start of the twentieth century the first gramophone recordings, while giving us an overview of singing practices, also subtly influenced and changed musical culture.[1] It is against this variegated, layered, and changing

[1] See Amlan Das Gupta, 'Women and Music: The Case of North India', in Bharati Ray (ed.), *Women of India: Colonial and Post-Colonial Periods*, New

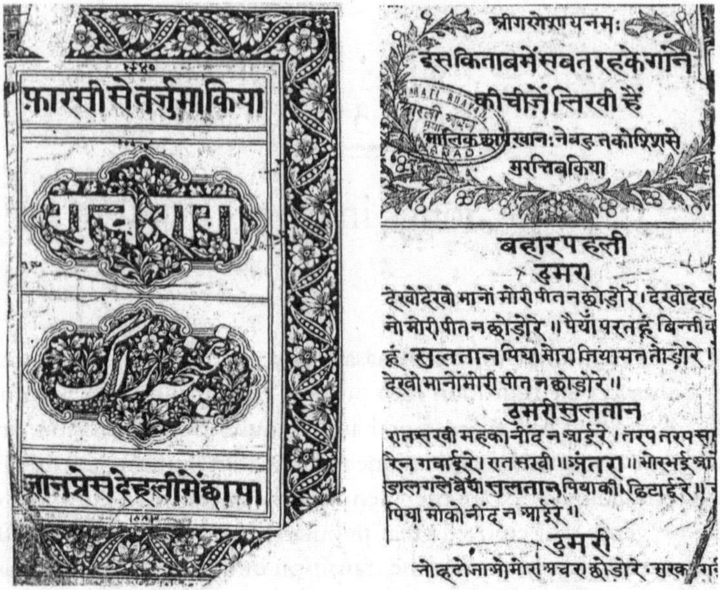

Fig. 7: Cover and p. 1 of *Ghuncha Rag*, "translated from the Persian", compiled by the owner of the press, printed at Gyan Press, Delhi, 1883.

landscape of entertainers and entertainment forms that we must understand the range of printed songbooks, the range of songs they contain, their compilers, and their readership.

Delhi: Sage, 2005, pp. 445–84; Janaki Bakhle's *Two Men and Music: Nationalism in the Making of an Indian Classical Tradition*, Ranikhet: Permanent Black, 2006, and Sheila Dhar's essays in *Raga 'n Josh: Stories from a Musical Life*, Ranikhet: Permanent Black, 2005, are also illuminating as histories of transition in music and musical life over this broad period. The work of Kathryn Hansen explores the development and transformation of theatrical forms in this period: 'The *Indarsabha* Phenomenon: Public Theatre and Consumption in Greater India (1853–1956)', in R. Dwyer and C. Pinney (eds), *Pleasure and the Nation: The History, Politics, and Consumption of Public Culture in India*, New Delhi: Oxford University Press, 2001, pp. 76–114; *Grounds for Play. The Nautanki Theatre of North India*, Berkeley: University of California Press, 1992; and 'Language Community and the Theatrical Public: Linguistic Pluralism in 19th Century Parsi Theatre', in S. Blackburn and V. Dalmia (eds), *India's Literary History*, pp. 60–86.

Singers and Performance Spaces

Ethnographic, scholarly, and memorial accounts reveal urban and rural spaces teeming with performers—in the streets, at melas, in kothas, at private recitals, in special arenas called *dangal*, in makeshift theatres, and so on.[2] The streets of Faizabad during Nawab Shuja ud-daula's rule were crowded with female performers: "there was such a multitude of bazaar beauties and dancers in town", writes Sharar, "that no lane or alley was without them." In Lucknow, apart from the famous courtesans and musicians esteemed at court, Sharar lists various groups of male and female dancers—Kathak dancers from Banaras and Rahasdharis from Mathura, Kashmiri *bhands* and local ones. *Domnis*, who used to sing accompanied by the tambourine (*daf*), had now "progressed" to singing with tabla accompaniment, in the manner of *randis* and male troupes, and to dancing and performing *naql* at women's *mehfils* and weddings, and were in great demand.[3] Radheshyam Kathavachak, reminiscing about Bareilly, suggests that singing, playing music, and watching performances were widespread: "Ordinary people in Bareilly had always been fond of singing and playing music— especially so in the [nineteenth] century. In every house the drum [*dholak*] was played and the *Ramayan* was sung. The story of Rukmini's marriage was recited; Raslilas, Ramlilas, Svang, theatre [*natak*], nautch sessions were all in great demand, especially during the

[2] William Crooke, 'Religious Songs from Northern India', *Indian Antiquary* 39, October 1910: 268–87 and December 1910: 321–45. 'Abdul Halim Sharar, *Guzishta-e Lakhnau*, New Delhi: Maktaba Jamia, 2nd ed. 1992, pp. 232–47. See also Mirza Jafar Husain, *Qadim Lakhnau ki Akhiri Bahar*, New Delhi: Qaumi Council Baraye Furugh-e Urdu Zaban, 1981. Musical-historical accounts of nineteenth-century North India have tended to focus either on changing musical tastes—with the rising popularity of the sitar and sarod, of kathak and thumri, and of regional styles in general—or on the establishment of Lucknow as a musical centre. See Allyn Miner's excellent *Sitar and Sarod in the 18th and 19th Centuries*, Wilhelmshaven: Florian Noetzel, 1993; Peter Manuel, *Thumrī in Historical and Stylistic Perspectives*, Delhi: Motilal Banarsidass, 1989, especially ch. 3; Madhu Trivedi, 'Hindustani Music and Dance: An Examination of Some Texts in the Indo-Persian Tradition', in M. Alam, M. Gaborieau, and F.N. Delvoye (eds), *The Making of Indo-Persian Culture*, Delhi: Manohar, 2000, pp. 281–306.

[3] Sharar, *Guzishta-e Lakhnau*, pp. 240–7.

four months [of the rainy season]. In such an atmosphere I not only learnt to play the harmonium, I was drunk with passion for it."[4] Ramgharib Chaube describes groups of itinerant singers of lavanis (also called *marhati* or *khyal*) who established relations of spiritual tutelage with members of the audience, imparted spiritual teaching through their songs, and occasionally competed among themselves. The singers met at several recognized places, known as *akhara*, and large crowds assembled to listen. "Money is deposited on both sides and the singer who can sing the greatest number of superior songs is awarded the prize. The prize won is expended in buying liquor and tobacco, which is distributed among the companions of the winner."[5] Sharar also grudgingly recognized their popularity: "Lower class people had also evolved special literary interests according to their tastes. For instance, one practice arose which was known as khyal. People composed extemporary verses and recited them when sitting in a circle . . . Several exponents of this art achieved great success and, although they had no connection with the best society or with educated people, still, if one considers the matter, one must admit that they produced real and natural poetry."[6]

What emerges from these accounts is not just the variety of performers, but also the fact that performances, and singing more generally, took place at specific times and on particular occasions. *Svang* songs in Saharanpur, notes Chaube for example, commenced about five days before the Holi festival,[7] whereas *kajlis* were performed by men and women in Mirzapur on the last day of Savan (July–August). After a ritual bathing, and a ritual involving barley saplings, women and girls would stand in a circle and perform a particular dance called *dhun muniyan* and sing kajli songs. "On the night preceding

[4] Radheshyam Kathavachak, *Mera Natak-Kal*, New Delhi: Rashtry Natya Vidyalay, 2004, p. 14.

[5] Ramgharib Chaube, 'Popular Singers in Saharanpur', *Indian Antiquary* 39, February 1910, p. 64; see also his note on 'Local Songs of Saharanpur' in the January issue of *Indian Antiquary* of the same year, p. 32. For the Deccani provenance of these singers, see Kathryn Hansen, *Grounds for Play*, p. 68.

[6] Abdul Halim Sharar, *Lucknow: The Last Phase of an Oriental Culture*, p. 93, quoted in Hansen, *Grounds*, p. 318.

[7] Chaube, 'Local Songs', p. 32.

Kajali Day, women of every Hindu family keep awake the whole night and sing Kajali", too.[8] Women's song genres were either connected to seasonal festivals like Tij or Holi, or else to specific activities like bathing or grinding, or with life-cycle rituals of weddings, birth or mourning.[9]

But women's seasonal songs in the nineteenth century were no longer exclusive to women. In the 1880s Badrinarayan Chaudhri "Premghan" of Mirzapur spoke of groups of bazaar singers (*gavaiyas*) who were singing kajlis that differed, in terms of vocabulary and mood, from those of ordinary women; they were closer to the mixed Braj Bhasha–Urdu poetic idiom of, for example, the barahmasa songs.[10] Besides, seasonal songs like kajlis had already become part of the *purabi* (eastern) repertoire of women singers (*bais* is the generic term). They were also eagerly written by members of the elite, from Nawab Wajid Ali Shah in Lucknow to Hindi literary people like Premghan and Bharatendu Harishchandra in nearby Banaras.[11] Premghan himself distinguished in his collection of songs (a) kajlis as sung according to different rhythms (*lay*) by ordinary women in "local women's language" (*sthanik theth stri bhasha*); (b) those sung by male singers (gavaiya) in "Banarasi rhythm"; (c) in the style of women actors (*natinis*); (d) in the "ornate Braj Bhasha" of women singers (*gavarins*); (e) and in the style/rhythm of randis, of *khanjaris*. He further added kajlis in Urdu and in Nagari (i.e. Khari Boli Hindi).[12] When sung *not* by local women but

[8] Ramgharib Chaube, 'The Origin of Kajali Songs', *Indian Antiquary* 39, October 1910, p. 325. Interestingly, both in the case of the *svang* songs in Saharanpur and the *kajli* festival in Mirzapur, Chaube claimed that it was a new festival.

[9] Crooke, 'Religious Songs'.

[10] Badrinarayan Chaudhri "Premghan", 'Kajli Kutuhal', vol. 1, Prayag: Hindi Sahitya Sammelan, 1845, pp. 508–12.

[11] Bharatendu Harishchandra published one kajli of his own in *Gulzare Purbahar*, Banaras: Benares Light Press, 1938Vi (1881), 2nd edn, 88 pp., printed (1000), and published, by order of the Maharaja of Banaras, *Malhar Hindola Kajli Jayanti Adi Sangrah*, Benares: Shrivajchand Yantralay, 1882, 11 pp., litho, a collection of seasonal songs on religious subjects from books like *Shri Shyamsudha*, *Shyamrang*, and *Ayodhyavindu*.

[12] "Premghan", 'Kajli Kutuhal'. Since his sobriquet appears in several of these compositions, it appears that he could imitate and write in all these styles.

by professional singers, seasonal songs thus maintained the mood and the musical identity of the song genre, but changed in linguistic variety, from local dialect—the Bhojpuri of either Mirzapur or Banaras—into a more diffuse "eastern" dialect or mixed Hindi–Urdu, thus moving from a purely local idiom to a supra-local one. As Amlan Das Gupta notes, the vast song repertoire of women singers in the purabi tradition "shows remarkable similarity no matter where these women were located."[13] Exactly the same phenomenon occurred with lavanis, which did not remain exclusive to the singers specified by Chaube but were taken up by other amateurs and by elite poets.[14] Radheshyam's father, a professional religious storyteller, was "addicted" to singing lavanis.[15] And Betab's father, a sweetmaker profession, used to compose svangs orally while someone else wrote down the text as he spoke it.[16]

It is in this expansion of song genres beyond their local, ritual spaces, at the hands of local amateurs and poets, wandering professionals, and bais that we must locate the production of songbooks, which captured the imagination of an audience already well acquainted with the

[13] Das Gupta, 'Women and Music', p. 9.

[14] Bharatendu, notes Kathryn Hansen, "was very fond of this form and would sit on the pavement with lavani singers and learn their compositions; his own lavanis were published as well"; Hansen, *Grounds for Play*, p. 68. See Harishchandra's *Phulon ka Gucchha*, Benares: Chandraprabha Press, 1882, 15 pp. (283 copies), printed, 3 annas, which preserves the combination of romantic/erotic and spiritual that Hansen describes as typical of lavani singers.

[15] Kathavachak, *Mera Natak-Kal*, p. 14. One lavani composer gave the following account for the competitive spirit of such gatherings and tried to distance himself from its more verbally aggressive aspects: "Some call it lavani and some marhati or khyal. Actually the composition and singing of it comes from the South, and it was created by two people: one was called Tuknigar and the other Shah Ali. They set up two different camps: *turra* and *kalangi*. Tuknigar held turra to be better, while Shah Ali preferred kalangi. They used to quarrel and each started their own group, both of which have many followers in this country even today, including some educated people. But I am sorry to say that [the two parties] exchange a lot of insults and go as far as having fights. For this reason honest folk do not like it, and I was involved in it since childhood"; Kashigiri Banarasi Paramahansi, *Lavani Arthat Marhatikhyal*, Lucknow: Naval Kishore, 1884, 4th edn, p. 1.

[16] Narayan Prasad "Betab", *Betab Charit*, p. 16.

forms.[17] Songbooks, as well as the theatre, gave further resonance to this rich and layered musical culture, and made all these various forms available together in the same space. One of the great puzzles that initially confronted me in this project was—who were the readers of so many songbooks? Since none of the professional singers usually mentioned—from ustads to bais, from domnis and mirasins to ordinary women—seemed in need of books for the transmission of their musical knowledge,[18] the answer seems to lie in the movement of songs beyond their original performers and performance spaces. It was men like Betab and Radheshyam who bought these books, and the women who came to Yashoda Devi's stalls in the 1920s asking for *Albela Gavaiya* and *Ghazal Sangrah*.

One more point before we turn to some of these songbooks. Often, accounts such as Sharar's or Mirza Jafar Husain's on the urban culture of nawabi Lucknow present a sharp distinction between on the one hand the nobility and respectable people (*'umara* and *shurafa*), and on the other ordinary folk (*'avam*) consisting of craftsmen, shopkeepers, and workers. This is reflected also in the way musical tastes are talked about: the spread of popular forms is voiced in terms of a "decline" in musical tastes. Quoting Asadullah Kaukab, the son of a famous Lucknow musician, Sharar says Wajid Ali Shah's reign witnessed a "decline in musical knowledge . . . In Lucknow Kidar Piya composed thumris

[17] For printed collections of lavanis and khyal, see *Guldasta-e Khyalat-e Turra,* by Gusain Anand Gir alias Nattha Singh, Talib of Khatauli, District Muzaffarnagar, Meerut: Dar-ul Ulum Press, 1891 (Urdu), 700 pp. (!) (500 copies), litho, 8vo, 4 annas; *Khyalat turra*, by Pt. Rangi Lal, Agra: Mathura Press, 1894, 68 pp. (1000), litho, 8vo, 2 annas. For lavanis, see Banarsi Das, *Lavani Arthat Marhati Khyal,* Lucknow, 1874 (Devanagari), 111 pp. (1000), litho, 8vo, 4 annas (Urdu edn, Kanpur, 1879, 106 pp., litho, 8vo); Nanhu Lal, *Lavani Navinavilas*, pt 1, Banaras, 1879, 194 pp., litho, 8vo; Raghunath Sharma of Banaras, *Lavani-Bahar*; Ghasi Ram, *Mohan ki Lavani,* Agra: Ijad-e Kishan Press, Agra, 1886 reprint, 32 pp. (1000), litho, 16mo, 9 paise; *Lavani Dilaram*, Banaras: Rajarjeshwari Press, 1888 (Devanagari), 33 pp. (1000), printed, 12mo, 3 paise; Pt. Devkinandan Tivari, *Bichitra Lavani,* 3 pts, Allahabad: Vidyadharma Vardhak Press, 1893 (Devanagari), 8 pp. (400), printed, 16mo, 3 paise.

[18] Not only was literacy among professional singers extremely limited, to this day they are known to prefer handwritten compilations (*bayaz*).

and spread them among the people, thus depriving music of its beauty."[19] Alternatively, musical knowledge among the 'avam is explained in terms of the beneficial influence of the nobility.[20] So, while aristocratic tastes are said to have been "corrupted" by ordinary people's tastes (*'amiyana mazzaq*), popular taste is said to have been refined by the cultivation of music at court and in aristocratic circles. It is with a tinge of surprise and local pride that Sharar declares of Lucknow that here even "people of the bazaar" and boys who sang in the streets could sing many different compositions, and even illiterates knew *she'rs* by heart and could sing popular raginis.[21] What we can derive from these accounts is a high degree of musical knowledge in society, as well as a preference for certain poetic song genres such as ghazals and seasonal songs among "people of the bazaar". It seems to have been a culture which ensured that as soon as people acquired a little literacy, they might well buy songbooks.

Music and Songs in Print

The *Quarterly Lists of Publications* for books connected to music reveal three broad categories of printed material: (1) Short treatises by aristocratic connoisseurs, published in Lucknow as early as the 1850s, continuing a long tradition of Persian treatises, though now the treatises were written in Urdu and published in lithograph form.[22] (2) Manuals for instruments.[23] (3) Songbooks, mostly in Devanagari, which include

[19] Sharar, *Guzishta*, p. 232: "*mausiqi ko behusn kar diya*".

[20] Husain, *Qadim Lakhnau*, p. 170.

[21] Sharar, *Guzishta*, p. 237.

[22] E.g. *Ma'dan al Mausiqi*, Lucknow, 1856; *Ghunchah-e Rag*, Lucknow, 1879 2nd ed., 1890 3rd edn, *Tarana-i Dilchasp*, Lucknow, 1886, all in Urdu. *Ghunchah-e Rag* was written by Muhammad Mardan 'Ali Khan, Nizam ud-Daula, who patronized schools and libraries and authored other books for the Naval Kishore Press: *Quarterly Catalogues of Publications* for the NWP for the relevant years [OIOLC: SV412/38].

[23] E.g. in Urdu: *Tahsil-e Sitar*, Kanpur, 1874, *Naghma-e Sitar*, Lahore, 1876; in Devanagari: *Ragamala, Tarjuma Ta'lim us-Sitar*, Delhi, 1876, *Harmonium Guide*, pt 1, Allahabad, 1893. About musical education in general: *Chautal*, Agra, 1890 4th edn, *Sangit Shiksha*, Lucknow, 1891, both in Hindi: *Quarterly Catalogues of Publications* for the NWP for the relevant years. Allyn Miner

both collections of mixed songs (*Ghuncha Rag, Dilbahlao, Sada Bahar*) and those dedicated to a single genre (*phag, holi, kajli, jhulna, khyal, lavani, jhagra, barahmasa*). These were mostly lithographed until the 1890s.[24] While the first two categories seem to reflect elite interest in musical forms—either in terms of continuing manuscript traditions or of the new respectability of musical education, it is the third group, by far the largest in terms of number of titles and editions, that really interests us as part of the story of commercial publishing. As we shall see, songbooks included material from at least four different sources. First, there were small booklets of single (usually women's) song genres such as *gari, jhagra*, or *lilas*. Second, there were more voluminous compilations such as the Hindi *Ghuncha Rag*, whose combination of ghazals, thumris and dhrupad reproduced a bai's repertoire. Third, there were mixed collections like *Sada Bahar* (1882), with "select pieces for reading and singing", which appear to be the product of bazaar poets—as well as more sophisticated literary versions of the same forms. Finally, we find songs included in theatre chapbooks and, increasingly from the 1890s, booklets consisting exclusively of songs from "theatrical plays", without the dialogues. The striking thing about these books is that, despite their different origin, outlook, and to some extent specialization, they all contributed to the circulation

---

suggests that there were distinct regional styles in these books, both in lithograph or print and in the language and contents according to the following groups: (1) Delhi, Lahore, and Rajasthan; (2) Lucknow, Banaras and Patna; (3) Bombay and Gujarat; (4) Bengal. The Bengal style stood quite apart from the others in terminology and in its nationalistic and pedagogic tone. Personal communication, 20 May 2008.

[24] E.g. in Devanagari: *Shrikrishna Phag*, Agra, 1868 2nd edn, *Majmu'a-e Dilbahlao*, Agra 1868 2nd edn, *Ghuncha Rag*, Delhi, 1883, *Prem Sudha Varshan*, Banaras, 1874, Harishchandra's *Gulzare Purbahar*, Banaras, 1879 (printed), and *Ras Barsat*, Banaras, 1882 2nd edn (printed); *Rag Pacchisi*, Shahjahanpur, 1880, *Gana Hulas*, Banaras, 1883 (printed), *Sada Bahar*, Fatehgarh, 1882, *Kajli Bahar*, Mirzapur, 1886, *Rag Naubahar*, Fatehgarh, 1886. In Urdu: *Gulshan-e Rag*, Lucknow, 1882 2nd edn, *Rabab-e Mughanni*, Kanpur, 1888, *Holi Bahar*, Mirzapur, 1889, *Majmu'a-e Gulshan-e Rag*, Meerut, 1889 (in Devanagari: Meerut, 1885 2nd edn). *Quarterly Catalogues of Publications* for the NWP for the relevant years.

of the same song types and to the currency of heterogeneous and (as we shall see) flexible musical-poetic tastes.

While ethnographers were eagerly collecting religious, life-cycle, and work-connected songs from village women, only a few of these song genres found an outlet in print. As we saw in the previous chapter, devotional songs connected to Krishna and Rama, whether in the form of short lilas or of barahmasas, were printed many times from the 1860s onwards.[25] Similarly, the songs of insults (gari or gali) that women sang at the bridegroom and his relatives at weddings were printed in the form of little narratives relating to the wedding of Krishna or Ram, as in the case of the very popular *Bara Gopal Gari*.[26] When the dazzlingly beautiful Krishna comes into the wedding pavilion, the gopis start singing the customary abuse: he has two fathers and one mother, his mother Jasodha eloped (*urhari*) from Mathura; his sister Sahodara made off with Arjun, and his father Nanda goes begging from house to house.[27] That women were the audience for such song booklets is confirmed by a colonial official, who noted about a barahmasi in 1879: "This tract, like others of the same class, is deficient in both language and plot, but is popular with women generally, as it furnishes them with songs."[28]

Other song genres that seem to fall within this category are jhagras and jhulnas. Jhagras were perhaps the first, most popular, and cheapest type of songbook to be published in Devanagari in substantial print-runs. They consisted of short stanzaic repartees between two opposing subjects—gold and iron, pearl and cotton-seed—spirited exchanges that reflected other poetic competitions. Jhulnas were spring songs

[25] See ch. 2 for the short *Barahmasa Benimadho* and Table 2.1 for a list of religious barahmasas. E.g. Parmanand, *Dan Lila* (Hindi), Fatehgarh: Dilkusha Press, 1867 2nd edn, 8 pp. 20 x 26 inches (800 copies), litho, 9 paise; or Narayan, *Shyam Sagai*, Hindi, printed at the same press, 1868, 16 pp. (1000), litho, 6 paise.

[26] *Bara Gopal Gari*, Banaras: Madho Prasad Bookseller, 12 pp. (2000), 16mo, 6 paise.

[27] Ibid., p. 4.

[28] *Statement of Particulars regarding Books, Maps, etc. Published in the North Western Provinces & Oudh* . . . fourth quarter of 1879, p. 9.

that women sung while swinging.[29] This is not to suggest that women were buying and singing only these songbooks, but that these songbooks were specifically targeted at them.

By contrast, a hefty compilation of thumris and ghazals, such as the Hindi Ghuncha Rag, made available to readers the repertoire of songs they would have listened to at bais' recitals.[30] Though usually taking place in courtesans' kothas or in the houses of the elite, such recitals would not have been inaccessible to ordinary people; they could attend by paying a small fee to the host.[31] Claiming to have been "translated from the Persian", no doubt to evoke the glamour connected with elite Persian poetry, Ghuncha includes pieces "collected with great effort by the publisher" (p. 1). It has a whole chapter on thumris, including pieces by famous poet-musicians such as Sultan, Haidar, Naqi, Kadar or Kidar, Alam, etc.;[32] a chapter on malhar and raga-raginis, including a *dhurpat*; a chapter "with many kinds of holi and khyals for sing-

[29] For examples of this genre in Devanagari, see Ram Ray, *Arsi Jhagra*, Delhi, 1868, 8 pp., litho, 16mo, 3 annas; Ambar Das, *Arsi Jhagra*, printed Pt. Keshab Das, Agra, 1868 3rd edn, 8 pp. (2000 copies), litho, 6 paise; another *Arsi Jhagra*, Agra: Sheonarayan, 1868 2nd edn, 8 pp. (2000), litho, 16mo, 3 paise. *Moti Binole ka Jhagra* (binola = cotton seed), Agra: Mufid Khalaiq Press, 1868, 8 pp. (2100), litho, demy 16mo, 3 paise; another edition Agra: Sheonarayan,1869 2nd ed., (2000), litho, 3 paise. *Sone Lohe ka Jhagra*, Agra: Sheonarayan, 1868 2nd, 8 pp. (2000), litho, demy 16mo, 3 paise; another edition Delhi: Hasani Press, 1868, 8 pp. (1000), litho, 12mo 3 paise. *Majmua Jhagra*, Agra: Mohammadi Press, 1869 2nd edn (1400) litho, 6 paise. For jhulnas: Pt. Gobind Sahay, *Jhulne Laila Majnun*, Meerut: Fakhr ul-Matabi Press, 1890 (Devanagari), 12 pp. (1000 copies), litho, 8vo, 3 paise; Kiddha, *Jhulne Bhakt Prahlad Ke*, Meerut: Chaman-e Hind Press, 1890, 48 pp. (1000), litho, 8vo, 1 anna, 6 paise; *Jhulne Rukmini Mangal Ke*, ibid., and *Jhulne Krishnaji Ke*, ibid., Mathura Singh, *Jhulne Sipahizada*, Meerut: Fakhr-ul Matabi Press, 1890 (Urdu), 20 pp. (1000), litho, 8vo, 5 paise (this was probably a version of the *Qissa Sipahizada*, see ch. 4 below). For lavanis, see fn. 17 above.

[30] *Ghuncha Rag: "farsi se tarjuma kiya"*, Delhi: Gyan Press, 1883, litho, 73 pp., Bharati Bhavan Library, Allahabad.

[31] Amlan Das Gupta, personal communication, Calcutta, January 2006.

[32] For a recent study of thumri texts, see Lalita Du Perron, *Hindi Poetry in a Musical Genre: Thumrī Lyrics*, London: Routledge, 2007.

ing" (p. 35), including some rather long khyals and khyals of spiritual instruction "called *marhati*, written by Banarasigir" and Devi Singh (p. 40); a chapter with "ghazals from *ustads* that are used for singing" (p. 46), including ghazals by 'Ali Gauhar, Atish, Zafar, 'Ustad Zauq', Mir Dard, Munis, etc.[33] It also includes a chapter on "khyals that are used for singing *qavvali*" (p. 65); and finally a chapter on dohas 'that are combined with song pieces' (p. 73). What is significant for us is, first of all, the range—from ghazals to thumris to seasonal songs; second, the diffusion of literary ghazals (and literary Urdu) to a wide audience through the medium of songs; and third, the fluidity of musical performance, so that a khyal could be sung as a qavvali and marhati/lavanis as khyals, as well as the fluidity between the erotic and spiritual registers and genres, so that courtesans could also sing the marhati/lavani songs of spiritual instruction popularized by lavani singers. It is this fluidity, typical of the flexibility of performance according to the context and the patron's demand, that left its imprint on the Hindi/Urdu commercial print culture as a whole.

The third group of songbooks seems to come straight out of the akharas of local poets and religious teachers.[34] Songs of spiritual instruction (sometimes called *haqqani*) are mixed with love songs of *'ishq* and *shringara*, which of course can also be taken to refer to spiritual love.[35] Let us take for example a popular title of a mixed collection of songs, *Dilbahlao* (Entertainment).[36] This particular chapbook contains

[33] Some of these were also quoted in Bharatendu's collection of ghazals and songs, *Gulzare Purbahar*: evidence of the shared nature of this repertoire and of the transmission of ghazals through bais.

[34] For khyal collections of lavani/marhati singers printed in Banaras, see Kathryn Hansen, 'The Birth of Hindi Drama in Banaras, 1868–85', in Sandria Freitag (ed.), *Culture and Power in Benares*, Berkeley: University of California Press, 1989, pp. 62–92.

[35] Or, as Kathryn Hansen puts it, "Such collections contained verses by Hindu and Muslim poets on devotional Krishnaite themes and on Indo-Islamic topics, for example, the love between *ashiq* and *mashuq* (lover and beloved)": *Grounds for Play*, p. 68. A cover of one such booklet (dated 1873), showing a group of singers with the main one in the centre holding a tambourine and another smoking a *chilum*, is reproduced on p. 69.

[36] The text I have had access to dates from 1882: *Dilbahlao*, Kanpur:

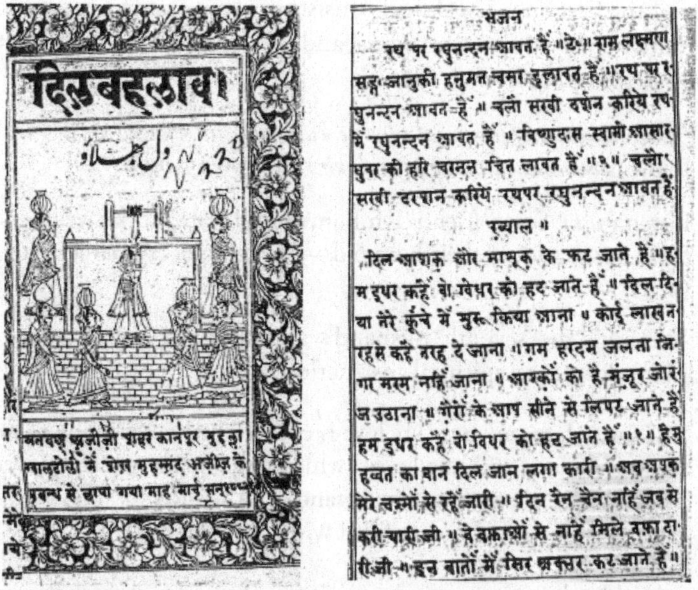

Fig. 8: Cover (left) of the song collection *Dil Bahlao* (Kanpur, 1882) with the seven friends at the well, and (right) p. 13 with a bhajan and <u>kh</u>yal.

thirty-four pieces (*chiz*): almost half are holi songs, while the rest are khyal, ghazal, thumri, dhrupad, rekhta, bhajan, *kabitt*, and "*rag pad*". Only a few songs contain a signature in the text, the rest are anonymous. Khyal here indicates longer, almost narrative, songs, at times consisting of a repartee between different singers or groups of singers, as in the

---

Matba Azizi, 1882 (Devanagari), 24 pp., litho, 16mo, held in the Bharati Bhavan Library, Allahabad. Quite possibly it reproduced earlier collections by the same name: e.g. *Majmu'a-e dilbahlao*, Agra: Shiv Narayan, 1868 2nd edn (Devanagari), 32 pp., litho, 16mo, 1 anna, 6 paise; *Majmua dilbahlao men lavani, khyal, holi, pad bhajan, thumri, rag rekhta, ghazal, chhand kabitt, doha hain*, Banaras: Rajkumar Mishra, 1868 (Devanagari), 32 pp., litho; *Dilbahlao*, Agra: Mohammadi Press, 1868 (Devanagari), 32 pp., (700), litho, 8vo, 1 anna; other edn, Agra: Latafat Press, 1868 (Devanagari), 32 pp., (1500), litho, 9 paise; other edn, Meerut: Amba Prasad, 1874 (Devanagari), 32 pp. (1000), litho, 8vo, 1 anna; other edn, Delhi: Hasani Press, 1872 (Devanagari), 32 pp. (1000), litho, 8vo, 1 anna.

case of the first one. This khyal consists of seven stanzas, each voicing the lament of a woman whose husband is prey to a particular addiction (*bhang*, *charas*, opium, *ganja*, etc.)

> *Sakhi sat ghar sen chali jal bharne kuen par sun gyani.*
> Refr.: *Nashe baz saton ke piya dukh roti bharen pani.*
>
> Listen *gyani*! Seven friends left home to fill water at the well,
> Refr: Seven addicts their husbands—the women cry filling water. (p. 2)

At the end, the seventh husband's addiction to "maya" turns the women's song into spiritual instruction.

> The seventh friend says: My love is crushed by his addiction to maya.
> *Maya* is its own antidote [*aksir*] which removes sorrow and poverty.
> Thousands come to flatter and stand at its service.
> [. . .] Giri, my ustad is ever filled with knowledge. (p. 5)

Another khyal urges amnesia in relation to the body—which the craftsman (God) has forged in the furnace of viraha and on which greed acts like fire—and to "drink the cup of love" (p. 6). Other khyals turn the ghazal template into a song of spiritual love. "I will awaken the *alakh* in your *kucha*", sings the author of one khyal, who vows to serve his master in all possible ways, including "singing in the khyal sabha of Dullaram Kalyansingh".[37] He himself will dress like a jogi but will bestow rich gifts upon his guru (p. 12). Another khyal is a spiritual ghazal (also by Debi Singh), in which the lover, "intoxicated with unity" (*vahidat men mast*), has no longer need for worldly beauties:

> *Mila hamen gulzar vo gulru ab gul khana nahin chahiye*
> *Men* [sic] *vahidat men mast hun may k̲h̲ana nahin chahiye.*
>
> I found the rose-faced, I no longer need to cauterize myself [*gulkhana*]
> Intoxicated with unity, I have no need for a tavern.

[37] The competitive context of the khyal sabha is evoked also in another khyal by Debi Singh, with the refrain, "I say something here, and over there he/they step back": *Dilbahlao*, p. 14.

Dil roshan kiya to phir tan badan jalana nahin chahiye.
Ah ki atish jale par ag jalana nahin chahiye.
Bahire ishq men bahe use dariya men bahana nahin chahiye.
Dube chah men jo phir kuan jhukana nahi chahiye.
Ishq ka sauda ho hamko ab aur divan nahin chahiye.

Once the heart is lit up, there is no longer need to burn the body,
You should not light a fire on the sigh of someone burnt by fire.
One who floats in the sea of love has no need to float in the river,
One who drowns in longing needs not go down a well,
Once I transacted love, I need no further court.

Men vahidat men mast hun . . .[38]

Besides these spiritual khyals and a few bhajans, the holi songs and thumris in this book evoke a somewhat different ethos of worldly or spiritual love. The holis engage in a playful banter with Krishna or chide Jasodha for her child's behaviour (p. 7). "Drench my *chunri* in colour, my love, Savan's spring has come. A new *chunriya*, a new youth and a new spring . . ." goes another song, evoking the joy and fulness of that special time. In a malar song a wife chides her husband for having left her to go abroad (p. 17), while another asks her husband to set up a swing in the garden (p. 18). A thumri clings to the image of the "enchanting face" of the dark lover which has "thrown magic" upon her (p. 9). What we see in this booklet, then, is the convergence of the repertoire of lavani singers, with their songs of religious instruction, of women's seasonal songs and of the purabi repertoire of bais, though the ghazals are less sophisticated. Unlike the ghazals by the masters in the collection *Ghuncha Rag*, language and spelling reflect spoken rather than written familiarity with Urdu, as the erratic use of the *izafat* construction suggests:

Na ho yar tau kya lutf zindagani men,
Firaq yar hai sab mausame javani men. [. . .]
Chala tu jan bhi hamrah tere jati hai,
Aziz rakhte hain jo dil me rang sabz tera,
Men kya karun kise thamun meri ravani men,
Unhen vaqa hai sada is jahan fani men. (p. 20)

38 This is the first of four stanzas. *Dilbahlao*, p. 10.

Without a friend, what pleasure does life have?
Separation from the friend in the season of youth [?].
If you go, my life will follow you,
Those who keep your youthful countenance dear to their hearts,
What can I do, who can I cling to in my flow,
They are immortal in this transient world.

Besides the popular Urdu of ghazals and khyals, most of the songs in this collection (holi, bhajan, kabitt, rag pad, and thumri) are in Braj Bhasha, and there is also one rekhta song about Krishna in Khari Boli.[39] The quality of the verses is unexceptional, but once again what is important for us is the range of poetic tastes that a songbook such as this encompasses, and the interface it shows between the non-elite musical-poetic activities of akharas and print.

A very similar assortment can be found in another lithographed collection, *Sada Bahar* (Always Spring, 1882), which promises on its title to page to be a "unique collection of the best and most select *bandana, dhrupad, basant, holi, des, mallar, sorath, eman, kandhara, bihag, khamanch, paraj, sohni, bhairavi, sarang, jogiya, pilu, chait, lavani, kaharva, kajjali, savani, barahmasa, kabitt, ghazal,* etc. *for both singing and reading.*"[40] The long list of songs and raga-raginis on the title page, and the combination of seasonal songs, ghazals, lavanis, and thumris points to the popular *rasik* milieu to which "Betab" and Radheshyam and their fathers belonged. The booklet begins with three religious songs, but soon the mood turns towards the flirtatious and erotic with a series of holi songs. The complaint voiced in this thumri, for example, typically opens up the attractive possibility of exposing the woman's body and the signs it bears of Krishna's passion:

[39] Though in fact the endings of masculine singular perfectives vary between Braj Bhasha "o" and Khari Boli "a" ("mero" is also a peculiar hybrid): "*Aisi sanvari surat aur mohani murat mere jiya ki. Surat hari phurat vane jadu aisa kina, chal lino jiya mero. Chave mujh men pan ave, meri jan nainan ke van, rasiya ke tan. Mopai jada aisa kino, chal lino jiya mero*"; *Dilbahlao*, p. 9. Cf. Peter Manuel, *Ṭhumrī*, p. 77.

[40] *Sada Bahar*, edited by one Jagadamba Sahay of village Kurhanni in district Muzaffarpur and printed in Fatehgarh by the Matba' Hasani, 1882, title page, emphasis added, Bharati Bhavan Library, Allahabad.

Pyare ne barjori kinhi apni or,
Main to paiyan parun kar jor jor.
Ghunghat khol kapol male mukh,
Ang urjhaye mori bahiyan maror. (p. 2)

My love forced himself on me,
I fell to his feet with folded hands.
He forced my veil open and rubbed his mouth on my cheeks,
Entwined his body and twisted my arms.

Various *khemta* songs instead evoke the atmosphere of nautch gatherings with dancing girls. This one is in the tone of a (male) lover's complaint, and accordingly the language tilts significantly towards Urdu:

Dil pher de pari tu hamara hamen. Bosa na diya dobara hamen.
Mehifil men jana, unko bulana, nainon se karti ishara hamen.
Ghairon se hansna, hamen tarsana. Ye bhi nahin hai gavara hamen. (p. 8)

Give me back my heart, you never kissed me again.
You go to the mehfil and call others while you encourage me with your eyes.
You laugh with strangers but me you tease, I cannot bear it any more.[41]

Finally, the ghazal that closes the collection is a peculiarly hybrid composition: as a *tarji' band*, where the *kafiya* of the first couplet is repeated in a line after every following couplet (here called doha) as a kind of refrain (AA, BBA, CCA). But what is peculiar about it is that, after the first stanza, which contains a lover's complaint in a faintly Urduizing register (*Za[b]ani hal yon kahna tun jakar namah bar* [?] *pahle. Hamari ah giriyan ki tun kar dena khabar pahle*),[42] the dohas switch to the Braj Bhasha idiom of thumris and barahmasas:

[41] By comparison, the lavani in this collection is a longer, stanzaic poem which voices the milkmaid's dismay and jealousy at having been abandoned by Krishna after having given up her "modesty" for him, pp. 11–12.

[42] 'First go and write a letter telling [him/her] of my condition. First inform him/her of my sighs'; *Sada Bahar*, p. 15.

Doha:

Tachyaun anch ab birah ki rahyau prem ras bhij,
Nainan main [*ke*?] *mag jal bahe hiyo pasij pasij.* (p. 15)

I burn in the fire of separation, drenched in the throes of love,
My molten heart is flowing through my eyes' path.

The tarji' line immediately after switches back to the Urduizing register again: "*Teri ulfat ke kuche men nafa pichhe, zarar pahle*" (In the lane of your affection, loss comes first, gain later). The shift between the two registers continues throughout the seven stanzas of the ghazal, creating a hybrid convergence of the two idioms of complaint—the thumri and barahmasa lament of viraha and the Urdu complaint about the lover as a "cruel hunter" (*sayyad zalim*).[43] This freedom to tamper with the ghazal—a freedom that would be difficult to imagine in trained Urdu poets—is significant because it shows how the self-taught poets of these collections, precisely *because* they were not formally educated, were free from the stringent rules of poetics and could mix their eclectic tastes as they liked. This freedom to be eclectic was to be crucial in the poets' thrilling encounter with the theatre.

The Impact of the Theatre

In order to grasp the changing and layered world of nineteenth-century songs and performance, one more element needs to be considered—the theatre. As the work of Kathryn Hansen and Anuradha Kapur has demonstrated, theatre was the site of numerous and far-reaching innovations. In terms of social and spatial location, the theatre moved from courtly and folk contexts into parallel and commercially organized urban and itinerant theatre companies (Parsi theatre and nautanki in North India). New technologies of stage machinery "changed the conditions of performance" and produced a new melodramatic mode defined by a "structure of excess or extravagance at the level of scenography, stage, effects, music, sound, language, suspense and colour".[44] Songs and music formed a very important part of the "attractions" of

[43] Ibid., pp. 15–16.

[44] Anuradha Kapur, 'Love in the Time of Parsi Theatre', in F. Orsini (ed.), *Love in South Asia: A Cultural History*, p. 211.

both Parsi and nautanki theatre, and their relationship with the wider world of music and song can only be called a symbiotic one of mutual exchange and influence. Once again, printed books managed to insert themselves into this virtuous circuit of pleasure, much to their advantage.

The story of the relationship between theatre, songs, and print in North India begins with Agha Hasan Amanat's *Indarsabha* (The Assembly of King Indra, 1853), a work rightly considered crucial in the "migration" of the theatre from the courtly milieu of the nawabs of Lucknow to the larger public domain. Kathryn Hansen has documented that *Indarsabha* was not only printed immediately upon composition but met with extraordinary success in print, with as many as seventy-seven editions and impressions over sixty years in Urdu, Devanagari, Gujarati, Gurmukhi, and even Hebrew scripts, and translations into Gujarati, Sinhala, and Malay![45] It is an eclectic work *par excellence*: in Kathryn Hansen's synthetic definition "an original text that assimilated Urdu *ghazals*, Braj Bhasha *thumris*, and Avadhi folk songs to a narrative base drawn from several popular *masnavis.*" It also "contained the earliest instance of the *chaubola* meter, and the six-line *chhand* that became the standard *doha* plus *chaubola*" of the svang and nautanki theatres.[46] Without a proper division of acts and scenes, Hansen notes, *Indarsabha* was largely "a pageant of song and dance connected by a thread of a story"[47]—and much of its popularity derived from the excess of visual and aural pleasures offered by the fairies (*pari*) who were named and clothed and sang songs connected with the colour of a gemstone. It is easy to see the songs as representing the purabi repertoire of women singers at court, now framed on stage as serial addresses to Indar/Indra as "deity, king, patron, poet and lover."[48] It is worth quoting Hansen's analysis and examples in full:

[45] Kathryn Hansen, 'The *Indarsabha* Phenomenon: Public Theatre and Consumption in Greater India (1853–1956)', in R. Dwyer and C. Pinney (eds), *Pleasure and the Nation*, pp. 76–114 (Appendix pp. 112–14 for printed editions in the British Library. The publication peaked in the 1870s).

[46] Hansen, *Grounds for Play*, p. 79.

[47] Hansen, 'The *Indarsabha* Phenomenon', pp. 78–9.

[48] Ibid., p. 84. According to a well-known oral tradition (one that Satyajit Ray incorporated in his film *The Chess-Players*), the role of Indar was first played by Nawab Wajid Ali Shah himself.

One moment a fairy takes on the voice of a *gopi* in a Hori . . . and chides the playful Shyam (Lord Krishna) for drenching her:

Pa lagi kar jori
Shyam mo se khelo na hori.
Clasping your feet I beg of you,
Please Shyam, don't play Holi with me.

Gauven charavan main nikasi hum sas nanand ki chori
Sagari chunar rang men na bhijovo inti suno bat mori. (#9)
I came out to graze the cows, stealing away from my in-laws.
Don't drench my whole garment in dye—this much I ask of you.

Next she mourns the absence of her lover (*piya*, 'beloved', one of Wajid Ali's pen-names) in the genre specific to the rainy month of Savan:

Bin piya ghata nahin bhave
Rah rah dil raund ho ave
Bijari ki chamak tarpave darave
Bin piya ghata nahin bhave. (#28)
With my Beloved/Piya, I cannot endure the rainy season:
My heart is oppressed with longing.
The lightning crashes—my body thrashes.
Without my Beloved/Piya, I cannot endure the rainy season.

Or, in the characteristic masochistic pose of the *ashiq* or lover in an Urdu ghazal, she complains of her beloved's naughty neglect and threatens suicide:

Takara ke sar ko jan na dun main to kya karun
Kab tak firaq-i yar ke sadme saha karun. (#11)
What should I do but dash out my brains?
How long can I bear the blows of separation from the Beloved?

Not only does the king's identity as the addressee slip between Indra, Krishna, and the nawab, Hansen notes also that the language of the songs moves easily back and forth between the Urdu ghazal and the Braj Bhasha thumri and seasonal song, creating a striking hybrid amalgam. He, the passive but powerful Beloved, emerges as a object of desires.[49] While *Indarsabha*'s popularity in print and performance alone would be evidence of the wide currency this hybrid amalgam came to enjoy, we also have evidence of the influence *Indarsabha* had on surrounding performance traditions. Sharar frames the phenomenon once again in terms of the influence of courtly tastes on the 'avam: It was Wajid Ali Shah's liking for popular theatre (*rahas*) that made "the ordinary people [*riyaya*] who watched it develop a particular taste for it", and it was on account of "this interest on the part of the *public*" (in English in the text) that

> Miyan Amanat, who was a famous poet skilled in poetic conceits and figures of speech, composed his *Indarsabha*, which was the first example of the Persian taste for *paris* mixed with Hindu gods. As soon as this *Indarsabha* was shown in the city, everyone became crazy about it. All of a sudden scores of *sabhas* were established in the city and they became so popular that the fashion for singers and dancing girls abated for a while. Then many people started other gatherings beside the *Indarsabha* where Urdu poetry may have been corrupted, and its language circulated among people coming from the countryside in the eastern region [*purab ki dehati*] and Hindus. [. . .] But then, suddenly, respectable society, which had established tastes in music, turned its back on this kind of spectacle and went back to singers and dancing girls. And the compositions that were popular in theatre remained limited to ordinary people and the people of the bazaar.[50]

In her study of popular theatre in this period, Hansen notes how the aristocratic Persianate tone of *Indarsabha* was imitated by svang through the adoption of Urdu diction and modes of address. "The folk vocatives *betaji* or *pyareji* (son, dear) used in early Sangit texts gave way to flourishes like *lakht-e-jigar* (piece of my lover, i.e. son or daughter) or *jan-e-man* (beloved of my heart)", and stories from the Persianate repertoire of masnavis, dastans, and qissas (see chapter 4) became more frequent topics.[51]

Indarsabha was thus clearly crucial for the wider circulation within the new commercial theatre—both cosmopolitan and "intermediary",

[49] Ibid., p. 85.
[50] Sharar, *Guzishta*, p. 249.
[51] Hansen, *Grounds for Play*, p. 79.

as Hansen defines nautanki—of the repertoire of ghazals, thumris, and seasonal songs that we saw was common to bais and lavani singers and was spreading far and wide among the 'avam. But this was only the beginning of a symbiotic relationship between theatrical songs and the wider world of singing in North India, especially after Parsi theatre companies based in Bombay switched to Urdu/Hindustani, and the Victoria Theatrical Company (1877), based in Delhi, and the Alfred Theatrical Company (1877), based in Calcutta, started touring North Indian towns.[52] "All the singers of Bareilly would sing the songs of New Alfred", Radheshyam Kathavachak recalled in his autobiography. Their annual tour with new shows was always eagerly awaited, and its singers impressed as much by the power of their voices ("chest-tearing songs") as by the allure of their acting.[53]

Through the recollections of 'Betab' and Radheshyam we also see theatrical songs acting as a kind of melting pot, churning out new tunes (*dhun*) which became instantly popular. These were learnt by heart and circulated further within society as the musical basis for new secular as well as religious songs. Radheshyam, for example, recalls that women would sing bhajans to the tunes of the new theatre songs (a practice still current today with film tunes), and his own first song composition was a bhajan with the words "*karo kripa guru maharaja*" (Have pity on me, my guru), based on the metre and rhythm of a song from the play *Chandravali* of New Alfred Theatres "*dahi vali ka taur dikhana*" (Show me the ways of the curd-churning milkmaid).[54]

[52] Hansen has convincingly argued that the "turn from Gujarati towards Urdu in the Parsi theatre was motivated by a number of complex considerations and did not represent an attempt to win over any particular group . . . The commercial expansion of the theatre certainly favoured the use of a lingua franca", she notes, "But more importantly, Urdu and the larger Indo-Muslim cultural heritage in which it was embedded were capable of bestowing on the Parsi theatre rich legacies of poetry, music and narrative"; Hansen, 'Language, Community and the Theatrical Public', p. 81.

[53] Kathavachak, *Mera Natak-kal*, p. 21. Radheshyam could still recall the titles of *all* the plays that New Alfred performed in Bareilly.

[54] Ibid., p. 21. As the title indicates, the play was based on the story of one of Radha's women friends, but it would have been performed on a secular stage with male actors performing female roles. Bharatendu Harishchandra had also composed a play on the topic: see Vasudha Dalmia, *The Nationalization of Hindu Traditions,* pp. 376–7.

Radheshyam not only learnt the song tunes orally from them, but also collected the chapbooks that New Alfred printed, and for a while specialized in writing songs of religious instruction based on theatrical songs. What we see, then, is commercial theatre in 1880s and 1890s North India not just passively consumed as a source of entertainment, but also influencing local popular musical flows, which used musical and poetic patterns that were acquired informally, dhun and vazan rather than raga and ragini. From a musical and poetic-linguistic point of view, theatrical songs continued the trend of amalgamating Urdu ghazals, thumris, and seasonal songs in mixed Urdu/Braj Bhasha.

The autobiographies and careers of "Betab" and Kathavachak thus document a shift from the local popular culture of lavanis, jhulnas, and bhajans in which their fathers had taken part. That had been a culture that could be acquired and transmitted purely orally by illiterate singers, composers, and listeners, and one that moved easily between religious and secular performances. Now, there is a transition to a popular musical and poetic culture which, thanks to the theatre, becomes inextricably enmeshed with the commercial world of print and professional performances. As we saw, despite dealing with a completely oral genre, songbooks were able to entice ordinary people such as Radheshyam Kathavachak—people with very limited means, minimal literacy, and no education.

Even for people deeply involved in the local world of singing and the folk stage, the visual and aural impact of the Parsi theatre was immense. "Betab" writes of the first play he watched at Rama Theatre in Delhi in 1900: "All those things for which Paradise is called Paradise—all of them I found in the theatre. Its actors were gods, the boys playing female parts were *apsaras*, the singers were *gandharva*s, and the comedians *yaksha*s and *kinnara*s. This *Indarsabha* threw such a veil over my brain that I became totally enamoured with them, who were witches by day and fairies by night."[55] In the cases of both "Betab" and Kathavachak, their encounter with the theatre proved to be the turning point in their lives. Theatre was for them not only an overwhelming experience, but a "paradise" that could be experienced every time one

[55] Kathavachak, *Mera Natak-kal*, p. 32. He later uses the same vocabulary to hint at his platonic passion for an actor playing female parts, a passion from which he was saved only by his poverty; pp. 35–6.

went to see a play. Theatre became also a professional opportunity that provided a focus for their otherwise dispersed and occasional poetic activities, and granted unimagined wealth and fame to the erstwhile sweetmaker and wandering storyteller.

Commercial theatre also created new expectations of pleasure—as Anuradha Kapur has argued. Songs became not just one of those pleasures but also gave the possibility of prolonging, augmenting, and appropriating that pleasure for oneself, into one's own ordinary life, a possibility publishers highlighted in their advertisements.[56] As is often observed with regard to film songs, theatrical songs thus had an extra-diegetic life, a life beyond the story. The emotions fused within effective and attractive wordings could also be appropriated and used in relation to one's own personal emotions.

I have here sought to situate songbooks and their audiences within the rich, layered, and changing landscape of musical performance in North India in the second half of the nineteenth century. I have, in brief, argued that while the professional and folk singers who are identified with musical traditions did not require books, the growth of a popular world of musical entertainment—which encompassed lavani and kajli singers, bais and women's songs, the powerful impact of *Indarsabha* on svang and on the emerging Parsi and nautanki theatres—all created an environment in which barely literate audiences craved songbooks and theatre chapbooks. Professional playwrights like Narayan Prasad "Betab" and Radheshyam Kathavachak, reminiscing about their lavani-singing fathers, their own musical-poetic upbringing, and their fateful encounter with the theatre help us give faces and profiles to the 'avam that writers like Sharar only mention. Their life-stories explain how music, theatre, and print came to be intertwined.

Wide-ranging in terms of forms, and shifting easily between multiple linguistic and aesthetic registers, songbooks contributed to the heterogeneous linguistic and aesthetic repertoire that was the hallmark of commercial publishing in North India over the second half of the nineteenth century. As we have seen, this was a highly intertextual

[56] See the Introduction, *vide supra*.

world even at the popular level—stories from masnavis and dastans became increasingly popular topics for nautanki plays.

In the next chapter we shall see another example of intertextuality—in the qissas printed in both Devanagari and Urdu scripts, some of which also incorporated the pleasures of songs and dramatic dialogue as part of their attraction.

4

Tales between Two Scripts

As a narrative form intended for oral recitation,[1] qissas or tales exemplify the typical oral-literate dynamic of Indian literature. The stories existed in written, often highly literary, forms, but they mostly circulated orally in a variety of social environments. Qissas are also central to the story of commercial publishing in North India. As simple prose texts of variable length, they had been one of the mainstays of language instruction at Fort William College. First printed by Calcutta printers (as we saw in the Introduction), they were subsequently taken up by publishers across North India who added old and new titles to the repertoire.[2] But cheap qissa booklets in Urdu and Hindi, costing only a few paise and containing either single or multiple tales together with popular verse, were also crucial to the boom of commercial publishing in the 1860s. Printed qissas reproduced, and also themselves spawned, a "broad repertoire covering heterogeneous narratives" drawing upon the Arabo-Persian and Indian repertoires.[3] But

[1] *Qissa sunana*, "to tell a qissa", is the verb used in Hindi/Urdu.

[2] All the qissas written by the munshis at Fort William College are reworkings of previous Perso-Arabic sources, e.g. *Qissa Chahar Darvesh* or *Bagh o Bahar* (1801), *Gul-e Bakavali* and *Qissa Hatim Ta'i* (1803), or else of Indian collections like the *Simhasan Battisi* (1801) and *Baital Pacchisi* (1802). Other popular qissas that came to be printed drew upon folklore (e.g. *Sarang Sadavrij* and later *Sit Basant*), and upon the rich lore on "women's wiles" (*Shuk Bahattari*, *Tiriya Charitra*, etc.): see Frances Pritchett, *Marvelous Encounters. Folk Romance in Urdu and Hindi*, Delhi: Manohar, 1985.

[3] Kumkum Sangari, 'Multiple Temporalities, Unsettled Boundaries, Trickster Women: Reading a Nineteenth-century *Qissa*', in S. Blackburn and V. Dalmia (eds), *India's Literary History: Essays on the Nineteenth Century*, p. 213.

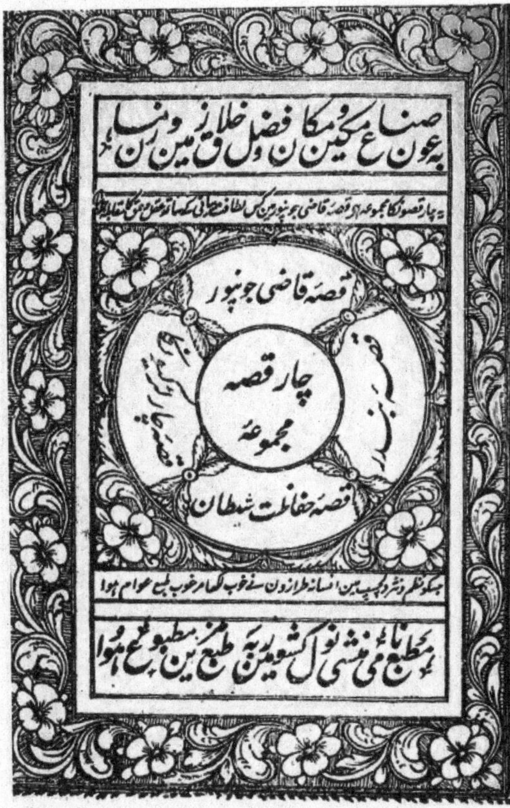

Fig. 9: *Majmu'a Char Qissa*, a collection of four qissas (*Qazi-e Jaunpur, Qissa-e Bandar, Hifazat-e Shaitan, Char Larkiyon ka*), published in 1882 by Naval Kishore, Lucknow.

while qissas are mostly associated with tales of chivalry and wonder, nineteenth-century printed tales also included a significant number of narratives of trickery and cunning about humbler, ordinary characters, and of competition between men and women. It is on these latter texts that this chapter will focus,[4] since they best exemplify the role qissas

[4] In particular, I focus on *Qissa Sipahizada* by Khushdil (1848), *Qissa Barhai o Sunar* by Tajammul Rasul Khan (1873?), *Qissa Qazi-e Jaunpur* by Farjan (1869?); *Kissa Tota Maina* (1870s) by Pandit Rangilal, and *Kissa Aurat Mard* (1882).

Fig. 10: Cover of another miscellaneous collection, including the qissas of *Sipahizada*, *Mahmud Shah*, *Saudagar Baccha*, and poems by Nazir Akbarabadi such as *Bhunchalnama* (On an Earthquake), *Hans Nama* (The Story of a *Hans* Bird), *'Ashiq ka Janaza* (The Lover's Bier) by Shahidi, etc., Lucknow: Naval Kishore, 1884.

played in creating a reading public by bridging the gap between oral storytelling and the printed book. Qissas also reveal how a pre-print genre changed after coming into print, belying the notion still prevalent in literary histories that the new is only to be found in genres like the novel and the essay. The novel is singled out as the modern genre in which all innovation took place; this chapter will show instead that qissas were also the site of considerable experimentation. Far from being purely traditional, printed qissas in the nineteenth century were a dynamic genre, intersecting "folktale, theatrical forms like *sangit*, and even reformist prescription."[5] The result was "multivocal" narratives combining adventure, romance, family rituals, and the voice of common sense. Their linguistic texture displayed a similar heterogeneity. Just as songbooks, barahmasas, and theatre chapbooks reflected a heterogeneous poetic and musical repertoire, qissas brought together, side by side, different registers and varieties of language, sometimes even within the same text—as in the striking case of *Kissa Tota Maina*. Even more than songs and barahmasas, qissas were usually printed in both Hindi and Urdu *without any changes*. This traffic of translation had important consequences for the currency of a broad and heterogeneous linguistic idiom and eclectic poetic tastes.

The authors of these short and cheap qissas—Khushdil, Farjan, Pandit Rangilal—are only names to us, as are the authors of the barahmasas, but it is precisely this lack of literary pedigree which signals that qissas offered the possibility of authorship outside the pale of high literature, and of courtly or government patronage.[6]

I begin with an overview of the genre and its transmission, and then focus on three short tales that were often reprinted, either singly or in majmu'as, at the cheapest end of the market. Subsequently, I look at two longer texts that exploited and developed the existing narrative trope of a competition between two narrators, the male parrot and the female mynah bird. Pitting tales of male cruelty against tales of female infidelity, *Kissa Tota Maina* (1870s) offered a number of gendered pleasures: the spirited defence of one's sex against accusations from the other sex, dismay at the cruelty of the other sex towards one's own, and the *frisson* resulting from witty repartees and the underlying sexual attraction between the parrot and the mynah. *Kissa Aurat Mard* (1882) clearly built upon the expectations of this sub-genre to present its own spirited critique of gender relations.

Two Genealogies of an "Oral-Literate" Genre

Qissas were both recited *and* read. The mass printing of qissas should not be taken as evidence of a linear transition from oral recitation to

[5] Sangari, 'Multiple Temporalities', p. 213.

[6] In fact, their popularity encouraged the writing of stories to convey all sorts of new reformist messages, as with Altaf Husain Hali's *Majalis un-Nisa*: see *Voices of Silence*, trans. Gail Minault, New Delhi: Chanakya Publications, 1986.

silent reading. Even a cursory look at the formal characteristics of these texts shows that printed qissas faithfully reproduced the constraints of oral presentation, with narrators and audience often featuring explicitly as characters.[7] Nor do we, as a rule, see the authors of printed qissas taking advantage of the potential complexities that writing allowed, e.g. by introducing disparity between the knowledge and values of the author and those of the narrator.[8] Instead, qissas adhered to the modes of oral storytelling, with straightforward narratives consisting only of action and dialogue and devoid of description or reflection. Simple tenses and verb forms were preferred to complex ones, direct discourse to indirect.[9] In terms of visual presentation, too, qissas ignored the new typographical conventions, such as paragraphs, quotation marks, and punctuation (apart from the caesura).[10] Thus, the only way to understand the text was by reading it aloud, or at least voicing it even when reading it in private. At the same time, this meant that the

[7] Even when the audience is not present as a character in the text, the narrator occasionally interrupts the flow of the narrative in order to address the audience (*suno*, "listen").

[8] See Pritchett, *Marvelous Encounters*, ch. 8, 'Qissa and Oral Narrative', pp. 144–61, which provides the basis for this analysis.

[9] The preferred syntactical structure is parataxis, with short sentences usually neatly fitting in each half line and connected by simple correlatives of time ("when . . ., then . . .") and absolutive constructions ("*having arrived* he sat down"), while *gharaz ki* ("in short") is used to round up a scene before passing to the next one. See ibid. In the particular case of *Qissa Sipahizada* the narrator has occasionally to intervene directly to manage two different locations at the same time, the soldier's house and the robber's house, with sentences like: "I have now told you all about here, now listen what happened over there" (l. 235), "I have told you the whole robbers' tale, listen now to the soldier's story" (l. 467). Khushdil, *Qissa Sipahizada ba Tasvir.* Delhi: Matba' Hindu Press, 1874 [OIOLC: VT 1167].

[10] This meant that changes of speaker had to be made explicit, although often without specifying who the speaker was ("he said" rather than "the old man said"). As Frances Pritchett notes, characters almost always "say" (*kahna*), with dialogue and inner thoughts distinguished only by the use of *dil men* ("in the heart") for the latter, and with simple absolutives expressing nuances of feeling ("*having become angry* he said"). "The pace and flow of the narrative", she writes, "are thus largely governed by such conventional speech-markers shared with most oral tales"; Pritchett, *Marvelous Encounters*, p. 154.

printed text which one *read* reproduced all the narrative conventions one was already familiar with from oral recitation; it did not require any new skills—unlike novels (see chapters 6 and 7 below). This fact, that qissas made less demands on the reader, may help explain the quick acceptance of these short, simple texts among neo-literates.

Following Frances Pritchett's pioneering study of Hindi and Urdu qissas, we are led to trace qissas back to medieval Persian folk narratives, a "form of orally recited prose romance created, elaborated and transmitted by professional narrators" or *qissa-khvans*.[11] Public narration in Urdu was part of the thriving urban culture of the early nineteenth century, with Urdu narrators active in Delhi and Lucknow in the 1830s, around the time when the term *dastan-go* became current and when the distinction between long dastans and shorter qissas also became current.[12] In Pritchett's account, the nineteenth-century qissa is really a short dastan, and the "core" of Hindi and Urdu qissas consists of "works in the main line of descent from Persian qissas, stories in which a noble hero achieves the goal of his quest."[13] This is undoubtedly true for adventurous qissas like *Gul-e Bakavali*, but the tales of ordinary folk which became just as popular in print point towards another genealogy—less courtly though also "oral-literate"—in the naql.

Naql, Christina Oesterheld reminds us, is an umbrella term covering all sorts of short stories and anecdotes based on tradition, written or oral or both. Written naqls vary in length between a couple of lines and several pages, but in most collections they are usually a page long. But naql refers also to a performative genre involving mimicry, parody, farce, or character sketch, usually enacted by troupes of actors (*bhands*).[14] Collections of anecdotes, also called *latifa* (Arabic plural *lata'if*), were

[11] Ibid., p. 1. Evidence shows that such narrators of Persian tales were employed at the Qutb Shahi court in Golconda and at the Mughal court; see ibid., p. 2.

[12] Ibid., p. 4. For Lucknow, see Mirza Jafar Husain, *Qadim Lakhnau ki Akhiri Bahar*, New Delhi: Qaumi Council Baraye Furugh-e Urdu Zaban, 1981.

[13] While tales of sexual encounters represent later accretions around the central core: see Pritchett, *Marvelous Encounters*, p. 27.

[14] Christina Oesterheld, 'Entertainment and Reform: Urdu Narrative Genres in the Nineteenth Century', in Blackburn and Dalmia (eds), *India's Literary History*, p. 16. For Bengali naql in the context of colonial urban culture, see

published by most of the munshis associated with Fort William College, since the form fitted, even more than did qissas, the requirement for short, simple prose material useful in language instruction.[15] But highly literate writers also composed and published collections of short stories and anecdotes in the nineteenth century. In these texts the ornate prose of the introductory and descriptive passages gives the work its literary status, whereas the narrative sections, reported dialogues, and jokes are in quite simple Urdu prose.[16] The characters, social types, and situations one finds in these texts are the same that one finds in the short qissas which this chapter focuses on: lovers betraying one another, cunning women, foolish or guileful qazis handing down

---

Hans Harder, 'The Modern Babu and the Metropolis. Reassessing Early Bengali Narrative Prose (1821–62)', ibid., pp. 358–401.

[15] Christina Oesterheld lists them in the article quoted above: Mir Bahadur Ali Afsos, *Naqliyat* (vol. 1: 1802, vol. 2: 1806?); Mir Bahadur Ali Husaini, *Akhlaq-e Hindi* (compiled 1802, printed 1803); *Naqliyat-e Luqman*; Lalluji Lal, *Lata'if-e Hindi* (written 1800, printed 1810, 1820, and 1840); Mir Sher Ali Afsos, *Bagh-e Urdu* (1802), and Hafizuddin Ahman, *Khirad-afroz* (1803); 'Entertainment and Reform', p. 172. She also notes that the Urdu translation and selection from the Persian *Jawami' al-Hikayat wa Lawami' ar-Rivayat* by Urfi, the *Jami' ul-Hikayat-e Hindi* compiled by Sheikh Salih Muhammad Usmani in 1825, went through six editions in Bombay between 1825 and 1856: C. Oesterheld, 'Urdu Tales and Anecdotes in the Nineteenth Century: A Case Study of Intertextuality', paper presented at the sixteenth European Association of Modern South Asian Studies, Edinburgh, 6-9 September 2000, p. 9n. Tales, usually called *hikayat*, featured also as illustrations of moral points in treatises and books about ethics and manners (*akhlaq* and *adab*).

[16] The collection that Christina Oesterheld has studied in detail, *Nauratan* by Sheikh Hakim Muhammad Bakhsh Mahjur of Lucknow, was first published in 1846 and went through at least eight editions between 1846 and 1888. While the use of ornate language and quotations from famous poets suggest, as Oesterheld points out, that Mahjur's text is firmly grounded in the literary culture of his time and addresses an elite comprising connoisseurs of Urdu poetry, the low price of some of the editions—as low as 3 annas for the 1870 Naval Kishore edition for a book of 184 pages—is striking and suggests that these "elite" books were becoming accessible to new audiences "sharif by educatio;". Oesterheld, 'Entertainment and Reform', p. 183. See Table 1.2 in the Introduction for details on publishing and prices.

judgements, clever or stupid traders getting cheated, opium smokers, misers, thieves, etc. Naql collections are closely related, as printed texts, to our qissas not only because of their colloquial language and stock of characters, but also for the high degree of intertextuality at the level of sources, for their "oral-literate" references to stories told and handed down by other narrators, and for the mixture of prose and verse (both gnomic and narrative). We must, therefore, envisage a dual genealogy for qissas: the dastan for the longer and adventurous qissas, and the naql for shorter qissas of ordinary people. The pleasures they offered also differed. While adventure tales, whether recited or read silently, transported the reader into another world, providing the kind of sensuous experience that Barthes called *jouissance*, the short, sketch-like tales were mostly farcical, inviting the reader to laugh at human folly and at the weaknesses of the mighty.

The genealogy, transmission, and transition into print of the longer qissas have been detailed by Frances Pritchett.[17] Briefly, professional dastan-gos, traditionally employed at court and by aristocrats, also began in the first half of the nineteenth century to ply their trade in public places.[18] A nostalgic, early-twentieth-century account of the "last dastan-go of Delhi", namely, Mir Baqar Ali, who specialized in the *Dastan Amir Hamza*, connects the end of the popularity of these regular public recitations with the post-1857 decline of old Delhi and the changing tastes of the new times.[19] In early-twentieth-century Delhi we see Mir Baqar Ali, sitting in his own courtyard on a cold winter night, huddled in thick, coarse, cotton clothes, reciting for two hours in front of a small group of aficionados and some visitors from Lucknow. Although the magic of his recitation still weaves its spell, we are led to feel pity for the grand old dastan-go, reduced to penury and obscurity, peddling chapbooks (!) and betel nuts for a living.

[17] In *Marvelous Encounters*, and in her fine study *The Romance Tradition in Urdu: Adventures from the Dastan of Amir Hamzah*, New York: Columbia University Press, 1991.

[18] See Pritchett, *The Romance Tradition*, pp. 14–21. She also mentions the fact that a qissa-khvan was employed also at Fort William College: ibid., p. 10.

[19] "Who asks for the old *dyot* when there is electric light?" Ashraf Sabuhi, 'Mir Baqar Ali', *Dilli ki Chand 'Ajib Hastiyan*, New Delhi: Maktaba Jamia, 1989, p. 48.

The publication of interminable dastans was one of the feats of nineteenth-century commercial publishing in North India.[20] The magic of the language, "rhythmic, repetitive, almost hypnotic, [giving] the narrator's vision a dream-like power and authority,"[21] seems to have worked just as well on the page as in the sound of the dastan-go's voice. The almost gluttonous pleasure to be had from "immersing oneself" in the reading of a printed dastan is testified to by illustrious readers, from Ghalib to Premchand.[22] Printed dastans were not cheap, though, and rarely came at less than Re 1 per volume.[23] Buying the whole forty-six volumes of the Naval Kishore edition required a serious investment.

But professional qissa-khvans and dastan-gos, whether employed in aristocratic households or reciting in public places, cannot have been the only reciters. Both the milieu evoked in some of the qissas and the much simpler, less flowery and sophisticated, language suggest a less elite environment. Usually in the qissas themselves the setting is the family home, where groups of women neighbours relax in-between household chores, or husband-and-wife couples spend their leisure time together.[24] Contextual evidence about the circulation of these popular tales is, however, notable by its absence. After suggesting that

[20] See Pritchett, *The Romance Tradition*, pp. 21–8. Although a few dastans had begun to be published in Urdu in the first half of the nineteenth century, she notes that it was only in the second half that the "real era of dastan publishing begun" with Munshi Naval Kishore: ibid., pp. 21–2.

[21] Pritchett, *Marvelous Encounters*, p. 6.

[22] As noted in the Introduction, "To Ghalib, dastan reading was an exquisite, escapist pleasure. In his old age, he wrote to a friend that was "in clover" [for] receiving one massive volume of the dastan of Amīr Ḥamzah, and one of *Bostān-e khiyāl*. And there are seventeen bottles of good wine in the pantry. So I read all day and drink all night. 'The man who wins such bliss can only wonder/What more had Jamshed? What more Alexander?'", quoted by Pritchett, *The Romance Tradition*, p. 28.

[23] E.g. Tota Ram, *Dastan Amir Hamza*, Urdu, 1869, 324 pp. (1100), litho, 1 rupee, 8 annas; Hafizuddaula, *Dastan Amir Hamza*, Lucknow: Naval Kishore, Urdu, 1871 2nd edn, 756 pp. (2200), litho, 2 rupees. The cheapest edition I could find was *Dastan Amir Hamza Bataswir* (ill.), trans. Khalil Ali Khan Bashak, Agra: Ijad-e Kishan Press, 1888 (1000), litho, 12 annas, 8 paise; *Quarterly Lists* for the relevant years. See also Stark, *An Empire of Books*, for the printing of the dastans.

[24] See *Kissa Aurat Mard* below.

oral tales were probably told in the bazaar, Pritchett admits that "[s]peculation is plentiful, but evidence scarce".[25] Going by the general argument that entertainment before print was typically embodied in professional performers, we would expect to find a body of professional popular storytellers. Indeed, the author of *Qissa Sipahizada,* whose ancestral home was Kiratpur near Anandpur Sahib in Punjab, claims to travel often to Delhi, Lahore, Kashi, Ayodhya, and Bijnore.[26] Internal evidence in qissas like *Aurat-Mard* suggests that stories of adulterous wives circulated within homes, possibly recited by *domnis*, while sketches about tricks at the expense of pompous people were performed in the streets and at fairs by bhands and naqqals (jester-actors).[27]

Without discounting the importance of chivalrous and wonderful stories like that of Amir Hamza—certainly the most elaborate and sophisticated example of dastan—the naql provides an additional genealogy which accounts for the unquestionable popularity in the second half of the nineteenth century of qissas on ordinary characters engaged in distinctly unheroic quests. The dastan's gallant and noble heroes, beautiful princesses and fairies, terrifying ogres and evil magicians, powerful spirits and magic puppets, treacherous enchantments (*tilism*) and clever helpers (*'ayyar*), all drew upon and added to a reservoir of characters and motifs that was enormously popular across genres in the nineteenth century. These genres went from masnavis

[25] Pritchett, *Marvelous Encounters*, p. 3. She quotes the opinions of Annemarie Schimmel and R.S. McGregor on the matter. Schimmel writes of this period: "Popular prose was, of course, always there; romatic fairy-tales or heroic legends were never lacking; although even those were more often than not converted into poetry"; *Classical Urdu Literature from the Beginning to Iqbal*, Wiesbaden: Harrassowitz, 1975, p. 203. McGregor speculates along similar lines: "It is very probable that alongside this poetry prose tales or fables based on the same sources or on the prose story cycles of early Urdu literature, or on everyday life, came to be circulated orally in some sort of standardized form, but little such material has come down to us in writing from this period." 'The Rise of Standard Hindi and Early Hindi Prose Fiction', in T.W. Clark (ed.), *The Novel in India: Its Birth and Development*, London: George Allen and Unwin, 1970, p. 142. Both quoted in Pritchett, *Marvelous Encounters*, p. 3.

[26] [Khushdil], *Qissa Sipahizada*, Lucknow: Naval Kishore, 1884, p. 2.

[27] Abdul Halim Sharar states that *domnis* "have started performing naqls at women's gatherings": *Guzishta Lakhnau*, p. 246.

to plays, from qissas to tilismi novels. And much as the ʿayyars stole the show from the princes in Devkinandan Khatri's *Chandrakanta* (chapter 6) and the *jasus* became the hero of the new detective novels, comedy, cunning, and subversions of authority took centre stage in the simple tales of the soldier's son, the donkey-cart driver, and the goldsmith and the carpenter.

Ordinary Quests

Tales of cunning, competition, and deceit are aplenty in the oral and written repertoire in India. Here is a case in which print and the print market impacted not so much upon the texts themselves, but upon the way they were presented, packaged, and distributed. In other words, while in the nineteenth-century story collections that Christina Oesterheld has studied, the simple naql or latifa was enclosed in elaborate introductions or frame stories—which conferred literary status on the text and its author and invoked an audience of connoisseurs—the short qissas of the teacher, the donkey-cart driver, and the qazi of Jaunpur, or the goldsmith and the carpenter, or the four friends that were printed and circulated as four- or eight-page chapbooks in straightforward rhymed prose (costing as little as three or six paise) suggest an audience with little patience for flowery language and the need to "understand everything immediately."[28] Though the impact of print on the texts themselves is perhaps slighter and more difficult to perceive, the format, price, language, and, to some extent, content all suggest a more popular audience for these tales. This is an audience less respectful of figures of authority, and ready to believe, like the donkey-cart driver, that sharafat could be bought through evidence of liberal consumption.

Qissa Sipahizada (The Story of the Soldier's Son), by Khushdil,[29] was the first and perhaps most successful of the new type of qissas.

[28] See fn. 29 below.

[29] In Blumhardt's *Catalogues* he appears as Khushdil Dehlawi, though the 1884 Naval Kishore edition features a short introduction, which is usually left out in the editions in which he appears to be a wandering storyteller. Although his "ancient *vatan*" is Kiratpur, he is in fact a great wanderer: "I am always on the move, wandering like Majnun. Sometime I go to Delhi and Lahore, sometime to Kashi, Ajodhya and Bijnore." Though conscious of his lack of literary

Published in Lucknow as early as 1848 by the Hasani Press, as a single text it went through no less than twenty-one editions between 1867 and 1877 in Delhi, Agra, Lucknow, and Meerut, often with attractive woodblock illustrations (see Table 4.1). Compared with the

Table 4.1

Editions of *Qissa Sipahizada*, by Khushdil in the British Library[30]

1848	U	Lucknow: Matba' Hasani, 1848, pp. 24, litho
1867	U	Delhi: Bhagwan Dass, manager Husaini Press, 8vo, pp. 16, Litho (2000 copies), 9 paise.
1868	U	Delhi: Lala Pyare Lal, manager Hindu Press, 8vo, pp. 16, litho (1000), 1 anna
1870	U	Delhi: Nasri Press, 8vo, pp. 16, litho (1000), 1 anna
1871	D	Agra: Matba Ijad Kishan Press, pp. 24, litho
1872	U	Delhi
1873	U	Agra
1873	U	Lucknow: Shagufa-i Oudh Press, pp. 12 (1000), 6 paise
1874	U	Delhi
1874	U	Lucknow

credentials ("if a poet finds any error or imperfection in my story, he should correct it. I do not say it's perfect, it's full of faults"), he finds credit in being a lover of wine and 'ishq, and feels the need to justify the fact that this tale is not about love: "This is a strange tale, very strange and wonderful." But "although love is mentioned, it is somewhat far from the path of love." He claims to have heard it from a beggar in Bijnore, who urged him to write it down. "Though it has no lofty theme for poetry, it is not lacking in eloquence. I wrote it clearly, so that everyone can understand it immediately" (*"Ibarat saf men likha usko is taur, Ke ave fahm men harik ke fi'l-faur"*). He does not appreciate verbosity: "I like brief writing": *Qissa Sipahizada* (in a majmu'a), Lucknow, Naval Kishore, 1884, p. 2 [Indian Institute Library, Oxford: 15 D 30].

30 Blumhardt, *Catalogues*. Note that four out of the twenty-one editions were in Devanagari, printed first in Agra in 1871 and later Lucknow and Delhi, without any change from the Urdu original. Prices ranged between 1 anna and 6 paise. I have used the Urdu edition in the Naval Kishore collection of qissas printed in 1884 (held in the Oriental Institute Library, Oxford), and compared it with the Devanagari edition printed in Delhi by the Matba' Hindu Press in 1874 [OIOLC: VT1167]. For this reason, references in brackets are to lines rather than pages.

1874	D	Lucknow
1874	D	Agra
1875	U	Delhi
1875	D	Delhi
1875	U	Meerut
1876	U	Delhi
1876	U	Lucknow
1877	U	Delhi
1877	U	Lucknow
1878	U	Delhi
1878	D	Delhi, reprint, 8vo, pp. 24, litho (1000), 9 paise
1878	U	Meerut: Lala Basudev, 8vo, 8 pp., litho (1000), 6 paise

As part of majmu'as (with *Mahmud Shah, Char Bagh, Saudagar-Bacchah* by Shah Rahman, *'Ashiq ka Janaza* by Shahidi, *Qasid-Namah* by Haidar, and six short poems by Nazir Akbarabadi)

1868	U	Kanpur: Naval Kishore, pp. 40
1869	U	Kanpur: Naval Kishore?
1875	U	Kanpur: Naval Kishore, 8vo, pp. 40, ill.
1876	U	Fatehgarh
1876	U	Lucknow
1877	U	Lucknow

"marvellous" world of the qissas that Frances Pritchett has focused on, the soldier's tale brings up a different set of characters, situations, and pleasures. Instead of princes, fairies (*paris*), and gods (*devs*), we have a struggling soldier, two cartoon-like robbers, and their aggravating father. Instead of heroic quests, the thrill and pain of love encounters, and the mysteries of enchantment (tilism), we have a failed attempt at finding employment and cunning stratagems of disguise that exploit the human weaknesses of opponents (lust, gullibility, greed). Instead of the pleasures of "marvellous encounters" and exotic journeys, we have the pleasures of familiar situations, of retribution for past offences and for human weakness and comic violence.

The story begins after the briefest introduction.[31] Places are unnamed ("in some *basti*", "a forest", "a court") and so is the protagonist.

[31] In most editions, the introduction is very brief: instead of the *na't* in praise of Allah and Muhammad, the narrator directly invokes God's guidance so that

Though endowed with hero-like qualities (he is "handsome, clever, and vigorous, and vigorous", 4), he has no hero's quest to embark upon. In fact, we first encounter him whiling away his time at home in the usual manner of unemployed youth, eating and drinking and enjoying himself with his wife and child with no thought of where the money for the provisions is coming from. It is his decision, though, once penury sets in, to leave home in search of employment. An "ordinary quest", rather than a heroic one. The quest ends soon enough when he finds employment with a courtier as a *sipahi*—here a guard rather than a soldier. We do not find out his employer's name, position, or accomplishments, discovering only that he is a bad master who "never willingly gave anyone his salary" (15). Typical of qissas of this kind is that while there is no "realistic" or "novelistic" attempt at particularization, the situations and troubles the characters find themselves in are ones the audience must have been familiar with—in this case the difficulty of getting one's salary paid by one's employer.[32] There is no suggestion that this is an unusual situation—quite the contrary. "You are not going to be ruined, are you?" the master chides the sipahi before telling him plainly that there is no cash to pay his wages for the time being. The sipahi should stop pestering him, and his desire to leave so soon ("after not even a year", 36) shows only his lack of common sense. The qissa's view of the situation, though, is strictly from the perspective of the employee, caught between his desire to leave a bad situation and the knowledge that leaving means forfeiting what remains his due.

The dispute between them escalates after the sipahi resolves that the only way out is to threaten to cause a ruckus if the master refuses to pay. Could it be that one of the pleasures offered by this section of the story

---

the author's speech may be eloquent and he may create "fresh writing" (*taza tahrir*, l. 1) and be remembered generously by those who will *read* it (*parhe jo ko'i*, l. 3). Two elements stand out in these few lines: the repeated mention of "fresh writing" and a "new story", not unusual per se but significant in this case because *Sipahizada is* an original story, and the reference is to the story being read, not (just) listened to. Whatever the real means of diffusion of this story, it was clearly also meant to be read, and its pictures to be looked at.

[32] A specific term is used for this, *na-dihandi*, "non-payment": see John T. Platts, *A Dictionary of Urdū, Classical Hindī and English*, reprint Delhi: Munshiram Manoharlal, 1997 (1884), p. 1110.

Fig. 11: The sipahi in front of his master the amir, and his servants. *Qissa Sipahizada ba Tasvir*, Lucknow: Naval Kishore, 1884, p. 3.

is that of seeing the sipahi argue on a par with his master, without any of the usual marks of reverence, thus offering a kind of vindication by proxy?[33] In fact, not once does the sipahi use the usual terms of respectful address, such as *sarkar* or *huzur*. In the end the only thing the master can offer is a bullock. Far from being a bad deal, though, the fine, strong bullock makes the sipahi hope that he will get a good lump sum on selling it, no less than sixty rupees.[34]

But when the sipahi is riding home on the bullock, ruminating over his good fortune, he is spotted by another set of stock characters, i.e. robbers.[35] They notice that the soldier is armed, so trickery is required rather than force. They show interest in buying the bullock and, using the excuse of needing a third party to name the right price for the bullock, they waylay the sipahi to their den, where their old father acts as an accomplice.

[33] Considerably longer (twenty-two lines) than the one-line description of the job itself.

[34] If we, instead of the narrator, calculate how much that would correspond to in terms of salary, we get close to Rs 10–12 per month, not an unrealistic amount.

[35] Literally, "thugs" (*thag*).

Fig. 12: The two robbers take the sipahi and his bullock to their father. *Qissa Sipahizada*, 1884, p. 5.

When the father names the paltry sum of six takas, the soldier realizes the deceit and swiftly abandons his bullock and any hope of gaining payment in order to save his life, though for form's sake he tells the robbers he is only postponing collecting the money.[36] From this print the qissa revolves around the soldier's elaborate attempts at revenge and regaining his bullock. That one of the pleasures of this text is the reversal of roles, with the victim tormenting his tormentors, is shown by the fact that the desire for revenge far overshadows the retrieval of the bullock, as the robbers themselves admit at the end.[37] The soldier

[36] As his later exchange with his own brothers shows, this arrangement is not so unusual: the deal has been struck, but instead of demanding cash payment upfront, the soldier enters a more prolonged transaction in which the purchaser delays the final payment by occasionally handing out small sums (*kharch* instead of *dam*). Of course, the implied robbery here consists in the fact that the price settled is so low (*chhatakke* is the idiomatic term used), something the soldier keeps reminding the old man at every meeting; the robbers have no intention to pay even this sum.

[37] The father exclaims after being beaten for the third time: "Alas, what guises he takes to come and torment me, what charms he displays! A good bullock indeed you brought, it will take my life alongside his! That man will not leave

goes from tricked to trickster, the robbers from villains to victims. Two of the three attempts involve disguises—another stock situation in qissas and dastans—first as a woman and then as a doctor-cum-holy man. Unlike in heroic dastans, then, the contest here involves not bravery and skill in armed combat, nor a supernatural challenge between the hero and fierce devs, but trickery and cunning. Physical attack, when it occurs, comes in the shape of mighty blows that leave people almost, but not quite, dead.

The first episode plays upon the familiar motif of the "old fool in love", clearly aiming at a few laughs. After hiring some palanquin bearers, the sipahi, dressed up as a bride, pretends to have been robbed and abandoned by her cruel husband near the robbers' home.

He plays the part of the bewildered, modest, and helpless bride ("who will have me now?") with conviction, and the robbers are charmed

Fig. 13: The sipahi disguised as a woman with the two robbers and their father. *Qissa Sipahizada*, 1884, p. 7.

---

us alone, how shall we survive? He is now plotting to take my life, but where can I go if I leave this house? If he keeps coming here, he will surely kill me one day" (394–8).

by her graceful indirect hint that she will be glad to accept their offer to go and live with them.[38] Typical of qissas, and confirming the moral dictum that the mere presence together of men and women leads to lust, the sight of a woman or her glances are enough to unleash passion. In fact for their father it is enough for him to see *one* eye of the disguised soldier to fall in love! In line with the greedy and comical behaviour of other figures of authority in these qissas,[39] the father decides to keep the woman for himself. His flimsy argument that she will cook rotis for him and for them, too, must have aroused a few peels of laughter in the audience. The old man's monologue is one of the very few descriptive passages in the text, evoking in concrete detail the life of leisure that the young woman can now lead thanks to him ("play the dholak and sing ragas to your heart's content", 155), the riches stored in his house, the ornate clothes that she can order and wear, the various body ornaments she can have made, and so on. He is happy to ascribe her reluctance to speak to her good birth and feminine "modesty", and yet he also longs for more: "How can I be satisfied? So far of you I have only seen one eye!" (167). The sipahi's strategy is to buy time by asking the old man for a proper marriage ceremony (*nikah*) to be performed by the town qazi: "There is nothing else we need", she says coyly, displaying a most pleasing lack of acquisitiveness. "Let me become your lawfully wedded wife and then you can fulfil all your heart's desires" (179). But when, on the appointed day, the sipahi manages to remain

[38] "Gracefully she looked them once in the eye and said: 'I am helpless in every way. What can I wish for now? Whoever takes me in, I will accept. If this poor servant does not remain here, where else can she go? Whoever will keep me in his home will do me a great favour'. When they saw her eyes lined with black kohl, both men fell in love with her there and then" (117–21).

[39] Cf. the qazi in the short *Qissa Char Yar* (Tale of Four Friends), only ninety lines long. Called upon to decide to whom the puppet-turned-into-woman belongs, after all four friends contributed to her creation, he claims that she is none other than his own slave (*kaniz*) who had fled with a lot of gold and other things. Now he asks them to hand her and all the wealth back to him, taking only some sweets in return (line 64). In short, the judge, far from delivering judgement becomes just one more deceitful claimant! Although often attributed to the famous poet Rangin, it is in fact despite the grandiloquent headings in Persian quite different from his *Char Chaman*; *Qissa Sipahizada* (*et al.*), Lucknow: Naval Kishore, 1884, p. 24.

alone with the old man, he takes off his disguise and beats the old man within an inch of his life, leaving him hanging ignominiously upside down inside the well, and looting the house of gold, silver, and cash. Why he does not take the bullock is not explained; functionally, this leaves the door open for further reprisals.

In her wonderfully probing essay on the qissa of *Chhabili Bhatiyari*, Kumkum Sangari has argued that the excess of retributive violence meted out on the female innkeeper, whose only fault had been to attract the prince's attention and compete for him with his respectable wife, is a sign of the misogynistic and anti-lower-class attitudes present even in non-prescriptive texts like qissas. While agreeing with her reading of the misogynist violence in that text, I cannot fail to notice a similar excess of violence in the case of the soldier and the robber's father, whose only fault has been to cheat the soldier by undervaluing a bullock. This is explicitly presented in the text as retributive violence; the robbers and their father are called "vicious" (*badzat*), but the mode of presentation is inescapably comic, especially in the two subsequent instances when the soldier beats the father on the head with his slipper. The difference with *Chhabili Bhatiyari* is that in this performed violence no one dies, no one is seriously hurt. Interestingly, when the qazi arrives with the two brothers to find no one at home, he believes that the old man, fearing that the qazi would not agree to a marriage between an old man and a young woman, has decided to elope. Thus, fragments of social discourse make their way into the world of the qissa.

The second episode plays on the popular qissa disguise of the hero or heroine as a wandering doctor and holy person, and on the gullibility of the old man. Thanks to, or perhaps despite, the sipahi's treatment, the old man's health improves and he feels ready to reward and discharge the doctor who, however, manages once again to remain alone with the old man and beat him senseless, chiding him all the time for those "chhatakke". In the third and final episode, the sipahi involves his brothers, who have been envious about his newly-acquired wealth and conspicuous consumption of food and sweets from the bazaar.[40] After spinning them a tale about a gentleman who bought his

[40] They say: "Where did you get so much gold from, that you are spending in a hundred different ways? Nobody spends so much. You seem to us to have

bullock and who is giving him spending money (kharch) from time to time, and about the man's two uncouth sons who are hostile, the sipahi sends his brothers to ask the old man for some kharch, too. While his unfortunate brothers are forced into a fight with the two robbers, the soldier takes the opportunity to beat and insult the old man a third time before riding home on his bullock.[41]

The sipahi's tale carries the humour and farcical violence of the naql into a longer narrative which can be called an "ordinary quest". The text's insistence on the quarrel between the sipahi and his master, and on the motifs of the old fool in love and the man cheated by a quack doctor, suggest that its primary pleasure is comedy, all delivered in plain language that could be reproduced in Devanagari without changing a single word—at this level, Hindi and Urdu are indeed one.

That comedy, or indeed farce, is the main pleasure offered by these popular tales about ordinary people is confirmed by a few other shorter and simpler texts which appear even closer, in their proclivity for comedy and cunning, to the naql tradition. The *Qissa Qazi-e Jaunpur* consists of only 82 couplets of rhyming half-lines printed on four small pages, and the first publishing record we have dates from 1869 in Delhi.[42] It is a very simple tale with only three characters, and although there is a real toponym, the city of Jaunpur, it exists more to signify the eminence of the judge rather than a specific location. The author presents the text explicitly as a naql (1), an extraordinary one (*turfa*) which he has recollected. Indeed, the whole story hangs upon a single sentence uttered by one of the characters: "From an ass I will make you a

---

a lot of gold. You have a lot of gold and you are very cunning, you are carefree and contented, why don't you turn your attention our way a little? We are in great distress these days and are never free from worry" (413–17).

[41] As consolation, he tells them he will give them part of the money when he finally manages to sell the bullock. This is where the qissa ends: "Enough, Khushdil, fasten your tongue, you have spoken long enough. This story is now ended, you have scattered enough pearls" (478–9).

[42] *Qissa Qazi-e Jaunpur*, Delhi: Akbari Press, 1869 (Urdu), 4 pp., 8vo, litho, 3 paise; another edition is Delhi: Muir Press, 1875 (Urdu), 4 pp. (1000), litho, 3 paise. The text was also often included in qissa collections, e.g. *Majmu'a Char Qissa*, Lucknow: Naval Kishore, 1882. Again, I refer to lines in the text instead of pages.

man" (17). The teacher utters this sentence to one of the pupils in his *maktab* and is overheard by a donkey-cart driver, who takes the sentence literally and asks the teacher to turn one of his donkeys into a man. It is a very difficult task, the teacher claims, but he promises to do it for fifty rupees. When the donkey-cart driver fetches the money and a donkey, the teacher promptly sells it for another fifty rupees. And when the driver comes back a year later to ask for his "man", the teacher tells him that, in the meantime, the man has become the qazi of Jaunpur, so he must go and reclaim him there. The driver proceeds to do so. After gaining admission into the qazi's house, he reminds the qazi in the strongest terms of his past existence as a donkey. Stunned and humiliated, the qazi hands him two hundred rupees to be rid of him. After sharing this reward with the teacher, the driver spends his own share on giving banquets at home, and goes every six months to the qazi to extract more money. In the end, by dint of offering feasts, the donkey-cart driver becomes a sharif (77).

What turns this naql into a qissa are a few deft touches. For example, the author takes his time in describing the lively scene at the teacher's maktab. Apart from the fateful sentence, this description does not contribute to the plot but acts as a funny, familiar scene and a build-up to the closing utterance:

Many students came to earn education, — they would respectfully bow and greet him.

Some read hadith and the Quran, — some the *Karima Mamuqiman*.

Some learnt the *Gulistan* stories by heart, — or helped others to remember their lesson.

Some practised from the *Insha-e Khalifa*, — others read qissas and latifas.

Some knew the *Bostan* by heart well, — some spoke aloud the names of God.

Some were experts in [Ghanimat's] *Zuleikha*, — others in [Khusrau's] *Sikandarnama*.

No one was silent in that maktab, — some argued, some recited

'*Ilahi ghuncha-e ummid bakusha'i,* — *Guli az rauza-ye Jawed banuma'i*'.

['God, disclose the bud of hope, — show me a rose from the eternal Garden.']

The teacher would shout at one,	correct another.
One got slapped hard,	another clacked or thumped.
One was rebuked,	another thrashed with a stick.
One got thumped by his fist,	another told to do penance.
One got boxed on his ears—	this is how he diverted himself.
Whenever he would feel sick of this life,	he would get angry and tell a pupil:
"Get this right, you wretched oaf,	from an ass I will make you a man." (3–17)

As always in qissas, characterization is by social type and not necessarily linked to the story. So, the teacher (*ustad*), who has been called "elderly, intelligent and honest" (2), feels no compunction in deceiving the donkey-cart driver who is, as it were, stupid by profession. The second pleasure of this text stems from the teacher's self-important declaration before the gullible donkey-cart driver:

The ustad said: "Are you stupid or what?	Are you a man or are you an ass?
Do you think that this task is easy?	*Are*, it takes a lot for an ass to become a man!
Although my tongue refuses it,	Your coming places me under obligation.
Because of your humble entreaty,	I will do it with much vigour and effort." (22–5)

We also laugh at the way in which the donkey-cart driver manages to get access past the guards to the eminent qazi of Jaunpur on the strength of their being compatriots (*hamvatan*) and then lashes out against the unsuspecting judge when he fails to recognize his past master:

Seething with anger he said: "Oh qazi, have you forgotten?	Your happy air here has changed you, it seems.
Look and remember what I have here:	the old sack and the old stick.
Have you lost all memory of the past?	Do you recall the old days or not?

The hot brick-kiln I took you to,	the furnace?
The load from daybreak to sunset,	day in day out, each and every day.
Now the qazi's seat has swollen your head,	you have forgotten my tapping, my clacking?
I am your master, salute me!	I paid a good hundred to make you a man.
I got that teacher to agree,	and from an ass he has made you a qazi . . ." (56–63)

Unusually for a qissa—and here we can see the old narratives changing into something new—is the short but expressive description of the poor qazi's embarrassment. Minute details and the use of four different past tenses (instead of the usual two: habitual past and perfective) in the space of three lines signal the new complexity of description:

Drenched in sweat from head to toe,	drops falling non-stop from his beard.
He would not lift his head in shame,	embarrassed he averted his glance.
Finally, humbly he drew out this plan	and with two hundred he got rid of the donkey-cart driver. (66–8)

As already mentioned, the tale ends with mutual satisfaction among the humble and mischievous characters of the story, the continuous blackmailing and humiliation of the only figure of authority, and the social rise of the donkey-cart driver to respectability through social spending on feasts and banquets. While not a tale of "subaltern resistance", it is certainly a tale of insubordination that pokes fun at both the stupid donkey-cart driver and the judge, but ends up with the former gaining the upper hand over the latter. We can compare it to *Qissa Barhai o Sunar* (Tale of the Carpenter and the Goldsmith), which also revolves around several tricks and an apparent metamorphosis, this time of children into bear cubs. In this case, after two friends ("clever, intelligent, *dag͟habaz*, 'ayyar and cunning, 15–16) have stolen some idols from a Hindu temple and hidden them, one of them tries to cheat the other but is cheated in turn.[43] After traversing the domains of the farcical and the ingenious, the story is wrapped up with a little couplet about deceit, borrowing a convention from moral tales:

> May God preserve from cheating, deceit is a bad, bad, bad thing.
> If a man ever deceives another, in the end he will repent. (204–5).

As in the case of the other stories, lively dialogues, fights, and insults all add spice to the tale and develop it into something more dramatic and elaborate than a sketch, a naql.

Tales of Women—and Men

Tales of "women's wiles" (*triya charitra*), synonymous in practice with adulterous women, were a staple of storytelling in India for centuries. Besides the famous collection of the Seventy Tales of the Parrot, *Shukasaptati*, which dealt exclusively with adulterous women, and which had entered the Persian repertoire as *Tutinama* at the beginning of the thirteenth century,[44] such tales were scattered all over the oral and written repertoire of tales. Many of these were printed in the course of the nineteenth century.[45] Worth mentioning are also the tales of women's treachery contained in the Persian *Bahar-i Danish* (The Spring of Knowledge, 1651) by 'Inayatullah Kanboh, because this book

[43] Tajammul Rasul Khan, *Qissa Barha'i o Sunar*, Delhi: Razawi Press, 1873. Tajammul Rasul Khan is also mentioned as the author of *Qissa Saudagar o Maina* (Tale of the Merchant and the Mynah Bird), also printed in Delhi in 1873: see *Quarterly List* for that year. References are to lines, not pages.

[44] The *Shukasaptati* was printed in Hindi as early as 1850 in Banaras at the Benares Akhbar Press (551 copies), at the price of 12 annas. Other editions include Banaras: Divakar Chapakhana, 1859, litho, pp. 91; *Shuk Bahottari Chitra Sahit* (ill.), Bombay: 1864, pp. 223; Delhi: Murari Lal Press, 1874 (reprint) 80 pp., 8vo (1000), litho, 2 annas and 6 paise; and Lucknow: Naval Kishore, 1874, pp. 87, Hindi (1250), litho, 3 annas; see Krishnacharya, *Hindi ke Adimudrit Granth*, p. 130 and *Quarterly Lists* for the relevant years.

[45] The second chapter of Mahjur's collection of naql, *Nau Ratan*, mentioned above, was devoted to tales of women's adultery; see C. Oesterheld, 'Entertainment and Reform'. The qissa *Triya Charitra*, about a woman killing her husband, was published at the end of the nineteenth century and is still in print: see Pritchett, *Marvelous Encounters*, p. 205.

found a certain success in print in the nineteenth century since it was part of the Persian curriculum and was translated into Urdu,[46] but also because the anonymous woman author of *Kissa Aurat Mard* mentions it explicitly, as we shall see. In *Bahar-i Danish*, the stories of adulterous women are told in order to dissuade Prince Sikandarshah from pursuing the path of love. Though unsuccessful in the task, the tales nonetheless present a terrifying picture of women's treachery: invariably the delicate and virtuous young woman who is pursued and wedded by the protagonist suddenly turns into a shameless and aggressive adulteress who not only betrays her loving husband but has no qualms about attempting to murder him in order to avenge the death of her lover.[47] Noble male heroes, of course, had always betrayed their wives in pursuit of other wives or women—indeed the hero with two wives is a motif of several folk epics which have played an important role in Indian literary history—but this was accepted as part of the order of things in a variously polygamous society.[48] While the epics recorded the suffering of the abandoned first wife, no blame accrued to the man.

In the last few decades of the nineteenth century, a new set of texts emerged in print which picked up and developed the theme of the battle between the sexes.[49] One particular text that became very popular, *Kissa Tota Maina*, reworked the repertoire in a way that put men's

[46] Editions of the Urdu translation of *Bahar-i Danish* by Tapish include Calcutta 1809, Calcutta 1845, and Kanpur 1874. The English translation by Jonathan Scott, published in London in 1799, is available online at http://persian.packhum.org/persian/pf?file=10301010&ct=0 (viewed on 11 September 2007).

[47] My favourite is the first story, in which the delicate and loving bride becomes the lover of the son of the town's *kotwal*. When they decide to elope she burns the family house to cinders so that they will believe that she died in the fire. The disconsolate husband is astonished to find her living happily with her lover in another town and convinces her to return home with him. On the road, however, the lover attacks the husband goaded by the wife, who insists on tying the husband against a tree and making love to her lover *in front of* her husband!

[48] See Stuart Blackburn, *et al.* (eds), *Oral Epics in India*, Berkeley: University of California Press, 1989.

[49] As already in the *baital*'s first story in *Baital Pacchisi*, quoted in Pritchett, *Marvelous Encounters*, p. 82.

and women's infidelity (*bewafai*) on the same plane. Another text, *Kissa Aurat Mard*, tried even more boldy to intervene directly with the repertoire in order to put across the woman's perspective. Both texts show the possibilities of print by combining the pleasure of familiarity with that of novelty, and the dynamism of the qissa as a genre. *Kissa Tota Maina* responded to the market's demand for multiplying "attractions" by stringing together a whole range of narratives with the additional pleasure of the banter and repartee between the parrot and the mynah, the two narrators. *Kissa Aurat Mard* clearly tries to capitalize on the expectation of such a contest to offer quite a different, and wholly partisan, narrative. Both texts also show how a commercial genre of entertainment like the qissa could carry elements of gender critique in ways that were quite different from the contemporary reformist calls for women's education.[50] In the case of *Kissa Aurat Mard*, the critical intention is explicit and beyond doubt: as its title indicates, it seeks to reject the "faults in women that men have imagined" (*purushkalpit stri dosh*). What is remarkable is that it should consciously use stories in order to combat a prejudice that was spread largely through stories. Pandit Rangilal's wholly commercial *Kissa Tota Maina* suggests, more intriguingly, how a multivocal text could include an element of gender critique for the sake of providing a new kind of entertainment.

Kissa Tota Maina (Fig. 14) is a microcosm of the processes qissas underwent as they came into print.[51] First, it shows how the various

[50] E.g. Hali, see fn. 6 above.

[51] Pandit Rangilal Sharma lived in or near Mathura and composed qissas, sangit, and Vaishnava devotional works. The owners of the Shyamkashi Press, one of the oldest and largest qissa publishers, interviewed by Frances Pritchett in 1977, claimed that Pandit Rangilal was their author and composed his works originally for the press, which was founded around 1870. Their own collection of old publications includes titles from the early 1880s, several by Pandit Rangilal. She suggests that *Kissa Tota Maina* must have been written sometime in the 1870s, for she also saw an Urdu edition in the Delhi University Library dated 1297 AH (1879–80), which unfortunately was not on the shelves when I check in August 2007. This edition, by Munshi Ibne Prashad (Delhi: Matba' Fauq Kashi, 1297 AH, 31pp.) was "Urduized not only in script but in vocabulary as well, no doubt by Munshi Ibne Prashad. The Hindi edition had probably been out long enough to become fairly popular by then." An edition of Pandit Rangilal's *Kissa Kesar Gulab*, printed in Agra in 1896, calls him

Fig. 14: Cover of a 1906 edition of *Kissa Tota Maina* published in eight separate parts on very brittle paper by the Mumbai Mitra Press, Mathura.

"Mathura *nivasi*", i.e. a resident of Mathura, while the S. 1955 [1898–9] Mathura edition of his *Champa Chameli* calls him "Vaikunth nivasi", i.e. a resident of Vishnu's heaven. He must have therefore died around 1897; Pritchett, *Marvelous Encounters*, pp. 96–7.

sources and traditions (Perso-Arabic, Indian) which made up the range of qissas became here a *combination* of motifs and sources *within* the text. Second, while marvellous adventures and romantic quests remain, they are only part of the narrative: other elements enter the frame—such as details of family rituals (especially concerning weddings), considerations of family loyalty, and social propriety. Third, the great variety of song forms, verse dialogue, and, on occasion, melodramatic monologue all manifest the intersection of qissas with the world of popular songs and theatrical plays—both as spectacle and as printed texts. The result is not a homogeneous prose and verse style but a very flexible and eclectic Hindi–Urdu idiom. This encompasses a wide range of registers and styles and moves easily between them, as we shall see.

In her chapter-length study of this text, Frances Pritchett has pointed out that Rangilal borrowed the framing motif of the male parrot and female mynah bird arguing with each other about the relative flaws of women and men from the third baital's story in the *Twenty-five Stories of the Ghost* (*Baital Pacchisi*).[52] "Pandit Rangilal's originality", she argues, "is to have created a frame story more interestingly and narratively effective than any of the individual dastans which it frames. He can take all kinds of liberties with the dastans, because they are not, individually and collectively, the center of his work. Rather, the heart of his work lies in the lively, malicious repartee between his two secondary narrator-characters, the misogynist parrot and the man-hating mynah." The argument between the two birds "is no mere formality", she argues, "nor is it confined to the beginning and end of the narrative: it is the moral and dramatic center of the whole work."[53] The individual stories, called dastans, are meant to illustrate either the treachery of the female character or the heartlessness and cruelty of men who desert or kill their wives: even when we expect a

[52] Pritchett, *Marvelous Encounters*, p. 82. As she suggests, "it seems that Pandit Rangilal recognized a clever frame story, and developed it at much greater length." The later *Qissa Sarhe Tin Yar* (Three-and-a-Half Friends) also features an adversary story, this time told by two human lovers. Other borrowings include the first story of *Baital Pacchisi* in the sixth dastan, and the eleventh statuette's story from *Simhasan Battisi* in the tenth dastan; ibid., p. 83.

[53] Ibid., p. 87.

happy ending, a cruel coda is added in which the unrepentant husband or wife will once again try to get rid of his or her spouse.[54]

The combination of motifs that is the hallmark of this text is evident, first of all, in the setting and characters of the fourteen dastans. The first one begins in "the famous city of Delhi in the country [*mulk*] of Hindustan", with Ahmad Ali, the son of a "Muslim belonging to the royal family" (p. 2). After leaving home, Ahmad Ali falls in love with an untouchable (*mehtar*) girl and insists on marrying her despite opposition—including from the girl's father. But after the relatively realistic setting of the first dastan, most of the following stories are set in imaginary cities. Even if they mention real cities, like Varanasi or Multan or Indraprastha, the characters are standard types—kings, princes, merchants, and faqirs, occasionally paris and gods like Shiva and Parvati. The gods are fully humanized, just as they are in the contemporary mythological plays of the Parsi theatre.[55] In the second story, for example, we find Shiva advising the protagonist against immolating himself along with his dead wife in the way a gruff elder would:

> Hey Rajkumar! You are so stupid. Why don't you try to understand that things in this world come and go all the time? One day we shall all have to leave this body. And you also know that you neither came into this world accompanied, nor will leave it in company. How can you sound so juvenile when you are so intelligent? If you remain alive, you will get many other queens just like this one, therefore believe me and stop mourning. (pp. 10–11)

Other stock characters who regularly crop up in the dastans are the king with four sons, the prince who leaves his virtuous and beautiful first wife to search for the beauty he has heard about, the faqir (either as the queen's lover, or as the disguise chosen by the lover, or even by the deserted wife), the cruel king and/or princess who imprisons all

[54] The edition that I have used is one of the earliest held in the British Library, a Devanagari edition printed in Banaras in 1910 [OIOLC: 14157.c.4(3)].

[55] See Anuradha Kapur, 'The Representation of Gods and Heroes: Parsi Mythological Drama of the Early Twentieth Century', in Vasudha Dalmia and Heinrich von Stietencron (eds), *Representing Hinduism,* New Delhi: Sage Publications, 1995, pp. 401–41.

the suitors who cannot answer her questions, the king who is so fond of music and dancing that he is ready to gift everything to a singing girl, the four princes who fall in love with four enchantresses, and so on.

While several dastans still broadly conform to the model of the romantic-adventurous quest, in most dastans this forms only one narrative element, and others combine to form a truly "multivocal" text in the Bakhtinian sense. Usually, the different segments and voices appear serially in the dastans. Madansen, like most other husbands, is at first truly in love with his wife and only at the end thinks of killing her off. This has led Frances Pritchett to remark that the brutal endings "must be forcibly imposed" on the tales in order to fulfil their illustrative role.[56] One could argue, instead, that this "patchwork" impression is not confined to the endings: the hero or heroine hold attitudes that are quite contradictory at different points of the narrative because of the linear and sequential structure of the qissa. It is because the voices change so much that we become aware of it. In particular, the romantic and adventurous "voices" that usually feature at the beginning of a dastan are counteracted in turns by the voice of the mynah or of women characters, by the text's attention to ritual events, by the pathetic voice of family ties (as in Madansen's dastan above), and by the "voice of society" echoed by other characters and ultimately by the male protagonist himself—and which leads him to reject the former object of his love-quest.

Let us take for example the seventh dastan, which offers a typical combination of the adventurous and the mundane. It is one in which the setting is ostensibly "realistic": the "famous and beautiful" city of Varanasi, with its wealth of dharamshalas and pathshalas for Brahmin boys. The protagonist is one such handsome Brahmin boy called Krishnadatt who, one day, joins other pupils to attend a feast offered by a wealthy merchant of a nearby town. Mundane are also the wedding customs (*rasmen*) for the marriage of the daughter of the local king to a prince. The "customs of the family" (*kul ki rit*) are all mentioned in great detail, anchoring the tale to the everyday and suggesting a female audience attentive to such details.[57]

[56] Pritchett, *Marvelous Encounters*, p. 84.

[57] The wedding rituals include: *toran marna, barothi, phera, bhamvar, negchar, kunvar kaleva;* pp. 70–1.

The element of adventure consists in the fact that Krishnadatt, who has lost the rest of his party and has been forced to sleep rough, is offered a thousand rupees if he undertakes to impersonate the bridegroom who is to marry the king's daughter: the groom is one-eyed and could therefore be rejected by the bride's family. After successfully playing the role and spending an intimate night with her, Krishnadatt is sent off with the reward by the bridegroom's father, and the one-eyed bridegroom takes his place. But here a new element comes in—the girl's voice. While other members of the bride's party wonder why this new bridegroom looks so different from the previous night's, the bride picks up the courage to address her father:

> "Father! This is not something I should say in front of you, but I have no option because this requires telling, and second my dharma will be ruined. This is why I am compelled to say something inappropriate in front of you. But it is written in the *dharmashastra* that: 'Give up your body, mind, heart and shame: you can forsake all this without regret if it is to save your dharma' and 'Give up your body, give up your mind, give up devotion but keep hold of your dharma. If you give up your dharma, you have lost everything.' And 'If you have to give up your life, so be it, but keep your dharma. With this in my heart I ask you in my sorrow.'
>
> So father! Because I remember these sentences from the dharmashastra I am afraid of losing my dharma and I want to tell you something." (p. 71)

Only now, with her father's permission granted, can she tell him that the man with a patch on his eye is not the same as the man who was with her the night before. It is once again the girl who takes the initiative and consoles her father—who has hastily and angrily dismissed the impostor and is now "exceedingly aggrieved and sad"—first with a lecture and then with a story and a gnomic verse to the effect that no one can change what is fated.

> "Father! Do not worry so much. One's mother and father are the companions of one birth [*janm*], not of one's karma. You have therefore no fault. You saw that his family was good.[58]

[58] She uses the colloquial term *ghar-bar*, p. 72.

Doha: What is fated to be will be, even if all have forgotten it. You realize it when what had to happen, does happen." (p. 72)

This not only earns her father's praise but also gives her the moral authority to suggest the stratagem that will retrieve her real husband. The stratagem leads us once again into the realm of the adventurous: posters are to be put up in big cities like Banaras announcing that the king's daughter will give a lakh of rupees to whoever can answer her question—one that only the man who has spent the night with her can answer. Eventually, Krishnadatt hears of the challenge and, of course, provides the full and complete answer. He is welcomed by her father with great respect and starts living with the girl as her husband. Love grows between them until one day the voice of family ties arises within him: "One day Krishnadatt thought: 'I have not had *darshan* of my parents for a long time. But how can I bring this Rani along? It will be awful, for when my parents see that I have married a *kshatri*'s daughter they will expel me from our caste. And if I go without her, the Rani will find out and follow me. What should I do?'" (p. 76). So, like all the other husbands in the mynah's stories, one night he kills his wife with a rod and leaves for his home with all her money and precious things. Morality is voiced only by the frame narrator, the mynah: "Don't lower your head, parrot. Answer me! Who is as heartless as Krishnadatt who killed his lovely and devoted wife?" (p. 76).

In this dastan, then, motifs common in tales of adventure—like the disguise, the search for the lost husband, the riddle—are mixed with the remarkable element of the woman's voice and her own version of the dharmashastra, while the caste angle really surfaces only at the end. This kind of multivocality is visible, to a greater or lesser extent, in all the stories.[59] In the fourteenth and final dastan, about one more

[59] In the first dastan, for example, after the adventurous and romantic beginning, we hear the "voice of society" in the shape of neighbours who urge Ahmad Ali to remember his religion and not marry the sweeper's daughter: "Miyan Sahab, come back to your senses, because you are a Muslim by birth and she is a sweepress [*bhangin*]. You should not fall prey to love to this extent; think of your faith as well [*din o iman*], because this youth and beauty will only last for four days" (p. 3). The household world of ritual events, relationships, and exchanges is also evoked at various points in the narrative, first when Ahmad

princely hero leaving his first wife behind in search of his love-interest Champaklata, the multiple voices include an original resolution to the contrast between the voice of love and that of society. This compromise solution is evidence of how the combination of various voices in these tales can lead to genre innovation. When Champaklata's mother, horrified at her daughter's romance with the hero,[60] hears that Champaklata is ready to poison herself if their union is forbidden, she counsels practical wisdom to her husband the king, who has set an impossible condition to his daughter's suitors. The Punjabi gnomic verse lends an element of earthy wisdom to the advice:

> "Look, nobody has been able to fulfil your vow [to bring a pearl bigger than an orange to match his own in order to marry his daughter] and Champaklata's youth has fully developed. Please listen to my request and marry her off. Also, the match is good this time and if you had to look for grooms God knows where you would have to go and look for them. Instead, sitting at home, God has sent you a bridegroom whom Champaklata likes. You will not get such a good opportunity again. As the poet has said:

Ali enjoys the mehtar's hospitality as a bridegroom, and then when he twice solicits substantial gifts from his wife's family. The wife's voice in this tale is mostly a submissive and suffering one: first she agrees to follow her husband back to his family, saying she is his obedient dependent [*tabedar*, p. 4], then she lies about her husband's crime. In the end when, despite feeling repentant and taking an oath before her, Ahmad Ali once again tries to kill her on the road home and leaves her despoiled of all her parents' gifts, "for her whole life that woman never mentioned that treacherous husband again' (p. 7). It is worth noting that while the violence meted out against the wife is indeed excessive (to use Sangari's term), her reaction is a "realistic" one—a reaction with which women readers could identify. At first she tries to hide her husband's fault in order to also safeguard her own reputation before her family and before strangers.

60 "My child! What a terrible thing you have told me today! What will people [*log lugai*] say when they hear of it! And what if by chance your father gets to hear of it, he will kill you and me. You are a Rajkumar's daughter and think such evil things!" (p. 148).

> *Kal karanta aj kar, aj karanta abb. Ausar bitau jat hai, pher karoge kabb.*
>
> Do today what you have to do tomorrow, and do now what you have to do today. The chance will slip away: when will you do it then?" (p. 149)

Written most probably in the 1870s, Pandit Rangilal's *Kissa Tota Maina* was already influenced by the new codes of theatre—as the combination of prose and verse, the extensive use of songs as attractions, and even an example of melodramatic monologue show. All these elements further contribute to making the prose of this qissa extremely eclectic. They also provided readers with the multiplicity of pleasures—strong dialogue, Urdu verse, folk songs—that audiences of the Parsi theatre were so clearly enthralled with.

Gnomic and love verse were already an element of qissas and dastans, but what we find in some of the *Tota Maina* stories—just as in Parsi, sangit, and nautanki plays—is a repeated use of songs and of verse dialogues when the effect sought is one of heightened emotion. "While the classic theory of melodrama in Europe suggests that the idiom of melodrama is principally visual, derived historically from mimed, popular entertainment rather than spoken theatre," Anuradha Kapur argues,

> the melodramatic mode of the Parsi Theatre has as much to do with dialogue, turn of phrase and rhyme. Dialogue and verse compel, drive, and herald action. The rich stage pictured is made more lavish by the extravagance of the word. Parsi Theatre uses prose, rhymed prose, verse, and metre and is linguistically coextensive to a wide range of social relationships: it uses Hindi, Urdu, Hindustani and dialect, and it includes well crafted didactic dialogue, the speech of war, politics, nationalism, and trade, humorous exchanges of abuse, vulgar speech, comic dialogue, everyday idiomatic vocabulary, and even formal argument in the shape of soliloquies.

She also notes that "the scope of its language is as wide as the variety of relationships emerging within a quickly urbanizing India. These extend to associations with domestic servants, tricksters, thugs, and crooks; with princes, epic lovers and gods, common housewives and everyday husbands".[61] While the range of social relationships in *Tota Maina* is not as wide, or rather not as differentiated—the mehtar and royal wives speak the same language— we do find the same rhetorical use of song, dialogue, and occasionally even of the melodramatic monologue that Parsi theatre cultivated in order to project the character's inner feelings against the enveloping backdrop of painted curtains. One instance, from the fourteenth dastan, could literally be a scene from a Parsi theatre play. The suitor has found out the impossible demand made by Champaklata's father of her suitors, and he addresses, with melodramatic accents, the garden where they made love:

> "The garden which we considered an abode of rest turned out to be a sea of troubles. The trees which blossomed out of gratitude for the fact that Champaklata had touched them, have now turned into wild forests so as to frighten me. O cruel garden! Were you made by a craftsman in order to kill poor lovers like me, apart from their beloveds? And O cruel craftsman! I scorn this craftwork of yours, because had you not created such a garden my bewitching Champaklata would not have come strolling in it and my life would not have been caught in the snares of love." (p. 140)[62]

Just as in plays and, later, in films, the narratives in some of the tales of *Tota Maina* offer "song situations" when, for example, a character becomes a jogi and wanders around singing, or when the lovers write letters to each other in the form of poems. The range of song and verse

[61] Anuradha Kapur, 'Love in the Time of Parsi Theatre', in F. Orsini (ed.), *Love in South Asia*, pp. 225–6.

[62] The dramatic inspiration of the tale is confirmed by a motif that we do not find in other tales. On the way back home the prince goes riding and leaves his faithful companion, the vazir's son, in charge of his wife. A ring slips inadvertently from the vazir's finger and Champaklata picks it up, thinking it her husband's. With an Othello-like ending, the prince kills his bride and also the vazir, thinking "How can one trust a woman? Who knows what she will do next." The parrot of the frame story confirms the prince's view against that of the mynah, who calls the prince "cruel" (*nirdayi*): "The wanton woman! She must have been full of vice. Had she told the story of the ring she would not have been killed. Don't you know how a man gets angry if his wife keeps something from another man? The prince was nowhere at fault": p. 152.

forms is as wide as in songbooks and plays, and each brings in its particular linguistic dialect: ghazals and she'rs are in Urdu, songs set to ragas and raginis in a mixture of Braj Bhasha and Khari Boli, and occasionally the result is a new kind of hybrid.

The fifth dastan is the one that most resembles a play text with its wealth of verses and songs throughout the tale. The merchant who comes and shows prince Madansen the picture of princess Chandrakiran uses a doha to tell him about her:

> *Kanchanpur ek shahar hai, base samandar par. Indrasen vahan ka nripati, uske rajkumar.*
>
> *Chandra badan si kamini, mrig se dou nain. Lakh lajat hai apsara, sarmavat ur main.*
>
> In the city of Kanchanpur, beyond the sea, lives king Indrasen. His daughter
>
> Is as fetching as the moon, her eyes like a doe's. A blushing apsara, she is shy in her heart. (p. 35)

The pathetic attempt by Madansen's father to dissuade him from leaving home is rendered instead with a ghazal explicitly "in the style of the *Indarsabha*":

> *Madansen beta chatur, kya dukh vyapa toy. Raj palat fakir banke, chhor chale ab moy.*
>
> *Kisne bahkaya tujhe, tu kah de sara hal. Chhor jai fi men mujhe, tu chala kahan se lal.*
>
> Madansen my clever son, what sorrow pervades you, That leaving the kingdom as a faqir, you are now leaving me?
>
> Who led you astray, tell me everything! Where are you going my little one, leaving me in anguished worry? (p. 36)[63]

The pathetic dialogue between Madansen and his mother and wife, instead, turns to verse, a convention in vogue in the Parsi theatre:

[63] Notice the very colloquial Hindi words (*beta, lal*) and a Braj Bhasha absolutive (*jai*) and pronouns (*moy, toy*) for pathetic effect.

Chala putr mere sang son, kaise ji samjhaun. Tum bin mere ladle, taraph taraph mar jaun.

How can I tell my heart that you are leaving me, my son? Without you, my dear boy, I will writhe and die. (p. 36)

Patka gahi kamin khari, kar solah shringar. "Chhod chale majhdhar men kahan mujhe bhartar?

The lovely bride was standing in full beauty, holding her sash: "Where are you leaving me in midstream, my husband?" (p. 36)

With Chandrakiran, instead, Madansen uses Urdu verse to express his romantic love, and he fittingly compares her with a pari:

Nazar ḳar tu meri taraf e pari. Muhabbat teri mere dil men bhari.

Look at me, you fairy! Love for you has filled my heart. (p. 37)

When his first wife goes looking for Madansen disguised as a jogin, she fittingly sings songs of love set to a ragini in Braj Bhasha, but also in the more Urduizing rekhta. The range and the linguistic and poetic registers are the same that we found in the songbooks in chapter 2:

Ragini Girnari:

Koi dilvar ka daras dikhay de re. [Refrain]

Lochan kaj, kutil bhrikuti, kach kanan, katha suna de re.
Rangilal, ab meri vaki chitt ki ganth mitay de re.
Jake rang ranga sab tan man, taki jhalak dekhay de re.
Koi dilvar . . .

Someone please show me my love.
Sidelong glances, furrowed brow, a tangle of hair, tell me your story.[64]
Rangilal says, now unwrap the mystery of his mind and mine.
Show me a glimpse of he who has coloured all my body and mind.
Someone . . .

[64] Notice the vocabulary and poetic devices of Braj Bhasha poetry such as alliteration: *lochan kaj, kutil bhrikuti, kach kanan.*

Rekhta:

Dildar yar pyare, galiyon men ri a ja. Ankh taras rahi hain, surat inhen dikha ja.

My beloved, my dear, come into my lane. My eyes are longing for you, do show yourself. (p. 41)

Kissa Tota Maina, then, displays the same phenomenon of eclectic confluence of song styles and the range of linguistic dialects pitched mostly at a middling level, that we found in songbooks and sung barahmasas. The phenomenon here is not limited to songs, but involves both the narrative grammar of the genre—the combination of motifs within the stories—and the mixing of narrative traditions. The result is both eclecticism and hybridization. This is a time when intellectuals and poets, who practised more than one poetic style side by side, were feeling more and more uneasy about their eclectic tastes and were striving to write in a language that mirrored a their new cultural identity. Popular genres that were linked to evolving traditions of performance, the growth of commercial entertainment and the proliferation of print went in the opposite direction, combining and mixing styles and forms.[65]

Kissa Aurat Mard

Kissa Aurat Mard is also a tale about "men and women", as the title says, and reveals a different aspect of the dynamism of the qissa genre. It is a remarkable text, seventy-five closely printed pages in Hindi, published in 1882 by the Naval Kishore Press in 600 copies for 4 annas and 6 paise.[66] Though not as successful in commercial terms—it appears to have been reprinted only once—the text nevertheless consciously inserted itself in the commercial market by calling itself a qissa and

[65] For the eclectic tastes of late-nineteenth-century Hindi poets and their growing ideological unease, see Valerie Ritter, 'Networks, Patrons, and Genres for Late Braj Bhasha Poets: "Ratnakar" and "Hariaudh"', in *Hindi and Urdu Before the Divide*, Delhi: Orient Longman 2008.

[66] A copy is held at the Indian Institute Library, Oxford [Hindi Qiss 1]. I am grateful to Emma Blake, in charge of the modern collections, for alerting me to the existence of this text. Page numbers refer to this edition.

sought to reproduce all the qissa conventions, from the frame to the embedded stories, the implied audience, and so on. At the same time, it reworked these conventions in significant ways, for example in relation to the characterization of the male and female protagonists, and the use of the implied audience—i.e. neighbourhood women who act as a kind of chorus to the woman narrator.

The book was published anonymously, ostensibly written by an "Agrawal woman of Jain beliefs from an excellent family" (*Agraval shreshth kul ki kulin jainmati stri ka racha hua*). The complete lack of admonition to women—either conservative or reformist—is what strongly suggests to me that this is not a case of a male author writing under an assumed female identity. Women in this text figure neither as objects of instruction or of a sensualized male gaze, nor as mute, self-sacrificing figures—the three typical modes of presentation of women in texts from this period. While the book is, as we shall see, a powerful gender critique—of the kind represented by Tarabai Shinde's *A Comparison Between Men and Women*—and is the work of an educated woman, it is not a reformist critique.[67] Reformist discourse was engaged in constructing a new role model of the educated and thrifty upper-class woman (*bhadramahila*). It counterbalanced appeals to women's education and public access with an exaltation of women's subservience to their husbands. *Kissa Aurat Mard*'s "traditional" point of view, by contrast, asserts that women, at least women from the author's own class, have *always* been educated and respectable, and what they aspire to is not equality but mutuality, i.e. a recognition of their dignity and of their crucial contribution to the household. Though its heroines subscribe to the *pativrata* ideal in theory, in practice they do not hesitate to contest or disobey their husbands in order to forestall their personal and family ruin.

The author's own relationship to textuality is complex.[68] Since, as the Indian saying goes, "the powerful gets twenty out of twenty"

[67] Cf. Rosalind O'Hanlon, *A Comparison Between Women and Men: Tarabai Shinde and the Critique of Gender Relations in Colonial India*, Madras: Oxford University Press, 1994.

[68] Not unlike the debates over "questions of truth" of seventeenth- and eighteenth-century novelists discussed by Michael McKeon, *The Origin of the English Novel: 1600–1740*, Baltimore: Johns Hopkins University Press, 1987.

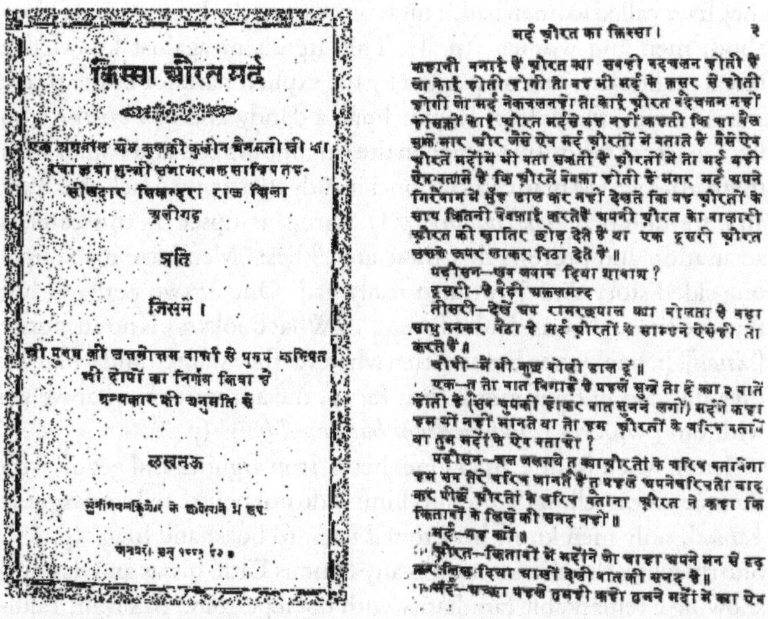

किस्सा औरत मर्द

प्रति

जिसमें।

लखनऊ

मर्द औरत का किस्सा।

Fig. 15: Cover and p. 3 of *Kissa Aurat Mard*: note that it is printed with moveable type and has paragraphs and indentations, like a novel. Lucknow: Naval Kishore, 1882.

(*zabardast ke bis bisve*) and decides what is good and what is bad,[69] "Though women do not have one-tenth of the faults that men have and there are thousands of tales [*dastan*] showing the goodness of women and the treachery of men, whenever men have written books

[69] At the beginning of the text, the author enrolls the "strong" discourse of Muslim hegemony vs Hindu defeat to strengthen her point: "The powerful call the weak bad and call themselves good, however good the weak may be. The history of Hindus and Muslims bears witness to this. When Muslims invaded India they did not excel in anything but the sword, whereas Hindus possessed every knowledge and skill to a high degree. But after the conquest everything Hindu became contemptible and everything Muslim worthy of praise. The same goes for men and women. Men are powerful and women are weak, so whatever fault men have wanted to find in women they have, and they have declared themselves good in everything", p. 1. For women's use of powerful cultural discourses in order to bolster their claims, see F. Orsini, *The Hindi Public Sphere*, ch. 4.

they have called women bad. This is the reason why I am writing a story about men and women" (p. 1). This argument against knowledge based on books is taken up again by the explicit narrator of the frame story, Sarupi, the wife of Ramrachpal, a dandy and *bon vivant* who likes to leer at beautiful women in the neighbourhood and banter with them. And yet the man can say nonchalantly that women lack character and are immoral (*badchalan*) (p.1). Sarupi is upset by this careless accusation and protests that these are all lies: "Men have made up a one-sided story. Are all women really bad? One or two perhaps, but that too through some fault of men . . . What books say is no authority [*sanad*]. In books men have written whatever they wanted and whatever they decided in their minds. But for us, the authority is what we see with our own eyes [*ankhon dekhi bat sanad hai*]" (p. 3).

Later, when Ramrachpal urges her to stop arguing and get on with the story she is telling, she rebuts him: "I do not how to tell stories [*kissa kahna*], only men know how to tell tales, to boast and brag" (p. 39). She then lists the characters of many famous Urdu qissas and dastans, showing a remarkable familiarity with the repertoire: Bakavali, Tajul-muluk, Benazir and Badremunir, Jan Alam, Azad and Husnara (from *Fasana-e Azad*, see chapter 5), and so on. All these are for her evidence that men have created stories according to their will, though never admitting that these were false, imaginary. Whereas, "poor women do not know how to make false puppets and then cover them with a veneer of truth. You judge, which book written by a man should one consider true? Should we consider the stories of women's wiles to be true? What about the whole of the *Bahar Danish*?" (p. 39). In other words, the author rejects the repertoire of stories of women's wiles as, first, invented, and, second, biased because written by men. She argues that the absence of tales written by women is not only due to the lack of women authors, but also to women's inherent truthfulness. But if, on the one hand, textuality is suspect because it has been used to spread lies about women—which are then believed on the strength of the text's own authority (sanad)—on the other hand *this* text, written to "set the record straight", must invoke its own claims to the truth. The way it does so is through the narrator's claims that her oral stories are true because they bear the authority of eyewitness and oral transmission among women.[70] "How do you know?" asks a suspicious Ramrachpal when his wife Sarupi starts telling him about their neighbours' personal affairs. "Do such things ever remain hidden from women?" is her pert reply (p. 7). In the course of the narrative, women speak to each other about their husbands' love, and if they refrain from speaking ill of them for fear that their friends will laugh at their misfortune, the others find out the truth anyway. Besides, maids and servants act as women's extended eyes and ears and report whatever goes on in the male part of the house, in the streets, and in other people's homes. In other words, the oral world of women living in seclusion, far from being cut off and steeped in ignorance, is construed as the realm of true knowledge.

In the case of *Tota Maina*, as we saw, the contest between competing stories became the organizing narrative structure through which claims and counter-claims were mounted and rejected without any resolution. In fact, the banter between the male parrot and the female mynah is one of the chief pleasures of the text. Here the banter between husbands and wives is indeed a pleasure proffered, but the contest of stories is only suggested. In fact, it is only the women characters who tell stories to their husbands. Their specific aim is to change their husbands' views and mend their ways, and in each case storytelling works as a cure.

Before going into the embedded stories, it is worth reflecting on the author's use of the implied audience. As is the case with qissas that have a frame story, the first implied audience is the character the narrator tells the story to, in this case Ramrachpal, who is sitting with his wife Sarupi inside the kotha. But in *Aurat Mard* there is another implied audience who performs the role of a chorus to the narrative—namely, women neighbours, who overhear from within their own homes the dialogue between husband and wife as well as the stories. With their laughter and comments they deflate the arrogant and empty claims of

[70] The first story regards a couple who lives in the same neighbourhood and with whose name they are acquainted, while the second, and much longer, story concerns a Muslim woman in Delhi; but these are only two of the "thousands of tales" that she "remembers" (p. 7).

the male characters and applaud the arguments of women.[71] When, for example, they overhear Ramrachpal's comment that "all women are bad", one of them says: "See what this wretch says, how he pretends to be a gentleman in front of his wife!" Another comments: "What a scoundrel! He himself is immoral [*badchalan*]. He says women are bad but then spends the whole day dressing and perfuming himself in the hope that some woman will be attracted to him" (p. 2). These women, themselves "eyewitnesses" to what neighbourhood men do, provide therefore a further "element of truth" to the wife's narrative and counterbalance the common sense notions upheld by men who, in this way, end up being thoroughly outnumbered. The result of this double implied audience is that while the qissa is ostensibly directed at men so that they can rethink their prejudices and see the truth, it is also directed at women who can "recognize" the truth in what the narrator and the chorus say—a very clever narrative strategy indeed.

In introducing the characters of the first story, the wife gives us a clear indication of the values that all the wifely characters in this text adhere to: "In our neighbourhood there lives a very wealthy man [*rais*], Kripashankar, an Agrawal by caste, of a good family" (p. 3). His forefathers used to be divans before the British came and were in charge of the whole treasury. They were "Rajas" by title, spent huge sums in charity (*kh̲airati*), and supported thousands of poor people. "At home their women were all educated [*parhi likhi*], intelligent, and clever, and old Brahmin pandits used to be employed to teach the girls" (p. 3). The women's authority over the management of the home was absolute, and men would always consult them even on matters of business. Women were much respected, and in turn they thought their men could do no wrong. Kripashankar's paternal grandmother, an intelligent (*aqalmand*), clever, and respected woman, was the head of the household and held it together (p. 5). This, then, is the socio-moral vision of our Agrawal author. Official recognition (through high posts, land grants, and titles) goes hand in hand with extensive charity, which is just as

[71] For example, when Sarupi protests that men leave their wives for the sake of mercenary (*bazari*) women, they exclaim: "What a great answer, well done!" "She is very intelligent [*aqalmand*]" (p. 3). At this point they turn from casual to attentive listeners.

important. Charity is as much a mark of the family's economic and social standing as of its moral fibre: as soon as Kripashankar's grandmother dies and her sons start moving apart, their charities decline, and so does their good name. Further—and this is the point which the embedded stories stress again and again—women are as much part of the household social and moral economy as men, and they often feel more responsible towards the household than men do. Far from speaking from a position of victimhood, then, the narrator speaks from this moral and social certitude. All the embedded stories, stories of ordinary desertion and adultery, place men's infidelity and cruelty to their wives in the wider context of the welfare of the household.

To return to the first embedded story: Kripashankar received a good education from his father and was married to an educated girl, Chandrakunwar, from a good family. She is the first of a gallery of daughters-in-law (bahus) who are beautiful, intelligent, and honest (*nekchalan*), a living disproof of the husband's claim that women are *either* beautiful *or* honest. For, he says, if they were both, no husband would desert his wife (p. 7). After an initial period of great love (*muhabbat*) between husband and wife, Kripashankar's father dies and Kripashankar becomes head of the household. Now he starts indulging in pleasures that endanger the good name of the family. Chandrakunwar is informed by her maids that "pleasure boys" have started coming to the house and she understands that she must act before it is too late. After a direct appeal gains no result, she asks Kripashankar's permission to tell him a story (introducing another story within the embedded story). Once again, this is a story about neighbours, one he does not know but whom she does, immersed as she is in the oral world of women.[72] Needless to say, the neighbour's story closely mirrors Kripashankar's own, with the cautionary message that keeping company with roguish boys (*badvaze launde*) leads to legal action, scandal, bankruptcy, and general ruin. (The scandal is presented very effectively through the voices of the neighbours which a servant faithfully reports to the women's quarter.) Even then, Chandrakunwar

[72] "I've never heard of her", Kripashankar says about the wife of the embedded story. "Who would tell *you*?" is Chandrakunwar's pointed answer, p. 9, emphasis added.

continues, the neighbour did not mend his ways—only, instead of keeping boys, he started keeping prostitutes. "He spent all that his forefathers had put together, mortgaged the house and ended up a pauper" (p. 12). The ghost of bankruptcy—as in the contemporary Hindi novel *Pariksha Guru* (1882) by Srinivas Das—is enough to make this errant young man see the light. Kripashankar stops calling boys to his home, though, just like his neighbour, he stops nurturing one vice only to nurture another.

Clearly, the reason why husbands desert their beautiful, intelligent, and faithful young wives and go on to waste heaps of money on faithless prostitutes is a great puzzle for *Aurat Mard* and its women. In Kripashankar's case, the prostitute he deserts his wife for is an ugly woman of dark complexion, with a flat nose, round eyes, a face marked by smallpox, "worse than your maid Bilaso", Chandrakunwar's maid Nando tells her.[73] The woman used to dance for a mere four rupees for low-caste men and now gives herself airs as a great courtesan and is full of demands (p. 14). The conclusion they reach is a dispirited one: "mankind is nobody's friend but its own, how can a good woman not burn with anger and jealousy?" (p. 15). Collective wisdom is invoked in the form of sayings: "Men are like that: they forsake a plate of kheer for the sake of millet pudding"; "Molasses from the shop taste sweeter than home-made sugar"; "Just like faqirs, they get addicted to eating morsels of food from different houses: even if you feed them to the full, they will still go and beg elsewhere" (p. 14). What these sayings signify, though, is that men are foolishly fascinated by what they do not possess: "they are in love with these women as long as they stay in the profession. As soon as the men set them up in a house they stop respecting them and start looking for someone else" (pp. 14–15).

The only person who can stop Kripashankar from ruin is, in fact, another woman—his mother. Chandrakunwar, who still refuses to complain about her husband, is reduced to a skeleton, though he takes no notice. Kripashankar's mother, however, first chides him by saying that men in their family have never shown such disrespect and

[73] All the women, including women servants, are named in this text—a very unusual feature in qissas. As we know, naming is usually a way of conferring individuality: thus even the attendant figures in the world of the women's quarter are recognized as playing a role.

disregard for their women, "and this is why our household still survives until today" (p. 17). Then she employs her strongest weapon: she asks to be allowed to go to a pilgrimage place and to not come back—ostensibly so that he can carry on as he pleases. But Kripashankar knows perfectly well that her permanent departure will bring ill repute (*badnami*) and would be a kind of moral death for him. So, when Chandrakunwar announces her intention to join his mother on the pilgrimage, he decides to accompany them—which is what his mother had hoped for all along. Before they return home, husband and wife have a spirited argument in which Chandrakunwar gains the upper hand.[74] She has him swear that he will never behave in the same way again.[75] It is thus women—wife and mother—who save Kripashankar from ruin and give the first story a happy ending. And whereas in *Pariksha Guru* the wayward young merchant is saved, and admonished, largely by his lawyer friend while his own admirable wife gives a silent helping hand, in *Kissa Aurat Mard* women both save and lecture their wayward men.

The second part of the qissa is wholly taken up by the story of Khurshaid Begam and her husband Nawab Manjhle (or Manjhle Miyan, as the less respectful characters in the story call him). If the stories in the first part deal with wealthy Hindu merchant families, the second story deals with the social world of the Muslim *ashraf*, the other prominent section of the urban elite.[76] The second story, though much longer,

[74] "It is a thousand times better for a wife to die than to be deserted", she declares. Kripashankar: "But scores of women do not care about their husbands at all." "That may be, but what should a woman whose aim in life is to look after her husband do if he deserts her?" Kripashankar: "She should leave him." "No woman from a good family will do so", is her reply, "for the sake of the family honour" (p. 19). In other words, the wife's ideal is not so much to serve her husband, whatever he may do—which is the usual understanding of the pativrata ideal—but to behave in a way that will protect the *family*'s honour.

[75] The narrator's wry comment is that Kripashankar was next to the Ganges when he swore, so he could not go back on his promise; normally, men break their oaths very easily (p. 20). Note the extensive use of false oaths between courtesans and their clients, for example in Devkinandan Khatri's detective novel *Kajar ki Kothri* (1902), see ch. 7 below.

[76] The story is prompted by Sarupi's chance remark that "such men are rare among Hindus but there are many among Muslims" (p. 20). Earlier, when,

closely resembles the first in terms of plot, characters, and the common ethos of elite families—repetition strengthens the author's argument. With its larger set of characters, more elaborate narrative, and greater focus on Khurshaid's thoughts and feelings, the qissa really gestures towards the new novelistic form—a form which the author must have known since she was familiar with Ratannath Sarshar's *Fasana-e Azad*, serialized only a few years earlier (see chapter 5).

Once again, the story begins by describing in precise terms the socio-economic setting of both male and female characters, and the webs of locality and friendship in which economic wealth is transient and what really counts is a good name.[77] When Manjhle Miyan, the second son of a nawab in somewhat straitened circumstances, but of good name, is suggested as a match for Khurshaid, the beautiful, bright, and accomplished only child of a rich nawab and his intelligent wife, her mother and father readily agree. A rather long subplot running through a fourth of the story involves the meetings of the affianced two after the match is arranged between their families. Plentiful detail and playful banter between the couple and their servants, and exchanges of soulful poetic messages all provide a significant pleasure in the text and show romantic fiction exerting a powerful pull. Manjhle behaves with all the restlessness of a true 'ashiq, while Khurshaid's longing is more subdued because of her modesty (*sharam*), so that the only way she can show her assent is by remaining silent, without protest. A meeting arranged at a local Sufi shrine—so that the two can catch a glimpse of each other—results in a comedy scene between the two women servants, Manjhle Miyan's *malin* and Khurshaid's *mughlani*, each eager to display her loyalty. That such a romantic twist

---

discussing the issue of "boys", her husband had protested that "Hindus have never praised the beauty of boys in their poems". She had replied, "Here we are not talking about Hindus and Muslims at all, here we are talking about men and women", p. 12.

[77] Manjhle Miyan's father lives in Kucha Mir Ashaq; reduced to an income of Rs 8000 a year after a grand past, the family still has a good name. In the words of an acquaintance "they live off renting properties, but the heart and mind are still the same. Thank God they are not beggars yet, they have all they need [*Allah ka diya hua sab kuchh hai*]": p. 23.

sits awkwardly in a tale about women's virtue is remarked upon by Ramrachpal, the husband of the frame story—"So you mean women help other women meet men?" (p. 38).[78] And while Manjhle falls completely in love after the first brief glance, Khurshaid reflects more wisely: "if only his character matches his good looks . . ." (p. 42).

The narrative glides quickly over the wedding, their first few happy years, and their first child to reach the onset of the crisis when Manjhle Miyan begins to change. "His heart began to lose interest in the dinner spread out at home and craved instead to lick other people's pans . . . Now as soon as he saw an ugly but youthful woman he would start drooling at the mouth" (p. 42). Once again, serious trouble starts only when the young and now wealthy husband gets into family money, in this case after the sudden death of Khurshaid's parents. The plot runs along familiar lines. Manjhle indulges in his pleasures unfettered and pays no heed to Khurshaid's attempts at reasoning with him. For weeks on end he stops going into the *mahalsara*, her part of the house, and when he goes he claims to have a headache in order to avoid her. A second attempt at giving him "good advice" ("a wife is to her husband like a vazir to the king", p. 48) results in a bitter argument. His hangers-on embroil him more and more in the company of low-born musicians and singers,[79] and, when an actress comes to town with a troupe, Nawab Manjhle is impudent enough to marry her on the spot, only to quickly tire of her, divorce her, and take in a prostitute instead. The height of disrepute, and an electrifying moment in the story, is reached when the two bazaar women fight inside the family courtyard (*divan-khana*), while Khurshaid watches stoically from her window (p. 55).

This is when Khurshaid decides to act, realizing that the only way to save the family from ruin is to separate Manjhle from the ancestral

[78] Sarupi retorts than men do not think twice about putting their honour in jeopardy, but then adds that there is no objection in the betrothed seeing one another before the wedding: p. 38.

[79] All musicians are lumped together as "bad characters", from *kalawants* to "randis, accompanists [*bharve*, also "pimps"], Kathak dancers, Khyal singers who sit in the house of bhang drinkers", p. 48. For the low social reputation of musicians and singers, see Katherine Brown, 'If Music be the Food of Love: Music, Masculinity and Eroticism in the Mughal Mehfil', in F. Orsini (ed.), *Love in South Asia*, pp. 61–86.

property over which she has ultimate control (*akhtiyar*). This supports Sarupi's claim that wives take better care of wealth than stupid husbands. Women may not produce wealth, but they keep it and spend it wisely. They spend generously when the family's reputation and honour are at stake (ceremonies, charity), or for the upbringing of children; they avoid wasting it in pursuit of pointless pleasures (*fizul vahiyat kharch*, p. 50). Sarupi's comment is important because it asserts the economic role of women from a traditional perspective: whereas the reformist emphasis was on thrift and the curtailing of "wasteful" expenditure at weddings and other family ceremonies, for this text such expenses, just like charity, are part and parcel of the social reproduction of the family.

Help comes to Khurshaid in the guise of old and faithful family retainers: acting on Khurshaid's authority, her old manager Divan Ramachand takes charge of the keys to the treasury (*khazana*), with the polite excuse that Manjhle Miyan is too busy and tired to look after the accounts. In the elaborate fiction of etiquette and politeness that follows, and that forbids Manjhle to fight with a dependant, Khurshaid finally gains the upper hand. Her arguments with Manjhle on the best use of money in order to increase one's social standing, on the balance between what God has fated and what man can achieve on his own initiative, and on the meaning of entertainment, all echo those between Sarupi and Ramrachpal. Manjhle is still unrepentant, but meanwhile Khurshaid has saved the family finances. Only the divan's advice to "follow the customs which have come down from old and from our forefathers" (p. 75) —which partly echoes the lawyer friend's in *Pariksha Guru*—has any impact on Manjhle, and soon the couple is reconciled within a happy ending. *Aurat Mard* itself ends on a conciliatory tone, and rather abruptly with a casual reference to the context of the narrative performance—it is after all late at night and any further story or discussion will have to wait until tomorrow. Once again, though, the last word belongs to the wife, Sarupi: "Men who think that women are bad and who attribute all sorts of faults to women are themselves riddled with faults. Excellent men believe that the only difference between men and women is one of gender [*jins*]; they do not consider women on a level with cattle [*bher bakri*, p. 75]".

Kissa Aurat Mard is a remarkable text that deserves to be more widely known as one of the earliest fictional narratives written by women in nineteenth-century North India. What is striking is that the author uses the commercially successful genre of men-and-women stories to convey her own, very specific and very gendered, view. While the author's desire to remain anonymous does not surprise us in the context of seclusion for respectable women, it is still remarkable that this Jain woman, who had clearly read and listened to Hindi and Urdu qissas, should decide to write her own qissa to counteract notions underpinning the texts she had encountered. The chorus of female neighbours who agree with the female characters and narrators of the stories all combine to create a strong voice for secluded women—the women who are usually missing from our picture of North Indian society at this time, or who are present only voicelessly.

Between Two Scripts

The overview of texts presented in this chapter highlights the range and dynamism of the qissa genre in the second half of the nineteenth century, and its active interaction with other forms of entertainment such as songs and plays. As Kumkum Sangari has perceptively remarked, "With the advent of mass publishing in the Hindustani belt, the Hindi/Urdu qissa became more capacious, it mingled and transformed various repertoires—oral, written, Persian, Arabic, Sanskritic. It enfolded multiple linguistic dialects and was intersected by several narrative traditions—folktale, theatrical forms like *sangit*, and even reformist prescription." Indeed, as she points out, a "literary history of the nineteenth century would be incomplete without the *qissa*."[80] While the shortest qissa texts at the cheapest end of the book market were among the simplest texts for neo-literates and favoured the farcical mode of the naql, the longer qissa texts gestured towards the novel, whether of adventure, romance, or instruction—in the case of *Kissa Aurat Mard*, for example, a combination of the last two. In this light qissas appear, very much like the early novels, as a kind of laboratory of narrative discourses.

With the exception of *Kissa Aurat Mard*, all the qissas noted above were printed in both Urdu and Devanagari. While the publisher's intention must have been purely commercial—to reach the widest

[80] Sangari, 'Multiple Temporalities', p. 213.

possible readership—this apparently simple act had significant consequences. While in the case of the oral tradition of folktales we surmise that it covered a broad and mixed spectrum of tales, in the case of printed qissas we know that the same audience read or listened to tales about princes and paris, King Vikram and the vampire, the soldier's son and the attractive innkeeper (*bhatiyari*). In the case of the oral tradition, we can imagine that it was a composite repertoire, while in the case of printed tales we can be sure of this. As we have seen, the anonymous author of the Hindi *Kissa Aurat Mard* was well familiar with the Urdu repertoire as well.

In most cases, publication in the other script involved only a simple transliteration which left all the vocabulary intact.[81] In other, much rarer, cases it involved a wholesale translation, which in Hindi could include a thorough sanskritization of register and the conversion of she'rs into dohas and kabitts.[82] Unlike the authors and publishers of "modern genres" like the novel, who eagerly explained their initiatives to their readers in detailed prefaces,[83] the publishers and translators of qissas did not go beyond the standard phrase "rendered with much effort". Therefore we can only speculate about the reasons behind such opposite translation strategies for the same texts, namely that two very different language ideologies were at play. Those who favoured plain transliteration must have believed that the script was the only obstacle to an otherwise common language. Those who changed the whole vocabulary probably subscribed to a view of Hindi and Urdu as two

[81] E.g. the Devanagari version of *Qissa Sipahizada* published by the Matba Ijad Kishan of Agra in 1872 and by Pyarelal of the Matba' Hindu Press in Delhi in 1874 [OIOLC: VT 1167].

[82] In the case of the Hindi translations of the popular *Fasana-e 'Ajaib* (1824), this included even the title, changed to *Mohani Charitra* and *Apurva Katha*. *Mohani Charitra*, trans. Pran Krishna, Delhi, 1869, pp. 180; *Apurv Katha*, tr. Ram Rattan Bajpeyi, Lucknow: Nawal Kishore, 1886, pp. 108, printed, 3rd edn (1200), 3 annas.

[83] E.g. the preface by Lala Srinivas Das to *Pariksha Guru* (1882), translated and analysed by Vasudha Dalmia in 'A Novel Moment in Hindi', in T. Damsteegt and V. Dalmia (eds), *Narrative Strategies*, Delhi: Oxford University Press, 1999, pp. 169–84.

separate literary languages that required different registers altogether. Thus, the two translation strategies for qissas show that while readers of qissas like *Tota Maina* were familiar with a substantial Hindi and Urdu vocabulary, a sanskritized register for written Hindi was finding its way into print among entertainment genres as well.

An important consequence of the translation traffic was that it produced a different kind of intertextuality from that prevalent in most Indian literary traditions. While intertextuality and translation flows are well attested to all levels and in all periods of Indian literature, usually the translation or adaptation involved a thorough *transcodification* into the language, register, and genre one had chosen. In other words, while Faizi's Persian version of the Nala and Damayanti story is explicit about the source of the narrative, the text in its presentation, discourse, and language fully adheres to the genre chosen by the Persian author, a literary masnavi. Similarly, the Punjabi qissas about Layla-Majnun and Shirin-Farhad may retell the story of distant Arabian and Persian characters, but their style and language are wholly consistent with the local qissas of Sassi-Punnun or Hir-Ranjha.[84] This kind of transcodification and assimilation of the source narrative into the target language and genre could be said to be the hallmark of literary intertextuality in India until the nineteenth century,[85] though of course a certain diglossia was also admitted—as between the introduction and the anecdotes in naql collections. As I have suggested earlier, the intertextuality of the qissas, especially of the later, more elaborate ones such as *Kissa Tota Maina*, is of an altogether different kind, much closer to that of the theatrical forms with which these qissas

[84] See e.g. Muzaffar Alam and Sanjay Subrahmanyan, 'Love, Passion and Reason in Faizi's *Nal-Daman*', in F. Orsini (ed.), *Love in South Asia*, pp. 109–41; Jeevan S. Deol, 'Love and Mysticism in the Punjabi *Qissas* of the Seventeenth and Eighteenth Centuries', unpublished M.Phil. thesis, School of Oriental and African Studies, University of London, 1996, and 'Acceptable Poetry: Muqbil's Mystical *Qiṣṣah Hīr Rānjhā*', *International Journal of Punjabi Studies* 3.2 (1996): 181–210.

[85] Which is why *rekhta* poetry that kept the two languages and registers of Persian and Hindi/Braj Bhasha apart, "macheronic poetry" as Imre Bangha has called it, is such an interesting and striking exception; see ch. 2.

clearly intersected. Though *Kissa Tota Maina* appears to be similar in content and form to story collections like *Shuk Bahattari*, a striking departure is the fact that the register, vocabulary, and verse quotations—both in the frame story of the parrot and the mynah and in the embedded tales—vary substantially. They range from moderately sanskritized to colloquial Urdu/Hindi, to literary Urdu in the rekhtas and she'rs, to a hybrid Braj Bhasha/Khari Boli on occasion, and to literary Braj Bhasha in the kabitt and songs quoted in some tales.[86] The same hybridity, we have seen, is found at the level of narrative and character. Not only is the range of register, poetic form, and narrative tradition wider in *Tota Maina* than ever before, but this heterogeneous linguistic and narrative range is written down without any attempt at homogenization.

Taken together with the hybridity of language and verse forms of contemporary songbooks and theatrical plays, this is proof that the translation traffic of qissas, theatre chapbooks, and song collections produced a repertoire that was intrinsically heterogeneous, and a public comfortable with such heterogeneity; in fact a public that most probably enjoyed this "assortment of pleasures". It was a linguistic pleasure that differed from the more highly literary pleasures of alliteration and other figures of speech and of thought, rhyming prose, and bountiful descriptions (of body, nature, war, etc.) of Sanskrit or Hindi courtly poetry and Persian or Persianized verse or ornate prose. These pleasures did not disappear. They were in fact valued and actively furthered by other writers, from Ratannath Sarshar to Bankimchandra.[87] But the pleasures offered by qissas such as *Tota Maina*, while less sophisticated, cannot be underestimated because they were accessible to the 'avam, the "common people" who were becoming more and more literate. The accessibility and entertainment value of these texts made reading and literacy all the more widespread, while the enduring

[86] See e.g. the language the goddess Parvati speaks on p. 10.

[87] For a discussion of beauty (*rupa*) in Bankimchandra, see Sudipta Kaviraj, 'Tagore and Transformations in the Ideals of Love', in F. Orsini (ed.), *Love in South Asia*, pp. 161–82. For Sarshar's pursuit of Persianized prose and Persian verse in *Fasana-e Azad*, see ch. 5 below.

dual oral-literate transmission systems eased the transition to the printed page.

In the remainder of this book I will consider three kinds of novels which, while differing sharply from the familiar experience of qissas and songs, became nonetheless "texts of pleasure" and managed to introduce readers to the new conventions of novelistic narration.

5

Generic Instability and Social Mobility

Pandit Ratannath Dar Sarshar's *Fasana-e Azad*

Thus far, we have seen commercial publishers successfully meet the challenges of low literacy and embodied pleasures by reproducing in print those genres that were connected to existing oral and visual pleasures, such as songs, qissas, and barahmasas.[1] These lithographed texts continued oral practices through voiced reading, retained the syntax of oral storytelling, and shunned high literariness in favour of a simpler style. Visually, lithographed booklets reproduced the hand of calligraphers and, in Urdu books, the "look" of earlier manuscript books. Hindi lithographed books introduced new conventions, such as paragraphs and indenting, and their copyists' hands strained to reproduce the standard look of type fonts. In terms of poetic tastes and narrative repertoires, songbooks and qissas were strikingly eclectic, partly because they continued performers' traditions, but also because they were printed in both scripts, thereby creating a common pool of forms and motifs. As a result, songs and tales evolved towards even greater eclecticism, and included a range of linguistic

[1] My thanks to David Lelyveld for his careful reading and invaluable comments on a previous draft of this chapter, and to audiences at seminars in Leicester, Sussex, and SOAS where that draft was first presented. I would also like to thank Jennifer Dubrow for generously letting me quote from her unpublished paper, sharing her discovery on the date of publication of novels, and painstakingly checking my Urdu translations and page references.

dialects and written registers within the same song or tale. These genres met with great favour among neo-literate groups and circulated well in towns and in the countryside through booksellers' stalls at fairs.

Parallel to these developments, education was creating an audience for books, a space for prose fiction and new generic expectations among both authors and readers. It is well known that the first Urdu novel, *Mir'at ul-'Urus* (The Bride's Mirror, 1869) by a Deputy Inspector of Schools for the North-Western Provinces, Nazir Ahmad (1830–1912), was initially written for his own daughters. After publication and the award of a government prize, it started a whole trend in educational novels, especially for girls.[2] Although the title suggested an advice-book for women to be given as a gift in preparation for married life, and the content of the book certainly warranted this notion, the novel did much more than that: it contained a story with both everyday events and dramatic upheavals, it had lively and recognizable characters, and it took pleasure in reproducing ordinary dialogue and familiar exchanges between girls. While other "first novels" found it hard to attract readers, *Mir'at ul-'Urus* was reprinted many times, totalling 100,000 copies by 1889.[3] And while the relationship between education and reading for pleasure remained as fraught in North India as elsewhere, it is certainly true that fictional narratives like *Bagh-o Bahar* and *Mir'at ul-'Urus* were allowed as reading matter for schoolchildren, when not part of the syllabus.[4] Thus, young men and women educated at

[2] See C.M. Naim, 'Prize-Winning *Adab*', in *Urdu Texts and Contexts*, New Delhi: Permanent Black, 2004, pp. 120–50; and Meenakshi Mukherjee, 'Novels of Purpose', in *Realism and Reality: The Novel and Society in India*, Delhi: Oxford University Press, 1985. A new edition of *The Bride's Mirror* carries a useful Afterword by Frances Pritchett: 'The First Urdu Bestseller', *The Bride's Mirror*, New Delhi: Permanent Black, 2001. For the influence of Nazir Ahmad's novel on Hindi, see Amrik Kalsi, 'Realism in the Hindi Novel', unpublished Ph.D. thesis, University of Cambridge, 1975, and Lise Smith, "Transmission and Reconstruction: The Role of Translated Texts in the Development of the Novel in Hindi, 1890–1920', unpublished Ph.D. thesis, University of Cambridge, 2005.

[3] Pritchett, 'Afterword. The First Urdu Bestseller', p. 204.

[4] On anxieties about mass literacy and novel-reading in nineteenth-century Britain, see Patrick Brantlinger, *The Reading Lesson*, Bloomington: University

government schools, at maktabs, pathshalas, at home, or at a combination of the three, not only acquired familiarity with printed books but also became potential readers who were ready for something else besides qissas and dastans. The popularity of the sensational novels by G.W.M. Reynolds, read in English but also widely translated in these decades, especially in Urdu, should be seen in the context of this burgeoning audience and of the new habits and expectations that education in the colonial context encouraged.[5]

It is in this framework that the novels analysed in this chapter and the next acquire particular interest, for they represent not only the conscious and successful engagement of educated writers with the commercial book market, but also famously document the familiarization of new readers with the novel form by means of narratives serialized as newspaper instalments. Both Ratannath Dar Sarshar (1846–1902) and Devkinandan Khatri (1861–1913) had received formal education and read their dastans as well as G.W.M. Reynolds.[6] Sarshar's *Fasana-e Azad* and Khatri's *Chandrakanta* were written with the commercial print market in mind: *Fasana-e Azad* (1878–85) was

---

of Indian Press, 1998. For the hostile attitude of Italian schooling towards pleasurable reading, see Ermanno Detti, *Il piacere di leggere*, Firenze: la Nuova Italia, 2002, new edition. For the popularity of *Bag̱h-o Bahar* in print, see fn. 100 in the Introduction.

[5] In her study of Hindi and Urdu translations of Reynolds's novels, Lise Smith has argued that "popular fiction (in the generic sense) becomes popular (in the quantitative sense) . . . because these texts satisfied the existing desires and expectations of their new Indian audience while simultaneously foreign novelties." She argues that "the two situations—the propensity for Indian authors to draw on pre-novel modes of description, characterisation and narration, and the widespread consumption of popular (or 'mediocre') fiction among readers and authors—are related to each other and also to the long-standing indigenous narrative traditions available to authors and readers in 19th century India": Lise Smith, 'The Mysteries of Translation. GWM Reynolds and the Development of the Novel in Hindi 1900–1920', unpublished M.Phil. thesis, University of Cambridge, 2001, p. 1. For Reynolds's popularity in English, see Priya Joshi, *In Another Country: Colonialism, Culture, and the English Novel in India*, New York: Columbia University Press, 2002.

[6] See Qamar Rais, *Ratan Nath Sarshar*, New Delhi: Sahitya Akademi, 1991, and Madhuresh, *Devkinandan Khatri*, New Delhi: Sahitya Akademi, 1980.

serialized in the Urdu daily *Avadh Akhbar* over the time Sarshar was the paper's editor. *Chandrakanta* spawned a commercial publishing house, the Lahari Press in Banaras (see chapter 6). The authors of both novels became professional novelists and capitalized on the success of their first fictions by running sequels. Unlike "novels of purpose" and other experimental "first novels" that set education and/or social reform as the chief aim of the narrative,[7] *Fasana-e Azad* and *Chandrakanta* subordinated ideas of social reform to a combination of pleasures and aesthetics: the older pleasures and aesthetics connected to tales and poetry, and the new pleasures and aesthetics of the novel—namely suspense, uncertainty regarding character and plot, verisimilitude of settings and characters, and so on. For example, while *Fasana-e Azad* was read both aloud and silently, just like qissas, it nevertheless surprised its readers with the characterization of its protagonists and the situations it placed them in—as we shall see.

As a consequence, even more than the earnest first novels, *Fasana-e Azad* and *Chandrakanta* display to a high degree what Michael McKeon has called "generic instability". This notion has been adumbrated in critical discussions of the often hybrid nature of early novels in India. Moving away from a simple paradigm of "foreign import"—in which the novelty lay all in the alien "original" genre and which Indian novelists copied but imperfectly, and to which they only added local colour—scholars like Meenakshi Mukherjee have stressed the importance of local genealogies and of reading early Indian novels against the grain, against their own declarations of imitative intent.[8] McKeon's notion of "generic instability" stems from a more general

[7] See Srinivas Das's "first" Hindi novel, *Pariksha Guru* (Experience is the Best Teacher, 1882); cf. Vasudha Dalmia, 'A Novel Moment in Hindi: *Parīkṣā Gurū*', in T. Damsteegt and V. Dalmia (eds), *Narrative Strategies*, pp. 169–84.

[8] "The assumption that the novel in India was a borrowed genre—the indirect outcome of English education introduced in the nineteenth century by the British rulers—had remained unquestioned for a long time. From 1860 onward, the fictional texts written in different Indian languages that were identified as novels came to be evaluated largely in terms of their closeness to Western models. The canon legitimized by literary historians was constructed on the unarticulated premise that there was a universal paradigm of novel writing, and because it began in Europe, all subsequent practitioners would need to be judged by the standards set there... It is only very recently, in the last couple of

attempt to explain the particular social and cultural mediations that genres perform, and the dialectical relationship between genres at any given point in history. We can first think of genres as providing "a conceptual framework for the mediation (if not the 'solution') of intractable problems, a method for rendering such problems intelligible", as McKeon suggests. Further, we can think of the novel emerging in early modern Europe in a *dialectical* relation with previously existing genres like the romance. From these vantage points we are led to conclude that the novel—which came into existence in order to mediate the change in attitudes towards epistemology (what McKeon calls "questions of truth") and towards social categories (what he calls "questions of virtue")—must reflect that instability. It is therefore not surprising, McKeon suggests, that European novels of the seventeenth and eighteenth centuries, far from projecting a simple "ideology of the novel" (representing the rising middle class, as in Ian Watt's original formulation), "should seem a contradictory amalgam of inconsistent elements".[9] McKeon not only debunks the idea of some pure or authentic model of the novel in Europe—which colonial writers then imperfectly adapted—but also urges us to explore which particular dialectical relationship early novels in India entertain with other genres, and which particular social and cultural mediations they are called upon to perform. Accordingly, I will not focus on the "local genealogies" of *Fasana-e Azad*, but rather on its formal and narrative innovations, all the while asking which social mediations the novel seeks to perform. In particular, I will argue that there is a clear link between narrative mobility in this picaresque novel and questions of

decades to be exact, that critics have begun to address themselves to the complex question of plural heritage, the multiplicity of determinants—that overlapped, interacted, and fused to make the shaping of this literary form a tangled and unique process in India… *The early novels in India need to be read closely, sometimes against the grain, to go beyond their state intentions and pry open the operations of the other, often subterranean forces in their formation*": Meenakshi Mukherjee, 'Epic and Novel in India', in Franco Moretti (ed.), *The Novel*, vol. 1, Princeton: Princeton University Press, 2006, p. 596, emphasis added.

[9] Michael McKeon, *The Origins of the English Novel*, Baltimore: Johns Hopkins University Press, 1987, pp. 20–1; Ian Watt, *The Rise of the Novel*, London: Penguin, 1957.

social mobility, as well as sharafat, that agitated North Indian society at this time and found their way into this entertaining novel. As David Lelyveld has argued, "*sharif* culture" was a "common vocabulary" for a wide range of professional and landed groups from a variety of social and ethnic backgrounds, geographic localities, and religious affiliations: for all of them the "*kachehri* milieu" provided a nexus in the wide and interlocking network of social relations and economic interests.[10] While sharif status was in theory based on birth and could only be inherited, Margrit Pernau has remarked that "this group would also include all those, whose social status denoted so much respectability that they could successfully claim foreign descent. Thus, within limits, it was lineage that followed status, and not the other way round." As a nineteenth-century saying went: "Last year I was a Julaha, a weaver, this year I am a Sheikh and next year, if prices rise, I shall be a Syed."[11] The many publications and debates on adab (culture, etiquette) and sharafat signal the urgent need to re-evaluate these terms and the values they denoted in terms of status, birth, and/or personal conduct in times of political, economic, and social upheaval.[12] *Fasana-e Azad* intervened in this debate on sharafat—though, typically for a novel, it offered varied points of view. I will be guided in this exploration by the narrative elements and characterization within the novel, as well as by the author's own running commentary and readers' letters: the latter offer a unique evidence of reception.

Fasana-e Azad as a Picaresque Novel

Fasana-e Azad (The Tale of Azad) was the first attempt at novel-writing by Pandit Ratannath Dar "Sarshar" ("Brimful"), a Kashmiri Pandit whose family had settled in the Kashmiri enclave (*mohalla*) of

[10] David Lelyveld, '"*Sharif*" Culture and British Rule', *Aligarh's First Generation*, pp. 35–101, especially p. 64.

[11] Margrit Pernau, 'Middle Class and Secularization: The Muslims of Delhi in the Nineteenth Century', in I. Ahmad and H. Reifeld (eds), *Middle Class Values in India and Western Europe*, New Delhi: Social Science Press, 2001, p. 23.

[12] Cf. the second story of Khurshaid Begum and Manjhle Miyan in *Kissa Aurat Mard*, ch. 4 above.

Lucknow.[13] Sarshar's father was a prominent merchant who died when Ratannath was only four years old. Ratannath was sent to a maktab to learn Arabic and Persian at the age of five, and then studied for a while at Canning College, where he learnt some English. Urdu writers and critics have tended to project onto him the qualities of his fictional hero: thus, Chakbast describes him as "free" from a young age, keen on Urdu and Persian poetry, and an early liquor addict. After becoming a teacher in the district Government School of Khiri, Sarshar began to send articles and satirical pieces to several Urdu journals, including *Avadh Panch* in Lucknow. He is reputed to have been a good translator from English into Urdu as well: he is said to have translated Cervantes's *Don Quixote* as *Khuda Faujdar*, which would partly explain his choice of the picaresque form.

Appointed editor of the Naval Kishore Urdu daily *Avadh Akhbar* in 1878, Sarshar had to write most of the paper himself, as was often the case with newspapers at the time, and decided to intersperse political news and articles with sketches and vignettes of contemporary urban life.[14] These humorous sketches, called *zarafat* (witticism), were writ-ten in a mixture of ornate and colloquial registers and became the nucleus of the novel, which was serialized daily in the paper from September 1878 to immediate acclaim.[15] The first volume came out in 1880, and, according to two chronograms at the end of the second and fourth volumes of the second print edition (1887)—Jennifer Dubrow has recently ascertained—the second volume came out in 1881 and the fourth in 1883.[16] Sarshar simultaneously started

[13] Rais, *Ratan Nath Sarshar*. For Kashmiri Pandits in Lucknow, see Stark, *An Empire of Books*, pp. 78–9.

[14] The newspaper was started as a weekly paper in 1858, it became a daily in 1877; Stark, *An Empire of Books*, ch. 6.

[15] First under the heading *Zarafat* from 23 September 1878, and under the title *Fasana-e Azad* from 1 July 1880, with the start of the second series: Firoze Mookerjee, *Lucknow and the World of Sarshar*, Karachi: Saad Publications, 1992, p. 79. Quotations from *Fasana-e Azad* are from the paperback edition, published by the Qaumi Kaunsil Barae Furugh-e Urdu Zaban, New Delhi, 1984–6; readers' letters and quotations marked suppl. or by a simple date are from the supplement within *Avadh Akhbar* at the British Library.

[16] Stark, *An Empire of Books*, dates volumes 1 and 2 to 1880, volume 3 to

another novel, *Fasana-e Jadid Aka Jam-e Sarshar* (The New Tale, or Sarshar's Cup) in June 1880.[17] Altogether, *Fasana-e Azad* runs to four parts over six volumes for a total of about 4000 pages, and it marked the beginning, and perhaps also the climax, of novel serialization in a newspaper. The novel's great length was certainly a result of daily serialization, but it was also functional to its narrative structure as a picaresque novel, and probably also due to the great popularity of the printed Urdu dastans (see Introduction).

That Sarshar should have chosen the picaresque novel warrants exploration since, to my knowledge, there are only a few such examples in Urdu after him.[18] What we see in *Fasana-e Azad* is the sketch of the "man about town", not unusual in colonial satirical literature, developed beyond measure into a sustained and composite narrative.[19] In the context of seventeenth-century Europe, McKeon notes that picaresque novels could represent either a progressive ideology (when the hero embodies the positive ideology of the new man) or a conservative one, as in the Spanish *Lazarillo de Tormes*, where the critique of the old aristocratic ideology with its arbitrary justice is matched by the equally arbitrary rise of the rogue hero. We will come back to whether Azad represents the positive ideology of the new man or not. McKeon also points out that the European picaresque novel of the seventeenth century is a literary form "peculiarly responsive to the crisis of status

---

1883, and volume 4 to 1887 (Appendix IV); I am grateful to Jennifer Dubrow for sharing this information with me.

[17] After five instalments, the publisher decided to print it as a separate supplement of 12–16 pages, for which readers had to pay an extra 8 annas per month. Despite that, the supplements sold well and demand exceeded supply. *Fasana-e Jadid* is a shorter novel, running into "only" 500 pages: Mookerjee, *Lucknow*, p.164.

[18] Dilip Menon has argued that peregrinations are part of the early low-caste novel in Malayalam as part of a process of reinvention of identity of low-caste protagonists: Dilip Menon, 'A Place Elsewhere: Lower-caste Malayalam Novels of the Nineteenth Century', in S. Blackburn and V. Dalmia (eds), *India's Literary History*, pp. 483–515.

[19] Other satirical heroes are opium-addicted Brahmins like Bankimchandra's Kamalakanta, and Balmukund Gupta's Shivshambhu of *Shivshambhu ke Chitthe*. I am grateful to Jennifer Dubrow for this suggestion.

inconsistency that was felt in different ways throughout early modern Europe." Thus, the picaresque anti-hero Lazarillo de Tormes "begins his life in the unstable and supremely mobile condition of an orphan, ripe for the discovery of aristocratic parentage but also for self-creation."[20] Though not represented as an orphan, nothing is known of Azad's parentage either, although he definitely considers himself a sharif and is considered so by others.

Typical of picaresque novels is the loose narrative structure and the focus on the street. The chapters of *Fasana-e Azad* are short and, in most cases, start with Azad waking up early in the morning when the cock crows, eager to go out into the street. He either meets someone or is attracted by a gathering or an event, which usually does not carry into the next chapter: if the episode is not over, it is left incomplete, and the next chapter starts with a fresh morning and a fresh adventure. This very loose open structure lasts midway through the first volume, when a continuous narrative begins to evolve: hence we can see the narrative structure change before our eyes.[21]

The novel's debt to the zarafat sketches is evident not only in this episodic and situation-centred structure, but also in the prominence given to spoken language and its pleasures. As Meenakshi Mukherjee has pointed out in her seminal study of the early novel in India, writers making the attempt had to grapple both with the new narrative form and the new use of prose. Both attempts are in evidence in this novel. Language works as an important structuring device, and multivocality, in Bakhtin's sense, is one of the main pleasures offered by the

[20] McKeon, *Origins*, p. 238.

[21] For example, Dubrow suggests, when Bi Allah Rakhi reappears later in the first volume, Sarshar is careful to connect her to previous episodes by making her the young woman who wrote an abusive letter to her old husband. She suggests that the structure is looser in the beginning of the first volume, before Sarshar knew the sketches would be so successful. By the time Bi Allah Rakhi returns into the plot, Sarshar knew that *Fasana-e Azad* would be a more sustained narrative. A continuous narrative comes together when Azad agrees to go to Turkey: after that, for example, even when the episode has nothing to do with it, continuous references are made to his imminent departure: Jennifer Dubrow, personal communication.

text—one recognized both by contemporaries and later readers.[22] The ability to speak well and deploy quick repartee is of course culturally valued in this milieu as eloquence (*fasahat*). Persian and Urdu she'rs and entire ghazals dot almost every page, certainly every polite gathering. The characters themselves are very attentive to language registers and use language as a marker of status. Their speech immediately reveals social standing. What is striking is the really wide range: instead of seeking a particular register for prose,[23] or else employing the ornate style of Perso-Urdu *belles-lettres* (*insha*), Sarshar shifts registers constantly. An ornate, Persianized style is used when Azad has to impress someone, or else in passages relating to poetry or to love, or else for mock-comic purposes. This moves down, along various gradations, to the very colloquial and idiomatic Hindi register of female and "lowly" characters, whose speech is reproduced with great relish—the forms evident in masnavis and qissas. Whereas in Urdu naql collections high literate and colloquial registers were distinctly apportioned to the frame and the short tales, in this novel they appear in a much more fluid and mixed way. Azad can recite Persian verse and shout earthy abuse, depending upon the occasion.

Franco Moretti has noted that the primary characteristic of the novel is its ability to mediate between "high" and "low", between sophisticated and popular cultural forms, characters, language, and values. *Fasana-e Azad* does this very actively, and to a very high degree. As a picaresque novel, most of the action takes place in the street. There are many descriptions of fairs, street activities, and performers—as also in the essays by Sarshar's contemporary and competitor Sharar.[24] Most descriptions, though, tend to be generic and consist of cumulative detail: at a poetry gathering there will always be (unspecified) "moon-faced" beauties (i.e. courtesans), gentlemen swaying drunk with wine and poetry, old men with white beards, and young dandies with locks

[22] Premchand, 'Sharar aur Sarshar', *Urdu-e Mo'alla* (1909), in A. Ray (ed.), *Vividh Prasang*, Allahabad: Hans Prakashan, vol. I, pp. 59–72.

[23] As in Mir Amman's *Bagh-o Bahar* or Srinivas Das's "first" Hindi novel, *Pariksha Guru* (Experience is the Best Teacher, 1882): see Dalmia, 'A Novel Moment in Hindi'.

[24] Sharar, *Guzishta-e Lakhnau*.

and tight-fitting clothes—all enumerated in the accretive style of dastans. Elements of modernity—the train, the newspaper, the lecture, the theatre—offer further possibilities of description. As the following passage shows, for instance, the railway restaurant adds to the appeal of opulent description without disrupting the narrative style:

> When [Azad] reached the Lucknow railway station, there was such a hustle and bustle, such a roil and turmoil, such a clamor and crowding, that shoulders were pressed up against shoulders. The reverend Brahmin with his water-buckets is forcing his way through the tumult: "Cold water!" The brass drinking-cups make their own clatter. The ordinary water-carriers with their large or small water-skins are making the rounds. Off to one side the hookah-man has filled the pipe with a sweet-and-bitter tobacco mixture and is burbling for customers; the rich aroma could turn one's nose into a perfumer's box. Next to the platform the potter has arranged his wares for sale. The clay toys are so ravishing that visitors hasten to buy them up and carry them off. Buyers push and shove other buyers; they fling down their money and grab the hookah. Immediately the water-carrier freshens the hookah, sprinkling water on its bowl. The hookah-man fills the hookah-bowl with tobacco; the customer wafts clouds of smoke into the air. The fruit-seller calls out: "Red juicy mulberries, mango nectar, qalami mango nectar! Safeda mangoes from the garden of Faqir Muhammad Khan himself! Langra mangoes from Banaras, Bombay mangoes from Charbagh! Oranges, tangerines, nectarines, pineapples, citrus-fruits, sharifa-fruits, guavas, apples—whatever you want, we've got it!" Elsewhere, in the confectioner's shop are displays of sweets—trays of white milk-sweets covered with silver leaf, sweets covered with crushed pistachio. Metal lanterns sway above them, so that the shop glitters with light.
>
> Now there comes a cry, "Biscuits—get your biscuits! Kabobs and bread-loaves!" Take a couple of steps another way, and the basket-man appears, making his rounds. Two-ply hats, pastel hats, brocade hats, reverse-embroidered hats, Murree-work hats, silk-and-gold woven caps, round caps—new fashions, unique and novel styles, he's showing them all in a heap together, very fast. Customer after customer, people are eagerly buying; five or ten hats are instantly sold, right out of his hand. Over a large area, travelers sit with their bed-rolls spread out—one sits on a saddle-cloth, another on a small carpet, all watching for the train. An uncouth fellow squats on his haunches, talking gibberish to himself.

> Azad said to himself, "Lord, what a carnival this station is! Is there any end to it? The crowd, the clamor, the bustle—really, Lucknow is quite a place! Lord, I've never seen such a station!"[25]

In most early Indian novels, either private or solitary spaces offer the possibility for individual characters to meet. In contrast, personal encounters take place in *Fasana-e Azad* either on the street, where young blades (*bankas*) are ever ready to stop and challenge passers-by of any social class, or in the mehfil, traditionally the elite male space in which courtesans, but not women of the household, can enter. Or there is the *sarai*, where female innkeepers provide quick wit and spirited dialogue, as we shall see.[26] The point about the street and the sarai is that they are by definition open spaces, where strangers meet. In *Fasana-e Azad* they are also the places where the high and low, those who belong to the old aristocratic culture and those who support the "new light" (Azad, mainly), interact.

Characters and Mediation

An important level at which the novel mediates society, genre, and culture is characterization. With Azad, Firoze Mookerjee observes, Sarshar wanted "to a create a character free from the tyranny of old conventions (hence the name) and spurred by a restless desire to move from place to place."[27] Azad is free of family ties, local attachments, and any commitment to the old order. In fact, he has no name other than Azad (lit. "free"), no occupation, and no obvious source of income. Is he a '"modern man", then? So it seems, in his initial encounter and exchange with Chhammi Jan, who by his name and appearance seems to represent the quintessential effeminate Lucknow dandy who

[25] 'Azad Goes to a Railway Restaurant', trans. F. Pritchett; available at http://www.columbia.edu/itc/mealac/pritchett/00fwp/published/txt_sarshar.html; originally published in K. M. George (ed.), *Modern Indian Literature: An Anthology*, vol. 2, New Delhi: Sahitya Akademi, 1993, pp. 1131–6. Slightly edited for the online version.

[26] Only during Azad's courtship of Husn Ara do we enter the private space of the women's quarter.

[27] Mookerjee, *Lucknow*, p. 98.

cares only for music and pleasure. Azad is on his way to a lecture by a "Professor Locke" on the excellence of Sanskrit (vol. 1, p. 15), while Chhammi Jan, who has never heard of the professor, is on his way to hear the famour Dhunni Khan, the celebrated interpreter of the song "*Tumhare ghunghariyale bal*" ("Your curly locks"). Azad immediately quotes back at him a Persian verse by Hafiz, to which Chhammi Jan replies, scandalizing Azad: "What tune is it set to?"[28] Azad repeatedly urges him to forsake his effeminate ways and become a "real man" ("*Lillah ab to mardue ban jao*": vol. 1, p. 16). Azad's masculine modernity is, like his appearance, hybrid rather than anglicized: "Khaki trousers, black jacket, yellow coat, loose-fitting waistcoat, half-boots and a beard thick enough for a rabbit to hide in" (vol. 1, p. 13).

Further, on several occasions we are treated to his reformist ideas and his profound learning, including his appreciation for "serious" (*haqqani*) Persian poetry—not for him the popular Urdu verse and songs of the day. After a visit to a local school, Azad is shocked by the low level of competence of the maulvi and writes a blistering report on publicly-affixed posters. When questioned by Husn Ara and her equally educated sister, he effortlessly displays his knowledge of everything from logic to mathematics, and of course his ability to compose poetry on the spot, correctly and in the given metre.[29]

Yet Azad is not a consistently reformist or serious hero—unlike the protagonist of Mirza Hadi Rusva's slightly later novel *Sharifzada* (1900). In the episode with Chhammi Jan, for example—after berating him for so long that he misses his lecture—Azad ends up following him to the musical mehfil, ready to show him that he will come out of the mehfil unscathed. At the mehfil, however, Azad behaves like everyone else and loses his heart to a beautiful courtesan. For the next three chapters he is suddenly transformed into the ailing lover of romantic masnavis—exactly what he was railing against. A similar ambivalence is evident in his attitude towards wine: ever ready to condemn it, along

[28] Chhammi reiterates the infinite pleasure of watching *nach* (nautch), and ends ups lamenting the lost glory of Lucknow, with its courtesans and its pomp; to this Azad juxtaposes the glory of Firangi Mahal and the famous poets and prose writers of Lucknow: *Fasana-e Azad,* vol. 1, p. 23.

[29] *Fasana-e Azad,* vol. 1, pp. 477 ff.

with all other addictions (opium, *ganja*), as the scourge of mankind, he nonetheless gets happily drunk from time to time when the company requires it.[30]

Even more intriguingly, Azad's free spirit and his tendency to intervene and speak his mind to all and sundry is perceived—at least by a comparably sharif character—to be at variance with the respectable code of conduct and closer, in fact, to the behaviour of street rogues. It is, literally, "barbarity" (*vahshat*) and it may, his friend Zarraf fears, ruin his chances of marrying Husn Ara. After watching Azad in a scuffle with a donkey-cart driver, he exclaims: "This is what they call barbarity. One could ask, 'Who are you exactly? Is what this person does any of your business, are you a Qazi, a Kotwal, a Mufti, just who do the hell do you think you are?' They're *his* donkeys, he can do with them as he likes. Who are you to interfere? (vol. 1, p. 472). To his friend Zarraf this attitude of Azad's is so incomprehensible that he interprets it as a character flaw, a question of temperament (*mizaj*), almost a mental illness to be cured by a doctor. Instead Azad, who has just manhandled the cart-driver for whipping his own donkeys and a bird-catcher for ensnaring his prey, justifies his actions as motivated by an innate sense of justice: he simply must answer the cry of suffering of the mute and helpless. His non-sharif behaviour is therefore excused in the light of a higher morality. Not always is Azad's intervention so morally justified, though, and he often likes to engage in altercations and physical fights with bullies, dandies, and women for the pleasure of exposing their pretensions and showing his superiority.[31]

[30] The same ambivalence seems to hold for Sarshar, who wrote many articles on the evils of drink but himself drank heavily and died of cirrhosis of the liver. True, his condemnation was sometimes qualified, as when he suggested restrictions on India-brewed drink but not on "*vilayati*" (foreign) liquor! See Mookerjee, *Lucknow*, p. 58. Dubrow notes that Azad drank even more in the zarafat sketches, but Sarshar edited some of the drink out in the first print edition, suggesting it was a topic of particular tension: Dubrow, personal communication.

[31] Premchand, appraising Sarshar thirty years later, had no doubts over interpreting Azad's actions in the light of social reform. "Here and there social ills are portrayed in this attractive way, even if they had little to do with the main narrative and it was not the author's intention that they should. Events relating

The mediations (generic, social, cultural) at play in Azad's character are most evident *vis-à-vis* his occupation and status: he claims to be, and is called by others, a sharifzada, a gentleman of good birth,[32] a crucial distinction in the social worldview of the novel, and yet his background and occupation are unspecified. When employed in succession by two nawabs as a companion (*musahib*), he constantly pokes fun at their gullibility, and as typical specimens of their class they appear only as objects of ridicule.[33] While the silence on Azad's lineage and status, coupled with his effortless grasp of classical and modern knowledge, does not refute Lelyveld's argument that "growing up *sharif*" entailed primarily a certain kind of education and code of conduct,[34] his lack of occupation does become problematic at least for one character in the novel—his fiancée Husn Ara.

The issue of Azad's (lack of) occupation emerges most directly at the time of his courtship of Husn Ara: she has no trouble in recognizing his virtues and his sharafat, but, as a respectable girl from a good family, she cannot be seen to be marrying a stranger (*pardesi*) with no name and no family.[35] Hence, he must make himself a name. How? Not by becoming a famous robber, she suggests, or by writing a book, but by

---

to ordinary life are written in such a humorous way that the reader keeps reading page after page, not knowing that s/he is been treated with a doctor's pill": Premchand, 'Sharar aur Sarshar', p. 63.

[32] The old boatman who plays an important role in bringing Azad and Husn Ara together comments, for example, that his being from a good family (*khandan*) shines through his face; *Fasana-e Azad*, vol. 1, pp. 469–70. For a discussion of "signs" (*lakshan*) in novelistic characterization, see ch. 7.

[33] One of the funniest episodes in the novel, wonderfully read aloud on stage by Zia Mohyeddin, is that of Saf Shikan, the favourite quail of the second nawab (both are left nameless on account of their stupidity), which has gone missing and whose intelligence and virtues the other courtiers compete to praise to the sky in order to curry favour with the distraught nawab. Azad has no qualms exploiting the nawab or cheating a moneylender, though this satire, playing—like the qissas of ordinary people—to the gallery contrasts with the novel's underlying assumption that nawabs are the people who matter.

[34] See Lelyveld, *Aligarh's First Generation*, ch. 2.

[35] "You are a traveller, an unknown stranger, a foreigner, you have no place to stay. Neither house nor home, a *khana barbad* [nomad]—if I mention you to anyone what can I say? Whose son are you, whose grandson, what is your

displaying bravery: he must go and fight on the side of the Ottomans against the Russians in the Crimea and come back as "Miyan Azad the *ghazi*". The path of bravery (*javanmardi*), is of course a well-recognized one for heroic narratives. Yet here it also inserts Azad into the world of contemporary news.[36] It is a path that Azad happily embraces, and by aligning him with the traditional dastan heroes it conveniently bypasses the question of his social status, as well as of course introducing exciting new adventures.

After his triumphant return to India, Azad is shown as devoting most of his energies to putting his ideas on education, commerce, and industry into practice. In the last chapter he re-establishes the local education department along innovative lines, changes the books prescribed in the syllabus, and suggests radical changes in the university system. He writes articles in Urdu and English in various Indian newspapers and has them published in England. He travels to Europe, spends six months in Paris, and a year in England. Back in India, he establishes a paper mill as well as a cotton mill, writes articles in favour of industry which have a tremendous impact, and goes on lecture tours throughout India. He then turns his attention to public health and publishes a vaccination bill. When his twin sons are fourteen he sends them to England to complete their education, and both distinguish themselves there.[37] In other words, Azad becames the prototype of the man of the "new light".

Yet, in order to highlight the unusual ("unstable") path through which Azad reaches this position, it is instructive to compare his transition to the new world and the new middle class with that of Rusva's

---

family, where is your ancestral home, what will I say? The news will spread in the whole city that Husn Ara has married a foreigner about whom nothing is known": *Fasana-e Azad*, vol. 1, p. 529. She insists that especially because she is educated, she must make sure that she makes no social *faux pas* which might attract opprobrium.

[36] The *Avadh Akhbar* reported extensively on the Russo-Turkish war, but the Crimean sub-plot probably owes a lot to G.W.R. Reynolds' *Omar*, which however was translated into Urdu only in 1903; did Sarshar read it in English (serialized 1855–6, it was published in book form in 1885), or was there an earlier Urdu edition available? See L. Smith, 'The Mysteries of Translation'.

[37] Mookerjee, *Lucknow*, p. 141.

Sharifzada (1900).[38] Born as an impoverished member of the old aristocracy who has literally fallen to the bottom of the economic scale, Rusva's hero has to start climbing it again within the new colonial set-up. After literally risking starvation he is happy to accept even menial jobs, first teaching Persian to the son of a Hindu coal-merchant inside his warehouse and then working for free at the draftsman's office. It is his hard work and unassuming demeanour, not his connections, that attract the attention of his British boss, and he slowly makes his way up, first as a draftsman and then as a surveyor—in a typical example of a reconfiguration of the law court (*kachehri*) milieu under British rule—and ends up comfortably as an Indian sahib. Nonetheless, he has learnt his lesson and keeps fast to the values of thrift and hard work, shunning all aristocratic pastimes and addictions: a sharifzada by birth, he has become one by character at the end, in the process changing the very meaning of the word. The same holds true of his wife, who had once saved them from starvation by embroidering hats, and who later becomes a thrifty and judicious housewife.

How are we to understand Azad's "instability" in comparison with Rusva's sharifzada? Given that the rounded character of the psychological-realist novel has yet to appear at this time, we cannot possibly dismiss the inconsistencies in Azad's characterization as either psychological or moral flaws. Rather, Azad's instability can be attributed to the composite demands on him and the composite character of the novelistic hero: ostensibly a modern reformer, a "new man", he must also be a zarafat character, witty and teasing, a valiant dastan hero and a romantic lover, morally improved by his heroine—as Khusrau was by Shirin or Bahram Gur by the seven princesses in the Persian masnavis of Nizami. In line with these models, Azad is in fact a serial lover, falling in love with every woman he encounters. Again, rather than seeing this element as a psychological character trait, it seems more correct to interpret it as a function of the "mediation" sought by the text. This mediation is between the desire to narrate a relationship between a man and a woman, and the impossibility of narrativizing

[38] Muhammad Hadi Rusva, *Sharifzada*, New Delhi: Maktaba Jamia, 1992. See also the extract in M.A. Farooqi, *The Oxford India Anthology of Modern Urdu Literature*, New Delhi: Oxford University Press, 2007, vol. II.

such a relationship—even quite fleeting contacts—in terms other than the existing one of 'ishq/muhabbat, especially if the man is the novel's hero. There is, literally, no other model of inter-gender behaviour available, outside familial models of sibling and conjugal relations.

The "problem" of imagining a fictional modern heroine and her relation with the hero was part of a general problem that the modern Indian novel was called upon to confront. Indeed, one could argue that one of the main tasks of Indian literature in the late-nineteenth and early-twentieth century was to tackle, in various guises, the problem of imagining relations between unrelated men and women, both in private and public. Novels in Bengali, for example, evolved the topos of childhood friends, neighbours, or quasi-affines (and later fellow students) who are later separated and whose close relationship—"innocent" by definition—provides occasions for fleeting but intense intimacy, verbal banter, and liminal sexuality. In later novels about Muslim households, the topos is that of banter and teasing among cousins.[39] But for Sarshar in the 1870s the challenge was to create a respectable and modern Muslim heroine at a time when debates on women's education and about women appearing in public raged in the public sphere.[40] Sarshar wrote several articles in *Avadh Akhbar* in favour of women's education and against purdah.[41] In *Fasana*, Husn Ara and her younger sister Sipahr Ara are both highly educated (at home) and appear not just as readers of Nazir Ahmad's didactic novels for women but as their embodiment: "Both sisters were, by God's grace, grown up [*siyani*] and carried the impetuous wind of youth, but were from start to finish chaste [*hayaparvar*] and pure, and on top of that they had also received a first-class education. They ha been through all the books on morals, ethics and chastity . . . (vol. 1, p. 464). Moreover:

> They cannot be more than about thirteen to fourteen years old—girls of good family [*sharifzadiyan*] and high social standing, very sensible, well mannered, and attractive. Bashful eyes, modest temperament. They

[39] See, e.g., Ismat Chughtai's *Terhi Lakir* (1944), translated into English as *The Crooked Line*, Oxford: Heinemann, 1995.

[40] See Minault, *Secluded Scholars*.

[41] Mookerjee, *Lucknow*, p. 62.

> veil their beauty, treasure their chastity, observe modesty, keep their gaze pure. Brought up in luxury but educated . . . both sisters are as fond of reading as can be. Reading, writing, outings on the river and walks in the garden—these are their only occupations. They are always reading the books of recent authors — the story of Asghari and Akbari, yes that one, *Mir'at ul-'Urus* and *Banat un-Na'sh*, and also *Fasana-e Hamid* and the *History of Germany* and *'Ali Band* and the *Akhlaq-e Kashi* and so on, and they really take them to heart. Both sisters are wonderful at needlework and embroidery, and both are excellent cooks.[42]

The girls pay attention to cleanliness and won't even sit in dirty houses. The emphasis on their wide-ranging reading, which includes history, ethics, and the new novels is striking. They also read the newspaper—which is providential since this is how they discover that the sharifzada boy (sharif only by birth) to whom Husn Ara was betrothed is actually a rogue who had robbed a moneylender and is now undergoing a jail sentence (vol. 1, p. 466)! Thus, Husn Ara's ability to read the newspaper is carefully unconnected from potentially dangerous interests and justified as a means of upholding the family honour, besides making her the agent of her own deliverance from danger.

Husn Ara is so passionate about women's education that a whole chapter in the novel is devoted to a lecture she plans to give on the subject. The chapter is replete with spirited arguments refuting women's incompleteness in matters of reason and of religion (*naqis al-'aql* and *naqis al-din*), references to past Hindu women of substance, and to the Annual Report on Public Instruction showing the swift progress made by girls once they start attending school.[43] Here, the fictional narrative incorporates the idioms and arguments of social reform articles and public speeches, reinforced here by the fact that the one penning them is herself a woman. Husn Ara promptly dismisses claims that educated women will become bad mannered and write love letters to their lovers. Women do not need letters to have lovers, she protests, and in fact education will make them more wary of such risky and dangerous steps. Most importantly, education will make women better mothers as well as *better companions for their husbands*. Her tone is solemn and

[42] Translated in Mookerjee, *Lucknow*, p. 106.
[43] *Fasana-e Azad*, vol. 1, pp. 511–14.

Persianized here: "Illiterate women are ignorant friends. Educated wives make wise companions. Schooled women usually look after the house as beautifully as the British look after their state" (vol. 1, p. 514). Earlier, she has announced that she will either wed an educated (and handsome) young man or remain unmarried, and offered her vision of a happy companionate marriage between educated spouses as one in which husband and wife take turns in reading to each other, converse on morality and poetry, and share entertaining stories and advice. An uneducated woman, clever though she may be, will always be ignorant (*jahil*) and will not be able to give good advice: she'll protest that she is ignorant and stupid (*murkh jahil*) and knows no better. "I can't understand how educated men can live with illiterate wives."[44] The lecture ends with her pledge to start a girls' school, to which all her friends are eager to contribute (vol. 1, p. 515).

Moreover, by giving the girls no father and only a mother who is ridiculed as a superstitious old lady,[45] fictional space is created for allowing Husn Ara to do what no Nazir Ahmad heroine would have done with such direct agency: decide on her own marriage partner. Husn Ara takes this responsibility very seriously: much as she is taken with Azad, she will not let him marry her just yet: "I don't object to marrying, but husband and wife have to spend a very long part of their lives together. If they don't get along or they disagree and quarrel or start bickering, life becomes bitter. The husband will kick his wife hard and she will curse him regardless of the consequences. He will sulk in one corner and she in the other. This kind of marriage is not for me, thank you" (vol. 1, p. 507). She therefore bluntly sets out six conditions with which he must comply. These six conditions virtually amount to

[44] Ibid. In this context see also Meera Kosambi's observations on Kashibai Kanitkar, the pioneering Marathi woman novelist: "She coaxes and cajoles male readers to see the situation from her point of view . . . educated wives would neither be remiss in their household duties, nor try to compete with men for jobs, but would be an asset to society and the nation." Meera Kosambi, *Feminist Vision or 'Treason Against Men?' Kashibai Kanitkar and the Engendering of Marathi Literature*, Ranikhet: Permanent Black, 2008, p. 21.

[45] Interestingly, the mother's standard of sharafat, based purely on lineage, is also ridiculed: for her it is enough that Azad should speak good Persian and claim to direct descent from Timur to accept him as a suitable match for Husn Ara; ibid., vol. 1, pp. 482 ff.

her definition of how to *become* a sharif, which has all to do with social conduct, respectability (visit the mosque, whatever your beliefs), and mastery of modern living (the bungalow):

> 1. Every fortnight you should organize a musha'ira, so that through these meetings people will get to know your name and will know that you are somebody.
> 2. Rent a first-class and beautiful bungalow or a smaller house [*kothi*] but on the main street, and furnish it in good taste so that people will realize that you are a well-mannered person and do not depend on others for your livelihood.
> 3. Do not entertain friendly relations with anyone who is not a gentleman or nobleman [sharifzada, *raiszada*], a member of the elite, a learned person, or a poet. Do not let scoundrels and riff-raff near you. Verse: "Let your companions be better than you, so that your intelligence and faith may increase."
> 4. Go to the mosque every week for the Friday prayer, so that Muslims will not say that you do not observe the fasts and prayers. Nobody thinks highly of an irreligious man. Whatever your own ideas may be, you have to observe the rules of the world and of appearance to a point.
> 5. Keep a carriage or a mount and go out mornings and evenings for a stroll [*havakhori*].
> 6. Come and meet Mother from time to time.
>
> If you agree with these points and do as I say, I have no objections whatsoever to the match. Think about it and let me have your answer. Of course both Sipahr Ara and myself are obliged to you, you have saved her life and thanks to you she has received a second life. I am your slave [*laundi*]. But since you are a learned man and you are serious and intelligent I have spoken in such clear terms. Had you been ignorant it would have been exceedingly difficult. (vol. 1, pp. 507–8)

Azad has no trouble agreeing to her conditions—just as he happily takes up her suggestion to make a name for himself by fighting for the caliphate in Crimea.[46] After his departure, Husn Ara appears in part the steadfast and patient heroine of dastans and masnavis, and in part the sensible Nazir Ahmad heroine.

[46] He only asks for permission to visit her from time to time, and will in fact subsequently spend most of his energy trying to see her every day.

What we see at play in her dealing with Azad, and the question of marriage, is clearly an imaginative attempt at creating a modern educated heroine. In her romantic behaviour with Azad only a thin line separates her behaviour as a respectable woman (*sharif bibi*) from that of a courtesan. In the intimate moments and spaces created by fictional licence—they spend a few days in a bungalow by the river after they are shipwrecked together—Azad and Husn Ara flirt. He plays the 'ashiq to the hilt and protests against her coldness, while she alternately sulks, exchanges witticisms, or warms to him; in one instance she even prepares *paan* for him and they exchange it in a seductive gesture. In this, Firoze Mookerjee has argued, Husn Ara and her sister follow the pattern of masnavi and dastan heroines who were modelled on real-life courtesans.[47] Perhaps one should say that the ideals of love, courtship, and flirtatious and sophisticated behaviour—those that were treasured in Indo-Persian culture and found expression in the poetry of ghazals and the fictional narratives of masnavis and dastans—could be realized in practice (and in public) only with courtesans. This was not just because of the gendered segregation of private spaces and monitoring of husband–wife relations in the zenana, but also because the wife and the courtesan embodied contrasting cultural ideals.[48] As a result, in *Fasana-e Azad*—as in the masnavis by Sarshar's fellow Lakhnavi Mirza Shauq composed and printed only ten years earlier—the two models of femininity, of the sharifzadi and of the courtesan, overlap in order to create a new type of attractive but respectable romantic heroine.[49] Clearly, the author was keen to maintain that the love between Azad and Husn Ara was "pure love" (*pak muhabbat, sachcha pyar*), and that she was a sharifzadi. As he wrote in one of his weekly commentaries:

[47] Firoze Mookerjee, *Lucknow*, p. 106. For example, she notices, they go out riding and on boat trips escorted only by an old man-servant—who is eager to help Azad gain access to them—and people gather to admire their beauty; ibid., p. 107.

[48] As Mookerjee puts it, Sarshar faced a real difficulty here. He wanted to depict a heroine who had all the educational and cultural accomplishments of men, and who moved freely and easily in their society, because this was his ideal of womanhood. But the only women in the society of his day who had these characteristics were courtesans; ibid., p. 107.

[49] See Nawab Mirza Shauq, *Zahr-e 'Ishq, Bahar-e 'Ishq*, Lucknow: Central Press, 1868 (1000), 1 anna; *Quarterly Lists.*

"Last week was all about the tête-à-têtes between Husn Ara, Sipahr Ara and Miyan Azad. Look at the effects of education and breeding! Husn Ara is at the age of burgeoning youth [*uthti javani*] and is very much impressed by Azad, and yet nothing has happened or has been said which would bear a stain of vulgarity or obscenity, or sully education and manners. [...] *Shabash*, Husn Ara! Very good! And why should it not be so?! (*Avadh Akhbar*, 2 August 1879, p. 2418). Unlike the equally fictional heroines of didactic and reformist models, however, the main heroine of *Fasana-e Azad*, while subscribing to the same ideals of modesty, chastity, and respectability, is also outspoken and flirtatious and speaks to Azad from a position of equality. Sarshar was aware that, despite realistic details regarding the girls' language and mischievous tricks, he was not representing some already-existing kind of woman but rather imagining a desirable ideal: "My heart's desire in this tale is not to speak of any particular person or any particular community or particular incident, but in a general way to caricature undesirable conventions and harmful ideas, so that men of discernment may give thought to these matters and come to follow the right path. It is just possible that two beautiful moon-faced sisters like Husn Ara and Sipahr Ara may exist somewhere" (*Avadh Akhbar*, 13 October 1879).[50] This combination of familiar models, fictional ideals, and credible characterization, dispensed day after day within the newspaper, gave rise to a new type of "sensuous reading", whether readers experienced it silently or were read to aloud.

A Novel Experience

> Early in the morning the whole family collects when the postman comes. We take the newspaper from him first, and as soon as I grasp the newspaper all my relatives come and we start reading the supplement [i.e. *Fasana-e Azad*]. Those who are present listen with their hearts and souls. Although we are thousands of miles away from you, our hearts stretch towards your pen. [We say] let's see what Pandit Sahab offers us in the novel tomorrow. Everybody is fond of you. No one has achieved the status you have . . . (Letter from Hyderabad, 12 November 1879, suppl., p. 172)
>
> Thanks to this *Avadh Akhbar* an assembly [*anjuman*] meets every day for two hours, and because of the elegant style those who can read start

[50] Quoted and trans. in Mookerjee, *Lucknow*, p. 109.

> arguing about who will read: "It's my turn", "I'll read." And when the reading begins there are loud comments on the idioms and style. (Letter from a district surveyor of district Montgomery, Punjab, 26.11.1879, suppl., p. 200)

> I was sitting in the train reading your *Avadh Akhbar* of 1st October, when at one station a group of men dressed in white clothes and some members of the general public came in the compartment next to mine. One of the six gentlemen asked me whether the *Zarafat* was also in the paper. Since I had finished with *Zarafat* I was reading a newspaper from Kabul, I handed it to him, and I also started to pay attention to their eagerness. That gentleman called his companions to attention and began reading the sheet, and I became engaged in watching the passengers in the compartment all listen so intently and with such eagerness to *Zarafat that they were not aware of their surroundings.* There was no other talk but of Miyan Khoji and Azad. [. . .] The point is that the people who were not interested in newspapers have now begun to be keen thanks to this *Zarafat.* May God bestow favour upon you for your prudence and the *benefit you have brought to ordinary people.* I for myself am very pleased at seeing this general eagerness. (Letter, 18 October 1879, p. 3268, emphases added)

There is little doubt that *Fasana-e Azad* marked a totally new experience for both author and readers. What were the elements in the readers' experience, the new "ambience" of realism, and the narrator's interven-tion that marked this fresh departure? Although daily serialization could not be sustained beyond the first year and a half, after which the novel appeared weekly, it allowed a whole new and intense relation between the author, the narrator, the readers, and the characters in the text. The weekly commentary in the newspaper ("*Sat din ki zarafat*") became a significant new space for author–readers interaction. Sarshar began by occasionally quoting and replying only to some readers' letters, but he must have gradually realized the potential that such letters had as publicity, since by the end of December 1879 the letters were published in full and appeared almost every day.[51]

Although the novel was not committed to absolute realism, the fact that the novel *as a genre* required standards of verisimilitude was not

[51] Jennifer Dubrow's Ph.D. thesis considers these features in greater detail.

lost on either author or readers. "Nature, nature, nature" was hailed as a major pleasure offered by the novelistic narration: "neither prose nor verse, neither story nor masnavi can offer the same pleasure as nature", proclaimed the narrator, complimenting himself on his attention to detail (29 November 1879, p. 3682). And in the name of "*nechar-nechar-nechar*" he played games within the text—to which readers gleefully replied. For instance, playing with the relationship between narrated time and real time, he said: "I'll find out about Azad when we get news by telegraph."[52] Or, in the emotional letter written by Sipahr Ara to Azad, we are told that the words are half-erased because "in her bewildered state she thinks she is writing one thing and another comes out of her pen" (15 November 1879, p. 3546). The affecting quality of dramatic realism is such that the narrator himself describes himself as moved and affected by what he is describing, be it a shipwreck or a hanging.

The readers' letters are precious evidence of the novel's popularity, and of the new readerly experience. From letters such as the ones quoted above we learn, first of all, that the readers' experience reproduced in some ways the oral one of the dastan, with a small audience collecting around the storyteller, though the experience was now one which could be repeated daily, at home or wherever one happened to be. In fact, the testimony of readers on the train evokes some kind of portable dastan experience and stresses the fact that the newspaper made this experience readily accessible to ordinary people, and many illiterates, through reading aloud. Moreover, the reference to the fact that the listeners got carried away and forgot their surroundings reminds us of the "sensuous reading" experience discussed in the Introduction. Detti argues that this kind of fundamental and deeply pleasurable experience is absolutely necessary to develop a taste for reading books. In order to acquire an enduring reading habit, "it is necessary to go through a phase in which the individual is able to relish reading so much as to long to relive that pleasure all through his life."[53] We could argue that *Fasana-e Azad* made those who had experienced deep pleasure listening to books being read out to them long to

[52] *Avadh Akhbar*, 29 November 1879, p. 3682.

[53] Detti, *Il piacere di leggere*, pp. 19–20.

relive that pleasure. Only now, in the absence of storytellers who would narrate Azad's story again and again, it was necessary to actually read a book in order to repeat the experience. Several letters underscore the fact that the novel offered pleasure to "ordinary people", literate and illiterate, thus turning non- and neo-literates into potential readers of novels: "Thank you so much for your counsels [*nasa'ih*]: anyone with even a little good sense will learn from them. The story of Azad has become so renowned and famous that everyone, young and old, lowly or mighty, *literate and illiterate* [*khwanda va nakhwanda*] is ever eager to listen to it" (Letter, 6 October 1879, suppl., p. 154, emphasis added).

Readers also appreciated the "realism" of the novel and its characters: this raised new expectations and engendered new games between the narrator and his readers, as readers began to look out for inconsistencies or the absence of verisimilitude in the story or the characters. One reader, for example, objected that it was not clear from where Azad had got the money to travel to Turkey. Sarshar first replied that, in the case of characters in a novel, it was not necessary to give out all this information and referred to the popular *Count of Monte Cristo*. But then, himself yielding to the pressure of this expectation, he concocted an explanation according to which Azad had received the money from a moneylender and from the wife of his friend Zarraf. Finally, playing with the conventions of fiction, Sarshar added that this had not been mentioned in the novel for fear of highwaymen (30 October 1879, p. 2732). A particularly interesting and long letter from an enthusiastic woman reader objected that the character of Husn Ara did not fit in any category of women she knew:

> You have created Husn Ara entirely according to your own tastes. Let alone omens [*fal*], she has not faith even in prayers [*du'a*]. Has she by chance received an English education? If not, there are only two ways in which she could reach this position—either under the influence of the company she keeps or under the influence of the books she has read. How can she have had the company of anyone who embraces English ideas? And as for her education, if it was in Persian how come she does not believe in omens? (12 December 1879, suppl., p. 247)

Clearly, this kind of demand for realism would not have been made in the case of a qissa or dastan character.

Another aspect of this new and intense reader experience, and of the perceived realism of the narrative, was the readers' desire to become part of the novelistic world and to see themselves represented in it. The same woman reader, writing in simple Urdu, urged Sarshar to tell the story of some sharifzadi who was *not* educated like Husn Ara and Sipahr Ara, hence probably more like herself: "Your qissa is good. And you are as good as people say you are, in fact even better. And you are good at writing the expressions Muslim women use in colloquial language, even if you are Hindu. But why don't you write about a sharifzadi who is not educated [*k͟hwanda*]? You will show even greater ability then."[54] The same reader asked him to leave out all those difficult Persian poems and instead write Urdu verses that people could understand, thus pulling the novel closer to the middling literariness of qissas and songbooks. Another reader asked the author to "bring" Azad to his home town,[55] while yet another begged Sarshar to tell him where Husn Ara's house was located.[56] One male reader attempted to enter the narrative world by sending a love letter to Azad to be printed in Husn Ara's name, directed at Azad, or in Humayun Farr's name addressed to Sipahr Ara. Interestingly, the grounds on which Sarshar refused to comply were not those of authorship but because "isn't Husn Ara a poet who can write the poem herself?"—thus carrying the game further.[57] Yet another male reader wrote to say he had fallen in love with Husn Ara's sister Sipahr Ara. Just as well he had not mentioned Husn Ara's name, Sarshar replied, otherwise Azad would have had to return from Turkey and duel with him![58] A captain (*subedar*) in the army compared his own fate unfavourably with Azad's: unlike Azad, *he* had to fight and was having no fun at all, nor did he have any moon-faced beauty to love him—"no one ever comes my way".[59] Other letters corrected factual mistakes and, as we have seen above, questioned authorial choices on the basis of the new expectations of verisimilitude.

[54] She was the wife of a subordinate judge, *Avadh Ak͟hbar*, 12 September 1879, suppl., p. 247.

[55] *Avadh Ak͟hbar*, 11 November 1879, suppl., p. 168.

[56] Ibid., 2 January 1880, p. 8.

[57] Ibid., 30 December 1879, suppl., p. 291.

[58] Ibid., 29 December 1879, suppl., p. 288.

[59] Ibid., 11 October 1879, p. 3192.

Another kind of reader's intervention generated by the serialization was repeated enquiries on what would happen next. Sarshar played skilfully with these expectations, anticipating them in his weekly comments but also feigning ignorance, as we have seen above. To delay the action and keep expectations alive was precisely, he pointed out, one of the pleasures of a novel.[60] Readers intervened in other ways, too—they suggested a weekly rather than a daily format so that readers would not miss instalments; others asked that the supplement be printed separately so that one could buy it without the whole paper.[61] The woman reader mentioned above urged Sarshar to keep enough written matter in advance so that readers would not be disappointed when he had to absent himself.[62]

The Novel According to Sarshar

Modern forms like the novel, the short story, and free verse in Hindi and Urdu have created among their critics what I think of as a "taxonomic obsession". By this I mean a compulsive desire to define the ideal characteristics of a literary form and then assess whether a particular text meets those standards or not. This has been especially true in the case of the novel, where "original" foreign models were posited as prototypes against which Indian novels could be judged—and usually be found wanting.[63] While this kind of compulsive exercise can be viewed (and dismissed) as an expression of the critic's wish to establish his own authority in the literary field, there is also another side to this business. In the case of *Fasana-e Azad* we see both author and readers trying to make sense of this fictional text, highlighting what appeared to be novelties compared with the familiar qissas and dastans, and suggesting how these novelties provided particular types of pleasure.

Sarshar often took advantage of the weekly commentary to express his authorial intentions. His awareness of the art of novel-writing and of the novel as a genre comes across in many comments about the

[60] Ibid., 23 August 1879, p. 2648.

[61] Ibid., 31 December 879, suppl., p. 296.

[62] Ibid., 12 December 1879, suppl., p. 247.

[63] See F. Orsini, *The Hindi Public Sphere, 1920–1940*, especially the reviews of Premchand's novel *Premashram* along these lines, pp. 166–71.

careful and gradual dispensing of information, the "natural" use of descriptions, the clever use of digressions (*gurez*) and subplots (for which he used the term qissa), and the different attractions (*lutf*) that novels offered in comparison to qissa–dastans. "A novel means that a reader should be interested from the bottom of the heart to read ahead and find out what all that is going to happen means. See, our readers were so eager to know what happened after what I wrote [about Husn Ara's courtship] at the end of last month that I have already received some eleven letters begging me for the grace of God not to let her chastity suffer taint."[64] "Don't think that Husn Ara and Azad will soon be married", he warned readers. "There is still plenty of time. The full pleasure of a novel is that the reader thinks that a certain thing is about to happen and will be announced in the next few days [but it is not]."[65]

He was proud of his powers of description, for example of realistic details of a shipwrecked pleasure boat: "These are the elements for which novels are esteemed and which make an impression on the heart."[66] "The attraction of a novel is not only to keep the story [dastan] going, but to present human feelings which provoke sorrow or joy in a way that paints a portrait of them."[67] Descriptions, he argued, should have nothing in them that goes against nature—a veiled sting at the supernatural worlds of dastan adventures—and should not be pure exercises in verbosity (*laffazi*) and verbal effects (*fiqrebazi*): they should have some point to them.[68] Nonetheless, he acknowledged that the dialogues between Husn Ara, Sipahr Ara, and Azad were "pure fun": "And in a novel these kinds of jokes [*mazzaq*] provide wonderful pleasure. Rarely is a novel devoid of them."[69]

Humour, wit, and nature are the keywords in Sarshar's perspective of the novel. In a lengthy note positing the novel as more desirable than the dastan, he contrasted the social comedy of his story to the gratuitous farce of dastans:

[64] *Avadh Akhbar*, 13 December 1879, p. 3747.
[65] Ibid., 26 July 1879, p. 2336.
[66] Ibid., 2 August 1879, p. 2418.
[67] Ibid., 6 September 1879, p. 2816.
[68] Ibid., 19 July 1879, p. 2256.
[69] Ibid., 2 August 1879, p. 2418.

I have started a new sub-plot in the novel. The attraction of a novel is exactly this: that from time to time digressions may appear in an interesting fashion, so that readers and admirers will feel even more eager to read it. In this sub-plot I have written nothing that goes against nature or that contradicts habit and reason in any way. Urdu masnavis and dastans are full of jinns, devs, paris, and magicians, and often nonsensical ideas are expressed which make intelligent, serious people of simple wit laugh their hearts out when they read them. *Mashallah*, the way they have spoilt the nature of the story! What they write is against reason. If someone rolls over, he will keep rolling for two hundred years. May the devil curse such a miracle! A man will be turned into a stone and a woman into a hen. The story of Miyan Azad is of the kind that in English is called a "comedy", that is, one which is full of funny things from top to bottom and which makes readers fall over with laughter at every step. But this should not be empty laughter or jest, it should be woven into the texture of witticism [zarafat] and should teach morals, which is exactly the specific effect of novels. The other kind of novel is called "tragedy". This contains such blood-stopping and fear-inducing events as to make readers shed floods of tears. One may tell of the death of a young man in such sorrowful accents that the reader will shed a few tears despite him/herself. Or else the separation between a lover and his beloved will be described in such a way that a human being will not be able to stop sobbing and sighing. The story of Miyan Azad belongs to the first kind, but it is not all about entertainment: "what humour is that which has no scent of morality?"[70]

Entertainment (*mazzaq*) and moral correction (*akhlaq*) are the two defining elements of the novel, then. While Sarshar was ever mindful of increasing the interest and pleasure (*shauq*) of the reader, at every stage he was keen to point out the moral of the incident. While we may argue that the moral and reformist intent seems much more prominent in Sarshar's idea of the novel than in the actual novel itself, it is clear that it was for him an important means of distinguishing the novel from the qissa-dastan.

Noteworthy in the programmatic passage quoted above is the definition of the novel by using terms like "comedy" and "tragedy", usually

[70] Ibid., 26 July 1879, p. 2336.

applied to drama. Yet, given the nineteenth-century North Indian context of colonial education, the inflow of English literature, and the burgeoning entertainment industry, the use of these terms is not so surprising. Partly, as we have seen, "comedy" and "tragedy" helped writers like Sarshar to distinguish their creations from indigenous narrative genres. And partly, his readers were striving to make sense of *Fasana-e Azad* by using as terms of comparison other genres and texts that they were familiar with. These could be either qissas and dastans or the "novels" of Shakespeare and Milton. In other words, what is significant here is more the attempt at making sense of the novel genre through familiar generic categories, and not so much whether such comparisons were correct. Several readers hovered between calling the story a qissa and a novel (*navil* in Urdu). "*Bandanavaz* Ratannath ji Sahab! The qissa of Miyan Azad brings amazing pleasure. I have come to the point that when I open the newspaper I first look at the Zarafat and then read the articles about the country and other matters. Now the qissa of Miyan Azad has become quite an excellent *navil*", wrote one reader.[71] Another compared *Fasana-e Azad* to "Shakespeare's novels", while yet another argued that such a comparison was not correct because Shakespeare's novels "are full of comedy and tragedy, which are called in Persian *razm-o bazm*, and they are all true and historical stories which have been embellished by poetic writing. The same is true of the novels of Italian opera." The same reader modified his judgement by saying that if *Fasana-e Azad* did not compare with Shakespeare's "novels", it was as good or even better than other English and French novels. He suggested that Sarshar had copied "our Arabic *Alif Laila va Laila* and the Persian *Bostan-i Khyal*."[72] Several readers cited the fact that "the pleasure [of *Fasana-e Azad*] is great because you write like Western novels".[73] One praised Sarshar's effort in modulating language in the novel in accordance with the action, serious or

[71] Ibid., 30 August 1879, p. 2832.

[72] Ibid., 15 November 1879, p. 3546. Although he admitted that he had not read *Bostan-i Khyal*, he had read the four volumes of *Alif Laila va Laila*, probably in Urdu translation; ibid., "You are the Shakespeare and Milton of our age", effused another possibly English-educated reader, Gobind Narayan Singh from Ghazipur: ibid., 29 December 1879, suppl., p. 288.

[73] Mir Ghaznafar Ali, writing from Hyderabad, Deccan, ibid., 29 July 1880, suppl., p. 84.

comic.[74] Another wrote in to say that he used to listen a lot to tales of adventures and wonder, such as *Fasana-e 'Ajaib*, "but now those really seem rubbish" in comparison.[75]

Through the letters, then, we see readers—accustomed to earlier narratives of adventure, or to modern novels and plays of exotic England—react enthusiastically to a narrative that seemed so much closer home. Equally, they responded enthusiastically to the dizzying possibility of influencing and even entering the novel's course. This deeply involving experience was one that Sarshar keenly encouraged, and which he tried to direct through his weekly interventions.[76] While the experiment of daily serialization and a daily immersion in the flow of narrative could not be physically sustained by him, it nevertheless provided a crucial experience of "sensuous reading", and the attendant yearning for more. Finally, it presented a successful precedent for other writers who tried to combine novel-writing with entertainment, and who found their path had been opened.

Narrative Mobility and Social Mobility

How different was *Fasana-e Azad* from the qissa-dastan tradition? There is little doubt that, despite identifying itself as a "tale" in the title and citing implicitly as a precursor Rajab 'Ali Beg Surur's *Fasana-e 'Ajaib* (*c.* 1824–5, but printed in 1850), *Fasana-e Azad* was a completely new kind of fictional narrative. Instead of princes and fairies, here were recognizable human characters from various walks of life. Instead of a consistent prose style, either ornate or simple, here was a whole range of language registers being used consciously to suggest social stratification and individual idiolects. Instead of a fable-like courtly milieu here was the street, the mehfil, and new spaces of sociability like the theatre and the train. In fact, aristocratic society and its culture

[74] Maulvi Sayid Abul Hasan from Lucknow, *Avadh Akhbar*, p. 87.

[75] Ibid., 11 October 1879, p. 3192.

[76] Though he was also careful to reintroduce distance, as when, for example, he came under fire for behaving "like drunken editors". He replied tongue-in-cheek: "I admit that editors drink wine. But which editors? Some European ones. I am a Hindu, and not just a Hindu but a Brahmin. And not just a Brahmin but a Panditji Maharaj. Then what do I have to do with alcohol?" Ibid., 5 January 1880, suppl., p. 10.

came under sharp critical scrutiny. Individually, these various aspects had already been taken up in Urdu by Sauda, Ghalib, Nazir Ahmad, and others; but here, in this work, they became part of a capacious narrative that appealed to "ordinary people". Despite Sarshar's insistence on calling realistic details and affective descriptions "nature", the result was less social realism and more an assortment of attitudes and textual pleasures that combined old and new literary forms, and elite and popular topoi. These were brought together for the first time, and were clearly enjoyed by both author and readers.

How far did Sarshar's inventiveness and narrative mobility mirror social mobility within the novel—to go back to McKeon's idea of genre as "mediation"? Earlier we saw that the novel answered the question "who is sharif?" by suggesting that wide knowledge and competent conduct needed to be supplemented by a certain assertiveness and curiosity about the world. At this point I would like to focus instead on the "lowly" characters in the novel—Khoji and Bi Allah Rakhi. Does their spatial and social mobility in the novel, typical of the picaresque, carry a "progressive" ideology or a "conservative" one—to go back to McKeon's terminology? Does social mobility embody the positive ideology of the new man? Or is it criticized as another sign of the decline of the times? Once again, readers' letters provide additional commentary to this debate.

For one thing, there is a definite "naturalness" about the way in which the social world depicted in *Fasana-e Azad* is, for its range of social figures, a completely Muslim world. Although there are narrative asides on differences between Hindu and Muslim customs, they do not become part of the narrative world, and there are no Hindu characters (while there are a few British ones). The impression is that the "Muslim sharif" is still the dominant cultural model, and therefore "Muslim sharif" stands for any member of the mixed elective group of the elite. And only one Muslim woman reader remarked upon the fact that Sarshar was a Hindu writing about Muslim characters.

There are two characters who most embody social instability and social mobility in the text. They are two "lowly" characters who, unsurprisingly, recall qissa characters: one the vocational stupidity of the donkey-cart driver, and the other the sensuality of the female innkeeper, the bhatiyari (see chapter 4). The first is Khoji who, judging by readers' letters, was the most popular of Sarshar's creations.[77] As a comic character, he is both a trickster and a laughing-stock figure who invariably gets beaten up, falls off his horse, or is otherwise frightened, while all the time bragging about his bravery (his pet sentence is "if only I had my dagger with me I'd gouge his eyes out"). As in the *Qissa Sipahizada* (chapter 4), here too the violence is of a comic kind, with Khoji bouncing back after every spectacular blow. Banter, linguistic peculiarity, and generic instability play an important role in his character. Bragging (*laffazi*) is one of his typical traits, and language is a source of comic effect, as when, after he has let his pony graze in a field, he abuses with choice, Persianized words an angry farmer who has come to shoo him away:

> '*Khabardar ye harkat-e, nashaysta se baz a, varna farqadan par yak bal baqi na rahega. Aur zarbat-e, paposh se baukhla jayega*'.
>
> 'I warn you, refrain from this uncivilized behaviour, else you will have no hair left on your extremities, and you'll be pulverized by my slipper.' (vol. 1, p. 563)

The farmer, "who knew neither Arabic nor Turkish", wastes no time in beating Khoji up with a club, and the farmer's wife lends him a hand in the thrashing. One can either cheer with the sturdy peasant who cares nothing for the power of elite language, or else laugh superciliously at Khoji's pretension to be an educated man using elite language as a class marker. While Khoji would like to think of himself as a sharifzada, others tend to think of him as a menial servant—he gets mistaken for a low-caste Muslim (a *julaha*) and then again for a groom (vol. 1, pp. 553, 569). His very name is a corruption of the respectful title Khwaja, signalling social as well as generic instability. Compared to the helpers ('ayyars) in the adventure dastans, as Firoze Mookerjee

[77] First introduced as one of the sycophantic courtiers of the silly nawab and as a weak old man hopelessly addicted to opium and always greedy for sweets, Khoji reappears a good 200 pages later, towards the end of Volume 1 (so much so that the narrator has to remind readers who he is) and follows Azad to Crimea, a devoted Sancho Panza to Azad's Quixote.

observes—and also to Tejsingh, the main 'ayyar in *Chandrakanta* (see chapter 6)—Khoji is an "undersized weakling": in his failure to defeat his opponents in violent encounters, as well as in his love for an almost wholly imaginary beauty, Bi Shitab Jan, he in fact resembles Don Quixote.[78] Called by the narrator a "dear friend" (*langotiya yar*) of Azad's, Khoji is definitely more of a helper and a menial than a peer.

In fact, Azad's unceremonious treatment of Khoji highlights one of the social faultlines present in the novel that counteracts the narrative drive to spatial and social mobility. For all its critique of the old aristocratic ways and its picaresque interest in low life, popular characters, and street language, the social ethos permeating this novel resolutely distinguishes between "sharif" and the "lower orders". Thus Azad, whose background, as we have seen, is unknown, is affronted when Khoji passes himself off as Azad's father—"That pig is a slave in our household, a slave born of a slave, a buffoon and scoundrel!" he thunders, and has no qualms about abandoning him when in trouble.[79] In this, Sarshar seems to reflect a not-uncommon attitude among even the reformist intellectuals of his time. In an article on education written for *Avadh Akhbar*, for example, he said that the government paid too much attention to the education of the lower classes, and expressed his desire that it would now see to the special needs of children of good families in order to reach a situation (obviously desirable in his view) within which education would be confined to the upper classes.[80]

A similar social faultline is evident in the character of the innkeeper Bi Allah Rakhi, perhaps the most socially mobile character in the novel. Her running sub-plot resurfaces from time to time in widely different circumstances. A composite character, Bi Allah Rakhi goes through several incarnations: she first appears as the young, beautiful, and impertinent wife of an old husband.[81] Asked by the old husband

[78] Mookerjee, *Lucknow*, p. 121.

[79] Transl., ibid., p. 103.

[80] See *Avadh Akhbar*, 20 February 1879, quoted in Mookerjee, *Lucknow*, p. 62.

[81] I have yet to ascertain whether the exchange of letters between them (she cursing his flabbiness and old age, he warming to her perkiness) is a kind of popular comical setpiece that Sarshar merely incorporates in the novel (it reappears in almost exactly the same words in a contemporary footpath

to deliver a letter to her, Azad is impressed by her beautiful (and unveiled) maids and their even more glamorous (and veiled) mistress; their eyes meet ("*ankhen char huin*") and he is immediately smitten.

Once widowed, Allah Rakhi wishes to remarry but her greedy mother refuses to let her, so she runs off and becomes an innkeeper. As Kumkum Sangari has shown in her analysis of the *Qissa Chhabili Bhatiyari*, the female innkeeper is a character of popular female seduction, placed by her trade in a public place, with easy mobility, and direct contact with many men. She is endowed with a sharp tongue and a quick wit that spares no one, high or low.[82] Once again, Sarshar's novel mediates between high and low genres and appropriates this figure of qissa lore. Azad meets her again as a bhatiyari and, needless to say, falls for her again—and indeed promises to marry her in a moment of abandonment. He is not really serious about it, but this provides material for a mock-romantic sub-plot in which Allah Rakhi tries in various ways to make Azad keep his promise: she writes him a letter, files a case against him, publishes an advertisment in the newspaper, sends the guards after him, and finally follows him to the city where he is courting Husn Ara. Azad, who never fails to be enticed (*farefta*) by her and is happy to flirt every time they meet, is nonetheless explicit about the social gap between them: "Listen Bibi! I am a *gentleman*, not a highway man, had you been a *lady* there would have been no problem, but you are after all an innkeeper. How can I possibly marry you? I admit that your beauty is devastating [lit. you are 'a tumult to the age and terror to body and soul']. But you are not a woman of good family [sharifzadi]. Gold brocade can only be matched with gold brocade, it would look odd to match it with coarse cloth" (vol. 1, pp. 363–4). When they meet just before Azad is ready to set off for Turkey, he worries that she

---

collection of Hindi love letters) or whether Sarshar created it—though Azad later tries to bemoan their match in serious-pathetic terms as an example of the social evil of mismatched marriages. Cf. my 'Love Letters', in F. Orsini (ed.), *Love in South Asia*, ch. 10.

[82] Kumkum Sangari, 'Multiple Temporalities, Unsettled Boundaries, Trickster Women: Reading a Nineteenth-Century *Qissa*', in S. Blackburn and V. Dalmia (eds), *India's Literary History*, pp. 213–50. The same is true of Carlo Goldoni's character Mirandolina in *La Locandiera* (1752).

might seek revenge by spoiling his chances with Husn Ara.[83] Allah Rakhi is in fact planning on revenge, but after seeing Azad and confessing to him that she, too, was born a sharifzadi after all, she is happy to step back. It will be enough for him to remember her as she will remember him.[84] In the last volume, Allah Rakhi does marry back into the fold of respectability. In fact, she does even better—marrying a nawab; and so her social status changes yet again.

Khoji's social pretensions and Allah Rakhi's narrative mobility designate the limits of upward mobility of the lower orders and highlight the distaste felt by the novel and its readers for this kind of mobility. This point is forcefully brought home by a rare letter from a woman reader, the wife of a subordinate judge (already quoted above): "I like this story very much . . . but here and there your pen has gone astray. Why on earth have you made Allah Rakhi the innkeeper a gentlewoman? It was a bad thing to do. There is no sin or anything offensive about it, but it just does not sound good to the ear. Why did you write like that? What did you achieve by it? What advantage, what result? Tell me."[85] Could this reaction be read as a sign of anxiety at the very social mobility that the novel's other, reformist side encouraged, and that this woman reader had witnessed all around her?

While it would be presumptuous to assume that social status was any less mobile in the pre-colonial period—as the spectacular careers of "low born" men *and* women in Mughal and eighteenth-century courts indicate—it could be argued that the political, economic, and social upheavals of the nineteenth century made the definition of "being sharif" all the more contested. This can be seen as the tension between old-world nobility, with nothing but its good name on the one hand, and on the other hand upstarts who believed, like the donkey-cart driver in the *Qissa Qazi-e Jaunpur*, that you only needed to throw a few parties in order to be accepted in respectable society.

[83] Given the fact that news about every character seep seamlessly into public knowledge.

[84] Incidentally, the fact that she is gentlewoman could make all the difference, for though Husn Ara knows of and cares little for his past entanglement with an innkeeper it would be a different question if the other woman were of a good family, *zat-e sharif*: *Fasana-e Azad*, vol. 1, p. 545.

[85] *Avadh Akhbar*, 12 December 1879, suppl., p. 247.

The choice of the picaresque and of a hero like Azad thus allows for a "generic instability" that encompasses precisely the contradictory impulses of this age of transition: reformist critique and popular scorn at the old elite, conflicting notions of sharafat, the predicament of the new serious yet also romantic heroine, the impossibility of narrativizing male–female encounters outside the realm of 'ishq-muhabbat and, finally, the impressive but contested mobility of Allah Rakhi. Within the broader developments of fiction and commercial publishing in nineteenth-century North India, we can read *Fasana-e Azad* as a text which stages its own generic change by establishing its co-ordinates in a dialectical relationship with European and Indian literary models, novels, drama, qissa, and dastan, and which also performs an important social and cultural mediation. The novel for the North Indian middle class is thus not a *Bildungsroman* or a novel of social manners. It is a novel which, through the character of Azad, refunctionalizes sharafat, the appeal of love poetry, the enjoyment and patronage of music, and the relations of dependence within courtly society for a mixed, established, and aspiring middle-class readership. Without any clear economic role, Azad is nevertheless free of the burden of courtly society. His ridicule is a way of measuring his mastery of and contempt for that outdated society. His own sharafat is based partly on knowledge and learning and partly on his intrinsic personal qualities. Further, through Azad's spatial and social mobility, the novel and its middle-class readers came to participate and intervene in everything—from a nawab's audience to a local school, from an aristocratic musical gathering to a grand marriage procession, from a street fight to Lucknow's famous Mohurram. All these pleasures now found a place on the printed page, within the capacious form of the new novel.

6

Chandrakanta and Early Hindi Fiction in Banaras

Chandrakanta, the first novel by Devkinandan Khatri (1861–1913), is considered significant because of the fame for which it became known. This was the novel for which thousands of readers learnt Hindi—or rather the Devanagari script. Within the history of Hindi literature, the phenomenal success of this novel counts therefore as an important victory in the difficult, but ultimately victorious, competition of Hindi with Urdu, a triumph that compensates for the negative critical assessment of the novel as such. In the words of a famous Hindi literary critic, "the aim of [novels such as *Chandrakanta*] is weird and wonderful events, not the supremacy of feelings or character building. They are really adventure narratives or tales [*qissas*] that make no attempt at depicting the various aspects of life, which is why they do not come under the category of literature [*sahitya*]."[1] In the history of modern Hindi literature, then, and of the Hindi novel in particular, *Chandrakanta* and the sub-genre of adventure as well as *tilismi* novels that it spawned are usually not thought of as literature but considered at best an unfortunate stage in the progress towards the realistic novel represented by the work of Premchand.[2]

[1] Ramchandra Shukla, *Hindi Sahitya ka Itihas,* quoted in Gopal Ray, *Hindi Upanyas ka Itihas*, New Delhi: Rajkamal Prakashan, 2002, p. 74.

[2] For an account in English, see e.g. Amrik Kalsi, 'Realism in the Hindi Novel', unpublished Ph.D. thesis, University of Cambridge, 1975. *Tilism,* as we shall see, is an enchanted space: the adventures that befall characters in these enchantments and their efforts to "break them" (*tilism torna*) are a major attraction of this sub-genre of novels.

Fig. 16: List of "books worth reading", available for purchase at the Lahari Press, Banaras, including editions of *Chandrakanta* in Urdu and in Nepali ("Gorkhabhasha"), shown on the back cover of Devkinandan Khatri, *Virendravir*, 1902 3rd edn, Banaras: Lahari Press.

Critics recognize Khatri's skilful manipulation of narrative elements, largely borrowed from Urdu dastans and contemporary theatre, as leading to the novel's unprecedented popularity and commercial success. A shrewd and perceptive critic of the Hindi novel like Gopal

Ray has also recognized Khatri's role in educating the reader to the new novelistic conventions; and the writer Rajendra Yadav reflected in a famous essay on the reader's experience from a subjective point of view, as well as on the cultural significance of the novel.[3] But, as in Ramchandra Shukla's case, a narrow definition of "literature" and the "novel" has mostly prevented a positive appreciation of Khatri's extraordinary innovation. From the perspective of commercial publishing, *Chandrakanta* was path-breaking in the way it managed to create a habit of novel-reading in Hindi. Like *Fasana-e Azad*, it represents the most successful attempt by a fiction writer to engage with the possibilities and requirements of entertainment in print, combining the attractions found in already current genres with new ones and creating, through serialization, the expectation of more. Instead of Sarshar's attempt to move away from Urdu dastans, Khatri adopted many of their conventions and adventurous ambience. At the same time, by manipulating the narrative elements and core values of dastans, he also managed to create a "novel experience" that proved to be as involving and satisfying as that of *Fasana-e Azad*, and accessible even to those readers for whom the Perso-Urdu literary world was alien.

The Longest Hindi Novel of the Nineteenth Century

At 300 pages, 4 parts, and 92 chapters, *Chandrakanta* was the longest book in modern Hindi written until then. The first part was written in 1887, as the author's introduction indicates, and published in 1888

[3] In 'Dayniy Mahanta ki Dilchasp Dastan' (An Interesting Story of Pathetic Greatness), Rajendra Yadav argues that the novel corresponds to the collective *imaginaire* of the period: "After the defeat of 1857, people accepted the material and social defeat, but not the intellectual and spiritual defeat. The celebration of vigilance [*chaukannapan*] and extraordinary intelligence in *Chandrakanta* can be linked to this. *Chandrakanta* does not accept defeat but transforms the terrible defeat of feudal prowess into intellectual cleverness—in other words a feeble attempt to prove one's intellectual excellence after one's material strength proved worthless"; first published in *Pandrah Upanyas* (Fifteen Novels) and now inserted as an introduction to the Rajkamal Paperbacks edition of *Chandrakanta*, New Delhi: Rajkamal Paperbacks, 1986, pp. 24–5. For the new novelistic conventions, see also Khatri's detective novels discussed in ch. 7.

in Banaras.[4] All four parts were published, all with moveable type, separately in 1891 and together in one volume in 1892. The success was immediate, so much so that in 1894 Khatri launched his own monthly novel magazine, 'Upanyas Lahari' (Wavelet of Novels) and started publishing the sequel to *Chandrakanta*, *Chandrakanta Santati* (Chandrakanta's Offspring), whose twenty-fourth and final part he completed by 1905. Meanwhile, *Chandrakanta* and *Chandrakanta Santati* appeared in a variety of editions, cheap and deluxe, Hindi and Urdu, under Khatri's imprint, the Lahari Press, though printed at other presses.[5] In 1907 Khatri started yet another sequel, *Bhutnath*, based on a character who had appeared in *Santati*. He managed to write and publish the first six parts of this before his death in 1913. His son, Durgaprasad Khatri, succeeded him at the helm of the Lahari Press and wrote another fifteen parts of *Bhutnath* between 1915 and 1935. All in all, *Chandrakanta* and its sequels compare in length with the achievement of the *Dastan Amir Hamza*. And yet Khatri had his reasons for telling readers, several times, that "from the beginning until now, I have been writing this small book in brief [*mukhtasar hi men*]."[6] Why did Devkinandan Khatri, who clearly had the Urdu dastans in mind when composing his novel, claim he was writing "in brief"?

Like the Urdu dastan about Amir Hamza and his companions, *Chandrakanta* is set in a chivalrous world of princes and princesses, of

[4] *Chandrakanta* was first published by Khatri's friend Babu Amir Singh, proprietor of the Hariprakash Yantralay. This edition is not now available. For this and the following information, see Ray, *Hindi Upanyas ka Itihas*, pp. 68–9.

[5] The *Catalogue of Publications* also shows a 1892 edition of the four parts separately, printed by the Hariprakash Press, Banaras (1000 copies), 8 annas; it also shows an Urdu edition published by Devkinandan Khatri and printed at the Said ul-Matba' Press, Banaras in 1898 (600 copies), at Re 1 for each part. Another Urdu edition published by Khatri was printed in 1898 by Dhundhiraj Press, Banaras, 600 copies, for the same price. A reprint of *Chandrakanta Santati* appeared in 1896 by the Hariprakash Press, Banaras (1000 copies), at Rs 3 for 844 pages. A reprint of its second part in 1897 by the Amar Press, Banaras, cost Rs 2 for 470 pages. Like all Hindi novels mentioned in this and the following chapter, *Chandrakanta* was printed, not lithographed (unlike most songbooks and chapbooks of plays).

[6] Devkinandan Khatri, *Chandrakanta*, Delhi: Rajkamal Paperbacks, 1997, 7th edition, p. 288. All page references are to this edition.

fighting and revelry, of war and the court (*razm o bazm*). The royal court, its etiquette and intrigues; the excitement and opportunity that battles offered for displaying one's valour (*javanmardi*); the splendid setting of palaces, royal gardens, and forests as hunting-grounds—all these elements are reproduced in the novel. Yet, as in the Urdu dastan, the splendour and chivalry of the princes and princesses here are somewhat overshadowed by the excitement offered by the activities of another kind of character, the 'ayyar. Male (and female) 'ayyars are introduced as "friends" of the princely characters but actually hold quite a distinct function and worldview.[7] Already in the Persian popular romances, 'ayyars had first made an appearance as literary figures despite the fact that conventions required that the hero be a prince and that he be superior to the 'ayyar. 'Ayyars were in fact the real protagonists, and it was their ideals that the romances embraced.[8] Elaborate descriptions of war (*razm*), of the splendours of the court (*bazm*), of beautiful women and love (*husn o 'ishq*), and of the elaborate tilisms and the clever tricks of the 'ayyar (*'ayyari*)—the four pillars of a dastan—were part and parcel of the dastan-go's oral art. In particular, to "stop the dastan" (*dastan rokna*) with long lists of items of a certain class was a mark of the narrator's virtuosity.[9] Though all these elements are present in *Chandrakanta*, descriptions are by comparison relatively short and the narrative never "stops". In fact, the pace remains swift throughout the novel. This is achieved primarily by short chapters which work like theatrical scenes: every chapter opens in a new locale and the sudden end of a chapter works like the curtain falling at a suspenseful moment. As Gopal Ray aptly puts it, *Chandrakanta* is an "extraordinary mixture of *qissa-goi* and theatricality."[10] One of the main theatrical innovations of Parsi theatre was its fast tempo and skilful manipulation of narrative pace: ". . . the new optics of the stage, the painted backdrops and stage effects, the footlights and curtains, the

[7] For a definition of the 'ayyar in the Urdu dastan, see Pritchett, *The Romance Tradition*, pp. 40–1, quoted below.

[8] See William Hanaway, 'Persian Popular Romances Before the Safavid Period', unpublished Ph.D. dissertation, University of Columbia, 1972. For 'ayyars as detectives, see ch. 7 below.

[9] Pritchett, *The Romance Tradition*, pp. 16–21.

[10] Ray, *Hindi Upanyas ka Itihas*, p. 75.

plot, narrative tempo, dialogue and song, the music and orchestration, actorly virtuosity and tableaux, identification and idealization, all combined in Parsi theatre to produce a cleverly synchronized performance style that employs velocity for emotional effects. The result was a new experience of the *drive of passion*, in a tempo that renders love both breathtaking and compelling, almost inexorable."[11] As with Parsi theatre, theatricality in *Chandrakanta* meant not only a new pacing of the action but also a multiplication of emotional effects, rashly juxtaposed. "Three-fourths of today have gone by in anxiety, anger and happiness, and not a morsel of food has passed anyone's lips" (p. 276), says the narrator in relation to a particularly eventful chapter, and there is little doubt that the same breathless emotional upheavals experienced by the characters were mirrored in the reader's experience. Moreover, while the qissas discussed in chapter 4 kept to the linear temporality of oral narration, *Chandrakanta* takes some significant liberties with this unwritten rule.[12]

But Devkinandan Khatri's manipulation of the dastan was by no means limited to contraction or a faster pace. His most significant innovation lay in the way in which he *naturalized* the dastan world. Naturalization included the Indianization of characters and locales, the ostensible explicability of all apparently supernatural characters and events, and the injection into the courtly ethic of dastan heroes and courts of local and "homely" elements through reference to caste beliefs, family relations, customs, and "Hindu religion and polity" (as the novel puts it) in a way not dissimilar to the multivocal *Qissa Tota Maina* (chapter 4), as well as to the homely aesthetic of printed

[11] Anuradha Kapur, 'Love in the Time of Parsi Theatre', in F. Orsini (ed.), *Love in South Asia*, p. 227.

[12] The most conspicuous case is the flashback in chs 14 and 15 of pt III, when we are told *how* Raja Jaysingh was kidnapped, an event simply mentioned two chapters earlier. The narrator does not highlight this deviation from linear time. Other, subtler, evidence is the narrator's analepses and prolepses in footnotes to the text, when he either reminds readers of clues or mysteries left unexplained in previous chapters, or suggests that what is left unexplained now may or may not be explained later—as in the case of the yogi splitting the earth with a kick: "whether it is possible or not to split the earth open will become clear in the fourth part": p. 231.

barahmasas (chapter 2). I would like to suggest that the "thrill of familiarity", added to the "thrill of the marvellous", contributed in great measure to the success of the novel. Princes and princesses, 'ayyars, female attendants (*sakhis*) and fairies (paris), masked characters (*naqabposh*), and villains are all found in this novel, as they were in Urdu dastans. But the fact that their adventures take place in the area around Chunar fort, a bare thirty-five kilometres from Banaras, and that royal mothers and fathers behave very much like ordinary parents, provided unprecedented pleasure to Khatri's readers.

Indianizing and Hinduizing the Dastan

Naturalization was long considered by literary critics to be a cosmetic intervention in what was essentially a phenomenon of borrowing—a phenomenon, moreover, that fundamentally invalidated a work, making it no longer "original" but a mere "imitation". In the case of early Indian novels, where naturalization or Indianization can often be seen, it supported the notion that the novel was an import. The assumption was that what counted was what was foreign, while the Indian features—the names, the locales, the language of dialogues, the narrator's occasional interventions—were simply local colour. As we saw in the previous chapter, Meenakshi Mukherjee was the first scholar to draw attention to the many and complex strategies that early Indian novelists put into practice in order to create texts that were new, both with respect to the "source" and the "target" literature, and also to the important presence of earlier narrative tradition in these "novel" texts.[13] It now seems commonplace to notice how translations and adaptations that do not diverge, not even in minimal ways, from their originals may still produce effects that appear new and meaningful to their new readers. *Chandrakanta* is a particular case, in that the "original" was already familiar to Indian audiences. The Arabo-Persian world of Amir Hamza—ostensibly the uncle of the Prophet Muhammad—and his companions was familiar in the way Greek myths, King Arthur's knights, and the Nordic sagas were familiar to European

[13] See Meenakshi Mukherjee, *Realism and Reality*, and idem, 'Epic and Novel in India', in Franco Moretti (ed.), *The Novel*, vol. 1, pp. 596–631.

audiences: as a coherent world which was at once distant and familiar, and whose characters were alive as types as well as destinies. By Indianizing this world, Khatri was not making the unfamiliar familiar. Rather, he made characters and adventures that existed only in the imagination move closer to the world of the everyday. The result was not a "realistic" novel but the thrilling possibility of imagining oneself as part of that wonderful world.

To all appearances *Chandrakanta* is a dastan. It tells the story of the contrasting love between Birendra Singh and Chandrakanta, the son and daughter of the two neighbouring rulers of Naugarh and Vijaygarh. Their fathers were once friends, until the divan of Vijaygarh successfully drew a wedge between them. Vijaygarh is the more powerful "petty kingdom" of the two, and both are tied to the ruler of Chunar, the famous fortress on the bend of the Ganges not far from Banaras. The divan of Naugarh, Jit Singh, was himself once an 'ayyar but gave up his calling when his son, Tej Singh, became proficient in the art. In Vijaygarh there is no divan-'ayyar but the divan's son—who is the main villain and is aptly named Krur ("Cruel") Singh—has two Muslim 'ayyars at his disposal, Nazim and Ahmad. Krur Singh's task is to prevent the love between Chandrakanta and Birendra Singh from resulting in marriage. In pursuit of this he does not hesitate to kill his own father in order to become divan himself and, when the plan misfires, he deserts to Chunar and incites its ruler, Shivdatt Singh, to move against Chandrakanta's father. Nazim and Ahmad and four of Chunar's own 'ayyars, including a Brahmin astrologer and expert at divination, Pandit Jagannath, are the main opponents of Birendra Singh and his only 'ayyar helper, Tej Singh, even though Chandrakanta's two sakhis, Chapala and Champa, are skilled at 'ayyari too. The first half of the novel consists of the repeated attempts of the 'ayyars to disrupt each other's plans and kidnap their opponents so as to put them out of action. The most common means is for an 'ayyar to change appearance (*surat banana*) and make the victim unconscious through a special powder (*behoshi ki dava*), which makes any kind of food, drink, and even scent perilous. Once unconscious, the victim is tied into a sack which the successful 'ayyar takes away on his (and, occasionally, her) back. Tej Singh places his victims in a special cave, which is similar to, but not quite, a tilism or enchantment. Once in a tilism, there is no way out, unless someone, designated by whoever set up the tilism, "breaks it".

The second half of *Chandrakanta* consists of the prolonged struggle by Birendra and Tej to dismantle, with the help of a "tilism book", the enchantment in which Chandrakanta and Chapala have wandered, only to find that the two women have disappeared into another, even larger, tilism annexed to the first. They are both helped and distracted in their quest by a group of women who wander in the forest on horseback. Their mysterious leader, called "Bankanya" or "Forest Girl", looks so remarkably like Chandrakanta that Prince Birendra falls in love with her at first sight, though not without feelings of guilt. In turn, the forest girl behaves very much like a pari in a dastan: she falls in love with the mortal man, declares her love openly, and for her help in recovering Chandrakanta sets the condition that Birendra should marry her at the same ceremony.[14] Her written messages are delivered by masked riders (*naqabposh*), also familiar figures in dastans and qissas.

In the end, after the threat of another, even more bloodthirsty, 'ayyar called Zalim Singh is averted, Chandrakanta is handed back to her lover and her father by another mysterious figure who calls himself Siddhanta Yogi. Though it is a shame to give away the ending at this point, this Yogi is none other than Tej Singh's father Jit Singh. He had mounted the whole elaborate masquerade so that Birendra Singh could break the first tilism and earn all the riches hidden in it, as customary, and so that Chandrakanta could break the second tilism and acquire all its wealth as dowry.

Razm, bazm, husn, and 'ayyari, all the four elements of a dastan exist here. How does Indianization work, then, and to what effect? To start from the descriptions, we find in *Chandrakanta* all the predictable depictions of forests, gardens, pavilions, and beautiful women. Yet subtle changes are at work. Take this description of the garden of the women's mahal inside Vijaygarh fort:

[14] Other supernatural, pari-like features include the fact that these women appear and disappear at will and the astrologer's divination (*ramal*) can ascertain nothing about them. When boating on the river one night they are described as an '*akhara* of paris' (p. 172), and they once appear in colour-coded dress, like the paris in *Indarsabha*: here one is a "*sabz sakhi*" (green sakhi) and the other a "*surkh sakhi*" (red sakhi): p. 277.

> The day is still lingering, Chandrakanta, Chapala and Champa are strolling in the garden. The scent of moist flowers mixed with the light breeze is delightful to the heart. All varieties of flowers are blooming. The thick mass of mango trees at the west of the garden and the sun rays shining through arouse a peculiar pleasure. Water has been sprinkled on the rows of flowerbeds, and the flower trees have been washed well with water. (p. 14)

The scene is the familiar one of the garden as a site of natural and female beauty and as the setting for love—this is the garden where, in a later chapter, Birendra Singh will visit Chandrakanta in secret. And yet, instead of launching into a long enumeration of poetic flowers, creepers, bees, and so on, this description uses a few light touches, including the "homely" detail of the daily sprinkling and watering of plants. Suddenly, the exotic palace garden with the princess and her sakhis has become any ordinary garden at dusk.

Even when the description is enumerative in the usual dastan way, the mention of *local* trees and animals is striking:

> The kingdom of Naugarh and Vijaygarh is a hilly tract covered by huge and dense forests, with the rivers Chandraprabha and Karmanasha flowing between the hills. Here and there inside the mountains you find gorgeous natural caves and ravines. Among the trees there are *sakhu, tend, vijaysar, sanai, koria, go, khaja, peyar, jigna, asan*, and others, and also many *parijat* among the wild trees. They are uncommonly interesting hills, if you find yourself in a village you only need to proceed for one mile in one direction or another and you will find yourself enveloped in dense forest and you will neither be able to find the way from which you came, nor know where you should go. During the rainy season the scenery is breathtaking, you will cross ten streams in just one mile. Among the wild animals you will see, besides antelopes, panthers, bears, leopards, ravine deers, langurs and monkeys, and also tigers occasionally, though not in the rainy season, because when there is too much water their dens are ruined and they move up to the higher hills. There are no deer in these hills, but many can be seen below. Among the birds partridges and peacocks are in abundance. In other words, these lovely hills are still there in the same way as I've written and are by all means worth seeing. (pp. 48–9)

This is not a literary description of nature as we would expect it, nor a general one of a "wild forest". The object is a specific area, with names of local trees and local animals.[15] It is partly a hunter's description—Khatri's pastime matched that of his dastan heroes—and partly a forest contractor's, which was in fact Khatri's occupation when he was writing *Chandrakanta*. However, nature is still a setting and suggestive of a mood, which in the case of the forest can be fear, intrigue, or encounter with strangers, and plays no other role in the narrative as yet.

The interiors of the tilisms, one with impressive ruins and the other with beautiful gardens and pavilions, are also described in great detail—and as if in moving sequence, following the point of view of the character who is exploring them. What is significant is that we are constantly urged to admire the arrangement (*sajavat*) of a garden and the splendid furnishings of a room or a pavilion.[16] In other words, nature is domesticated and spaces adorned for handsome living.

A similar shift occurs in the description of female beauty. Here, as with nature, literary convention was particularly strong, and Khatri did not abandon it completely. But whereas every heroine would be introduced by an elaborate "head-to-toe" (*nakh-shikh*) description, in the chapter quoted above—in which we catch the first glimpse of Chandrakanta and her sakhis—no physical description is offered. We *assume* she is beautiful since she is the heroine. We are told that she is at various points in the novel and her picture (as the forest girl) is indeed described, but the absence of elaborate description cannot fail to strike us as an authorial decision.[17] Women in the novel are

[15] Local trees and creepers appear also in the first description of the cave-tilism, whose secret entry only Tej Singh knows: the fruit trees mentioned here are *karjani, ghumchi, ber, mukoiche, chiraunji*, etc.: p. 28.

[16] Though the narrator explains such detailed descriptions otherwise: "Reader, I will not utter praises of a garden at every step and describe each and every flower and leaf, because I have been writing this small volume in brief from the beginning until now. Besides, the gardens in this cave are not so big as to justify wasting reams of paper on them, though I have to say that all the gardens in this cave, whether big or small, are arranged in a nice fashion, and not just in terms of flowers: the hillocks and the leafy greenery are also attractive to the extreme": p. 288.

[17] We can recall the unease of another great nineteenth-century novelist, Bankimchandra Chattopadhyaya, at describing his heroine according to the usual, highly sensual, conventions: see Sudipta Kaviraj, 'Tagore and the Transformations in the Ideals of Love', in Orsini (ed.), *Love in South Asia*, pp. 161–82.

beautiful, as they always are in dastans, and they never fail to attract and enamour men. Chunar's ruler Shivdatt Singh is immediately smitten with Chapala, who arrives disguised as a singer in order to look for the whereabouts of Tej Singh, kidnapped and held captive inside Chunar fort. But this is how she is described:

> Chapala was no ordinary woman. Apart from beauty and elegance [*khubsurati aur nazakat*], she also had strength. To fight with two or three men and capture them was but a trifle for her. She was fully competent in the art of using weapons. And apart from the art of 'ayyari she had many other qualities. Masterful at singing and playing music, expert in dancing, very fond of making fireworks—what else can I write? There was no art in which Chapala was not skilled. Her complexion was fair, her body shapely in every way, her delicate hands and feet suggested that to strike her with a flower would be a crime. Whenever she needed to go out she would consciously spoil her beauty or disguise herself. (p. 62)

The notion of beauty at work here is the usual one of fairness and delicate features, but, in the case of this female 'ayyar, exquisite beauty hides a tough, fearless, and resourceful woman. Chapala knows the feminine arts and will flirt with Shivdatt Singh in order to obtain what she wants, but she can also carry an enemy 'ayyar on her back.

What about Chandrakanta herself? Surprisingly, her only physical description is in the shape of a painting of the mysterious forest girl, as already mentioned, admired by Birendra Singh himself. As in the case of the interiors and gardens, her beauty is a mixture of bodily features and adornments, in this case jewels, and shies away from explicit sensuality:

> Oh, what a good and clear picture this is! It shows her natural height, the same large eyes whose lines are drawn so sharply. Aha! How the rosiness of her cheeks has been depicted, her smile, the redness of betel on her thin lips. The large earrings in her ears, the mark on her forehead and her nose ornament are all there, but how beautiful and clear is the *gop* around her neck, whose gem in the middle and gold leaf work at the sides show that the highest craftsmanship has been expended in its making. Not only the *gop*, all her jewels are exquisite. The chain around her neck, the armlets, *kangan*, wristlets, bracelets, rings, everything is perfectly crafted . . . (p. 195)

It could be argued that this list of jewels is in line with the dastan-gos' tradition of enumerating all the items of one class, yet, if taken together with the description of the tilism's interiors (and other elements that we will come to later), it is hard to escape the impression that the aesthetic evoked is one of wealth rather than princeliness.

Descriptions in *Chandrakanta* are thus not structurally different from those in dastans, though by being shorter they serve the novel's faster and more dramatic pace. The mention of local features conveys a sense both of specificity and closeness. Descriptions of natural locations and individuals no longer necessarily conform to literary and aesthetic conventions, and when they do, as in the case of gardens and women, the emphasis is less on wondrousness and sensuality than on an aesthetic of wealthy pleasure.

Several critics have pointed out that supernatural objects, events, and characters, so typical of the dastan world, do not disappear in *Chandrakanta* but are all "explained" so as to bring them within the order of the natural sciences.[18] The author takes great care when explaining how the tricks (*tarkib*) of the 'ayyars work: whenever someone is rendered unconscious by the ubiquitous "drug of unconsciousness" (*behoshi ki dava*), we are told where and when exactly the 'ayyar mixed it in the victim's food or drink or sprinkled it over flowers.[19] The 'ayyars' prodigious ability at disguising themselves is explained by taking recourse to the performing art of certain disguise artists

[18] "Although the multiform activities of the 'ayyars cannot altogether be explained logically, Khatri spares no effort to make them believable . . . Strange and wonderful descriptions of herons and snakes made of powder, the stone man, self-playing instruments, a laughing stone dog, walls that make you unconscious at the mere touch, doors that automatically open and shut, fake doors and marvellous tunnels are all found in Khatri's narratives. But Khatri has painstakingly and scientifically described the mechanical structure of these tilismi marvels. This is what makes Khatri's narratives, which he called novels, different from Persian stories of 'ayyars and tilism. Even if Khatri drew inspiration for these descriptions from Persian and Urdu dastans, in nature they differ completely from them. The tilism of his novels is no magical spectacle like that of *Tilismi Hoshruba* but shows the *clear imprint of the new mechanical age*": Ray, *Hindi Upanyas ka Itihas*, pp. 72–3, emphasis added.

[19] For example, Chapala tricks the 'ayyar Nazim, who has entered the palace garden disguised as Champa, by placing some "powder of unconsciousness" in

(*bahurupiye*), who still practised (or were said to practise) their feats of disguise in India then. The magic world of tilism is explained by way of mechanics: when hit in a particular fashion, stone slabs reveal secret doors and chambers; long tunnels are actually excavated in the rocks, secret doors can be opened with special locks and hidden knobs. The stone figure of a man reading reclined over a platform which "magically" moves when touched is actually moved by a steam coming out of his mouth (p. 147). As with the 'ayyars' disguises, these explanations do not fully account in the end for the tilism devices, but what matters is the consistent attitude towards their explicability. It is as if the author and readers, both well acquainted with the wonderful world of tilism and 'ayyars from the dastans, mutually shared a novelistic pact according to which one of the novel's new *expectations* was accountability, and natural or mechanical explanations had to be provided. (While, for example, astrology and other forms of divination were considered wholly within the natural world.[20])

The same requirement is at play in the characterization of the Bankanya. As mentioned, Chandrakanta and her sakhis reappear in the tilism as "forest girls" and behave in an imperious way that strongly resembles the fairies of Perso-Urdu dastans. Khatri uses the motif of the fairies as a dissembling device, confident that his readers will readily accept the event of a fairy princess falling in love with the human hero, as well as the playful tricks that fairies play on human characters. The function of the forest girls is also similar to that of fairies in dastans in that they sometimes help and at other times hinder the hero in his quest. Only, here the forest girls are *not* fairies, they are not supernatural beings and do not perform supernatural feats, they are only women in disguise. Moreover, as we shall see, the confusion and unease felt by Prince Birendra when he is attracted to the forest girl, and the feeling of guilt he feels for thinking less of

---

her ear and asking Champa/Nazim to check what is it in her ear that is troubling her: p. 16.

[20] In particular, *baladavi*, telling the future by swirling until one faints, and *ramal*, divination by drawing lines or figures on the ground. The astrologer Pandit Jagannath makes great use of ramal to discover the whereabouts of things and people, though ramal is powerless with tilisms and with the special metal of the amulets (*taviz*) that the forest girls wear: pp. 30, 56.

Chandrakanta and accepting marriage with the forest girl, are functional to the specific ethic that the novel proffers.

The final area of Indianization, or in this case Hinduization, worth considering regards the insertion of familiarizing elements pertaining to caste, family, and religion. The most obvious change introduced by Khatri is that all the main characters are Hindu: the princes and 'ayyars of the Perso-Urdu dastans are replaced with local Rajputs. Bengali novelists had elected Rajputs as the heroes of their historical novels,[21] and the casting of Rajputs as protagonists makes *Chandrakanta* a historical novel by default. This is despite the fact that these are local Rajputs from the Banaras region rather than from Rajputana, and despite the historical period of the novel being unspecified. As we shall see, elements of modernity enter the novel at the level of genre ideology, making it a "dastan for a new age", but they do so surreptitiously, while the overall courtliness and adventurous quality of the novel suggest a more heroic age.

Transmogrifying the chivalrous ethic of Hamza and his companions in the Perso-Urdu dastans into *kshatriya dharma* was not a difficult move, since the ideals of heroism, magnanimity, generosity, and justice were common to martial groups across religious lines. The kshatriya ideal Birendra Singh subscribes to is defined by the same term used for dastan heroes, *javanmardi*, "gallantry", whose virtues include manliness, courage, and a magnanimous heart. Chunar's ruler Shivdatt Singh is no *javanmard* because, among other things, he does not try to win Chandrakanta through his courage and generosity of heart (p. 96).[22]

[21] Notably, R.C. Dutt's *Rajput Jivan Sandhya* (1879), already translated in Hindi and published in Banaras probably in the early 1890s by the Bharat Jivan Press (see ch. 7); Gopal Ray, *Hindi Upanyas Kosh*, vol. 1, p. 312.

[22] Actually, since 'ayyars with their feats dominate this novel, as they did in the dastans, the Rajput hero has only a few occasions to display his bravery, though his virtue is nonetheless never in doubt: "Your courage and *javanmardi* are not in doubt", Tej Singh's father reassures Birendra Singh while dissuading him from pursuing the 'ayyars who have kidnapped his friend Tej: p. 59. Birendra shines only on the battlefield, where he initially suggests that he and Shivdatt Singh should fight each other singly, so as to spare the "unfortunate poor soldiers": p. 95. His proposal is refused, but he easily carries the day anyway.

Not only the princely heroes but even the divans and 'ayyars are predominantly Rajputs. This makes for a very cohesive social and ideological environment. In fact, here and there we find echoes in the novel of the anti-Muslim prejudices that, Shahid Amin has argued, found a wide echo in this period.[23] In passing, the mutinous villain Krur Singh claims that he has all the Muslims on his side, which makes the raja of Vijaygarh keep a wary eye on his Muslim soldiers and subjects (pp. 33, 39). And when an armed confrontation ensues between the ruler of Chunar and the raja of Vijaygarh, once again the threat of a mutiny of Muslim soldiers is voiced: they are made to fight in front, with a cannon right behind them (p. 84). Caste is mentioned only once in the novel, in relation to Chapala and her potential marriage to Tej Singh, but the discussion arising about it suggests that the novel is negotiating several stances at the same time. Intriguingly, it is Pandit Jagannath who raises the question:

> *Jyotishi*: "So, Tej Singh, is Chapala of the same *jati* as you?"
>
> *Tej*: "I don't know about her caste, but once love has happened, whatever the caste . . ."
>
> *Jyotishi*: "But doesn't she have a guardian, anyone responsible for her? If she is not of your own caste, how will her parents agree?"
>
> *Tej*: "If anything like that happens I will kill her and then I'll kill myself."
>
> *Prince* [*Birendra Singh*]: "If you give me a reward I'll tell you what caste Chapala is . . . Chapala is of the same caste as we are. Her father was a very big landowner and an 'ayyar through and through. Her mother died when she was seven days old. Her father brought her up and taught her 'ayyari, he died only a few years ago . . ." (p. 245)

While the Pandit is introducing a realistic concern, in line with current social norms (the decision is not Chapala's but of whoever is her

[23] Shahid Amin, 'On Representing the Musalman', in S. Mayaram, M.S.S. Pandian, and A. Skaria (eds), *Subaltern Studies XII: Muslims, Dalits, and the Fabrications of History*, New Delhi: Permanent Black and Ravi Dayal Publisher, 2005, pp. 1–35.

"guardian", *varis*), Tej reacts like a literary hero, to be precise a masnavi hero: caste, like religion and other worldly distinctions, does not matter when facing the power of love. And if their love cannot be accepted, they will be together in death. Birendra Singh's solution introduces the typical novelistic motif of agnates. The two lovers are not only of the same caste, but also of the same social standing: while so far we only knew that Chapala was a female attendant to Chandrakanta, now we know that she is a zamindar's daughter, thus perfectly fit to marry the divan's son.

Behind these various Indianizing touches there lies a more basic Hinduization of the novel. Hinduizing is certainly involved in the presence of a Brahmin 'ayyar like Pandit Jagannath, who on one occasion doubles as a messenger bearing a wedding proposal, a typical task of Brahmins and a nice touch (p. 73). Occasionally, sadhus and yogis also make an appearance, though mostly as a convenient and impressive form of disguise.[24] Thus, Jit Singh disguised as a yogi does not allow the rajas to prostrate themselves before him because he is not *really* a spiritual authority (p. 282). The vanquished Shivdatt Singh declares that he will abandon his kingdom in order to perform austerities in the forest—a culturally accepted practice—though in fact he is plotting revenge (p. 238). Just as in the first volume of *Fasana-e Azad* every chapter began with Azad waking up and going out into the streets, again and again here a new chapter opens with a new dawn. And every time a new day begins for Birendra Singh and his companions, we see them taking a bath, performing puja as well as the *sandhya* ritual. Such examples can be multiplied. When Chapala is desperate trying to find Tej Singh, who has been kidnapped, she vows that she will fast and take no food or water (*anna-jal*) until she finds him: only when she discovers his whereabouts (through the power of her austerity?) does she allow herself to eat (p. 63). Finally, one of the sure proofs that Krur Singh is an unredeemable villain is not only that he has blithely killed his own father, but that he disregards the state of impurity and mourning (*sutak*) after his father's death. When he hears that Birendra

[24] E.g. the 'ayyar Devi Singh who, disguised as a Ramanandi sadhu, sings a song that informs Tej Singh about Krur Singh's actions. Tej Singh's father also disguises himself as a great yogi (*mahapurush*) "with a very long beard and matted hair": pp. 36, 230.

has managed to enter Chandrakanta's garden, he runs to inform her father, Raja Jaysingh, as he is, "naked and with his head like a pan turned upside down" (p. 33).[25]

The "domestication of the mythological"—and of the courtly we may add—and the "mythologization of the domestic" were, according to Anuradha Kapur, crucial to Parsi melodrama, "a mode which mediated the transition from courtly culture to the new domesticity and nationalism of the emerging middle classes." Love, she points out, "was critical to this process, as it domesticated the mythological and mythologized the domestic."[26] In this novel about chivalrous adventures and courtly characters inspired by dastans, we can see the very same domestication at work. It is at work in the royal characters, whose reactions are those of ordinary parents. Thus, when Chandrakanta and Birendra are in any danger, their fathers and mothers worry and fret. When Raja Jaysingh is warned by Krur Singh that his daughter Chandrakanta is dallying with Birendra in the garden and goes and finds no one there because Birendra has already left, he is doubly angry with Krur for "giving his daughter a bad name with no good reason" (*jhuth-muth badnam karna,* p. 28). And finally, when courtly and kinship etiquettes clash—as when towards the end Raja Jaysingh, who has already resolved to marry Chandrakanta to Birendra, visits Birendra's father—it is kinship etiquette that prevails. Courtly etiquette—and note the Perso-Urdu terms—would require that Surendra Singh, Birendra's father, welcome his neighbourly ruler (*istiqbal* is the term used) and offer him hospitality and refreshments (*ziyafat*, p. 281). But Jaysingh refuses the hospitality without giving any explanation, though Surendra Singh understands: Jaysingh's position as the father of the prospective bride overrules his role as an overlord to whom honour is due and puts him in a subordinate position in this situation.[27]

Sometimes domestication is evident in the idiomatic expressions used. For example, when Tej and Birendra first discuss Krur Singh as

[25] Jaysingh is astonished to see him: "Krur Singh, you left your impure state and mourning for your father to come here—this astonishes me": p. 33.

[26] Anuradha Kapur, 'Love in the Time of Parsi Theatre', p. 227.

[27] Two other instances occur inside the tilism towards the end of the novel: the mysterious yogi (actually Jit Singh, Tej's father) first asks Birendra and Tej not to speak about Birendra's love and impending marriage to the forest girl to

one of the obstacles to Birendra and Chandrakanta's marriage, Tej observes that Raja Jaysingh will not "give his daughter to the son of his minister"—using the common expression "*larki dena*" (p. 12). The reservations against Birendra being Chandrakanta's prospective husband are removed pretty quickly in the novel, but even before then the princess's mother fondly recalls the time, before Chandrakanta's birth, when the child Birendra used to visit them often and the two fathers were "like one man". After Chandrakanta was born the two children played together, "and this was how their love for each other was born" (p. 40). The terms used for the intimacy between the two houses and the love between the two youths are domestic and domesticating ones, for she is trying to justify a love that has since become known and, hence, potentionally objectionable.

Indianization, Hinduization, and domestication go hand in hand in the novel, then, bringing the wonderfully exotic world of the dastan tantalizingly closer home. In the same direction, another change emerges towards the end of the novel in relation to the very meaning of the adventure: this could be called a re-ideologization of the tilism.

The New Novel as a Dastan for a New Age

The trend in *Chandrakanta* towards elucidating supernatural and magical elements in terms of mechanical or quasi-natural "devices" (tarkib) has been rightly linked by critics like Gopal Ray to Khatri's

---

anyone outside: "You may talk about it between yourselves as much as you like, but if her parents find out won't they be displeased? Because for a girl of good family to meet a male stranger and correspond with him and make him an offer of marriage is very objectionable": p. 265. Later, the yogi asks Birendra to enter the tilism before the two fathers. The reason is that he wants Birendra to meet Chandrakanta safely out of sight of the two elders: "Usually, when one loses something one desires a lot and then finds it again after much effort or by surprise, one falls upon it just as a famished hawk falls on its prey. I know that you and Chandrakanta love each other very much, if you see each her or if she sees you suddenly in front of the two rajas, I would not be surprised if you or Chandrakanta were to do something disrespectful [*beadabi*], or if in a fit of passion you were to go and stand next to her. This would not be appropriate. Therefore I consider it better for you to meet the princess before them . . .": p. 283.

attempt to reconcile the dastan with modernity and with the modern genre of the novel. This trend is accompanied by a related intervention in the value system of the genre. In Perso-Urdu dastans the function of tilisms and of the other adventures of princes and 'ayyars was to provide entertainment. Ideologically, as we have already seen, the dominant courtly values of the princely characters were shared by all. Even though punctured and offset by the 'ayyars' irony, their earthy humour, and their greed, the 'ayyars themselves worked by their strict code of honour. To all appearances, *Chandrakanta* reproduces this dynamic balance between courtly ideals and the 'ayyars' counter-values; but towards the end of the novel a new explanation is offered for the existence of tilisms. This explanation, proffered by Siddhanta Yogi (Jit Singh in disguise), is worth noting, for while it is in line with the other attempts to "explain" the supernatural features of dastans, its foundations are not in courtly values but in wealth:

> *Baba*: "A tilism is set up by a man who has a lot of wealth and treasures and no heir. He then asks the best astrologers [*jyotishi* and *najumi*] if a brilliant or worthy son is likely to be born in his family or his brothers' families. When finally the jyotishi and najumi inform him that after so many years a boy in his family is going to be brilliant and they write up his horoscope, a tilism is "tied" [*bandhna*] to his name, holding many treasures and beautiful precious objects.
>
> Nowadays, the rule for setting up a tilism in somebody's name is that you put a little bit of money and treasure and then sacrifice one or two animals for it, which become ghosts or snakes and protect it and do not allow anyone, apart from the designated man, to take any money away. Earlier, the rule was different. In the old days, whenever kings needed to set up ["tie"] a tilism, jyotishis, najumis, vaidyas, craftsmen, and tantriks were gathered. In order to set up the tilism the ground would be dug up according to their instructions, then the treasure would be hidden in the ground and a tilism building would be erected on top. The jyotishis, najumis, vaidyas, craftsmen, and tantriks would then set their spells, each according to their strength, so as to hide the tilism, but they also kept in mind the astrological chart of the designated man. (p. 293)

The yogi/divan's explanation sets up an interesting historical narrative of ritual "simplification". According to this the elaborate tilisms found in dastans and in the novel belong to an earlier period, when rajas conducted elaborate and expensive rituals with scores of specialists of religion and magic. They are not to be found "nowadays", not because they belong to a wonderful world as against reality, but because now tilisms are so small that they are hardly noticeable and cannot be distinguished from ordinary sacrifices (*bali*).[28] Even more striking, and in line with other shifts in the novel, is how the magical and wonderful world of tilisms is explained on the basis of the two co-ordinates of wealth and inheritance (cf. chapter 7). Why did Jit Singh become Siddhanta Yogi and prolong Birendra's search inside the tilism by distracting him with the forest girl and by hiding Chandrakanta in the second tilism? It was so that, by each breaking a tilism, Birendra and Chandrakanta could acquire the wealth hidden in the tilisms. As he explains:

> "To bring the princess and Chapala outside the cave or bring them home would have been no big task for me, but I was inclined to have the princess break this small tilism with her own hand so that everything in it would become hers. Not just myself, everybody must know that the prince was breaking the Chunar tilism in order to free Princess Chandrakanta from captivity, and that he had no desire [*lalach*] for wealth and treasures. Had I taken the princess out of here myself and brought her to you, he would have stopped breaking the tilism and the treasure in it would have remained buried, too. I want you to prosper. I would never have accepted that so much wealth should go waste and that neither the prince nor Princess Chandrakanta should not get it." (p. 295)

"*Mal-asbab*" is the term most often used in this passage, a term usually employed for household belongings.[29] The effect is reinforced

[28] Interesting also is how the various specialists of secret knowledge are grouped together: what they perform could be called magic, but this could also be viewed as their accepted secret and powerful knowledge.

[29] When Prince Birendra finds the treasure of the first tilism, the instructions written in the book order him to transfer all the boxes out of the tilism: the process of carrying the boxes out and back to Naugarh takes all of ten days. The prince frets at this delay in the search for Chandrakanta, but the book is adamant: he can make no progress until he becomes master of all the wealth: pp. 192–3. In the case of the second tilism, the precious things it contains can

when Chandrakanta's father exclaims: "May those people be thanked who accumulated all this wealth [*daulat*]. Had I wanted to sell my whole kingdom in order to put together things for the dowry [*dahez ka saman*], I would not have been able to put together more than one fourth of this!" (p. 298). Although the prince's official values of javanmardi are reconfirmed, the wonderful tilism is here re-ideologized as a means to acquire wealth and dowry. If we juxtapose this statement with the aesthetic of adornment that we found in physical and natural descriptions, we begin to see that the dastan's courtly splendour has been transvalued into an aesthetic of wealth. Wealth is no longer an attribute of princely courtliness, a means to the display of awesome splendour. Wealth is an end and a necessity, both for the hero and the heroine, and inheriting it is the only way in which they can acquire it (see also chapter 7).

A third and final aspect of this modernization of the dastan is the ubiquitous presence of written documents: letters, undertakings (*iqrarnama*), marriage agreements, posters (*ishtahar*), and books. While in detective fiction (as in the two novels by Khatri analysed in the next chapter), the emphasis on written documents is a function of the new genre—letters and wills act as crucial proofs—in *Chandrakanta* written documents enter more incidentally. The visible presence of such documents can even in a novel be related to the greater visibility and role they played in the life of ordinary Indians.

Major Stock Characters: The *'Ayyars*

'Ayyars were undoubtedly the most popular characters in dastans, and the same is true of the 'ayyars in *Chandrakanta*.[30] Their genealogy lies in Persian popular narratives. Historians have traced the existence of

---

remain there since it will become a pleasure residence for Chandrakanta and Birendra: p. 300.

[30] "Talk to any readers of *Chandrakanta* or *Santati* and they will speak with much greater enthusiasm of the marvellous tricks of [the 'ayyars] Tej Singh, Bhairo Singh, Badrinath, Jit Singh, Bhutnath, and so on, and of the tilisms at Chunar, Jamaniya, and Rohtasgarh, than of the love stories of Birendra Singh and his children": Ray, *Hindi Upanyas ka Itihas*, p. 71.

'ayyar confraternities in Iraq and Iran from the ninth to the twelfth centuries. They embodied the concept and institution of javanmardi, which indicated: (a) a set of virtues such as chivalry, generosity, magnanimity, bravery, and virtuous youth; and (b) an organization of men devoted to these principles. Though contemporary court historians in Iran often spoke disparagingly of 'ayyars, their deeds were celebrated in popular romances which portrayed the ideals of javanmardi. 'Ayyars often stole the show from brave but rather less sensationally skilled princes.[31] In Perso-Urdu dastans 'ayyars are part of the courtly retinue. In Frances Pritchett's succinct definition:

> They specialize in reconnaissance, espionage, disguise (impersonating women with implausible ease), commando tactics (scaling walls, tunnelling into fortresses, killing sentries, knocking enemies unconscious with drugs), and other forms of guerrilla warfare, thievery, and dirty tricks. '*Ayyars* are not really part of the courtly elite, and so they have less dignity to uphold; they are tremendously given to playing practical jokes, especially vulgar ones, to each other and on their enemies . . . ['Amar, the chief 'ayyar] is responsible for virtually all of the considerable amount of humor in the dastan.[32]

While 'ayyar-like qualities, such as omnipresence, omniscience, and perfect disguise, are manifest in the detective or detective-like characters in Hindi detective novels (*jasusi upanyas*, in the next chapter), in *Chandrakanta* the jasus characters act as mere spies and the 'ayyars are more like helpers. It seems that in *Chandrakanta* Khatri started out with 'ayyar characters that were very similar to the trickster figures of

[31] See Hanaway, 'Persian Popular Romances', and also ch. 7.

[32] Pritchett, *The Romance Tradition in Urdu*, pp. 40–1. According to one Persian romance, these were the attributes of the 'ayyar: "The *'ayyar* must be a master of stratagems and have many ways of doing things. He must be clever and have a ready answer. He must speak softly and be able to deal with everybody and not be at a loss. He must make the obvious unseen and not mention a person's faults, and hold his tongue and speak little": *Samak-e 'Ayyar*, II, p. 220, quoted in Hanaway, 'Persian Popular Romances', p. 153. 'Ayyars share a secret language and a special attire, first and foremost the satchel (*batua*) containing all their necessary implements and ingredients.

the dastans: greedy, humorous, mischievous.[33] But then Khatri gradually emphasized the 'ayyars' adherence to a strict ethical code and to the values of their princely rulers. In fact, as mentioned, most of the 'ayyars in the novel are Rajputs or their Muslim "equivalents", Pathans. They are incorporated into the courtly elite as ministers or ministers' sons: they are granted *jagirs*, royal embraces, and "equal status" (*barabari ka darja*) in exchange for their services.[34] The 'ayyars' ethical code includes the refusal to use force in order to extract information from enemy 'ayyars, and they absolutely forbid their masters to harm and punish other 'ayyars except with imprisonment. This means that, even in times of war, 'ayyars are never unduly upset about what other 'ayyars do: if one manages to kidnap an 'ayyar or even an overlord, eventually they will be freed. This makes for a peculiar kind of warfare, in contrast with the brutal killing of soldiers in battle,[35] but also for a lighter

[33] The only instance of greed on the part of an 'ayyar takes place towards the beginning of the novel in chapter 9 of part I, when, in a comic scene, Tej Singh manages to wrestle Rs 10,000 out of the munshi of Raja Jaysingh of Vijaygarh, only to then go to his own master, Birendra Singh, asking for more: "*Yar*, this is devil's money, add something to it so that it becomes pure . . . but it should be no less than the amount because your status is higher": p. 32. Disguises, and especially cross-dressing, of course give rise to many humorous incidents, as when Tej Singh enters Chandrakanta's private garden disguised as one of her sakhis. She then starts bantering with Chapala, and in the ensuing scuffle Chapala grabs one of her fake breasts, p. 12. This kind of sexual frisson is found also in contemporary Parsi theatre: see Anuradha Kapur, 'Impersonation, Narration, Desire, and the Parsi Theatre', in Blackburn and Dalmia (eds), *India's Literary History*, pp. 87–118; and Kathryn Hansen, 'Stri Bhumika: Female Impersonators and Actresses on the Parsi Stage', *Economic and Political Weekly*, vol. xxxiii, no. 35, 29 August–4 September 1998: 2291–2300.

[34] While female 'ayyars, like Chapala above, are skilled at singing and dancing just like qissa heroines, status makes the case of male 'ayyars more ambivalent: Tej Singh is very skilled at playing the flute, but when Chapala makes him accompany her singing in front of Chunar's ruler in order to free him from captivity, he jokes about the lowly status of the accompanist as contrasting with his own status as a divan's son: 'I became your accompanist (*safarda*). I had to do what my fathers and grandfathers never did!', p. 68.

[35] A fact commented upon in the only real battle scene in the novel, pt II, ch. 5.

mood, in contrast with the often dejected air of the princes. Also, though Tej Singh conducts a romance with Chandrakanta's sakhi Chapala, 'ayyars are otherwise chaste and never take advantage of their disguises to, for example, enter the women's quarters of their victims.[36]

The chief 'ayyar of the *Dastan Amir Hamza*, Pritchett notes, has a wicked, and often scatological, sense of humour, in sharp and no doubt pleasurable contrast with Hamza's dignity.[37] In *Chandrakanta* this contrast is blunted, and whatever little humorous contrast there is in the exchanges between Tej Singh and Birendra Singh results more from the 'ayyar's pungent irony at the prince's *lack* of princely dignity than from the 'ayyar carrying counter-princely values. When Birendra is about to eat a pear allegedly peeled by Chandrakanta herself and delivered by her sakhi Chapala (but actually from an enemy 'ayyar in disguise), Tej scolds the prince for disobeying his warnings: "The hell you recognized that this was Chapala or an 'ayyar! Enough, you only needed to listen to a wench [*randi*] sweet-talking you and you were duped!!" (p. 43). Later, Tej teases the prince on several occasions for his sudden love for the forest girl and lesser love for Chandrakanta: "He falls in love at every step, he is yet to come out of one misfortune and

[36] E.g. when Tej Singh disguises himself as the divan of Vijaygarh, he sleeps in the divankhana at night: p. 40. But, again as a mark of incorporation, the divan assures him that he would have taken no offence had he slept in the inner quarters because "you are more than my own son to me": p. 43.

[37] "Not only is the content of 'Amar's humor entertaining, but the very fact of its presence is notable as well, for humor has been held to be dangerous to the 'high style' of the romance . . . But in chapter nine, the sublime heights of Ḥamzah's rapture over Mihr Nigar, and the scatological crudity of Baḳhtak's being forced to foul his clothing and carpet, occur literally in the same room at the same time—yet thanks to the interposed figure of 'Amar, Ḥamzah's dignity is not jeopardized. By the same token, Ḥamzah keeps 'Amar's unbounded, cruel humour within some kind of necessary restraint": Pritchett, *The Romance Tradition in Urdu*, p. 41. There is only one instance of scatological humour in *Chandrakanta*, when Tej Singh's disciple and 'ayyar, Devi Singh, taunts the enemy 'ayyars: they ask him permission to feed their fellow 'ayyar Badrinath, who is held captive because he refuses to admit to having stolen the tilism book. "You can go and fetch food for him, grants Devi Singh, but what will you do when he has to go and crap" (*disha jana*)? p. 156. Devi is the rudest 'ayyar, positively insulting Maharaja Shivdatt Singh of Chunar: p. 93.

he is ready to acquire a new one" (p. 164).[38] The ease with which the 'ayyar teases the prince and with which the prince accepts the teasing stems from a less hierarchical relationship than that between master and servant: Tej and Birendra are friends (*yar*), and while in the official space of the darbar Tej must pay obeisance to the prince, in private they are on more familiar terms: Birendra positively depends on Tej for everything. Can we read the ambivalence in this hierarchical relationship as another sign that the courtly world of the dastan had been reinterpreted for a new class of readers who inhabited a more fluid social world?

Commercial Acumen and the Simplification of Hindi

What made Devkinandan Khatri the first commercially successful Hindi writer—much more than the towering figure of his compatriot Bharatendu Harishchandra? Gopal Ray, who has long reflected on the question of readers' tastes,[39] puts it down largely to a single crucial factor: works by Bharatendu's contemporaries were written with the aim of "enriching" Hindi literature; they wanted to educate their readers rather than meet their existing tastes and linguistic repertoires. "As a result, the novel of Bharatendu's age could not attract ordinary readers. Devkinandan Khatri easily filled this gap between novels and readers with his commercial acumen. Khatri was the first novelist in Hindi who created narratives keeping in mind the readerly competence and taste of contemporary prospective Hindi readers, who were barely literate and were well acquainted with colloquial Urdu words and expressions but ignorant of Sanskrit and who, despite their huge numbers, were neglected by writers."[40] Ray quotes Devkinandan Khatri himself as saying:

> When I began writing *Chandrakanta* there were poets and writers like *Kavivar* Pratap Narayan Mishra and *Panditpravar* Ambikadatt

[38] See also pp. 169, 175, 210.

[39] See Gopal Ray, *Hindi Katha Sahitya aur Uske Vikas par Pathakon ki Ruchiyon ka Prabhav* (The Influence of Readers' Tastes on Hindi Narrative Literature and its Development), Patna: Grantha Niketan, 1965.

[40] Ray, *Hindi Upanyas ka Itihas*, p. 70.

> Vyas. [. . .] At that time there were Hindi writers, but no buyers of Hindi books; now there are buyers but not such writers. Many of my friends speak of the ingratitude of Hindus, pointing out that they did not buy the excellent books of a patriot like Babu Harishchandra. But what I say is that if Babu Harishchandra had made his language a little simpler, our friends would have no cause for putting such blame on their own society, and by mixing natural words [*svabhavik shabd*] Hindi's passenger train would have become an express mail . . . I am the one who can ascertain which type of Hindi is mine, and I know that one does not need to reach for the dictionary in order to read it. When I started *Chandrakanta* I had no idea that it would become so widely read, I wrote it for my own amusement. But later when I saw how fond people were of it I also became attached to it and turned the book into a means for spreading those ideas which I had not been able to publish until then, and I wrote ordinary things in simple language which would make me the darling of that developing circle. [. . .] I am delighted to have been successful in this task and to have found such a good circle of buyers for my book. Many are aware of the fact that scores of men and women learnt the Nagari script in order to read *Chandrakanta*, and even those who never had to learn Hindi did so for this purpose.[41]

Khatri's colloquial register shunned "literariness" even for set pieces like natural and physical descriptions, a bold move for a writer of that period. Khatri included Perso-Urdu vocabulary whenever appropriate, e.g. for example for mechanical devices or terms relating to courtly transactions. As we have seen, he Indianized and Hinduized his characters, so that a pari became a bankanya, but by and large he maintained the Persianizing register that Rajput petty rulers would also have used. As Ray suggests, this was a judicious move. This was the language that Hindu and Muslim neo-literate people like "Betab", who were acquiring a basic Hindi and Urdu literacy, would have been familiar with. As a matter of fact, *Chandrakanta* was printed in the Urdu script as early as 1898, an indication that this Indianized and modernized dastan found favour among Urdu readers too. It could well be that readers already familiar with dastans, and those who were new to them,

[41] D. Khatri, *Chandrakanta Santati*, pt XXIV, ch. 8, quoted in Ray, *Hindi Upanyas ka Itihas*, p. 70.

found different echoes in the text. For the former, *Chandrakanta* would have represented an addition to an already existing palimpsest formed by earlier dastans. For the latter it would perhaps have represented an autonomous work or a particular version of the Rajput palimpsest. Whatever the case, the long-lasting popularity of *Chandrakanta* suggests that its particular kind of eclecticism—mixing "Rajput heroism" with the dastan's 'ayyars and the marvellous with the familiar—became an integral part of the pleasure of print.

Chandrakanta was the most spectacular success of nineteenth-century Hindi publishing and created a wide audience for Hindi novels in the 1890s. In the next chapter, I will situate it within the development of commercial writing and publishing in Banaras in order to show the novelty it introduced, not just as a text but as a "field of possibilities" for commercial Hindi writers in the 1890s. This field came to be largely occupied by detective novels, which became the most widely published and read genre of Hindi fiction for at least the two ensuing decades. As a genre introduced, and not reproduced, from existing oral or literate traditions, detective novels raise a specific set of issues concerning genealogy and adaptation, as also the introduction and familiarization of new pleasures.

7

Detective Novels

One of the main arguments of this book has been that publishing became a veritable "field of action" in which old and new literate groups came to work.[1] Books and ephemera were created in response to different kinds of needs: educational, religious, practical, and literary. Publishing was initially fuelled by patronage, but as its commercial scope increased it became concerned with the need to bring out something "new", timely, attractive, useful. Among what was published and found favour in the commercial market we have distinguished between genres reproduced, such as barahmasas and qissas, and genres introduced, such as theatre chapbooks and, of course, novels. This final chapter is about detective novels, a new genre which met with immediate commercial success. With its easily reproducible formula and monthly issues, it generated a flurry of writing and publishing activity. The detective novel was a genre introduced first from English into Bengali, and then from Bengali into other Indian languages at the end of the nineteenth century. Like all *genres introduced*, it raises particularly interesting questions of cultural translation, adaptability, and intelligibility. Like the novel itself,

[1] A version of this chapter was first published in S. Blackburn and V. Dalmia (eds), *India's Literary History*, pp. 435–82. I would like to thank Richard Cullern of the Oriental Collections Reading Room in the British Library in London, and the staff of the Bharati Bhavan Library in Allahabad, for their invaluable help; Priya Joshi for her bibliographic suggestions; Vasudha Dalmia and the participants of the workshop on New Literary Histories for South Asia for helpful comments; and Professor C.A. Bayly for reading and commenting on an early draft.

the detective novel was brought into India "ready-made", without the intellectual and historical substratum that had generated it in Europe.[2] As always in these cases, one has to ask how meanings travelled. What was new and appealing about detective novels for Indian readers? What was changed, lost, or gained in adapting detective novels to Indian situations? What concerns and attitudes did this form allow that had not been expressed before? With their novelty worn self-consciously on their sleeves, detective novels prove to be surprisingly useful texts for asking these questions pertaining to cultural translation.

Visually, detective novels came in a format that was different from that of lithographed qissas, songbooks, and theatre chapbooks. Invariably printed with moveable type, unmistakably modern in pagination, and accompanied by flashy advertising that stressed the serial novelty of each title—one a month—detective novels highlight the fact that *reading*, and reading *novels*, was becoming an established pleasure in North India.[3] Indeed, detective novels arguably contributed in a significant way to the creation of reading for pleasure as a habit. Preliminary research into library borrowings shows that novels became, around this time, the books most issued by public libraries. Habitual readers sometimes borrowed one novel a day, and the detective novels and translations of G.W.M. Reynolds figure prominently among the novels borrowed.[4] In other words, the commercial success of detective novels may be linked not to a widening habit of book-buying but to

[2] See Carlo Ginzburg, 'Clues: Morelli, Freud, and Sherlock Holmes', in U. Eco and T.A. Sebeok (eds), *The Sign of Three: Dupin, Holmes, Pierce*, Bloomington: Indiana University Press, 1983, pp. 81–118; and D.A. Miller, *The Novel and the Police*, Berkeley: University of California Press, 1988.

[3] E.g. this ad for *Jasusi Kutta* (Detective Dog): "The marvellous acts of a loyal dog who lands his impoverished master to the position of 'Lord'; enjoyable and instructive: how an honest man can attain great progress, with 3 beautiful half-tone photographs": from the publicity list of the Burman Press, Calcutta, which listed twenty-four of its own detective novels but also advertised forty-two titles published elsewehere but available at the press. Every issue of its monthly fiction magazine *Daroga Daftar* had a 'beautiful ghastly eventful picture": publicity at the back of *Hatyakari Kaun Hai?* (Who is the Murderer? 1910).

[4] See footnote 15 below.

a more intensive use of public libraries, and testifies to the fact that reading novels had found its way among ordinary *taimpas* (timepass) activities.

Here I outline the many novelties involved in writing, selling, and reading detective novels in Hindi. That genre-writing is often in the vanguard of new narrative techniques is a point literary critics have made before.[5] We will see that the "detective function" in these novels introduced the new conventions of novel-reading and writing in an easy and attractive format. Conventional characterization persisted side by side with a new attention to details of individual psychology, while dramatic dialogues and techniques were put to good use in prose to create an effective idiom for dialogue. The process of translation and adaptation carried through detective novels reveals significant social implications as well. We will also see that *straightforward translations* replicated a "Bengali modernity", revealing a society already fully adapted to British rule, one which had accepted the agencies of the colonial state and the hierarchy inherent in "colonial subjecthood". *North Indian adaptations*, instead, depict a policy that is still self-regulated and self-policed by local elites and is pursuing its own trajectory of adaptation to the colonial regimes of knowledge and of law.

Enterprising Khatris

As I argued in the Introduction,[6] a fully-fledged Hindi print culture developed in Banaras only in the 1870s, mainly through the initiative, talent, and indefatigable activity of Bharatendu Harishchandra. A member of the merchant elite and of many important networks in the city, Harishchandra saw the possibilities and usefulness of print for immediate communication, and for the new public and independent role of the intellectual. He put into print lectures, essays, translations, periodicals, historical researches, drama, satires and sketches, devotional and occasional poems, songs: the list is endless. Through almost every

[5] See Ken Worpole, *Dockers and Detectives,* London: Verso, 1983, p. 31.

[6] And also in my 'Pandits and Printers in Banaras', in A. Gupta and S. Chakravorty (eds), *Print Areas: Book History in India*, New Delhi: Permanent Black, 2004, pp. 103–38.

month of his short but intensely productive adult life, some writing or the other of his appeared in print, and was often *written precisely to be printed.*[7] Such a regular output must have created a habit in his circle of readers and admirers, and in poets the sense that one's poems now ought to appear in printed form for there was a readership and a market, even when sales were slow to follow. In a word, Harishchandra's activism certainly established a "field of action" for writers in Hindi. It is well known that he encouraged many of his contemporaries to write and publish, wherever they were: the "Bharatendu circle" had its centre in Banaras but extended over several cities in the United Provinces and Bihar, and included aspiring novelists such as Devkinandan Khatri (chapter 6).

As Harishchandra's own production shows, the Hindi literary print culture that developed in Banaras was a mixture of genres reproduced and genres introduced. It fed on and reproduced the taste of Braj Bhasha poetry circles in Banaras and eastern UP; it introduced newspaper essays, skits, and drama as a form of social and political commentary, and it looked further afield to Bengal for models of fiction writing.[8] Harishchandra's lead was followed by the Bharat Jivan Press, established in 1884 by the dynamic Ramkrishna Khatri, alias Varma

[7] Although it is not yet clear to me how the process of publishing actually worked in his case (e.g. whether he was paid or had to pay, or both alternatively), it seems that he published every work with more than one publisher (one in Bihar, one in Banaras), and that he spread out his publications catholically over several printers (ten in Banaras alone).

[8] As Vasudha Dalmia has demonstrated, in establishing a literary field for Hindi Harishchandra drew upon the widest possible sources, including devotional and courtly poetry, Urdu verses and metres, Sanskrit, Bengali and popular drama, seasonal songs, and the variety of colloquial styles and idiolects that obtained in the cosmopolitan city of Banaras: Vasudha Dalmia, *The Nationalization of Hindu Traditions.* In a more recent article Dalmia has, however, drawn attention to the novel written by the Bengali child-widow (and Harishchandra's companion) Mallika, entitled *Saundaryamayi*; ostensibly a translation from Bengali, it is, according to Dalmia, an original work: Vasudha Dalmia, 'Generic Questions: Bharatendu Harischandra and Women's Issues', in Blackburn and Dalmia (eds), *India's Literary History*, pp. 402–34. The publishing details are: Mallika Devi, *Saundaryamayi*, Banaras: Amar Press, 1887, 65 pp. (1000), printed, 4 annas.

(1859–1906): his career and choices as a publisher well reflect the next stage in the development of Hindi commercial publishing.

The orphaned child of a petty grocer, after struggling to acquire an education Ramkrishna Varma set up a small bookshop, patronized and encouraged by Harishchandra. In 1884 he made a trip to Calcutta to buy a second-hand press and thereafter started publishing the works of contemporary Braj Bhasha poets from Banaras and the adjoining region. Because he was secretary of the Kashi Kavi-Samaj, a local poetry circle, many of his authors were his friends. Some collections were printed "by order" of the author or of a wealthy patron and distributed free.[9] Other poetry books were printed and distributed commercially and clearly found a market: in fact, out of 256 titles published between 1884 and 1900 by the Bharat Jivan Press, 119 (46 per cent) were collections of poems or songs in Braj Bhasha, mostly of the *shringara rasa* variety. Only a fraction of them were "classics": the rest were the works of contemporary authors, or manuals of metre and rhetoric—halfway between manuals and collections of verses. In this way Braj Bhasha poetry, which had until then circulated at courts and in private circles of poets, was made public and became part of commercial print culture. And despite the moralistic condemnation of this erotic poetry by literary reformers, it took several decades before an alternative poetic taste developed in the area.

At the same time, Ramakrishna Varma took the cue from Harishchandra and looked to Bengal for new literary models. His three publications, using moveable type, of stories "of fifty years ago" about thugs, police officers, and Company officials in Bengal, translated from Bengali into lively and colloquial Hindi prose, were clearly meant as gripping reading for the reasonably well-to-do and were a novelty in Hindi publishing.[10] In fact, Ramkrishna Varma spanned the whole range of genres reproduced and introduced, from daily prayers to

[9] E.g. the poems (*nakhshikh* and *shadritu*) by Diwakar Bhatt, printed in 1884 in a thousand copies and distributed free, or the collection of *ghanaksharis* by Jagannath Das Ratnakar, published in 1897 by Gosvami Balkrishnalal, himself a member of the Kavi-samaj, and distributed free. Ramakrishna Varma also printed the proceedings of the Kavi-Samaj and their "poetic riddles" (*samasyapurti*).

[10] See Ramakrishna Varma (tr.), *Thag Vrittantamala*, 1889, 782 pp. (1000), printed, very expensive at Rs 3, 9 annas, *Pulis Vrittantamala*, 1890, 122 pp.

reformist pamphlets, from grammars to calls for cow-protection (six titles in 1888 alone): clearly Hindi, too, had by now become a public print-language in Benedict Anderson's sense.

Significantly, Ramkrishna Varma published some of the first translations of Bengali novels.[11] This paved the way for the explosion in fiction writing that took place in Banaras in the 1890s. Apart from the novels of Bankimchandra Chattopadhyaya,[12] who was renowned in North India too, most Bengali novels that were translated appeared without the author's name: it was the template that was important, not the author. Besides, the work of Karttikprasad Khatri, an associate of Ramakrishna Varma at the Bharat Jivan Press, both a translator and an original novelist, shows how the introduction of Bengali translations was soon followed by original attempts in Hindi.[13]

Bengali novels provided a model for a new kind of fiction which broke away from qissas and dastans in terms of narrative conventions, social setting, and characterization. The impact of Bengal was so strong at this stage that many derided Hindi as a "literature of translation". Writers on their part freely acknowledged that they made trips to Calcutta in order to pick up Bengali novels to translate, sometimes even from junk shops (*raddikhana*)![14] Ranging between 100 and 200

(1000), printed, 8 annas, and *Amla Vrittantamala*, 1895, 172 pp. (1000), printed, 12 annas, published and printed at the Bharat Jivan Press.

[11] E.g. *Saccha Sapna*, trans. Pandit Vijayanand, 1890, 2nd edn, 42 pp. (1000), printed, 2 annas: in other words, short, printed, and cheap.

[12] His novel *Durgeshnandini* was translated and published in Banaras first by the Hariprakash Press in 1882, 99 pp. (500), 6 annas, and then by the Chandraprabha Press, 1896 2nd edn, 122 pp. (1000), 6 annas and six paise.

[13] Among Karttikprasad Khatri's translations were *Madhumalati*, 1897, pp. 258 (1000), 6 annas, and *Dalit Kusum*, 1898, 144 pp. (1000), 6 annas, while *Premlila* was a prose translation of *Romeo and Juliet* (1896, 242 pp. (1000), 10 annas): all published by the Bharat Jivan Press. *Jaya* (1896) was an original novel by Karttikprasad Khatri. *Dinanath*—published by Friend & Co. Mathura and printed in Banaras, 104 pp. (1,000), printed, 5 annas—is an interesting and "candid" account of the slow rise and fall of a self-made man as advocate in Banaras.

[14] See Kishorilal Gosvami's statement in the translator's note to *Premmayi* (1914, 2nd edn), a Bengali novel he translated after picking it up with many other books in a junk shop in Calcutta in 1889.

pages and printed with moveable type, these novels were priced middlingly, at 6 annas. Select evidence has shown that public libraries became important spaces for the circulation of these novels and that novels were the genre most borrowed.[15]

Gradually, then, a field for new fiction was established in Hindi and many potential writers, almost all of them centred in Banaras, were tempted to try their hand at writing novels. Some, like Kishorilal Gosvami (1865–1932), were scions of scholarly pandit families and took some time to switch from their highly sanskritized literary models to a more colloquial prose style.[16] Others, like Devkinandan Khatri, combined Urdu models with the new novelistic and dramatic conventions (as we saw in the previous chapter). Most, however, like Gopalram Gahmari (1866–1946) and Harikrishna Jauhar (1880–19?), mainly drew upon Bengali models. One crucial innovation all these writers introduced was professional: they very soon became their own managers and developed a new means of distributing their "product" (i.e. fiction). Almost all of them started their own monthly fiction magazines and began publishing their own books. In short, they all became professional writers.

After the experiment of *Avadh Akhbar* with *Fasana-e Azad* in Urdu in the late 1870s, it was monthly fiction magazines, a new concept in Hindi which started in the 1890s, that established and expanded the habit of novel-writing and reading in Hindi. Fiction monthlies solved the two problems that had plagued commercial publishing from the start: the problem of distribution and that of irregular demand. Fiction magazines promised and delivered to subscribers (individuals as well as public libraries) regular monthly instalments or full novels at the reasonable price of 4 to 6 annas, and at the

[15] For English novels, see Priya Joshi, *In Another Country: Colonialism, Culture, and the English Novel in India*, New York: Columbia University Press, 2002. For evidence of borrowing from Bharati Bhavan Library in Chowk, Allahabad, based on the issue catalogues for a slightly later period (1920s), see Lise Smith, 'Transmission and Reconstruction': see footnote 77 in the Introduction above.

[16] See his early novel *Pranayini Parinay* (1890) and drama *Mayankamanjari* (1891) for evidence of his debt to sanskritic models and literary language.

same time aroused high expectations for the next instalment. In this way, profit was guaranteed to writers, and entertainment and novelty to readers, all thanks to the postal service and the railways. Since journals required a constant output, a veritable fiction industry emerged as a result.

Serial publication set specific conditions upon writers and their work: crucial for its success was the ability to maintain a grip on readers, to manipulate their attention and arouse dependence in them, a craving for more. With their easily recognizable and easily reproducible formula, detective and mystery stories were ideally suited for the purpose, and two fiction monthlies came out solely devoted to detective novels, *Jasus* (Detective, 1900) and *Hindi Daroga Daftar* (Hindi Constabulary, 1910).[17] Suspense, mystery, dramatic reversals, and denouements became the bread and butter of many a Banarasi writer. But before we turn to the actual nuts and bolts of Hindi detective fiction, an outline of the activities and careers of the authors will help us to appreciate the many improbable ways in which a litterateur became a commercial Hindi writer, and the extent to which commercial fiction came to constitute an important dimension of the Hindi literary sphere.

Devkinandan Khatri's was the most sensational success story: a forest contractor in Chunar, near Banaras, and a literary friend of Harishchandra, he started writing fiction after he had read Bankimchandra Chattopadhyaya and the English novelist G.W.M. Reynolds of *Mysteries of London* fame.[18] As mentioned earlier (Chapter 6), after the success of *Chandrakanta* he launched a fiction monthly,

[17] *Jasus*, published by Gopalram Gahmari, brought out a full novel of between 44 and 60 pp. every month for an annual price of Rs 6, free of postal charges; a single issue sold for 6 annas. *Daroga Daftar*, "an illustrated monthly relating to detective novels", brought out issues of 48 pp. every month, "a fat volume of 600 pages every year"; the annual subscription was Rs 2, inclusive of postage, while a single issue sold for 4 annas.

[18] As mentioned in ch. 5, numerous novels by Reynolds were translated into Bengali, Urdu, and Hindi from 1880 onwards. Khatri was so taken by Reynolds that he planned a fiction journal solely devoted to translations of his works; only one novel, *Pravin Pathik* (*Leyla, or the Star of Mingrelia*) was translated, by Khatri's younger brother Devi Prasad Khajanci; the likely date is 1899;

'Upanyas Lahari', and acquired his own printing press, the Lahari Press (1898), in order to bring forth a continuous stream of stories about Chandrakanta's descendants. Khatri became a very rich man, and it is easy to imagine what the spectacular success of the novel must have meant for his Hindi contemporaries: wealth, stability, and fame in a market that had so far been notoriously grudging of them. The novel and its sequels (continued after Devkinandan's death by his son Durgaprasad) remained continuously in print in Hindi and Urdu, and in different formats suited to every pocket, and the Lahari Press became one of the foremost commercial publishers in Banaras. In this chapter I analyse Khatri's two forays into detective fiction, *Virendravir athva Katora Bhara Khun* (Virendravir, or the Bowl Full of Blood, 1895) and *Kajar ki Kothri* (The Dark Cell, 1902), early original attempts at the genre.

If Khatri was something of a phenomenon, Kishorilal Gosvami, the grandson of a famed acharya and scholar of the Nimbarka order in charge of ritual service at a temple in Vrindaban, epitomizes the unlikely career of a commercial Hindi novelist.[19] His first, programmatic, attempt at novel-writing, *Pranayini Parinay* (The Beloved's Marriage, Bharat Jivan Press, 1890),[20] was followed by a series of translations of Bengali novels, and his language changed accordingly: descriptive

---

Gopal Ray, *Hindi Upanyas Kosh*, Patna: Grantha Niketan, 1968, vol. 1, p. 224. For Reynolds's popularity in Hindi, see Lise Smith, 'The Mysteries of Translation'.

[19] Kishorilal had been through a typical Sanskrit education. He lived with his father in Arrah (Bihar), and dabbled in religious and educational activities until he settled in Banaras under the shelter of his maternal grandfather, who counted Harishchandra as one of his literary disciples. Here Kishorilal received an informal Hindi literary education and, under the inspiration of Harishchandra and Shiva Prasad, wrote his first novel.

[20] This 'new kind of supernatural fantasy' (*ek apurv abhinav prakar ki alaukik kalpana*), as Gosvami called it, was meant to remedy the absence of "excellent novels . . . in our beautiful Nagari [characters], though actually novels had originated in India." With its kings, thieves and Brahmins, the plot clearly looked back to classical Sanskrit novels as models, and the language was equally sanskritized: K. Gosvami, *Pranayini Parinay*, Banaras: Bharat Jivan Press, 1890, pp. 1–2.

passages in a conventionally ornate style alternated with lively dialogue in colloquial language; the predominant tone was heroic for historical novels and pathetic for "social" ones. The narrator's voice became confident, humorous at times, and bold enough even to suggest an alternative ending.[21] In 1898 Gosvami started his own monthly fiction magazine, *Upanyas Masik Pustak* (Novel Monthly), for which he translated and wrote over sixty-five novels.[22] The detective novels he wrote for *Upanyas Masik Pustak* were probably translations or adaptations from Bengali originals. He even tried to launch a monthly devoted only to detective fiction called *Guptachar* (Spy) in 1906, whose first issue was the novel *Zinde ki Lash* (Live Corpse), but the project did not take off.[23]

Jayramdas Gupta was one of those "potential" writers of Banaras who tried their hand at novel-writing almost as a joke, as he told the readers of his first novel, the detective story *Bina Savar ka Ghora* (The Riderless Horse, 1904), published by the Bharat Jivan Press. After writing one more novel, in 1904 he started editing a monthly fiction magazine, *Kashi Upanyas Darpan* (The Banaras Mirror of Novels). He must have discovered a talent for publishing for, in 1907, he launched his own magazine, *Upanyas Bahar* (The Prime of Novels) and his own publishing house. Unlike Kishorilal Gosvami's journal, *Upanyas Bahar* offered a complete novel with every issue instead of keeping readers in suspense. At Rs 2 per annum it was cheap, and no postal charges were demanded of ordinary readers.[24] Jayramdas Gupta himself wrote several detective and mystery novels, as well as loftier historical ones.[25]

[21] For example, in *Premmayi*, a Bengali "social novel" about *kulin* marriage, he changed the ending from a sad one to a happy one: K. Gosvami, *Premmayi*, Vrindavan: Sudarshan Press, 1914 2nd edn, p. 28.

[22] For details and a critical assessment of Gosvami's novels, see Ray, *Hindi Upanyas Kosh*, and *Hindi Upanyas ka Itihas*, pp. 78–93.

[23] See Ray, *Hindi Upanyas Kosh*, vol. 1, p. 122.

[24] "Of course, rich people like rajas and maharajas, seths, moneylenders, and others may send according to their power and their gift will be gracefully accepted": from the notice at the back of *Kalgras* (no date), Bharati Bhavan Library, Allahabad.

[25] Among his detective and mystery novels were *Do Khun* (Two Murders, 1907), *Chandrashala va Yuvati Chori* (Chandrashala, or, the Kidnapped Girl,

An amateur actor with the local theatre company Nagari Natak Mandali, he later specialized in publishing "theatrical plays", and collections of songs from Parsi plays as well as from the Hindi playwrights on the Calcutta stage. The Upanyas Bahar Press became one of the most flourishing commercial publishers of Banaras in the early twentieth century, and its books are still sold in the Chowk area of the city.

Two more writers-publishers deserve to be mentioned. The first is Gopalram Gupta, better known as Gopalram Gahmari, from the name of his town of Gahmar (district Ghazipur) in eastern UP. After trying his luck in Bombay, back in Gahmar in 1900 he launched the first Hindi monthly solely devoted to detective fiction, *Jasus* (Detective). Much like the others, Gahmari too first tried his hand at other, loftier genres, translated some Bengali novels, and finally settled upon detective fiction: it was the genre which made his name. The rich and apparently inexhaustible mine of Bengali detective fiction proved invaluable to Gahmari, who specialized in translating the novels of Panchkauri De, the most acclaimed Bengali practitioner of the genre. Panchkauri De had already done to the Bengali detective novel what Gahmari and other detective writers were doing to the Hindi one: he had naturalized foreign characters and settings while maintaining the glamour of the detective's fast life and smart brains. Thus, he had turned Sherlock Holmes into Govindram and Watson into Dr Bose.[26] For *Jasus* Gahmari translated several of De's novels, usually serialized over many issues. In general, even when the translation was not acknowledged, the Bengali characters and setting gave its origins away. But Gahmari also maintained foreign settings and with him readers travelled to France, England, and other countries.[27] By 1917 Gahmari

1907), *Langra Khuni* (The Lame Murderer, 1907, 1911, 2nd edn), *Bhuton ka Dera* (The Ghosts' Haunt, 1911): Ray, *Hindi Upanyas Kosh*, vol. 1, pp. 117–18.

[26] Ray, *Hindi Upanyas Kosh*, vol. 1, p. 99.

[27] Among De's novels translated by Gahmari are *Manorama* (as *Jadugarni Manorma ya Panch Khun*, Manorama the Sorceress, or, Five Murders *c.* 1900), *Mayavi* (1901–2), *Nilvasana Sundari* (*c.* 1904), *Bhishan Bhul* (as *Bhayankar*

had written, from the provincial town of Gahmar, about 107 detective stories alongside original works, translations, and adaptations.

Gahmari was not the only one to translate the prolific Panchkauri De: Karttikprasad Khatri, Ramakrishna Varma, and Ramlal Varma of R.L. Burman, Calcutta, were among the other translators.[28] Ramlal Varma (1885–1930), also from Banaras and initially an associate of Ramakrishna Varma, became one of the chief commercial Hindi publishers in Calcutta—in the 1920s he published Premchand's novels, for instance. In 1910 he launched a detective monthly, *Hindi Daroga Daftar* (Hindi Constabulary), which brought out mostly translations of Bengali detective stories, many of them by Panchkauri De. Detective novels were only one branch of Burman publications; another important enterprise was the multi-volume translation of Reynolds's best-selling *Mysteries of the Court of London* as *Landan Rahasya* (54 volumes, 1905–22). Not all detective writers became enterprising publishers like the ones mentioned, but they all became professional writers. And this overview would not be complete without mentioning Harikrishna "Jauhar", who is best known for his novels of tilism and 'ayyar, which followed Khatri's example.[29]

Detective Fiction

The term for "detective fiction" in Hindi is *jasusi upanyas*. Actually, this term includes stories that actually feature a *jasus*, a detective or spy,

---

Bhul, 1910) and among the "Govindram/Sherlock Holmes novels": *Chhadmavesh* (as *Kapat Rupvala*, 1905) and *Govindram* (1905): see Ray, *Hindi Upanyas Kosh*, vol. 1, pp. 234–40.

[28] Karttikprasad Khatri's son Manoharlal Varma claimed that De himself had asked his father to translate his novels; his brother translated *Parimal* (1904); Ramakrishna Varma translated *Kulta va stri buddhi pralayankari* (1900); Ray, *Hindi Upanyas Kosh*, vol. 1, pp. 243–4.

[29] Among Harikrishna Jauhar's early detective novels are *Daku Upanyas* (The Dacoit's Novel, 1899), *Jadugar Chhati ka Chhura* (The Magician's Chest-knife) and *Jawaharat ki Peti* (The Jewel Casket, both 1901), *Nirala Nakabposh* (The Wondrous Masked Man, 1902), and *Bhayanak Khun* (Fearsome Murder, 1903).

and thrillers and adventure stories that do not. This already points to the continuities and discontinuities in the genre: continuities, because detectives did have Indian forebears. And discontinuities, because the fictional template and the modern slant of the genre were true novelties for Indian readers.

As seen in the context of *Chandrakanta*, the use of characters and terms like 'ayyar and jasus points back to the history of state and private spying and investigative operations established by the Mughal and post-Mughal regimes and modified by the British. Rulers relied on the services of newswriters, posts, runners, carriers, and spies for information and political surveillance on other rulers, distant officials, and the local populace. Extreme mobility, verbal skills, endurance, an aptitude for disguise and, of course, discretion were recognized as the markers of news carriers and spies.[30] Again, as we saw in the previous chapter, the word jasus also hints at a genealogy in Persian popular romances and Perso-Urdu dastans. In romances and dastan narratives, every king, good or bad, had spies or jasus who collected information and were sent out to discover the enemy's plans. Called 'ayyars, these spies were invested with almost magical skills of perfect disguise, superhuman feats, and omnipresence. They also featured prominently in the direct successors of dastans, those novels of adventure and magic of which Devkinandan Khatri's *Chandrakanta* was the first example in Hindi. As we shall see, 'ayyar-like qualities such as omnipresence, omniscience, and perfect disguise are evident in the detective or detective-like characters of Hindi detective novels.

But what about the method? In his brilliant essay entitled 'Clues: Morelli, Freud, and Sherlock Holmes', Carlo Ginzburg has shown how an epistemological model based on the deciphering of clues emerged in the sphere of the social sciences in the late nineteenth century which, though claiming "scientificity", had its roots in ancient methods of divination.[31] Thus, Sherlock Holmes's brilliant deductions from clues had ancient and even specifically Indian forebears: the

[30] See C.A. Bayly, *Empire and Information: Intelligence Gathering and Social Communication in India, 1780–1870*, Cambridge: Cambridge University Press, 1996.

[31] Ginzburg, 'Clues'.

very term 'serendipity,' coined in 1754 by Horace Walpole to indicate happy and unexpected discoveries by "accidental sagacity", was taken from the story of the three princes of Serendip, who "were always making discoveries by accidents and sagacity, of things they were not in quest of: for instance, one of them discovered that a mule blind of the right eye had travelled the same road lately, because the grass was eaten only on the left side, where it was worse than on the right."[32] This story had first appeared in Europe in mid-sixteenth century Venice in an Italian translation of a Persian text, which was none other than the masnavi *Hasht Bihisht* (Eight Paradises, 1301) by Amir Khusrau of Delhi (1251–1325). Thus, the concept had travelled to and fro between India and Europe. It provided the Hindi jasus with a local genealogy and, we can surmise, Indian readers with an immediately familiar cognitive model. Yet, not all was the same.

In late nineteenth-century Europe this conjectural method that lay at the basis of a number of new disciplines like phrenology or palaeontology acquired a specific "scientific" status. Above all, it was medicine which confirmed its scientificity, and it was within the realm of forensic medicine that modern methods of identification (for example through fingerprints) were devised which had a direct bearing on the making of the detective story.[33] Critics have long pointed to these connections: if Sherlock Holmes's conjectural method was old, its trappings were those of modern, systematic scientific knowledge. In fact, although in his introduction to *Chandrakanta Santati* Khatri took special pains to justify the knowledge and skills of its 'ayyars in "scientific", i.e. non-supernatural, terms, they were still a long way away from Sherlock Holmes. In Sherlock Holmes's stories the detective is a rational being who can connect clues and disguise himself, and who possesses astounding knowledge; more importantly, every act of his is *rationally explicable*. We do not find the same exigency for total accountability in Hindi detective novels: threads are left pending, detectives can behave like 'ayyars. To give just one example, the 'ayyar-like

[32] Worpole (1754), quoted in Angelo M. Piemontese, *Gli "Otto Paradisi" di Amir Khusrau da Delhi*, Roma: Accademia dei Lincei, 1995, p. 335.

[33] The classic study is R. Messac, *Le "detective novel" et l'influence de la pensée scientifique*, Paris: Champion, 1929.

character Naharsingh in Khatri's *Virendravir* (1895, see below) is acquainted with the plot of the wicked king and follows him around like a ghost. Even in the king's court he appears in the guise of a voice saying: "I am a ghost who is with you at all times and knows everything about you[;] see! Even now I have reached you here."[34] Yet quite how he reached there and how he acquired his knowledge is never made clear. Rather than considering this a failure and imputing it to an inaccurate application of the European model, we can read this difference as a trace of the partially different genealogy and context of reception of the Hindi novel. It therefore comes as no surprise that the trappings of scientificity figured more prominently and coherently in Bengali translations of English detective novels than in those of Hindi adaptations.

Despite these continuities, jasusi upanyas were immediately distinguishable from qissas and dastans. What distinguished them was the novelistic formula. Rather than recognized by the plot—someone has been killed or kidnapped and the hero/es must find him or her and uncover the murderous plan—jasusi stories were recognized as such by their narrative arrangements and by certain key elements. As we all know, any story can be turned into a mystery story by taking a certain perspective and "cutting" it in a certain way. It was these key elements that distinguished detective novels from suspenseful qissas and dastans, and which set them apart as a genre.

One particularly interesting thing about detective novels (I will refer to jasusi upanyas as such) is that authors *had to* be aware of the rules of the genre: without suspense, without keeping the reader guessing, a detective novel just would not work. Sensational events and titillating titles were not enough: certain narrative techniques had to be employed to achieve this effect. In particular, focalization (the narrative "viewpoint") and the controlled release of information were crucial. These two elements represented the break from previous narrative traditions and marked detective novels as the heralds of modern fiction in Hindi.

Suspense had been an element in Perso-Urdu qissas and dastans, which thrived on the marvellous and on sudden breaks in story lines

[34] Devkinandan Khatri, *Virendravir athva Katora Bhara Khun*, Banaras: Lahari Press (1895) 1902, 3rd edn, p. 30. Page numbers will refer to this edition.

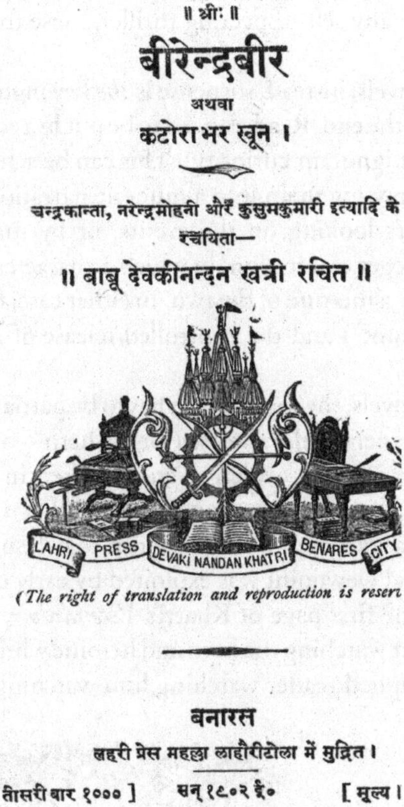

॥ श्रीः ॥

वीरेन्द्रबीर

अथवा

कटोरा भर खून।

चन्द्रकान्ता, नरेन्द्रमोहनी और कुसुमकुमारी इत्यादि के

रचयिता—

॥ बाबू देवकीनन्दन खत्री रचित ॥

LAHRI PRESS DEVAKI NANDAN KHATRI BENARES CITY

(The right of translation and reproduction is reser

बनारस

लहरी प्रेस महल्ला लाहौरीटोला में मुद्रित।

तीसरी बार १०००] सन् १९०२ ई० [मूल्य।

Fig. 17: Devkinandan Khatri, *Virendravir*, 1902, 3rd edn, Banaras: Lahari Press.

structured like Chinese boxes. In Mir Amman's *Bagh-o Bahar*, for example, we have the enigmatic character of the dog-worshipping (*sag-parast*) merchant who keeps his brothers in a cage and treats his dog like a prince. It is in order to find out who he is and why he indulges in such monstrous behaviour that the minister's daughter undertakes many adventures; and it takes the merchant many more pages and stories to explain his reasons. Dog-worship is meant here to arouse curiosity (as it does in the king of the story) and to activate further narratives. But in most cases the curious details are only meant to move the plot further; they are mere narrative devices, and the readers' curiosity can well be left unsatisfied once the narrative has turned their attention elsewhere: unlike any self-respecting thriller, loose threads here need not be tied up.

In detective novels, instead, suspense is *the* key ingredient and must be maintained to the end. Readers need to be put in a condition of curious ignorance (or ignorant curiosity). This can be achieved in various ways: either by drawing them into a mimetic narration in which they are like spectators looking on the events, or by making them the addressees of a diegetic narration, in which a character tells them how things went, or by a mixture of the two. In either case, focalization (the narrative "viewpoint") and the controlled release of information are crucial.

In detective novels, the focalization has to be partial, either internal to a character—generally the detective or the hero—or to the narrator who acts, like the implied reader, as an onlooker. In either case, the narrator refrains from mentioning anything that the hero or the implied reader cannot see. The ambiguity that results from such a limited and partial viewpoint was exploited by early detective writers to the full. On the first page of Khatri's *Virendravir*, the focus shifts from the character watching the hero and heroine while hiding behind a trellis to the implied reader watching him watching them.

Fig. 18: *Virendravir*, opp. p. 2. Note the combination of traditional style of profiling human figures with the new demands of setting, details, and composition.

The story begins *in medias res*, itself a novelty, and the absence of a frame introducing the scene is manipulated to great effect: the character who seems to be the narrator (for he speaks in the first person) begins by uttering words that sensationally defy common morality: "People say that 'virtue is virtue's reward and evil is evil's reward', but this is not true, just see how I am going to be wicked to a virtuous and devoted wife [;] if I succeed I'll be the king's divan tomorrow, then who will be able to say that an evil-doer cannot enjoy happiness and that virtuous men cannot find sorrow . . . (stops) Let's see who is coming" (p. 1). Such a beginning, which clearly owes a lot to theatrical asides, momentarily confuses the reader: can this really be the author, preaching such a wicked message? The doubt is cleared up in the next paragraph, but only slightly, for though we can hear the character we cannot see him. "Inside a garden, hidden behind a grapevine trellis, a man is muttering the words mentioned above. It is very difficult to say what this man looks like because first the dark night hides him well, secondly he has concealed himself in dark clothes, thirdly the thick grape foliage has thrown a curtain over him as well as his vices. Whatever the case[,] further on his condition will not remain hidden, at the moment he is looking at a bungalow standing in the middle of the garden, gnashing his teeth" (p. 2). Next we follow his gaze to the bungalow and its two occupants: only in the course of their conversation do we gradually pick up their names, but since the conversation is highly self-referential we are left with more questions than before. A "bowl full of blood" is mentioned with regard to the heroine's father, and an air of danger hangs over them. But when Birsingh (the hero) thinks out a plan, he is speaking so softly that "we cannot hear" (p. 5).

In its outline—a good ruler killed by a wicked servant who has taken his place and now on the throne plots to get rid of the surviving heir, who knows nothing of his real identity—the plot of *Virendravir* could be that of a traditional story. What is new is the narrative in all its aspects: temporality, the mode of regulation of narrative information, and the selection of the narrative agent.[35] Information is only gradually released, and the narrative agent is either part of the story or claims a

[35] For a detailed description of these elements, see Gerard Genette, *Narrative Discourse: An Essay in Method*, Ithaca: Cornell University Press, 1980.

partial perspective. In fact even the earliest Hindi authors of detective novels were so aware of the peculiar rules of the genre that they introduced a high number of suspense-inducing clues in the first few pages. In *Virendravir*, for example, the first two chapters show the protagonists in some danger, and hint that the heroine's father was once forced to kill somebody and fill a bowl with blood. This person is now forced (by whom? why?) to kill his beloved daughter. The king's son and heir has been killed (by whom?) and his corpse thrown in Birsingh's garden—all this in the opening two chapters.

Alternatively, in a diegetic narration events are *told* by a character. In *Virendravir*, most of the mysteries (*bhed*) are disclosed by the supposed dacoit Naharsingh, who is in fact the hero's elder brother. Other mysteries are cleared up by other characters and even by the culprits themselves under the title of "So-and-so's story", as in Jayramdas Gupta's *Bina Savar ka Ghora* (The Riderless Horse, 1904). Often, in later detective stories, it is the detective himself who recounts in the first person the events as they happened. In this retroactive or analeptic narration, ignorance is secured by emphasizing the limited perspective (and knowledge) the narrator had *then*, and by successive denouements. One example of diegetic narration is Kishorilal Gosvami's *Chandravali va Kultakutuhal* (Chandravali or the Mystery of the Fallen Woman, 1904), in which the detective is told the circumstances of the case first by a friend and then by a servant. The shifting focus ensures that ignorance is dispersed only gradually, for until the next revelation we do not, literally, have a clue. Once the confessions are over, all the detective has to do is inform the local magistrate so that the culprits are arrested and hanged; all the action takes place on the last page![36]

[36] The device of internal focalization could be taken to extreme and sensational consequences: in Agatha Christie-like fashion, Panchkauri De's story *Hatyakari Kaun Hai?* (Who is the Murderer?) is told by one of the characters, Yogeshchandra, who has seen his childhood sweetheart, Lilavati, married to Shashibhushan, a despicable man who beats and abuses her. Yogesh is allowed to watch over her because he had promised her mother to do so before her death, but clearly his enduring relationship with Lilavati is a source of tension and Shashibhushan threatens to kill her. The next day she is found dead and Yogesh employs a detective, Akshay Babu, to find the culprit. Suspicion of course

What we have then is a new genre with a new contract between author and readers and new rules that the authors have first to spell out: "All that I talked about with Mayank bears no connection with our novel and therefore I will not retell it here", declares Nalinimohan, the narrator of Ishwariprasad Sharma's *Kokila va Pap ka Bhishan Pratiphal* (Kokila or the Terrible Fruit of Sin, 1908). The title of chapter five "promises" a life-threatening situation ("*Jan sankat men*") and begins with a scene in which a masked man threatens another with a knife until a bullet flies just past him. In order to achieve suspense, information on who they are and why they are fighting is withheld, until the narrator relents—"because I do not want to throw my readers into confusion."[37] He then explains that the man being threatened was detective Nalinimohan and the man who fired the shot that saved him was his brother Mayank.

The template of jasusi upanyas was a rather simple one. This made a detective novel immediately recognizable from the first page, whether it was seven pages long or a hundred and fifty.[38] Novels began either with a suspenseful moment—a shot in a dark and stormy night—or with a sudden summons for the detective to attend a new case. The call generally came by telegraph, emphasizing the urgency of the matter and the rapidity of the technology. The detective reacted just as dynamically, usually by taking a train the very same night. Other trademarks of the genre included stormy nights, bullets fired in the dark, kidnappings with a lot of blood splashed around, a masked figure (*naqabposh*), some mysterious voice, an anonymous letter, a dark prison (*kothri*

---

points to the profligate husband, who is arrested and kills himself in jail, but the detective is able to prove through professional means (fingerprints, shadowing, cross-interrogation of witnesses) that the killer was actually . . . Yogesh, the narrator himself! The frame of the story, which would have revealed the truth, is uncovered only at the end—Yogesh is telling the jailer his strange story just before being hanged. Panchkauri De (trans. Ramlal Varma), *Hatyakari Kaun Hai?* Calcutta: Burman Press, 1910 2nd edn (2000).

[37] Ishwariprasad Sharma, *Kokila va Pap ka Bhishan Pratiphal*, Banaras: Bharat Jivan Press, 1908, p. 13.

[38] See e.g. the seven-page long *Thiyetar me Khun* (Murder at the Theatre), in Ramlal Varma, *Chaturang Chaukri*, Calcutta: Burman Press, 1918, 2nd edn (2000), 5 annas.

or *tahkhana*), a band of goondas, and the detective's tools: examination of the scene of the crime, fingerprints, interrogations, disguises, shadowing, and, of course, the ability to formulate hypotheses and decipher clues.

These elements constituted the basic template, but several novels displayed some "generic instability" (McKeon) and included elements pertaining to other genres. The "head-to-toe" (*nakhshikh*) description of the beautiful captive heroine (or of the vamp) borrowed conventions from erotic poetry; the life-story of a goonda borrowed from fashionable "confession" narratives,[39] while love interludes introduced motives from contemporary social and romantic novels. Interestingly, in the first and last cases some authors feared the possible fault (*dosha*) of rasa incompatibility, a breach in the protocol of the detective novel: "In a sad situation like this to describe her beauty appears quite inappropriate and we have to abandon this topic", wrote one author.[40] Another could not resist the temptation and exclaimed: "What have I done! Why did I raise my pen on this difficult topic? [. . .] But by the grace of Lord Krishna I have succeeded in my responsibility towards the readers."[41] These sub-plots and additional elements reveal the detective novelists striving to maximize entertainment by drawing upon appealing features from other genres.

Whereas in Europe and America the detective story "first emerge[d] as an aborted function *within* the novel" and only later "arrived" as an independent genre with Conan Doyle, Agatha Christie, Ceraux, and others,[42] the opposite argument could be made for the detective novel in Hindi. The attention to details, facial expressions, and conversations as "clues", the narrator's controlled release of information, the reader's limited perspective, his active involvement in deciphering clues and drawing conclusions—all these elements prefigured the novel and

[39] See P.M. Taylor's *Confessions of a Thug* (1839) and W.B. Hockley's Anglo-Indian "confession" novels; see Javed Majeed, 'Meadows Taylor's *Confessions of a Thug*: The Anglo-Indian Novel as a Genre in the Making', in B. Moore-Gilbert (ed.), *Writing India, 1757–1990*, Manchester: Manchester University Press, pp. 86–110.

[40] Khatri, *Virendravir*, p. 5.

[41] Sharma, *Kokila*, p. 45.

[42] Miller, *The Novel and the Police*, p. 51.

prepared readers accustomed to qissas and dastans for novelistic representation. By carefully distinguishing between the unusual detail (the clue) and normality, did not detective novels train the reader accustomed to "marvelous encounters" to expect normality on the page? As David Miller has argued, the attention to trivial details which inevitably indicate, betray, or conceal a defining something else, typical of the novel, becomes programmatic in detective novels "where the detail literally incriminates".[43] Trivial details and causal connections, after all, make the fabric of the novel; ordinary Hindi readers first encountered them systematically in detective novels. As in the case of *Fasana-e Azad* and other novels of this period, we should not rush to equate this verisimilitude with absolute realism. In detective novels, for example, we see the fascination for the magical skills of the 'ayyars persist. Yet, when turning to their own society in search for suitable crimes, settings, characters, and dialogues for their detective novels, Hindi writers were forced to introduce elements of verisimilitude and a modicum of realism.

Bengali Detectives and the North Indian Community

Early Hindi detective novels document not merely a shift in taste from the marvellous to the verisimilar. This shift in taste was the result of a cultural transaction in colonial India that paralleled other transactions: between old and new types of societal arrangements, legal systems, authorities, elites, and dominant cultures. Quite unlike those serious "first" Indian novels which directly confronted the question of colonial society and colonial subjects,[44] detective novels reflected these issues rather less self-consciously. Yet questions about delinquency and policing can guide us in investigating how detective novels refracted changes in the social world: refracted, not reflected, since detective novels used and recomposed the social and political material in combination with old and new fictional templates, as the discussion of "proofs" and "*lakshans*" (signs) will show.

[43] Ibid., p. 29.

[44] See e.g. Mukherjee, *Realism and Reality*, and idem (ed.), *Early Novels in India*, New Delhi: Sahitya Akademi, 2002.

Following David Miller, I will therefore ask who does the detecting in the novel, who holds the "detective function". A parallel question concerns the world of delinquency—"not just the delinquents themselves, but also the persons and institutions supposed to reform them or prevent from forming them."[45] Finally, there is the crime: the prevalence of murders or kidnappings of a female heir in order to secure her inheritance has to be connected, I will argue, to colonial interventions in matters of civil law and rules regarding inheritance, part of a restructuring of the indigenous legal system under the colonial "regime of law".[46]

Hindi detective novels were either translations from Bengali, or original works. Behind the obvious generic similarities, the differences between them show two sides of the same coin of cultural influence, both of them crucial to colonial culture. I want to argue that *translations* and *adaptations* were not only quite different processes, one replicating the novelty in a familiar setting, the other looking for local models to rewrite them in the new template. In the case of detective novels, we can look at translation and adaptation as two different responses to colonial rule (and the new regime of law) and two different versions of colonial society. Here I will therefore explore issues of policing, delinquency, and crime in the detective novels along the two axes of translation and adaptation.

Early translations from Bengali carried the glamour not only of the template of the detective novel, but also of the new colonial society. They always featured professional inspectors from the Calcutta police, detectives from the special intelligence branch, and sometimes private detectives. As a rule, they maintained the Bengali setting and Bengali characters with their glamorous aura of colonial modernity. Detectives held most of the "detective function" in these novels. They possessed all the scientific knowledge and powers of deduction of a Sherlock Holmes, deployed with ease the tools of the trade, and moved smoothly in a fast world full of the glittering symbols of modernity: the railway, the telegraph, the newspaper headline, the police "case".

[45] Miller, *The Novel and the Police*, p. 4.

[46] See Radhika Singha, *A Despotism of Law*, New Delhi: Oxford University Press, 1998.

For readers of Hindi translations, Bengaliness worked as a shorthand for (colonial) modernity. Detectives often appeared as graduates, and in one instance the inspector figures even as an eligible groom for the zamindar heiress: he is "worthy, unmarried, respectable and rich", so her uncle thinks of what is, literally, a marriage between the landed elite and the new class of colonial (police) servants.[47] A similar match between a police officer and a member of genteel society, Miller reminds us, would have been unthinkable in an English equivalent such as Wilkie Collins's *The Moonstone* (1868).

As for the crimes, we must remember that Bengali novels, which set the pace for Hindi adaptations, were themselves translations or adaptations. The social setting they chose was that of bhadralok zamindars with their extended families and retinues of servants. Murder and kidnapping—rather than sensational thefts or robberies—appear to be *the* typical offences in Indian detective novels. The motive? Almost invariably, inheritance. This obsession with inheritance, and with female inheritance in particular, reflects, I would argue, an engagement with the new colonial regime of law and its fixed laws regulating inheritance. True, Company rule apportioned matters like inheritance to "personal" rights, to be dealt with in the civil courts through the religious law code of the parties concerned. Still, the existence of unified codes, of law courts and of a regime of law could not fail to impress Indian society. Also, as Radhika Singha has argued, "disputes about defying the domain of domestic authority constantly put pressure on [the] distinction" between personal right and matters of public interest, to be dealt with by the magistrate.[48] The circumstances of an abduction or murder would definitely consign the matter, now a criminal case, to the jurisdiction of the police and the court. This is the situation most thematized in detective novels, which display a keen interest in wills, especially in the case of female heirs. In *Kajar ki Kothri* the will is quoted in full: Sarala, the only child of the wealthy zamindar Lalsingh, will inherit his entire property (*jaydad*); her husband will have full control over it as manager but will not become the owner; she will not part with any of it without her husband's consent. After her, the inheritance will

[47] Sharma, *Kokila*, p. 55.

[48] Singha, *A Despotism of Law*, p. 121.

pass on "in accordance with the dharmashastras."[49] To the narrator, this elaborate will is evidence of the zamindar's capriciousness (*zid*); there is a hint that the zamindar is in some way responsible for the events, and that fate has not granted him a son because of his ungenerous behaviour. Yet, under the new regime of law the will is valid, the novel does not query that fact. A clause in the will about the choice of bridegroom in fact provides the loophole that spurs one of Lalsingh's nephews to act: he kidnaps Sarala and plans to get her married to somebody else so that he and his brothers may inherit in her stead. For that purpose it will be enough for her to say in front of some family elder or respected man that she married of her own fre will.[50] As he tells Sarala in a rare moment of truthfulness: "This will has been like death for you."[51] It is to take possession of an inheritance that the female heir is killed in *Chandravali*, and kidnapped in *Kajar ki Kothri*, *Kokila*, and *Virendravir*.

The motif of the kidnapped or murdered heir sheds an interesting light on the related issue of delinquency: if the crime is always located within the family, the criminal is generally not far away either. In Ishwariprasad Sharma's *Kokila*, the kidnappers of the young heiress are actually a gang of dacoits whose chief plans to marry Kokila and acquire her property, but the immediate suspect is her brother Bhupendra.[52] In *Kajar ki Kothri* the whole plan is masterminded by a poor relation. On the matter of delinquency, David Miller reminds us that among nineteenth-century English novelists Dickens, for example, made delinquency an enclosed world from which it was all but impossible to escape. Oliver Twist is exceptionally able to escape because he was not really a born delinquent. Dickens's willingness to see coercive systems where it was traditional to see only bad morals, Miller argues, was an index of his progressive attitude. At the same time, Dickens drew a kind of *cordon sanitaire*, isolating delinquency from the respectable middle-class world of private life.[53] To the question of how delinquency is apportioned in Indian detective novels the answer must

[49] Khatri, *Kajar ki Kothri*, p. 17.
[50] Ibid., p. 79.
[51] Ibid., p. 51.
[52] Sharma, *Kokila*, pp. 6, 16, 25.
[53] Miller, *The Novel and the Police*, p. 5.

be twofold. Certain marginal groups in the lower rungs of society like badmash, goondas, and mercenary women (*randis*) are recognized as being intrinsically delinquent, but generally the plotters and instigators are within the family. In most novels, the active criminals may be thugs, but the masterminds belong to the family. In Bengali novels these criminals, though called *daku*, dacoits, have rather the appearance of urban underworld gangs, sometimes with a vamp attached[54]—the type of delinquency that would later resurface in Hindi films.

The situation is altogether different in North Indian adaptations. Here, the "detective function" is less concentrated in the hands of the detective, who is less individually characterized and whose authority is inflected or undermined in various ways, for example by stronger claims of loyalty to family or friends. Often, there is no detective at all: in his place we find either a jasus-'ayyar figure or a representative of the community. In Kishorilal Gosvami's *Chandravali*, the Bengali detective called in to solve a murder case in Banaras is first summoned by a friend of his, who is in fact the prime suspect in the case: he has the detective swear that he will stay true to their friendship even after hearing his confession. Far from being professionally appalled, the detective is only too ready to place the claim of friendship above that of duty: "Even if you are the one who killed that prostitute", the detective says, "I will let you go scot free, and even if there's no place left in hell for me when I die I will not betray a friend."[55] In fact, in this novel the detective hardly does any policing at all: instead, he listens to and believes his friend's confession and arrests the culprit the friend has accused (see above). In other novels, as in *Bina Savar ka Ghora*, the detective function is dispersed among several characters, including the detective's brother, an assistant, and an anonymous helper.

In the case of Devkinandan Khatri's novels there *is* no police, and the detecting work is done either by members of the community (*Kajar ki Kothri*) or by a jasus-'ayyar figure (*Virendravir*). In *Kajar ki Kothri* the hero, with his friends and relatives (including his future in-laws), initiates a counter-plot to discover the identity of those who have kidnapped his bride, a course of action that has the approval of the local raja who is informed of every move. As we shall see, a courtesan

[54] See e.g. Sharma, *Kokila*.

[55] Kishorilal Gosvami, *Chandravali va Kultakutuhal*, p. 6.

is centrally involved in the plot and monopolizes a large part of the narrative. In *Virendravir* it is a mysterious dacoit with all the qualities of an 'ayyar who aids the protagonist, a prince unfairly ensnared by the evil raja and usurper of the throne in a plot aimed at discrediting him, the rightful heir. Once he has collected enough "evidence" the 'ayyar-jasus can convince a "panchayat of fifteen big landlords" and the agent of the raja's overlord, the king of Nepal, of the raja's conspiracy. At a secret meeting (for the raja has his spies, too) they decide that the final showdown will take place in full public view at the next royal darbar: there, one by one, the victims stand up as witnesses, and in the ensuing scuffle the raja has his eyes gouged out in a bloody act of retribution. Peace and good rule are restored: the new king is just and merciful and extracts no further revenge from the raja's family (see below).

If the plot of *Virendravir*, Khatri's first jasusi novel, owes so much to the chivalrous world of royal claimants and counterclaimants, his *Kajar ki Kothri* appears more anchored in North Indian society. Here too the crime is the apparent murder of a female heir, masterminded by a poor relation with the help of a few thugs and a courtesan. As observed above, though the existence of a delinquent underworld of goondas, dacoits, and badmashes is acknowledged as an inescapable fact, much in the same way as prostitutes are hired and desired and feared and tolerated, delinquency is shown not to be socially confined to them alone. Rather, in a world where not cash but property (what the Italian realist writer Giovanni Verga called "la roba") was the key to social existence, and where poor relatives had to bear the burden of maintaining appearances while living at the mercy of the charity of wealthy heirs, inheriting is shown to be the only way for them to change their fortunes.

To recapitulate, Bengali translations depict a colonial society that is already fully adapted to British rule, its agencies, and its racial hierarchy. The colonial state and its police system are already paramount and readily accepted by the population. When a crime is committed the police intervene, culprits are arrested, sentences are passed by a judge in a court of law, and murderers are executed in jail.[56] Bengali detectives work within an established pattern of naukri and a hierarchy of sub-inspectors, inspectors, and a white officer at the top;

[56] See Sharma, *Kokila*, and Varma, *Chaturang Chaukri*.

they themselves are members of the urban, educated middle-class (some add BA to their name) and represent the colonial order to the local population; as such, they are treated with respect by the local elite. Their mobility is aided by modern systems of communication—the rail, the telegraph, and newspapers—and replicates colonial control over the territory when they go on missions to "Hindustan," i.e. North India.[57]

By contrast, original Hindi works adapted the novelistic template to a rather different North Indian society: often there is no police and no visible sign of British presence. The social world is that of self-policing Thakur landlords and their retinue, the polity that of partly independent rajas with their spies and courtiers; detectives are replaced by more explicitly 'ayyar-like figures. As I argued above, adaptations looked for indigenous models and rewrote them in the new template: thus, the picture of feudal society we get in Hindi adaptations can arguably have more to do with an existing model of society than with actual North Indian society, compromised as it was already (the first novels date from the 1890s) with colonial rule. Yet, the currency of this model and the difference from Bengali translations are nonetheless striking.

A comparative study of Bengali translations of English detective novels would give us a more complete picture of cultural *translation* and undoubtedly provide a more nuanced picture. In the following section I will analyse in some detail the two most significant examples of Hindi *adaptations*, Devkinandan Khatri's *Virendravir* and *Kajar ki kothri*. This is in order to provide a more concrete sense of these novels, to highlight the use of pre-existing motifs and new techniques, and to focus on some themes that document the cultural transactions accompanying the shift to the new regime and the new colonial society: the theme of "marks" (*lakshan*) and "proofs," that of the courtesan and that of inheritance.

Two Detective Novels: *Virendravir* and *Kajar ki Kothri*

Familiar motifs and new techniques are combined in Devkinandan Khatri's first jasusi novel, written three years after the runaway success

[57] See e.g. Gosvami, *Chandravali*.

of *Chandrakanta.* In *Virendravir* (1895) the social world is largely the same: chivalrous princes, royal courts, and swashbuckling adventurers. But, in line with the genre, gory details and mysteries abound. A large number of mysterious clues and suspense-inducing techniques are employed in the first few pages: every chapter ends at a critical moment, and each following chapter takes us to a different scene.[58] In following the narrative thread of the novel, I would like to concentrate on a crucial issue: the tension between the visible "marks" of one's character and "proofs." What we have is a confrontation between different systems of validation: the written proof, the clues provided by appearances, and, finally, the marks of one's nature. The notion that "marks" (*lakshan, nishani*) on the body reflect and reveal a person's inherent nature (*svabhav*), astrological fortune, and reputation is still widespread in India. In literary texts, it merged with social classification and the universal tendency to describe characters in fixed terms: the hero and heroine (*nayak* and *nayika*) were invariably of high rank; heroines always bore the marks of beauty whether young or old, noble men of high birth were always brave and strong whether on the right or the wrong side of the story; "bad" marks were found predominantly in the lower rungs of courtly society and in prostitutes. In detective novels, "marks" now worked in the physical description of characters as revealing "clues" which told you whether a character was good or bad.[59] Yet, they now had to compete with other, more powerful clues: those provided by written and other evidence (such as *flagrante delicto*).

After the first scene, in which Birsingh and his wife are sitting in the garden, spied upon by someone who turns out to be her father and to have murderous intentions (see above), the plot thickens when Birsingh is attacked by a mysterious group of men. Suspecting more trouble, he returns to the garden, only to discover a corpse lying on the ground,

[58] This is remarked upon apologetically by the narrator when he returns in ch. 11 to the hero's wife, abandoned at the end of the first chapter when she was about to be murdered by her own father; Khatri, *Virendravir*, p. 81.

[59] It is also worth pointing out that in European detective novels, as well as in other genres (Gothic novels, melodramas), facial and bodily marks work as clues to a character's nature, in accordance with the long-standing interest in physiognomy and the nineteenth-century "science" of phrenology: see Ginzburg, 'Clues'.

in the rain. No, it's not his wife: from the jewels and clothes he recognizes the raja's younger son. Further, before he can hide the corpse, it has disappeared! Instead, two guards appear to summon Birsingh into the king's presence. When the corpse is found on their way to the court there is general consternation (Fig. 19).

Here we have the first instance of the dilemma: the guards correctly report to the king that although Birsingh had declared to them that he was innocent and had been indoors, his wet clothes revealed that he had in fact been outside and must therefore be lying. This incriminating evidence contradicts Birsingh's universal good name. As the king says, after some reflection: "All around people know Birsingh to be good, honest and kind-hearted, but if what you say is true then I must doubt Birsingh." Against this evidence, Birsingh cites his own logic of loyal service: "What [the courtier] said is completely true. But Maharaj! How is it possible that I could have committed such a huge crime against my lord [*malik*] who is my provider and is like god for me [*annadata, ishvar-tulya*]?"[60]

This is the dilemma that we will encounter again and again in Khatri's novel: evidence cannot be denied, but if it contradicts the "marks"

Fig. 19: *Virendravir*, opp. p. 18. The headless corpse is found on the way to the court.

[60] Khatri, *Virendravir*, p. 21.

(which determine and include one's general good name), then it cannot be true. On this occasion, for example, the raja exhibits for the first time what appears to be "strange" and most unkingly behaviour: he is furious with Birsingh and insults his wife ("she is a bad woman. No doubt she must have run away with somebody").[61] Later the narrator points out the remarkable absence of signs of grief on the king's face but tries to mislead readers with a different explanation (Fig. 20): "Here readers will say that the king's son has been killed and the king must be ritually impure, but why was there no sign [nishani] of grief on his face? To answer that, one can only say that in earlier times those who sat on the throne did not light the funeral pyre and did not shave their heads like mourners, and nowadays several royal families still observe this custom; besides, here the matter of the dead prince was somewhat strange and will be cleared up later" (p. 28). Despite the misleading explanation, designed to send readers on the wrong track, the clue is in fact right: the king is not mourning because his son's killing was just a show, a plot to incriminate Birsingh. For the time being, though, evidence accumulates against Birsingh: a knife with his name on it and belonging to him (it was stolen from him, he protests) is found on the prince's corpse.

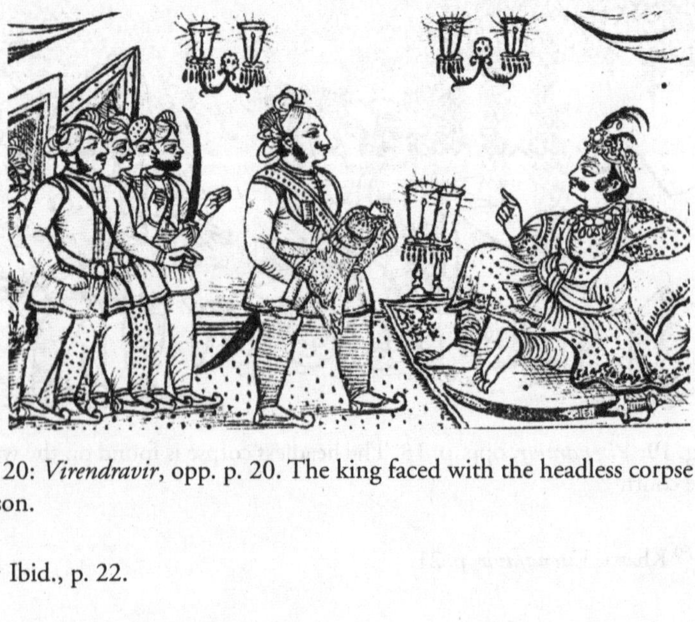

Fig. 20: *Virendravir*, opp. p. 20. The king faced with the headless corpse of his son.

[61] Ibid., p. 22.

Fig. 21: *Virendravir*, opp. p. 22. The curious underground cell.

Before we find Birsingh again, locked in an impenetrable prison underground (Fig. 21), we are introduced to a mysterious figure who will play a large role in the novel, in fact a larger and more active one than Birsingh himself, quite in line with the 'ayyar–prince pairing in dastans.

This mysterious figure is Naharsingh, a famous dacoit, the one Birsingh was supposed to hunt down. We now find him clad in black, posted outside Birsingh's house, where he ambushes a servant of the raja who was trying to steal Birsingh's seal. The dacoit tells Birsingh that the "fraudulent king" is mounting a plot to ensnare him and claims to know the mystery of the "bowl full of blood" (p. 27). We encounter this mysterious character next when he frees Birsingh from his prison. Birsingh is most surprised to hear that his saviour is Naharsingh, and even more surprised because his appearance shows him to be a noble man: "On your face there is no sign whatsoever that proves you are a dacoit or a criminal. I think Naharsingh must be some other man" (p. 35). In keeping with the detective novel's need to withhold information, Naharsingh does not reveal his or Birsingh's real identity for the moment. His suggestion that the raja is plotting against him at first appears implausible to Birsingh, but on second thoughts he admits that the king has none of the *marks* that distinguish kings. Yet there is no *proof* (p. 36). The proof soon arrives in the guise of a letter (i.e. *written* evidence) from the raja to a friend, which Birsingh and Naharsingh intercept. Naharsingh gradually reveals the story of the raja, whose real name is Karansingh Rathu, and of Birsingh and Naharsingh's father, the real Karansingh, over the course of the next few chapters, anchoring the novel in the socio-political world of North India. Karansingh had been a small landholder in Patna who lived happily with his wife, two sons and a daughter. Unable to pay land tax, after a couple of bad harvests he had been evicted by the inflexible king and left for Nepal in search of employment with the king of Nepal, leaving his family in charge of his superintendent. Moved by his sad tale, the king of Nepal had employed him in his army, and after Karansingh had distinguished himself in capturing some dacoits the king had granted him the collection of revenue over an area (*pargana*) in the border region of the Tarai. Two years later, Karansingh was given hereditary rights over it. His superintendent, Karansingh Rathu, had long wanted to wrestle control of the pargana from him. Finally, taking advantage of a journey from Nepal to the estate, he killed Karansingh and his elder son and on arrival declared himself to be Karansingh. The two younger children he had passed off first as his own, then as a friend's, and he had won over the new king of Nepal with rich gifts. In an emotional denouement, Naharsingh reveals that Birsingh is that younger son and he himself is no dacoit but the elder brother (whose real name is Vijaysingh), who in fact had escaped murder; the two brothers embrace (p. 51).

The mystery now shifts to the palace, where a woman is kept imprisoned with the fateful bowl full of blood. We now find out indirectly that it was Tara's father, Birsingh's father-in-law, who was commissioned to kill young Vijaysingh. But who is this woman, called Sundari? The mystery remains. Meanwhile, in the night a secret "committee" of local zamindars discusses with the envoy of the king of Nepal the possibility of ousting Raja Karansingh (Rathu) since he is an unjust and cruel ruler. All agree that Birsingh should be made king in his place. But the raja's spies are there.

The scene shifts again, this time to Tara, Birsingh's wife, who has been miraculously saved from her father's clutches by an old sadhu. Now she tells him that in her childhood she used to be friends with a girl in the palace, whom the raja wanted very much to marry. But after the girl disappeared for a while and returned with a daughter, Tara saw her own father being ordered to kill the young child. As a witness to the murder, Tara, too, has to die . . . The child's blood was put in a bowl, the same bowl (we realize) that was artificially kept "with some masala" (p. 101) next to Sundari's bed in order to bend her will. Sundari, then, is none other than Birsingh's long-lost sister, whom the raja had wanted to marry in order to strengthen his claim to rule.

Before the final showdown at the raja's palace, an interesting episode takes place that leads back to the issue of marks and proofs: the old sadhu who saved Tara appears at the secret committee and declares his intention of joining them, dressed as a chieftain (*sardar*). At first he is ridiculed, but after a good shave and with some proper clothes his "marks" appear unmistakable. Although this is not yet revealed (and he leaves the assembly wearing a mask), he is in fact Karansingh the father, who had also miraculously escaped being poisoned. At the darbar the next day, the witnesses speak up, one by one. The raja's letters detailing the plot are shown publicly as proofs, and lastly the sadhu walks up to the throne without the mask. "I am the final proof", he cries, and before the false raja can attack him a tussle breaks out. In the fight, the real Karansingh throws the usurper on the ground with considerable force and takes his eyes out. Still covered with blood, Birsingh, "whom the people here really loved", is made to sit on the throne (p. 125). Consistent with the 'ayyar–prince pairing, it is Birsingh who becomes king rather than his elder brother. The narrator in fact feels obliged to justify the decision, saying that Birsingh was designated since Naharsingh/Vijaysingh was celibate and did not want to reign.

In the economy of truth of this novel clues incriminate, and proofs, especially when written, are compelling; yet the Hindi detective writer is reluctant to rely on them alone for *truth*. Thus, though readers are encouraged to pick up clues and establish causal links, they are also directed to suspect appearances—even proofs!—and to believe in the true "marks." This tension between embodied and bureaucratic knowledge, between reading a person's signs and the demand for forensic evidence, highlights another critical transaction from pre-colonial to colonial society.[62] Even in a novel like this, where there is no trace of

[62] See Bayly, *Empire and Information*.

colonial presence as such, the paramount authority of evidence and proof over and against a person's marks or good name, is undenied. And yet this is felt to be an impossible strain and is ultimately shown to be invalid: even though all the evidence weighs against Birsingh, he cannot be the villain. For the man-who-returns-as sadhu, a familiar topos of contested identity, it is enough to remove the disguise for the marks of his true identity to be manifest. He himself is, as the novel puts it, "the final proof". At the same time, proofs *are* necessary and marks are insufficient against them. When Naharsingh reveals to Birsingh that the king is actually a "great devil and badmash" and is his "worst enemy", Birsingh is at first incredulous and then says: "(After some thought) There is no doubt that he has none of the things (qualities) which should be there in kings, but we have yet no *proof* that all his generosity towards me was forced" (p. 36, emphasis added).

This ambiguity, on which Hindi detective novels thrive, points to a deeper tension between different validating systems: are written proofs, as the regime of law tells us, more valid than "marks" and one's reputation in the community? Technically, under the new regime of law, if there is a conflict between proofs and lakshan, a proof wins *even when it is not true*. In the novels, however, the tension is only resolved when marks and proofs coincide; only then can closure take place.

Deceptive and reliable evidence, marks and proofs, also lie at the heart of *Kajar ki Kothri*, Khatri's other detective novel. Yet here deception is practised equally by the heroes, the villains, and, of course, the courtesan. If *Virendravir* transposed the system of raja and jasus within the new framework of the detective novel, *Kajar ki Kothri* transposes the behavioural code of courtly society, where the courtesan plays a crucial, and ambivalent, role. It is significant that although Bandi the courtesan is only a minor accomplice and plays a rather small role in the kidnapping plot, she monopolizes a significant share of the narrative. Indeed, she is at the centre of the web of deception woven by Parasnath, the villainous nephew, and Harnandan, the hero: the former is hopelessly in love with her and a mere plaything in her hands; the latter only pretends to be in love but actually exploits her for his own ends.

Daud Ali has argued that Indian medieval erotic literature acts as a kind of *tableau* upon which the anxieties of male courtiers are played out with regard to the two poles of independence and dependence.[63] Within a context of dependence upon a ruler or a superior, he has argued, the values of independence (of means, of emotions) and of dependence are often expressed in terms of love and of erotic affection. The ability to attract others to oneself is valued in a woman as well as in a courtier or king, while losing oneself to another, falling into their power, is supremely dangerous in both cases. One of the sad characters in Sanskrit dramas is the *vita*, the man who was once an educated, wealthy, and well-born member of courtly society but who has squandered all his wealth on courtesans and is now dependent on the charity of others. The courtesan then becomes the fulcrum of discourses and values that are important to courtly society in general: she is exalted as a model of behaviour for her ability to attract others, and despised for the dangerous hold she acquires over men which allows her to extract the greatest possible wealth from them. Dissembling and the ability to master a courtesan without being overwhelmed by her are, then, the attributes of the successful courtier, the *nayaka* of Sanskrit literature. They are also the attributes displayed by the hero of *Kajar ki Kothri*, a real nayaka in terms of birth, disposition, and wealth.

After his fiancée has been kidnapped on their wedding day and is feared dead, Harnandan is found chatting away with Bandi, one of the nautch-girls at the party, to the shock and shame of his relatives and friends.[64] Significantly, instead of reporting the matter or seeking help from anyone, Harnandan starts reflecting and acting on his own. For the moment, a crumpled chit of paper recovered near the nautch-girls' camp is his only clue. Like his father, prospective father-in-law, and friends, Harnandan is described in terms that combine character and type. His father Kalyansingh is a typical old-style zamindar: "though not quite a short-tempered and decadent aristocrat [*bigrail aiyash*], he

[63] See Daud Ali, 'Anxieties of Attachment: The Dynamics of Courtship in Medieval India', *Modern Asian Studies* 36.1 (2002): 103–39.

[64] Devkinandan Khatri, *Kajar ki Kothri* (1902), new edn, Delhi: Rajkamal Prakashan, 1991, pp. 14–15. (Page numbers are from this edition.) Note that, in order to stress the point, the event is narrated three times, every time producing a reaction of shocked surprise in the listeners.

was nonetheless a self-indulgent and jovial man" who enjoyed a bit of flirtation with nautch-girls (p. 9). His friend Surajsingh is "much respected" by the local raja (whose name is nothing less than Dharmasingh), and his son Ramsingh, Harnandan's friend, is already administrator and revenue-collector of twelve villages. He has earned the raja's respect for his just administration and especially for his intelligence. He and Harnandan are true nayakas: "careful, clever, wise and courageous, lovable and handsome", with remarkably well-built and muscular bodies (p. 12). Lalsingh, the father of the bride, is only good really because he belongs to the same class; as an individual, though, he "had a very bitter character". Easily angered, he paid no heed to years of friendship and amicability. Though not quite a miser, he nevertheless spiced his generosity with taunts and humiliations. Immensely rich but with no sons (a sign of divine retribution?), he has only one much-loved daughter, Sarala. "Though he had brothers and nephews he had written all his own property, which he had accumulated through his own efforts, in her name; he had deposited the will with the raja and had left his brothers and nephews, who were in dire straits for money, empty-handed. True, he did not let anybody go hungry . . ." (p. 16).

This character description sets the stage for the fateful will. "After reading this will, our readers must have realized what a stubborn character Lalsingh was" (p. 18). In this framework, the will in favour of the female heir is therefore presented as the whimsical desire of a "stubborn character" who has an unusually exclusive claim over his property because it is personal, rather than family, wealth. His love for his daughter is commended as the only emotional side in his unforgiving nature, yet his preference for his daughter over male relatives (brothers and nephews) borders on the obsessive. Treated on a par with servants, who have access to the master's food but not his money, the latter have good reason to be disgruntled.

On finding out that she has disappeared after leaving behind a pool of blood, the distraught father nonetheless goes and investigates for himself (*tahqiqat*). Surprisingly, all the traces of blood are inside the room and there is nothing on the threshold. The news that Harnandan has been gallivanting with the courtesans, delivered by a messenger sent to Kalyansingh's house, leaves Lalsingh almost mad with grief and anger. His four nephews add oil to the fire with their remarks on Harnandan's deceitful appearance: "I had already suspected his behaviour but people used to praise him so much . . . This is the way with clever *aiyash* . . . they get so extremely proud of their cleverness" (pp. 19–20). One nephew, Parasnath, goes so far as to insinuate that Harnandan must be responsible for Sarala's murder. Lalsingh wants *proofs*, while Parasnath can only offer "his heart as witness" (*dil ki gavahi*), yet he vows that he will undertake the task of recovering Sarala . . . for a fee (Rs 10,000 now and Rs 25,000 on recovery). Lalsingh is typically suspicious; after all Parasnath's "marks" are not good. "Though I have no faith or trust in you, I will act blindly and foolishly and be ready to spend some money on you", he says (p. 21). As for the motive, Parasnath suggests that since Harnandan wanted to marry somebody else, a poor girl whom his father would not accept, he has secretly arranged Sarala's abduction so that her name will be sullied and marriage with her will become impossible.

The rest of the novel is devoted to Parasnath's attempts at fabricating evidence to incriminate Harnandan, and Harnandan's attempts at gaining information regarding Sarala's whereabouts. Both attempts centre around Bandi, the courtesan. As in an Italian *opera buffa*, her kotha in the bazaar of Darbhanga is the stage for multiple double-games, false protestations of love—with Bandi swearing separately to Parasnath and Harnandan that she loves them and cares nothing about money or any other man—and truth-telling asides. In front of Parasnath, for example, she claims that she pines for him and has to ask him for money only because of her mother, the matron ("I swear by you that I care nothing for wealth and riches. I only want you and I am ready to give my life for you, but what can I do, my mother is a witch": p. 25). While to her mother she confesses: "The bastard, whenever he comes he hangs around forever." "What can you do, my daughter?" replies her mother: "This is after all our job" (p. 27). Bandi's plot, together with Parasnath and another accomplice, is to bring Lalsingh face to face with Harnandan at her kotha in order to shame him and exclude him as a possible son-in-law.

Harnandan plays into this plot by feigning disdain for Lalsingh and for Sarala whenever he visits Bandi in her kotha. He makes a formal promise of maintenance and enters into an agreement with her mother for a monthly allowance: he will write an estate with a revenue of Rs 500 a year in her name, and will pay an allowance of Rs 400 plus extras for dancing sessions, clothes, and jewels. He too swears his love for her ("I swear by you, how can I lie to you?" p. 32) and appears to enjoy her love-talk and mannerisms. Is he really infatuated? The ambiguity is maintained over the next few pages, and it is in fact thematized in the very next chapter by his friend Ramsingh, who even after hearing about Harnandan's real motive and strategy is still worried that he may lose his self-control with the courtesan after all. Harnandan replies that though he cannot promise that he will not, every morning he prays to God to preserve him from the danger (p. 37). Ramsingh reiterates his fears in a later chapter: since at first courtesans seem so innocuous, it is very easy to be captivated. In the face of the young Thakurs' discomfort, Kalyansingh's relaxed attitude to courtesans seems to be a thing of the past: when Harnandan indirectly refers to it, he says that "ancient scholars" maintained that men cannot become accomplished, clever (*chatur*) without them (p. 75). Can we see signs of a new morality coming in?

Their next move is to let in Sarala's father, Lalsingh, on Harnandan's true behaviour and his plan, without his nephew or his informers finding out. For this reason, Surajsingh visits him one night with the chit of paper (the written proof) and more "oral evidence" (*zabani sabut*). Lalsingh believes him "because you are a respected man" (*pratishthit purush*): "Rumours in the air and the [colourful] fabrications of my nephews had utterly fooled me", he admits (pp. 40–1). Bandi has assured Harnandan that Lalsingh's daughter is in Parasnath's hands; now Surajsingh instructs him to be short with money with his nephew, so that Bandi will be eager to break up with him. Meanwhile, Harnandan has implanted into Bandi's house a maidservant who will work for them.[65]

[65] Character types were of course complicated in novels: thus, the woman servant who plays a double-game in the house of the prostitute in *Kajar ki Kothri* has the traits of a typical go-between (*kutini*), shrewd and cunning with words. But while to others she is just the type, an "old devil", a "wicked old woman", she perceives herself to be "one of the beauties" and is not averse to flirting (see pp. 79, 69, 64). It is in this new attitude to physical description, half-formulaic and half-searching for psychological clues, that we may find the beginning of novelistic characterization.

Parasnath is indeed informed of the night visit, but not of the visitor's identity: "As is often the case with the fellows of bad characters, the information contained many more lies than truths", is the narrator's comment (p. 43). Information, too, depends on character. Lalsingh himself now starts playing a double-game with Parasnath, evading his questions and showing less inclination to support his plan. A frustrated Parasnath finds that he cannot prod him further as it is improper to goad one's elder.

Meanwhile, Sarala is imprisoned in a dark cell; to describe her beauty now would be a breach of decorum, the narrator declares, and her thoughts are locked up in her mind, yet Sarala comes across as a spirited young woman with a mind of her own (p. 48): "intelligent" and "honest" are the two words most used to describe her. "Despite her young age she had learned honesty and intelligence from her devoted and intelligent mother and could thus understand a bit of the world" (*unchi-nichi baten*: pp. 51–2). When the cell door is opened and Parasnath enters pretending to have been caught himself, Sarala confronts him directly with her suspicions: she thought that *he* had been involved in her kidnapping because he had been the one calling her through a secret door that had led her into the hands of the criminals. Parasnath sheepishly shifts the topic to Harnandan's strange reaction and his own efforts at finding her: he has "discovered" that the mastermind is Hariharsingh, an acquired relative (the husband of a deceased cousin on her mother's side), he tells her. "But if he marries me you will also get half of the inheritance", she quickly retorts. Finally, Parasnath's hopes are dashed when she declares that she cannot possibly marry "twice:" in her heart she is already married (to Harnandan). In a lively exchange that shows off her spirit, she declares that she would rather kill herself. Suicide is forbidden by the dharmashastra, Parasnath objects. Nonsense: even if she has not read the dharmashastras she knows their "essence" (*marma*), which is that anything that appears bad to her conscience and is a source of shame must be forbidden there somewhere.[66] Parasnath leaves the cell empty-handed.

[66] We find here an echo of the argument advanced by the princess in the seventh dastan of *Tota Maina* (ch. 4), who similarly "recalled" the "sentences from the dharmashastra" in order to support her claim that she could not marry anyone other than the young Brahmin Brahmadatt: "Give up your body, give up your mind, give up devotion but keep hold of your dharma. If you give up

In the second half of the novel the multiple double-games of Bandi, Harnandan, and Parasnath continue, a "*tamasha* worth watching" (p. 65). Meanwhile, Lalsingh has disappeared, causing further despair in his household. It is the familiar motif of the man-dead-to-the-world, the sanyasi, here with a direct bearing on the plot: with Lalsingh technically dead, the will is going to be enforced. The message he has sent through a stranger says as much, and Parasnath secretly rejoices with his accomplices because now that his uncle is "like dead", there is no need to kill him off (p. 78).

The climax presses on when the maidservant, who has been playing her own double-game with Bandi-Parasnath and with Harnandan, announces that she has finally managed to bring Sarala round. A letter shows that Sarala has agreed to marrying somebody other than Harnandan and to give half of her inheritance to Hariharsingh after the wedding: the letter and the agreement, *written* evidence, are quoted in full (p. 83). The man she has named is a stranger to us readers, and in order to allay our curiosity the narrator reveals that he is a poor young man known to all the parties, whom Bandi has chosen for her (p. 84). Amidst the gang's jubilation, the wedding is hastily prepared. Shivanandan, the appointed bridegroom, has set some conditions: his face will be covered and he will be alone with Sarala inside the marriage pavilion. After the wedding ceremony, in a sudden twist Sarala produces another letter which reveals that despite all the treachery of her cousins and her tribulations: "God has protected my honour and in the end I have been able to marry Harnandan Singh, according to my father's wishes" (p. 86). As the reader might have suspected already, Shivanandan was no one else but Harnandan in disguise. Just then Lalsingh breaks in, Parasnath is shamed, the culprits are sent to jail, and the others go home to celebrate. But at the end of the day, "people will say that it was thanks to Bandi the harlot that Harnandan Singh found out about Sarala", concludes the narrator (p. 88). As Ramsingh, Harnandan's friend, had cautioned: befriending a courtesan is like a sooty room: "However wise a man enters it, he never comes out untarnished" (p. 76).

---

your dharma, you have lost everything." And "If you have to give up your life, so be it, but keep your dharma." This seems to be the "essence" that Sarala refers to.

In this novel, too, a labyrinth of clues, marks, appearances, and proofs is at work; yet only those proofs and clues which agree with the marks of one's inherent nature will eventually prove right.

The contemporary landed elite replays in this detective novel the dynamics of courtly society: self-control and control over a courtesan are the marks of the true hero and enough to bring about his success; the landed elite can be its own police and rid itself of illegitimate claimants to property. Though Lalsingh's lack of generosity towards his kin is not commended, and the written will is a source of trouble, their authority is never called into question. There are some contrasting signs, too. Behind the appearance of a self-contained and self-policing community, *Kajar ki Kothri* opens, like other detective novels, dangerous possibilities of expression. Prostitutes are deceitful by definition; but, as one character adds in a passing remark, "aren't zamindars false and deceitful, too?" (p. 76). Although all zamindars in the novel are honest and upright and the remark does not develop into social criticism, the mere fact that it can be voiced signals new avenues for expression within the world of fictional narratives. Similarly, the courtesan comes also under the attack by a new generation of moral and efficient rural elite. In the end, it is the lawfully wedded couple who are reunited and win. It is this world of (paternalistic) rural elite, romanticized in visions of Rajput chivalry, that occupies Khatri's imagination; it is an indigenous ideal of social order that urban colonial modernity has yet to dislocate.

Lively Dialogue and Punchlines

One of the most original and interesting features of Hindi detective novels is their language, consistent with the genre's conventions of verisimilar representation. The model of dramatic dialogue was brilliantly adapted to create a new colloquial idiom. As recent scholarship on nineteenth-century Indian fiction has shown, language was a thorny question indeed, not least where new genres and new styles of prose were concerned; the same was true for Hindi.[67] In tune with other early attempts at novel writing, would-be detective writers like

[67] See Mukherjee, *Realism and Reality*; Vasudha Dalmia, 'A Novel Moment in Hindi: *Parīkṣā Gurū*', in T. Daamsteegt and V. Dalmia (eds), *Narrative Strategies*, pp. 169–84.

Gopalram Gahmari and Kishorilal Gosvami had adopted high literary models in their early works. This model involved sanskritized vocabulary and complex syntax: even dialogues aimed at literariness rather than liveliness. Bengali historical novels, eagerly translated into Hindi from the 1880s onwards, provided a similar model for writing historical novels: the lofty style of description and dialogue emphasized historical "aloofness" and the high status of the characters. Bengali social novels, dealing with contemporary life, introduced a slightly different solution: a lofty literary style for descriptions and set pieces but a lively colloquial idiom for most dialogue, that is for all except the most dramatic. Dialogue was obviously the area in which language could be most easily colloquialized, yet this was not the path most often chosen by early Hindi novelists, who were rather trying to establish literary credentials for the genre in their language. Detective novels, by contrast, valued effect and conciseness over literariness, and this was reflected in the choice of language style, too, which came much closer to the colloquial register of qissas:

> *Nahin, main jane na dungi*!
>
> *Pyari! Dekho tum mujhe mat roko nahhin to log* tana marenge *aur kahenge ki Birsingh dar gaya aur ek zalim daku ki giraftari ke liye jane se* ji chura gaya, *Maharaj ki ankhon se bhi main gir jaunga aur meri neknami men* dhabba lag jaega.
>
> —No, I won't let you go!
>
> —My dear! Look don't stop me otherwise people will tease me and say that Birsingh got scared and when he had to arrest a terrible dacoit he beat about the bush, I will also fall in the king's eyes and my honesty will be stained . . . (p. 3, emphasis added)

Note in the Hindi sentences the (romanized) use of idiomatic expressions and of the compound verbs so much used in colloquial language. Also noteworthy is the number of clues "hidden" in the lines even before we find out who the characters are: the man's name, the fact that he is a courtier of the king, that some dacoit needs to be captured and that some danger hangs over him. Dialogue is at the service of the controlled release of information.

Another novelty was the quality of description, with an accurate topography of rooms, gardens, and houses that prepared the setting for dramatic entrances and exits. Even natural description acquired new nuances in the direction of greater realism, as we already saw in Khatri's *Chandrakanta*. Notice the details and mixed vocabulary in this scene from the same novel, when Birsingh, after having discovered the corpse of the king's young son in his garden during the night, brings it to the palace:

> *Asman par subah ki sufaidi chha chuki thi jab lash liye hue Birsimh kile men pahuncha, vah apne hathon par kunvar sahab ki lash uthaye hue tha [.] Kile ke andar ki riyaya to aram men thi keval thore se buddhe jinhen khansi ne tang kar rakkha tha jag rahe the aur udyog men the ki kisi tarah balgam kil jay aur unki jan ko chain mile.*
>
> The morning light had already spread in the sky when Birsingh reached the palace with the corpse; he was holding the corpse of the young prince in his arms[.] Inside the palace the people were sleeping peacefully[,] only a few cough-ridden old men were awake trying to find a way to expel the phlegm in order finally to get some peace. (p. 19)

Such anti-climactic effects were rare. Sometimes the characterization of the detective could be self-ironic, as in *Chandravali*, when the detective introduces himself as follows: "My name is Yadunath Mukherjee. Even though I studied up to BA I am held in chains of subjection, that is, I am inspector in the detective police department.[68] More often, language was put at the service of suspense and of underworld roughness. Notice the laconic quality of the opening of *Bina Savar ka Ghora*: "Bang bang, two shots were fired and two bullets grazed the young man's temple."[69] A voice is heard: "Hey Gopisingh! Don't meddle with us otherwise your corpse will be found. You think you are very clever but we are special guys and your deadly enemies [*jani dushman*]."[70] Perhaps the most extreme example of such compact dialogue is in Ishwariprasad Sharma's *Kokila*—so extremely compact as to

[68] Gosvami, *Chandravali*, p. 1.

[69] '*Day day do fair huin aur is javan ki kanpati se do goliyan nikal gayin*': Jayramdas Gupta, *Bina Savar ka Ghora*, Banaras: Bharat Jivan Press, 1904, p. 1.

[70] Ibid., p. 3.

become ludicrous. At the beginning of chapter 5 (see above), Inspector Nalinimohan is confronted by a masked man who asks him why he is involved in the case. Nalinimohan retorts:

> *'Tab to tuhi khuni hai?' Ghabrakar vah bol utha, 'So kaise jana?' Maine hanskar kaha 'Tumhari batchit se'. Ispar krodhit hokar voh bola, 'Bare batchit se khuni ka pata lagnevale bane hain'. Mainne kaha, 'Tujhe giraftar kiya.'*
>
> "Then you must be the murderer?!" He winced and cried: "How do you know?" I answered with a laugh: "From what you just said." At this he got furious and exclaimed: "Here is our great detective who can find a man out by what he says!" I said: "You are arrested."[71]

As a matter of fact the man overwhelms Nalinimohan, who is providentially saved by his (cleverer) brother, as on other occasions. These few examples suffice to show that detective novels employed a kind of language, both in mimetic and diegetic narration, which was substantially different from the more literary register of other kinds of novels, a register closer to everyday idiom and to the language of qissas. Such an expressive, and occasionally dramatic, language served well the purposes of adapting the novelistic formula to North Indian realities.

Espousing the argument that genre-writing is often at the vanguard of new literary techniques, this chapter has analysed the novelistic conventions that detective novels pioneered. Partial focalization, a controlled release of information, trivial details, and causal connections were first systematically introduced in jasusi upanyas, and their significance explained to readers by solicitous narrators. It was this kind of fiction, geared at consumption and entertainment, which induced a demand for, and a habit of reading, fiction that more serious writers were to exploit in the following decades. The fact that detective novels belonged squarely to the realm of entertainment, of *manoranjan*, and aimed at providing an absorbing reading experience is reflected in the promises of the advertisements: "You will not be able to put it down"; "Every volume has a beautiful ghastly eventful picture." Titles and chapter headings hinted at the fearful pleasures to be derived by

[71] Sharma, *Kokila*, p. 14.

reading them. Often, the plot did not quite live up to the gruesome title (as in *The Bowl Full of Blood*), but the title nonetheless signalled that the book belonged to the genre of detective fiction. While little is known about the readership of this genre when it was first introduced in Hindi, library issue registers from a slightly later period point to a varied readership of students, traders, shopkeepers, and clerks who usually read them one after the other. One of the significant novelties of texts like detective novels was, in fact, that they were meant to be read only once.

What light can Hindi detective novels throw on the process of cultural translation that took place under colonialism and in which literature, and the novel in particular, played a significant part? I have tried to suggest that detective novels are an excellent example of how genres of entertainment, too, mediated or assimilated political or cultural change. For example, I have distinguished between straight translations and adaptations, though they ought in fact to be seen as part of a combinatory continuum in which the weight shifted from the foreign to the familiar. In translations, the emphasis was all on the novelty: translations spelt out the formula in all its components—suspense, mystery, clues. The focus was on the unfamiliar and mysterious character of the detective and his glamorously modern methods. The geographical and social setting appeared unobtrusively: that the adventures of detective so-and-so took place in Calcutta instead of the French Riviera seemed incidental and irrelevant to the adventure itself, as did the fact that the adventures were told in Bengali (or in Hindi) rather than in English. Yet, this unobtrusiveness masked a crucial step in the translation process: when the formula was grafted on the Calcutta landscape, it proved that the detective, or modernity, or romance, *could* happen in Calcutta, too. I have argued that the society depicted in translations from Bengali was one that had fully accepted the colonial order of which detectives and their "scientific" methods were a glamorous part. Hindi adaptations, by contrast, partly fell back on indigenous genealogies, as with the figure of the jasus–'ayyar, and depicted a society in which the ruling rural elite could do very well without the colonial state. Yet the treatment of courtesans in the novels also revealed that subtle processes of self-reform were going on there, too. The predominance of crimes over inheritance as the major theme of detective novels was intimately connected to this propertied class (which included landowners as well as merchants in the city), but it also indicated a fraught engagement with the new colonial regime of law. The same fraught engagement was manifest in the contention between "marks" and "evidence" as sources of truth. The stringent rationality of clues, proofs, and causal connections clashed in Khatri's novels with the inherent morality of "marks". If evidence without the validation of marks could be misleading, marks were effective only if supported by evidence. With considerable contortions, the morality of the "marks" remained in place; only now it had to be supported by the strength of written proofs. In drafting the old idioms of the 'ayyar and of virtue shining through bodily marks onto the new formula of the detective novel, Hindi detective writers made the new intelligible, for themselves and for others, and participated in the recomposition of identities that was the hallmark of colonial modernity.[72]

[72] In this perspective, one could, as David Miller and others have done, write a history of detective novels as a history of social perceptions and preoccupations with crime and with the function of policing. It is noteworthy, for example, that the most famous Urdu detective novel of the early twentieth century, Zafar Umar's *Nili Chhatri, ya Shahan-e Dehli ka Poshida Khazana* (The Blue Pavillion, or the Hidden Treasure of the Kings of Delhi), published by the Indian Press, Allahabad, in 1916, 138 pp., 12 annas, written by a Muslim deputy superintendent of police, splits the detective function between the police and a clever student from Aligarh Muslim University, features the "hidden treasure of the emperors of Delhi" as the historically prized object (as well as several murders), and involves a very public competition between the hero and the villain through the pages of Delhi newspapers! For a perceptive historical analysis of Urdu detective novels of the 1920s and 1930s, see Markus Daechsel, 'Zalim Daku and the Mystery of the Rubber Sea Monster: Urdu Detective Fiction in 1930s Punjab and the Experience of Colonial Modernity', *Journal of the Royal Asiatic Society*, 13 (2003): 21–44.

8

Conclusions

India, Europe, and the Far East

This book has presented facets of print culture in nineteenth-century India. The significance of this print culture in North India is easier to grasp if we place India in a comparative perspective. As Elizabeth Eisenstein has demonstrated, in various parts of Western Europe the technology of print may have come at a time when fifteenth-century scriptoria were already straining to meet the demand for manuscript books. But precisely because of an already well-developed infrastructure—consisting of a literate population with the leisure and means to purchase and read books, and of market mechanisms to distribute goods like printed books to customers—printing took off immediately. In less than half a century it had established itself as the primary means of book production.[1]

On the other hand, in societies such as those of East Asia the technology of woodblock printing was developed by the eighth century at the latest, and that of metallic moveable type no later than the twelfth century, but several centuries elapsed before it was commercially exploited in Ming China and seventeenth-century Korea and Japan.[2]

[1] Elizabeth Eisenstein, *The Printing Press as an Agent of Change: Communications and Cultural Transformations in Early-Modern Europe*, Cambridge: Cambridge University Press, 1979.

[2] Tsien Tsuen-hsuin, *Paper and Printing*, pt 1 of vol. 5 in Joseph Needham, *Science and Civilization in China*, Cambridge: Cambridge University Press, 1985; Joseph P. McDermott, *A Social History of the Chinese Book: Books and Literati Culture in Late Imperial China*, Hong Kong: Hong Kong University

The cases of India and Russia are substantially different in that the technology was purposefully introduced but failed to establish itself for some time. For North India we need only compare the paltry number of Hindi titles in the first forty years of printing, a mere 126—as against thousands of manuscript titles—to realize that manuscripts and copyists were still fulfilling the textual needs of society. Similarly, in Russia the introduction of printing in the sixteenth century led to equally paltry numbers of printed titles until Peter the Great attempted, in vain, to foist a European-style print culture on a Russia that did not, in the event, prove ready for it until the end of the eighteenth century.[3] As Gary Marker has argued, the delay in the take-up of the new technology is instructive, reminding us that technology is not all and that it fails to take off unless the infrastructure necessary to support a commercial print culture is in place.[4] Thus, printing can be said to have developed comparatively late in the day in Europe but to have developed or been introduced in many other societies well before it was in a position to flourish.

Thus, for nineteenth-century North India it is clear that commercial publishing in particular faced two daunting challenges: the challenge of low literacy, and the widespread habit of pursuing cultural pleasures orally and visually—as embodied in various kinds of professional and non-professional performers. How did the transition to print take place, then? Unsurprisingly, we saw that one of the strategies pursued by North Indian commercial publishers was to anchor the printed book to familiar pleasures and habits, reproducing genres that enjoyed currency in oral practice and performance: songs, sketches, and tales. Oral song traditions came into print "filtered" through urban "akhara" poets, who composed in a less localized Hindi–Urdu linguistic idiom. As is also true of barahmasas, they emphasized the sensuality of happily

---

Press, 2006; Peter Kornicki, *The Book in Japan: A Cultural History from the Beginnings to the Nineteenth Century*, Leiden: Brill, 1998; and Boudewijn Walraven, 'Reader's Etiquette and Other Aspects of Book Culture in Choson Korea', forthcoming.

[3] Gary Marker, *Publishing, Printing, and the Origins of Intellectual Life in Russia, 1700–1800*, Princeton: Princeton University Press, 1985.

[4] Ibid.

married women and their festivals over the suffering of the virahini. In the case of qissas, commercial publishers repackaged short tales either singly or in miscellaneous collections, taking them out of literary frames that had traditionally encased them for literate readers. What was new about print in this case was not the content of the books so much as their easy availability as small, cheap publications, *both* in Devanagari and in Urdu. There was the additional fact that many titles were available for the same genres, and that commercial publishers often mixed songs and tales that belonged to different traditions. In drawing attention to the wide range of Urdu small and cheap booklets, this book has hopefully helped dispel the perception that Urdu literary culture was completely and inherently elitist. At this stage at least, it certainly was not.

A second important strategy that commercial publishers pursued to maximize readership was to print the same texts and genres in both Urdu and Devanagari. In a society where people did not have language but linguistic repertoires—as David Lelyveld has aptly put it—and parallel avenues of education and types of literacy coexisted according to background and professional orientation, it made a lot of sense in such a context to try and reach the widest number of readers by printing both scripts. Thus, while Benedict Anderson's arguments about the emergence of standardized print vernaculars at the expense of other varieties is pertinent to Urdu and particularly Hindi in the nineteenth century, neither script could claim complete dominance. And while the Hindi–Urdu controversy between intellectuals and in the field of education and government employment has been read as a competition between two elites, in the field of commercial publishing there was a contrary process of mutual reinforcement between Urdu and Hindi, as well as of the consolidation of a common pool of genres and stories. This "traffic between scripts", as I have called it, partly mirrored already existing elements of linguistic and poetic hybridity in oral entertainment forms, but it also undoubtedly pushed this hybridity even further. As we saw in the case of *Kissa Tota Maina*, narrative tropes and song forms from both Perso-Urdu and Sanskritic repertoires came together, or, in the case of the peculiar *tarji' band ghazal*, with *she'rs* and *doha* alternating in a new mixed fashion. Thus, while print and modern linguistic and literary identities at the higher end of the literary field produced increased exclusivity, within the wider sphere of commercial publishing the opposite was true. And it was this same hybridity that marked the modernity of Parsi melodrama and, later, cinema.

Despite the impressive concentration of publishing activities in Lucknow at the hands of Naval Kishore, the largest Indian capitalist of the region (as Ulrike Stark has shown in her monograph), commercial publishing in North India played a geographically much more dispersed field than, for example, Bengal with its metropolitan centre in Calcutta. This posed particular distributional challenges that publishers operating in large cities like Paris, London, St Petersburg, Beijing, or Edo (Tokyo) did not have to face, for they could depend on the infrastructural support they needed within the confines of a single city. By contrast, no North Indian city offered at this stage a comparable level of support—not even Lucknow. In North India administrative, educational, and pilgrimage towns were the most likely centres of book publishing, for here shifting populations of office-workers, students, and pilgrims became additional customers. In the continuing search for a customer base, booksellers endeavoured to produce a varied menu of songs and tales as well as religious books and heavily targeted urban and rural fairs. Advertisements for novels, by contrast, point to a distribution network through the postal service or at select urban shops. In general, however, novels tended to be borrowed rather than purchased: borrowing records at neighbourhood libraries such as Bharati Bhavan in Chowk, Allahabad, confirm Priya Joshi's findings *vis-à-vis* Bengal libraries about readers' predilection for borrowing novels.[5] Can we speak of two almost independent avenues of circulation—namely, flimsy books distributed at fairs, and novels and more literary books sold through urban depots—a pattern we still see nowadays? More research and more records are needed before we can draw any substantive conclusions.

Literacy in the nineteenth century, I have argued through the examples of Narayan Prasad Betab and Radheshyam Kathavachak, was not synonymous with the literacy acquired through formal schooling. And while books of entertainment reproducing oral forms were crucial in bridging the transition to print and in instilling a habit of reading,

[5] Lise Smith, 'Transmission and Reconstruction'; Priya Joshi, *In Another Country*.

I see those who acquired literacy on the side—"neo-literates", as I have called them—swelling the numbers of readers *tout court*. The profusion and popularity of simple adab books can be taken as witnesses to this gradual rapprochement between neo-literate groups and the traditional literati. Thus, while Urdu and Hindi newspapers and journals in the second half of the nineteenth century were clearly aimed at a literate elite which was familiar with Persian, Sanskrit, or Braj Bhasha, by the 1920s newspapers like *Aj*, *Pratap*, and *Vartaman* directly targeted peasants and industrial workers.[6] Within this gradual process of the expansion of newspapers and books, the fact that by the 1890s the most commercially successful genre was the detective novel, a *genre introduced* with no previous local tradition, looks like a social and cultural landmark. Here was a genre that thrived on novelty and which consisted of titles published and read only once. It was a genre moreover that required its readers to be used to the conventions of novel-writing and of moveable type—proof that reading had become a habitual and widespread pastime. The success of detective novels also coincided with the emergence of a professional class of writers wholly dependent on commercial publishing, itself a sign that commercial publishing was beginning to transform the conditions in which texts were created.

Whereas "popular literature" and its audiences have been sometimes viewed as heroically resisting reformist concerns, such as the sanitization of women's spaces, I have argued in this book that we should consider commercial publishing as an enterprise that followed its own imperatives of entertainment and profit. In aiming to offer an "assortment of pleasures", commercial publishing of course appeared to reformist intellectuals (or Christian missionaries) recalcitrant, sometimes even antithetical to their concerns, but this was surely due more to the intrinsic logic of commercial enterprise than because of some counter-reformist intentionality. The "politics" of commercial publishers and their audiences need to be read not as a function of elite reform but rather in the light of the studies by Gyanendra Pandey, Sandria Freitag, and Nandini Gooptu on the political culture of the urban and rural

[6] F. Orsini, *The Hindi Public Sphere*. In the early decades of the twentieth century commercial publishers would aim further at specialized segments of the book market, targeting women or young readers.

poor.[7] Commercial publishers clearly exercised self-censorship when they did not print popular songs celebrating the heroes of the 1857 revolt, songs that circulated in the countryside. But already the cow-protection campaigns of the 1880s and 1890s saw the circulation of Hindi prints, pamphlets, and handwritten leaflets for propaganda purposes in the countryside.[8] In the early twentieth century, as Nandini Gooptu has shown, bhakti publications provided a focus for political identity. Christopher Pinney and Anuradha Kapur have drawn attention to the *affective* politics of allegory created by mythological plays and lithographed prints. These created an "interocular field" that reinforced the messages produced by each medium and easily crossed the threshold of literacy. Commercial texts such as *Kissa Tota Maina* and Parsi plays were, after all, multivocal texts that easily incorporated reformist or political messages within their logic of offering an assortment of pleasures.

One final point. In spite of all that has been said about the emerging print society in nineteenth-century North India, it behoves us not to forget the vast numbers of manuscripts copied in the nineteenth century, especially in Braj Bhasha and the regional varieties of Hindi. These included copies of printed books, and by far outnumber manuscripts from earlier centuries for the obvious reason of preservation. The persistence of manuscripts is of course a phenomenon that has its parallels in most print societies.[9] The weight of the present book is not to suggest that printed books had come to occupy the whole of the textual field in North India, for bookselling and distribution systems had not yet rendered copying by hand obsolete.

[7] Gyanendra Pandey, 'Rallying around the Cow: Sectarian Strife in the Bhojpuri Region, *c.* 1888–1917', in R. Guha (ed.), *Subaltern Studies II*, Delhi: Oxford University Press, 1983, pp. 60–129; Sandria Freitag, *Collective Action and Community: Public Arenas and the Emergence of Communalism in North India,* Berkeley: University of California Press,1989; Nandini Gooptu, *The Politics of the Urban Poor in Early Twentieth-century India,* Cambridge: Cambridge University Press, 2001.

[8] Pandey, 'Rallying', pp. 109–10.

[9] David McKitterick, *Print, Manuscript and the Search for Order, 1450–1830*, Cambridge: Cambridge University Press, 2003.

Glossary

(H. = Hindi, P. = Persian, U. = Urdu)

adab	good conduct, civility
akhara	wrestling ground
anjuman	association
'ashiq	lover
ashraf [*pl. sharif*]	persons of aristocratic or eminent family
'avam	common people
'ayyar	spy with almost magical skills of perfect disguise, the prince's companion in a dastan
bai	woman singer
baital [*vetala*]	ghost
banka	dandyish thug
barahmasa	song of the twelve months
barwai	Hindi metre of nineteen instants, which requires great concision
bewafai	being unfaithful
bhadramahila	gentlewoman
bhajan	Hindu devotional song
bhakha	lit. "language", the vernacular
bhand	itinerant actor
bharva	pimp

bhatiyari	female innkeeper
chhand	metre
chaupal	a covered assembly place (in the village)
chhat	rooftop
chhatakke	lit. "six copper coins"
chilum	clay bowl with stem for smoking tobacco or hashish
chunri	woman's light cotton shawl
daan	donation, gift
daf	tambourine
dangal	poetic contest
dastan	long story, usually told orally by a *dastan-go*
dev	U. demon; H. god
dharmashastra	code of Hindu law
dhun	melody
divankhana	public room of a house
doha, dohra	H. rhyming couplet
domni	woman from the Dom community, who sang for women and at women's festive rituals
fasahat	P. eloquence
gali	insult
ganja	cannabis
gavaiya	singer
ghazi	a Muslim victor over unbelievers
haqqani	related to divine truths
hikayat	story, tale
huzur	sir
insha	P. *belles lettres*

'ishq	love
jasus/jasusi	detective (n. and adj.)
javani	youth
jhagra	poetic and song genre in which two characters argue with one another
jhulna	song sung when swinging on swings
joban (*yauvan*)	youth; also a woman's breasts
kabitt	H. a poem with thirty-one syllables per line
kachehri	local law court
kajli	a song sung in the rainy month of Savan
kalawant	musician/vocalist of the highest order
kharch	expenses
khelna	to play
khemta	a type of song
khyal	a style of music and singing
kotha	courtesan's house
kothi	a large house, a bungalow
kotwal	chief police officer of a town
kundali/kundaliyan	H. a six-line stanza
latifa	a witty story, a joke
lavani	a type of popular song
lila	performance dealing with the story of either Ram or Krishna
mahalsara	private apartment, woman's private apartment
majmu'a	collection
maktab	local school where elementary Persian was taught
malhar	a raga of the rainy season

malin	woman gardener
manana	to win over, to console
mardana	manly
marhati	Marathi
marsiya	U. elegy for the death of Hasan and Hussain
masnavi	U. narrative poem
mazzaq	joke
mehfil	poetic or musical gathering
mehtar	a sweeper
mizaj	mood
mohalla	locality, neighbourhood
mughlani	a woman servant in the women's apartments
munshi	secretary, scribe
nach/nautch	dance performance
naql	sketch, either told or performed
naqqal	performer of naql
na'‘t	praise of the Prophet Muhammad
nechar	"nature"
nikah	wedding
papiha	papaya
pardes/pardesi	'abroad'/a husband who has gone away, usually for work
pari	P. fairy
pativrata	loyal and devoted wife
phag	a type of song sung at Holi
qasam	oath
qasba	provincial town
qissa	tale

ragini	"female" raga
rais/raiszada	wealthy man/son of a wealthy family
randi	common prostitute
rasik	connoisseur
riti	H. sophisticated poetry that strictly follows metrical and rhetorical rules
sakhi	female friend
sangit	music; type of musical dramatic performance
sant	holy man and devotional poet
santan	offspring
saqqa	water carrier
sarai	lodging in the market
sarkar	government
sharafat	the quality of being *sharif*, which includes good birth, good breeding, good education
sharif/sharifzada	man of good birth, good breeding and/or good education/son of a sharif family
she'r	U. poetic couplet
shringara	erotic mood; adorning oneself in preparation of a romantic or erotic encounter
sipahi	guard, soldier
suhag/suhagin	lit. "good fortune": the quality of being a married woman; a woman whose husband is alive
svang	musical folk-drama
tadbhava	words derived from Sanskrit but whose orthography has changed over the centuries
tamasha	spectacle

tazkira	biographical dictionary-cum-anthology of poets or Sufis
tilism/tilismi	enchantment; enchanted
turfa	wondrous, rare
ustad	master
ustani	female teacher
vahshat	terror
vatan	homeland
vazan	U. metre
vilayati	foreign
viraha/virahini	pain of separation from one's beloved/woman pining for her beloved
vratkatha	story about a failed or successful ritual observance of a vow to a deity, and its punishment or reward
zarafat	witticism

Bibliography

Ahmad, Nazir. 1976. 'Development of Printing in Urdu, 1743–1857'. Unpublished M.Phil. thesis, University of London.

Ahmed, Amineh. 2004. '"The World is Established through the Work of Existence": The Performance of Gham-Khadi among Pukhtun Bibiane in Northern Pakistan'. Unpublished Ph.D. thesis, University of Cambridge.

Alam, Muzaffar, and Sanjay Subrahmanyan. 2006. 'Love, Passion and Reason in Faizi's *Nal-Daman*'. In F. Orsini (ed.), *Love in South Asia: A Cultural History.* Cambridge: Cambridge University Press, pp. 109–41.

Alavi, Tanvir Ahmad. 1988. *Urdu Mein Barahmase ki Rivayyat. Matala' aur Matn.* Delhi: Urdu Academy.

Ali, Daud. 2002. 'Anxieties of Attachment: The Dynamics of Courtship in Medieval India'. *Modern Asian Studies* 36.1: 103–39.

Ali, Mir Bahadur. 1803. *Nasri Benazir.* Calcutta: Hindustani Press.

Ali, Mushtaq. 1989. 'Hindi Sahitya ke Itihas Men Ilahabad ka Yogdan, Indian Press ke Vishisht Sandarb Men'. Unpublished Ph.D. thesis, University of Allahabad.

Allahbakhsh. 1877. *Allahbakhsh ka Barahmasa.* Fatehgarh: Matba' Hasani Press.

Amin, Shahid. 2005. 'On Representing the Musalman'. In S. Mayaram, M.S.S. Pandian, and A. Skaria (eds), *Subaltern Studies XII: Muslims, Dalits, and the Fabrications of History.* New Delhi: Permanent Black and Ravi Dayal Publisher, pp. 1–35.

Ashk, Upendranath. 1947. *Girti Divaren.* Allahabad: Neelabh Prakashan.

Banerjee, Sumanta. 1989. *The Parlour and the Street: Elite and Popular Culture in Nineteenth-Century Calcutta.* Calcutta: Seagull.

Bara Gopal Bari. 1909. Banaras: Madho Prasad Bookseller.

Barthes, Roland. 1975. *The Pleasure of the Text.* Translated by Richard Miller. New York: Noonday Press.

Bayly, C.A. 1996. *Empire and Information: Intelligence Gathering and Social Communication in India, 1780–1870.* Cambridge: Cambridge University Press.

"Betab", Narayan Prasad. 2002. *Betab Charit.* New Delhi: Rashtriya Natya Vidyalay.

Blackburn, Stuart H., *et al.* (eds). 1989. *Oral Epics in India.* Berkeley: University of California Press.

———, and Vasudha Dalmia. 2004. *India's Literary History: Essays on the Nineteenth Century.* Delhi and Ranikhet: Permanent Black.

Blumhardt, James Fuller. 1889. *Catalogue of the Hindustani Printed Books in the Library of the British Museum.* London: British Museum.

———. 1893. *Catalogue of the Hindi, Panjabi, Sindhi and Pushtu Printed Books in the Library of the British Museum.* London: British Museum.

———. 1900. *Catalogue of the Library of the India Office.* Vol. 2, pt 2, *Hindustani Books.* London: India Office Library.

———. 1902. *Catalogue of the Library of the India Office.* Vol. 2, pt 3, *Hindi, Panjabi, Pushtu and Sindhi Books.* London: India Office Library.

———. 1913. *A Supplementary Catalogue of the Hindi Books in the Library of the British Museum Acquired during the Years 1893–1912.* London: British Museum.

Brantlinger, Patrick. 1998. *The Reading Lesson: The Threat of Mass Literacy in Nineteenth-Century British Fiction.* Bloomington: Indiana University Press.

Brown, Katherine. 2006. 'If Music be the Food of Love: Music, Masculinity and Eroticism in the Mughal Mehfil'. In F. Orsini (ed.), *Love in South Asia: A Cultural History.* Cambridge: Cambridge University Press, pp. 61–86.

Chakrabarty, Dipesh. 1991. 'Open Space/Public Place: Garbage, Modernity and India'. *South Asia,* XIV, 1: 15–31.

Chaturvedi, Jawaharlal. 1965. *Braj Bhasha Riti Shastra Grantha Kosh.* Allahabad: Hindi Sahitya Sammelan.

Chaube, Ramgharib. 1910. 'Popular Singers in Saharanpur'. *Indian Antiquary* 39 (February): 64.

———. 1910. 'The Origin of Kajali Songs'. *Indian Antiquary,* 39 (December): 325–6.

Chughtai, Ismat. 1995 [1944]. *Terhi Lakir*. Translated into English as *The Crooked Line*, by Tahira Naqvi. Oxford: Heinemann.

Crooke, William. 1910. 'Religious Songs from Northern India'. *Indian Antiquary* 39 (October): 268–86 and (December): 321–45.

Daechsel, Markus. 2003. 'Zalim Daku and the Mystery of the Rubber Sea Monster: Urdu Detective Fiction in 1930s Punjab and the Experience of Colonial Modernity'. *Journal of the Royal Asiatic Society*, 13: 21–44.

Dalmia, Vasudha. 1997. *The Nationalization of Hindu Traditions: Bharatendu Harishchandra and Nineteenth Century Banaras*. Delhi: Oxford University Press.

———. 1999. 'A Novel Moment in Hindi: *Parīkṣā Gurū*'. In T. Damsteegt and V. Dalmia (eds), *Narrative Strategies*, Delhi: Oxford University Press, pp. 169–84.

———. 2004. 'Generic Questions: Bharatendu Harischandra and Women's Issues.' In S. Blackburn & V. Dalmia (eds), *India's Literary History: Essays on the Nineteenth Century*. New Delhi and Ranikhet: Permanent Black, pp. 402–34.

Das, Sisir Kumar. 1978. *Sahibs and Munshis. An Account of the College of Fort William*. Calcutta: Orion Publications.

Das Gupta, Amlan. 2005. 'Women and Music: The Case of North India'. In Bharati Ray (ed.), *Women of India: Colonial and Post-Colonial Periods*. New Delhi: Sage, pp. 454–84.

De, Panchkauri. 1910. *Hatyakari Kaun Hai?* Translated by Ramlal Varma. Calcutta: Burman Press. Second edition.

Deol, Jeevan S. 1996. 'Love and Mysticism in the Punjabi *Qissas* of the Seventeenth and Eighteenth Centuries'. Unpublished M.Phil. thesis, School of Oriental and African Studies, University of London.

———. 1996. 'Acceptable Poetry: Muqbil's Mystical *Qiṣṣah Hīr Rānjhā*'. *International Journal of Punjabi Studies* 3.2: 181–210.

de Tassy, Garcin Joseph-Héliodore-Sagesse-Virtue. 1850. 'Analyse d'un monologue dramatique indien'. *Journal Asiatique*, October: 310–28.

Detti, Ermanno. 2002. *Il piacere di leggere*. Firenze: la Nuova Italia. New edition.

Du Perron, Lalita. 2007. *Hindi Poetry in a Musical Genre: Thumrī Lyrics*, London: Routledge.

Dvivedi, V.P. 1980. *Bārahmāsā. The Song of Seasons in Literature and Art.* Delhi: Agam Kala Prakashan.

Dyson, Ketaki Kusari. 1978. *A Various Universe. A Study of the Journals and Memoirs of British Men and Women in the Indian Subcontinent, 1765–1856.* New Delhi: Oxford University Press.

Farooqi, Mehr Afshan. 2007. *The Oxford India Anthology of Modern Urdu Literature.* New Delhi: Oxford University Press. Two vols.

Faruqi, Shamsur Rahman. 2001. *Early Urdu Literary Culture and History.* New Delhi: Oxford University Press.

Flint, Kate. 1993. *The Woman Reader, 1837–1914.* Oxford: Clarendon Press.

Friedlander, Peter. 2006. 'Hindustani Textbooks for the Raj'. *Electronic Journal of Foreign Language Teaching*, 3, Suppl. 1: 39–56.

Gaborieau, Marc. 1994. 'Late Persian, Early Urdu: The Case of "Wahhabi" Literature (1818–1857)'. In F.N. Delvoye (ed.), *Confluence of Cultures: French Contributions to Indo-Persian Studies.* New Delhi: Manohar, pp. 170–96.

Gauridatt, Pandit. 1966. *Devrani Jethani ki Kahani.* Patna: Grantha Niketan.

Genette, Gerard. 1980. *Narrative Discourse: An Essay in Method.* Ithaca: Cornell University Press.

George, K.M. (ed.). 1993. *Modern Indian Literature: An Anthology*, vol. 2. New Delhi: Sahitya Akademi.

Ghosh, Anindita. 2006. *Power in Print: Popular Publishing and the Politics of Language and Culture in a Colonial Society, 1778–1905.* New Delhi: Oxford University Press.

Ginzburg, Carlo. 1983. 'Clues: Morelli, Freud, and Sherlock Holmes'. In U. Eco and T.A. Sebeok (eds), *The Sign of Three: Dupin, Holmes, Pierce.* Bloomington: Indiana University Press, pp. 81–118.

Gosvami, Kishorilal. 1890. *Pranayini Parinay.* Banaras: Bharat Jivan Press.

———. 1904. *Chandravali va Kulta-Kutuhal.* Banaras: Kalpataru Press.

———. 1914. *Premmayi.* Vrindavan: Sudarshan Press. Second edition.

Goswami, Manu. 2004. *Producing India: From Colonial Economy to National Space.* Chicago: University of Chicago Press.

Gray, J.N., and D.J. Mearns (eds). 1989. *Society from the Inside Out: Anthropological Perspectives on the South Asian Household.* New Delhi: Sage.

Grierson, George A. 1884. 'Some Bihārī Folk-Songs'. *Journal of the Royal Asiatic Society of Great Britain and Ireland*, XVI: 196–246.

Griffith, R.T.H. 1880. *Report on Public Instruction in the North-Western Provinces and Oudh.* Allahabad: Government Press.

Gupta, Charu. 2001. *Sexuality, Obscenity, Community: Women, Muslims, and the Hindu Public in Colonial India.* New Delhi: Permanent Black.

Gupta, Jayramdas. 1904. *Bina Savar ka Ghora.* Banaras: Bharat Jivan Press.

Hali, Altaf Husain. 1986. *Majalis un-Nisa.* English translation: *Voices of Silence*, by Gail Minault. New Delhi: Chanakya Publications.

Hanaway, William. 1972. 'Persian Popular Romances Before the Safavid Period'. Unpublished Ph.D. dissertation, Columbia University.

Hansen, Kathryn. 1989. 'The Birth of Hindi Drama in Banaras, 1868–85'. In Sandria Freitag (ed.), *Culture and Power in Benares.* Berkeley: University of California Press, pp. 62–92.

———. 1992. *Grounds for Play. The Nautanki Theatre of North India.* Berkeley: University of California Press.

———. 1998. 'Stri Bhumika: Female Impersonators and Actresses on the Parsi Stage'. *Economic and Political Weekly*, xxxiii, no. 35 (29 August–4 September): 2291–300.

———. 2001. 'The *Indarsabha* Phenomenon: Public Theatre and Consumption in Greater India (1853–1956)'. In R. Dwyer and C. Pinney (eds), *Pleasure and the Nation: The History, Politics, and Consumption of Public Culture in India.* New Delhi: Oxford University Press, pp. 76–114.

———. 2002. 'Parsi Theatre and the City: Locations, Patrons, Audiences'. *Sarai Reader 02. The Cities of Everyday Life.* Delhi/Amsterdam, pp. 40–9.

———. 2004. 'Language Community and the Theatrical Public: Linguistic Pluralism in Nineteenth-Century Parsi Theatre'. In S. Blackburn and V. Dalmia (eds), *India's Literary History. Essays on the Nineteenth Century*. New Delhi and Ranikhet: Permanent Black, pp. 60–86.

Harder, Hans. 2004. 'The Modern Babu and the Metropolis: Reassessing Early Bengali Narrative Prose (1821–1862)'. In S. Black-burn and V. Dalmia (eds), *India's Literary History. Essays on the Nineteenth Century* New Delhi and Ranikhet: Permanent Black, pp. 358–401.

Harishchandra, "Bharatendu". 1938. *Gulzar-e Purbahar*. Benares: Benares Light Press (reprint of second edition of 1883).

———. 1882. *Malhar Hindola Kajli Jayanti adi Sangrah*. Benares: Shrivajchand Yantralay.

———. 1882. *Phulon ka Gucchha*. Benares: Chandraprabha Press.

Husain, Mirza Jafar. 1981. *Qadim Lakhnau ki Akhiri Bahar*. New Delhi: Qaumi Council baraye Furugh-e Urdu Zaban.

Jauhar, Harikrishna. 1908. *Jawaharat ki Peti*. Banaras: Kalpataru Press. First published in the monthly *Mitra* (August 1901).

Jones, Kenneth. 1976. *Arya Dharm: Hindu Consciousness in Nineteenth-Century Punjab*. Berkeley: University of California Press.

———. (ed.). 1992. *Religious Controversy in British India: Dialogues in South Asian Languages*. Albany: State University of New York Press.

Joshi, Priya. 2002. *In Another Country: Colonialism, Culture, and the English Novel in India*. New York: Columbia University Press.

Kalsi, Amrik. 1975. 'Realism in the Hindi Novel'. Unpublished Ph.D. thesis, University of Cambridge.

Kapur, Anuradha. 1995. 'The Representation of Gods and Heroes: Parsi Mythological Drama of the Early Twentieth Century'. In Vasudha Dalmia and Heinrich von Stietencron (eds), *Representing Hinduism*. New Delhi: Sage Publications, pp. 401–41.

———. 2004. 'Impersonation, Narration, Desire, and the Parsi Theatre'. In S. Blackburn and V. Dalmia (eds), *India's Literary History. Essays on the Nineteenth Century*. New Delhi and Ranikhet: Permanent Black, pp. 87–118.

———. 2006. 'Love in the Time of Parsi Theatre'. In F. Orsini (ed.),

Love in South Asia: A Cultural History. Cambridge: Cambridge University Press, pp. 211–27.

Kashigiri Banarasi Paramahansi. 1884. *Lavani arthat Marhatikhyal.* Lucknow: Naval Kishore. Fourth edition.

Kathavachak, Radheshyam. 2004. *Mera Natak-Kal.* New Delhi: Rashtriy Natya Vidyalay.

Kaviraj, Sudipta. 2006. 'Tagore and Transformations in the Ideals of Love'. In F. Orsini (ed.), *Love in South Asia: A Cultural History.* Cambridge: Cambridge University Press, pp. 161–82.

Kempson, M. 1870. *Report on the Progress of Education in the North-Western Provinces for 1869–70.* Allahabad: Government Press.

Khan, M. Siddiq. 1961. 'William Carey and the Serampore Books (1800–1834)'. *Libri*, 11, 3: 247–8.

Khatri, Devkinandan. 1895. *Vīrendravīr athvā Kaṭorā Bharā Khūn.* Banaras: Lahari Press. Third edition 1902.

———. 1991 [1902]. *Kajar ki Kothri*. New Delhi: Rajkamal Prakashan.

———. 1997 [1892]. *Chandrakanta*. New Delhi: Rajkamal Paperbacks.

King, Christopher R. 1994. *One Language, Two Scripts. The Hindi Movement in Nineteenth Century North India*. New Delhi: Oxford University Press.

Kissa Aurat Mard. 1882. Lucknow: Naval Kishore. [Indian Institute Library, Oxford: Hindi Qiss 1.]

Kolff, Dirk. 1990. *Naukar, Rajput, Sepoy*. Cambridge: Cambridge University Press.

Kornicki, Peter F. 2005. 'Unsuitable Books for Women? *Genji Monogatari* and *Ise Monogatari* in Late Seventeenth-Century Japan'. *Monumenta Nipponica* 60, 2: 147–93.

Kosambi, Meera. 2007. *Crossing Thresholds: Feminist Essays in Social History*. Delhi and Ranikhet: Permanent Black.

———, ed. and trans. 2008. *Feminist Vision or 'Treason against Men'? Kashibai Kanitkar and the Engendering of Marathi Literature.* Delhi and Ranikhet: Permanent Black.

Krishnacharya. 1966. *Hindi ke Adimudrit Granth,* Delhi: Bhartiya Jnanpith.

Lelyveld, David. 1996 [1978]. *Aligarh's First Generation: Muslim Solidarity in British India.* New Delhi: Oxford University Press.

McGregor, R.S. 1970. 'The Rise of Standard Hindi and Early Hindi Prose Fiction'. In T.W. Clark (ed.), *The Novel in India: Its Birth and Development*. London: George Allen and Unwin, pp. 142–78.

———. 1974. *Hindi Literature of the Nineteenth and Early Twentieth Centuries*. Wiesbaden: Harrassowitz.

McKeon, Michael. 1987. *The Origins of the English Novel: 1600–1740*. Baltimore: Johns Hopkins University Press.

Madhuresh. 1980. *Devkinandan Khatri*. New Delhi: Sahitya Akademi.

Majeed, Javed. 1996. 'Meadows Taylor's *Confessions of a Thug*: The Anglo-Indian Novel as a Genre in the Making'. In B. Moore-Gilbert (ed.), *Writing India, 1757–1990: The Literature of British India*. Manchester: Manchester University Press, pp. 86–110.

Malhotra, Anshu. 2002. 'The Emergence of Bazaar Literature: Jhagrras, Kissas and Reform in Early Twentieth Century Punjab'. *Studies in History* 18, 2: 297–321.

Mallika Devi. 1887. *Saundaryamayi*. Banaras: Amar Press.

Manuel, Peter. 1989. *Ṭhumrī in Historical and Stylistic Perspectives*. Delhi: Motilal Banarsidass.

Mehrotra, Arvind Krishna (ed.). 2007. *The Last Bungalow*. New Delhi: Penguin India.

Menon, Dilip. 2006. 'Reading *Sarasvativijayam*: Caste and Colonial Modernity'. In *The Blindness of Insight*. Pondicherry: Navayana Publications, pp. 110–44.

Messac, R. 1929. *Le "detective novel" et l'influence de la pensée scientifique*. Paris: Champion.

Metcalf, Barbara D. 1982. *Islamic Revival in British India: Deoband, 1860–1900*. Princeton: Princeton University Press.

Miller, D.A. 1988. *The Novel and the Police*. Berkeley: University of California Press.

Minault, Gail. 1998. *Secluded Scholars: Women's Education and Muslim Social Reform in Colonial India*. New Delhi: Oxford University Press.

Miner, Allyn. 1993. *Sitar and Sarod in the 18th and 19th Centuries*. Wilhelmshaven: Florian Noetzel.

Mookerjee, Firoze. 1992. *Lucknow and the World of Sarshar*. Karachi: Saad Publications.

Mukherjee, Meenakshi. 1985. *Realism and Reality. The Novel and Society in India*. New Delhi: Oxford University Press.

———. 2006. 'Epic and the Novel in India'. In F. Moretti (ed.), *The Novel*, vol. 1: *History, Geography and Culture*. Princeton: Princeton University Press, pp. 596–631.

Naim, C.M. 2004. 'Prize-Winning *Adab*: Five Urdu Books Written in Response to the Gazette Notification No. 791A (1868)'. In *Urdu Texts and Contexts*, New Delhi: Permanent Black, pp. 120–50.

———. 2004. 'How Bibi Ashraf Learnt to Read and Write'. In *Urdu Texts and Contexts*. New Delhi: Permanent Black, pp. 202–24.

———. 2004. 'Ghalib's Delhi'. In *Urdu Texts and Contexts*. New Delhi: Permanent Black, 2004, pp. 250–73.

Naregal, Veena. 2001. *Language Politics, Elites, and the Public Sphere: Western India under Colonialism*. New Delhi: Permanent Black.

Note. 1850. *Note on Native Presses in the North-Western Provinces for the Year 1850*. Banaras: Ukhbar Press.

———. 1860. *Note on Native Periodicals and Presses, 1858*. Allahabad: Government Press.

Oberoi, Harjot. 1995. *The Construction of Religious Boundaries: Culture, Identity and Diversity in the Sikh Tradition*. New Delhi: Oxford University Press.

Oesterheld, Christina. 2000. 'Urdu Tale and Anecdotes in the Nineteenth Century: A Case Study of Intertextuality'. Paper presented at 16th European Association of Modern South Asian Studies, Edinburgh, 6–9 September.

———. 2001. 'Nazir Ahmad and the Urdu Novel: Some Observations'. *Annual of Urdu Studies* 16: 27–42.

———. 2004. 'Entertainment and Reform. Urdu Narrative Genres in the Nineteenth Century'. In S. Blackburn and V. Dalmia (eds), *India's Literary History. Essays on the Nineteenth Century*. Delhi and Ranikhet: Permanent Black, pp. 167–212.

O'Hanlon, Rosalind. 1994. *A Comparison between Women and Men: Tarabai Shinde and the Critique of Gender Relations in Colonial India*. Madras: Oxford University Press.

Orsini, Francesca. 2002. *The Hindi Public Sphere: Language and Literature in the Age of Nationalism*. New Delhi: Oxford University Press.

———. 2004. 'Pandits and Printers in Banaras'. In A. Gupta and S. Chakravorty (eds), *Print Areas: Book History in India*. Delhi: Permanent Black, pp. 103–38.

———. 2006. 'Love Letters'. In F. Orsini (ed.), *Love in South Asia: A Cultural History*. Cambridge: Cambridge University Press, pp. 228–58.

———. Forthcoming. 'Hindi and Urdu Barahmasas'. In F. Orsini (ed.), *Hindi and Urdu Before the Divide*. New Delhi: Orient Longman.

Papanek, Hannah, and Gail Minault (eds). 1982. *Separate Worlds. Studies of Purdah in South Asia*. Delhi: Chanakya.

Parshad, Munshi Debi, and Munshi Nathhan Lal. 1875. *Guldasta-e Adab*. Lucknow: Naval Kishore.

Pernau, Margrit. 2001. 'Middle Class and Secularization: The Muslims of Delhi in the Nineteenth Century'. In I. Ahmad and H. Reifeld (eds), *Middle Class Values in India and Western Europe*. New Delhi: Social Science Press, pp. 21–41.

Petievich, Carla. 2007. *When Men Speak as Women: Vocal Masquerade in Indo-Muslim Poetry*. New Delhi: Oxford University Press.

Piemontese, Angelo M. 1995. *Gli "Otto Paradisi" di Amir Khusrau da Delhi*. Rome: Accademia dei Lincei.

Pinney, Christopher. 2004. *Photos of the Gods. The Printed Image and Political Struggle in India*. New Delhi: Oxford University Press.

Platts, John T. 1997. *A Dictionary of Urdū, Classical Hindī and English*. Delhi: Munshiram Manoharlal. Reprint of the 1884 edition.

Prasad, Bhagavat. 1925. *Mela Ghumni*. Published by the author, Muzaffarpur.

Premchand. 1985. 'Sharar aur Sarshar'. In Amrit Rai (ed.), *Vividh Prasang*. Allahabad: Hans Prakashan, vol. I, pp. 59–72. Originally published in *Urdu-e Mo'alla* (1909).

"Premghan", Badrinarayan Chaudhri. 1949. 'Kajli Kutuhal'. In *Premghan Sarvasva*. Prayag: Hindi Sahitya Sammelan, vol. 1, pp. 508–12.

Pritchett, Frances. 1985. *Marvelous Encounters: Folk Romances in Hindi and Urdu*. Delhi: Manohar.

———. 1991. *The Romance Tradition in Urdu. Adventures from the Dastan of Amir Hamzah*. New York: Columbia University Press.

———. 2001. 'The First Urdu Bestseller'. Afterword to *The Bride's Mirror* by Nazir Ahmad. New Delhi: Permanent Black, pp. 204–21.

Qissa Qazi-e Jaunpur. 1869. By Farzan. Delhi: Akbari Press.

Qissa Sipahizada ba Tasvir. 1874. By Khushdil. Delhi: Matba' Hindu Press [1848]. [OIOLC: VT 1167].

Qissa Sipahizada, 1884. Lucknow: Naval Kishore.

Quarterly Lists of Publications Published and Registered under the Provisions of Act XXV of 1867 [for North-Western Provinces, Oudh, Punjab], 1867–.

Raheja, Gloria Godwin, and Ann Grodzins Gold. 1994. *Listen to the Heron's Words: Reimagining Gender and Kinship in North India*. Berkeley: University of California Press.

Rai, Alok. 2001. *Hindi Nationalism*. Delhi: Orient Longman.

Rai, Amrit (ed.). 1985. *Vividh Prasang*. Allahabad: Hans Prakashan,

Rais, Qamar. 1991. *Ratan Nath Sarshar*. New Delhi: Sahitya Akademi.

Rangilal, Pandit. 1894. *Khyalat Turra*. Agra: Mathura Press.

Ray, Gopal. 1965. *Hindi Katha Sahitya aur Uske Vikas par Pathakon ki Ruchiyon ka Prabhav*. Patna: Grantha Niketan.

———. 1968. *Hindi Upanyas Kosh*. 2 volumes. Patna: Grantha Niketan.

———. 2002. *Hindi Upanyas ka Itihas*. New Delhi: Rajkamal Prakashan.

Reid, Henry Stewart. 1859. *Report on the State of Popular Education in the North Western Provinces for 1856/57 and 1857/58*. Banaras: Medical Hall Press.

Ritter, Valerie. Forthcoming. 'Networks, Patrons, and Genres for Late Braj Bhasha Poets: "Ratnakar" and "Hariaudh"'. In F. Orsini (ed.), *Hindi and Urdu Before the Divide*. New Delhi: Orient Longman.

Robinson, Francis. 2000. 'Technology and Religious Change: Islam and the Impact of Print'. *Modern Asian Studies* 17, 1 (1993): 229–51. Reprinted in *Islam and Muslim History in South Asia*. New Delhi: Oxford University Press.

Russell, Ralph, and Khurshidul Islam. 1994. *Ghalib: Life and Letters*. New Delhi: Oxford University Press.

Rusva, Mirza Muhammad Hadi. 1992. *Sharifzada*. New Delhi: Maktaba Jamia.

Sabuhi, Ashraf. 1989. *Dilli ki Chand 'Ajib Hastiyan*. New Delhi: Maktaba Jamia.

Samiullah. 1989. *Fort William Kalij: Ek Muta'lla*. Sultanpur.

Sangari, Kumkum. 2004. 'Multiple Temporalities, Unsettled Boundaries, Trickster Women. Reading a Nineteenth-century *Qissa*'. In S. Blackburn and V. Dalmia (eds), *India's Literary History. Essays on the Nineteenth Century*. Delhi and Ranikhet: Permanent Black, pp. 213–50.

———. 2006. 'Love's Repertoire: Qurratulain Hyder's *River of Fire*'. In F. Orsini (ed.), *Love in South Asia: A Cultural History*. Cambridge: Cambridge University Press, pp. 259–88.

———, and Sudesh Vaid. 1989. 'Introduction'. *Recasting Women. Essays in Indian Colonial History*. New Delhi: Kali for Women, pp. 1–26.

Sarshar, Ratannath. 1984–6. *Fasana-e Azad*. New Delhi: Qaumi Kaunsil baraye Furugh-e Urdu Zaban. Six volumes.

———. No date. 'Azad Goes to a Railway Restaurant', available at http://www.columbia.edu/itc/mealac/pritchett/00fwp/published/txt_sarshar.html. Originally published in K.M. George (ed.), *Modern Indian Literature: An Anthology*, vol. 2. New Delhi: Sahitya Akademi, 1993, pp. 1131–6. Slightly edited for the online version.

Schimmel, Annemarie. 1975. *Classical Urdu Literature from the Beginning to Iqbal*. Wiesbaden: Harrassowitz.

Selections. 1854. *Selections from the Records of the Government, North Western Provinces* (containing *Notes on Native Presses in the North-Western Provinces for the Year 1848*). Agra: Secundra Orphan Press.

———. 1855. *Selections from the Records of Government* (containing *Notes on Native Presses in the North-Western Provinces for the Year 1853*). Agra: Orphan Press.

———. 1866. *Selections from the Records of the North-Western Provinces of Agra and Oudh* (containing the *Report on Native Presses in the North-Western Provinces for the years 1862, 1863, 1864 and 1865* by M. Kempson). Allahabad: Government Press.

Sharar, Abdul Halim. 1989. *Lucknow: The Last Phase of an Oriental Culture*. Trans. and ed. by E.S. Harcourt and Fakhir Hussain. New Delhi: Oxford University Press.

———. 1992. *Guzishta-e Lakhnau*. New Delhi: Maktaba Jamia. Second edition.

Sharma, Ishwariprasad. 1908. *Kokilā vā Pāp kā Bhīṣhan Pratiphal.* Banaras: Bharat Jivan Press.

Shaw, Graham. 1981. *Printing in Calcutta to 1800: A Description and Checklist of Printing in Late 18th-century Calcutta.* London: Bibliographical Society; New York: Oxford University Press.

———. 1998. 'Calcutta: Birthplace of the Indian Lithographed Book'. *Journal of Printing Historical Society* 27: 89–111.

Singha, Radhika. 1998. *A Despotism of Law.* New Delhi: Oxford University Press.

Smith, Lise. 2001. 'The Mysteries of Translation. G.W.M. Reynolds and the Development of the Novel in Hindi 1900–1920'. Unpublished M.Phil. thesis, University of Cambridge.

———. 2005. 'Transmission and Reconstruction: the role of Translated Texts in the Development of the Novel in Hindi, 1890–1920'. Unpublished Ph.D. thesis, University of Cambridge.

Sprenger, Aloys. 1979. *A Catalogue of the Arabic, Persian and Hindustany Manuscripts of the Libraries of the King of Oudh.* Osnabrück: Biblio Verlag. Reprint of 1854 edition.

Stark, Ulrike. 2004. 'Hindi Publishing in the Heart of an Indo-Persian Cultural Metropolis'. In Stuart H. Blackburn and Vasudha Dalmia (eds), *India's Literary History: Essays on the Nineteenth Century.* Delhi and Ranikhet: Permanent Black, pp. 251–79.

———. 2007. *An Empire of Books. The Naval Kishore Press and the Diffusion of the Printed Word in Colonial India.* Delhi and Ranihet: Permanent Black.

Statement of Particulars regarding books, maps etc. published in the North Western Provinces & Oudh... fourth quarter of 1879; see *Quarterly Lists.*

Suvorova, Anna. 2000. *Masnavi: A Study of Urdu Romance.* Karachi: Oxford University Press.

Talwar, Vir Bharat. 2002. *Rassakashi: 19vim Sadi ka Navajagaran aur Pashchimottar Prant.* Delhi: Saramsha Prakashan.

Thornton, Reginald 1850. *Memoir on the Educational Statistics of the NWP.*

Trivedi, Madhu. 2000. 'Hindustani Music and Dance: An Examination of Some Texts in the Indo-Persian Tradition'. In M. Alam,

M. Gaborieau and F.N. Delvoye (eds), *The Making of Indo-Persian Culture*. Delhi: Manohar, pp. 281–306.
Vaishya, Melaram. 1932. *Gande Git Vahishkar*. Bhivani. Second edition.
Varma, Ramlal, trans. 1918. *Chaturang Chaukri.* Calcutta: Burman Press. Second edition.
Vaudeville, Charlotte. 1986. *Barahmasa in Indian Literature*. Delhi: Motilal Banarsidass.
Vedalankar, Shardadevi. 1969. *The Development of Hindi Prose Literature in the Early Nineteenth Century*. Allahabad: Lokbharati Publications.
Wadley, Susan W. 1983. 'The Rains of Estrangement: Understanding the Hindu Yearly Cycle'. *Contributions to Indian Sociology* 17, 1: 51–85.
Watt, Ian. 1957. *The Rise of the Novel.* London: Penguin.
Yang, Anand. 1998. *Bazaar India: Markets, Society and the Colonial State in Bihar*. Berkeley: University of California Press.
Worpole, Ken. 1983. *Dockers and Detectives*. London: Verso.
Zaidi, A.J. 1993. *A History of Urdu Literature*. New Delhi: Sahitya Akademi.

Index